GUIDE TO

Motorcycles

Fifth Edition

by *Motorcyclist* magazine with John L. Stein

ALPHA

A member of Penguin Group (USA) Inc.

This book is dedicated to all of those who have tried motorcycling and understand. And to those others who soon will.

ALPHA BOOKS

Published by the Penguin Group

Penguin Group (USA) Inc., 375 Hudson Street, New York, New York 10014, USA

Penguin Group (Canada), 90 Eglinton Avenue East, Suite 700, Toronto, Ontario M4P 2Y3, Canada (a division of Pearson Penguin Canada Inc.)

Penguin Books Ltd., 80 Strand, London WC2R 0RL, England

Penguin Ireland, 25 St. Stephen's Green, Dublin 2, Ireland (a division of Penguin Books Ltd.)

Penguin Group (Australia), 250 Camberwell Road, Camberwell, Victoria 3124, Australia (a division of Pearson Australia Group Pty. Ltd.)

Penguin Books India Pvt. Ltd., 11 Community Centre, Panchsheel Park, New Delhi—110 017, India

Penguin Group (NZ), 67 Apollo Drive, Rosedale, North Shore, Auckland 1311, New Zealand (a division of Pearson New Zealand Ltd.)

Penguin Books (South Africa) (Pty.) Ltd., 24 Sturdee Avenue, Rosebank, Johannesburg 2196, South Africa

Penguin Books Ltd., Registered Offices: 80 Strand, London WC2R 0RL, England

Copyright © 2011 by Source Interlink Media LLC

International Standard Book Number: 978-1-61564-070-6
Library of Congress Catalog Card Number: 2010912368

13   12   11   8   7   6   5   4   3   2   1

Interpretation of the printing code: The rightmost number of the first series of numbers is the year of the book's printing; the rightmost number of the second series of numbers is the number of the book's printing. For example, a printing code of 11-1 shows that the first printing occurred in 2011.

Printed in the United States of America

Publisher: *Marie Butler-Knight*

Associate Publisher: *Mike Sanders*

Senior Managing Editor: *Billy Fields*

Senior Acquisitions Editor: *Paul Dinas*

Development Editor: *Jennifer Moore*

Production Editor: *Kayla Dugger*

Copy Editor: *Amy Borrelli*

Cover Designer: *Kurt Owens*

Book Designers: *William Thomas, Rebecca Batchelor*

Indexer: *Tonya Heard*

Layout: *Ayanna Lacey*

Proofreader: *Laura Caddell*

Contents

Introduction

The motorcycle world is hard to understand from the outside. Most nonmotorcycle people are hesitant to join in because everybody knows that motorcycling is dangerous. I'm guessing that buying this book means you're on the outside, wondering whether to enter. Well, come on in; things probably aren't what they seem.

I remember being on the outside myself. I can cast my mind back to being a kid at my grandpa's house in England, and being hypnotized by his motorcycles. My dad drove a car, and all that meant to me was paint, wheels, and seats. His dad was different, though—he rode bikes, and to my baby blues they were freaky things. They looked so complex when you got up close, with their weird pipes and levers, exposed engines covered in elaborate fins, shiny metal here, dull metal there. It all looked so functional, so raw, so focused.

Back then I was too young to realize what a true motorcyclist my grandfather was. He spent his entire career working at Norton Motorcycles, one of the most famous manufacturers of the day. This meant that bikes were more than just a mode of transport to him, they were his life. When the inevitable happened and I wanted to ride, too, I was immediately told "no" by my father. Motorcycles were too dangerous.

That all seems like a long time ago now; I've been inside the motorcycle industry for most of my life. Currently I spend more time writing about bikes than riding them, but for a long time it was the opposite. Obviously, I defied my dad and got a license, but later I took it one stage further and became a full-time motorcycle instructor. For five years I introduced others to motorcycling, and I did it in Britain, where licensing often requires five full days of intensive training.

The point is that I spent all of those years watching new riders just like you come walking through the door, and most of them had similar concerns as my father. It would always take some time to alleviate those concerns and gain their trust, but I'm proud to say that I always did. It was one of the most satisfying experiences of my life to watch them walk out of the same door, license in hand, knowing they were as safe as possible and that they really "got it."

This book has been designed to achieve the same end result as the training school, to turn you from a hesitant new rider into a fully informed motorcyclist—somebody who not only understands the potential dangers of motorcycling, but gets how to dramatically reduce those risks.

That's the trick, really; every new rider has to accept motorcycling for what it is.

We choose to ride an exposed piece of machinery in a world filled with other road users, people with wildly varying levels of skill. Smart motorcyclists understand those xiv   The Complete Idiot's Guide to Motorcycles, Fifth Edition

dangers and do everything possible to minimize them. True motorcyclists understand the need to ride defensively, and they get how vital it is to protect their bodies with the right bike gear. For this kind of motorcyclist, it's a surprisingly safe sport.

If you can walk the line between having fun and knowing when to take it seriously, the motorcycle world's enormous community will embrace you. They're a great bunch of diverse people, who all subconsciously respect each other's commitment to being a true motorcyclist. Don't be surprised if you meet some lifelong friends along the way: my wife, best man, my closest friends—in fact, nearly all of my friends—are people that I initially met just because we all ride motorcycles.

For those of us who understand the risks and are always prepared, bike riding is one of the most exhilarating experiences in existence. To be "at one" with such an ergonomically designed machine, defying gravity through twists and turns—and effortlessly accelerating away from everything else on the road with just a drop of your wrist—is, quite simply, addictive.

So yes, motorcycling can be dangerous, *in the wrong hands*, and that's what it comes down to. You've already gotten off to a great start by taking it seriously enough to buy an informative book, so I don't have to worry about you. Just take it all in, respect your bike, and I'll see you out on the road someday.

How to Use This Book

This book follows a linear, step-by-step structure, and takes you through the entire motorcycle experience from start to finish. The book is structured this way to help you minimize the risks associated with motorcycling, to help make your entry into the sport safe and enjoyable.

I've divided the book into five parts, each designed to take you to a new level of enjoyment in a safe, orderly fashion.

Part 1, Biker Basics, sets the stage for the adventure you are about to embark on, providing a general overview of why we ride, the history of motorcycling, and the types of bikes available.

Part 2, So You Want to Buy a Bike?, helps you identify what type of motorcycle you need and teaches you how to buy your first motorcycle. You get detailed discussions about the parts of a motorcycle and, more important, how those parts relate to you, the rider.

Part 3, On the Road, is probably the most important part of this book. It helps you actually get out and ride. This is where you put your knowledge to the test, where theory translates into reality.

Part 4, Living with a Motorcycle, condenses the entire spectrum of the motorcycle-ownership experience into chapters that cover maintenance, repair, customization, and collecting.

Part 5, The Motorcycling Community, discusses the many places in which you'll meet fellow motorcycle enthusiasts, including motorcycle clubs, races, and rallies. It also covers the growing trike niche and the new breed of electric bikes.

I've also included four appendixes that you'll find useful. Appendix A lists all the new bikes for sale in the United States, along with the bikes that are best suited for beginners and the bikes I believe are best buys. Appendix B features a comprehensive list of used bikes that make ideal first motorcycles. Appendix C highlights useful motorcycle-related resources, and Appendix D is a glossary of the terms you'll encounter in this book.

Extras

Throughout this book you'll find tips and information that will help you ride better and safer, without looking like a dork in the process. This information is highlighted in sidebars:

CYCLE BABBLE

Definitions of technical motorcycling terms that pop up throughout the book.

MOTORCYCOLOGY

Tips and inside information providing insights into safe, enjoyable motorcycling.

STEER CLEAR

Advice on practices and hazards to avoid if you want to choose the right kind of bike, keep the shiny side up (which means not falling down), and get the most enjoyment out of motorcycling.

MOTORCYCLE MOMENTS

Anecdotes of historical and personal moments in the history of motorcycling.

A Note About the Fifth Edition

There's been a lot going on recently in the motorcycle world. After years of keeping a fairly low profile, motorcycling suddenly got a lot of exposure in the form of several television shows. The theme was consistent throughout all of these programs: the chopper—more specifically, building custom choppers from scratch, with the shows' format being either a judged competition, or a soap opera filled with drama, mystery, and suspense (or filled with none of the above, depending on your perspective).

At the exact same time, another segment within the motorcycle community experienced a dramatic growth: stunt riding. Young guys were taking ultralight sportbikes and abusing their abundant power, making them do things they were never designed for. The poor bikes.

Other factors contributing to motorcycles' recent ascent include the high gasoline prices of the late 2000s, which drove many budget-conscious commuters onto two wheels. And finally, there are the baby boomers. With kids out of the nest, many of them are returning to the motorcycling passion of their youths, or else finally trying it for the first time.

What this all means is that a whole bunch of new riders have joined the motorcycling community in recent years, and despite the world's recent financial troubles, they've stuck around. And with the introduction of new safety features and automotive-style fuel injection and traction control on bikes, plus the promise of a new breed of electric motorcycles coming into the market, motorcycling looks ripe for still more growth.

This is great news for everyone, because more people riding bikes means more money coming into the industry, and that means more choices for bike riders.

This guide has been constantly evolving since the first issue. In this fifth edition I've updated the content throughout, totally revised the "Biker's Buying Guide to New Bikes," added a new chapter covering trikes and electric bikes, and updated the photos in the color section.

In short, this book should still be the most thorough introduction to motorcycling available. So whatever brought you into the motorcycle world, I'm glad you're here.

Trademarks

All terms mentioned in this book that are known to be or are suspected of being trademarks or service marks have been appropriately capitalized. Alpha Books and Penguin Group (USA) Inc. cannot attest to the accuracy of this information. Use of a term in this book should not be regarded as affecting the validity of any trademark or service mark.

Biker Basics

Congratulations! As a beginning biker, you are about to embark on an adventure that will change your life. No other hobby will affect you at such a fundamental level as motorcycling. It will start subtly: at work, you'll find yourself daydreaming about going for a ride while you stare at the gibberish on your computer screen; in meetings, you'll look right through your boss and instead see the road outside the window. In your mind, you'll be riding on that road. Before you know it, you'll have a pet name for your motorcycle, which, of course, you'll tattoo on some hidden part of your body.

In other words, you will become a biker.

You are about to enter the community of motorcyclists. In this part of the book, you'll learn about that community, its history, and all it has to offer you—including an introduction to the joys of motorcycling.

The Motorcycle Mystique

In This Chapter

- Why motorcyclists love to ride
- Motorcycles as "chicken soup for your soul"
- The cultural impact of motorcycles
- How motorcycle films have shaped generations of motorcyclists
- The advantages of owning a motorcycle

Perhaps one word best sums up the appeal of motorcycles: *fun*. Fun is what I had the first time I rode my neighbor's minibike nearly three decades ago. It's what I had this morning when I took my bike out for a ride.

But it's a complex fun, composed of many facets. Part of the pleasure of riding comes from the freedom and mobility the machine gives you. The exhilaration you feel as you power effortlessly up to cruising speed provides a portion of the fun. Part of your enjoyment comes from developing your riding skills—your ability to control the machine.

In this chapter, I show you why motorcycle riding can be such a rewarding, exhilarating, and liberating experience.

The Thrill of the Open Road

The sun creeps over the treetops, its warm rays driving the chill from your limbs as you open the garage door and wheel your motorcycle onto the driveway. You prop up the bike and check to make certain everything is okay, which it will be because you take good care of your machine. You don your helmet and jacket and pull on your gloves, and then start your engine. The beast jumps to life and then settles into a patient, powerful idle. You look over the bike one last time, and then mount up and ride away. Now the fun begins.

At about the same time, your neighbor, co-worker, friend, or family member is unloading his—or her—dirtbike at a local off-road park. He goes through the same rituals, giving the machine a thorough preflight inspection, donning protective gear, and then mounting up, snicking the machine into gear, and riding away. Now the fun begins.

You take it easy at first, waiting for your tires to warm. You shift through the gears, feeling the satisfying mesh of the cogs, and breathe in the cool, clean morning air. The vibration through the handlebars and footpegs feels reassuring, making you aware of your machine's mechanical presence.

As you ease onto the practice track, looking for oncoming riders, you do a warm-up lap. With each lap, you increase your speed, getting air over the jumps. The bike responds perfectly to every weight shift, to every control input.

As your tires warm, you start accelerating harder through each curve. You snake through a series of S-curves, settling into a rhythm among you, the road, and your bike, engaged in a dance as elegant as any ballet.

As your muscles warm, you start riding harder, hitting the triple section perfectly, and taking inside lines where others are taking the longer, slower outside one. You and your bike find the track's rhythm, one that's less of a ballet and more of a break dance. This is what it's all about.

It doesn't matter whether you're riding a brand-new electric bike, a cutting-edge sportbike, a heavyweight cruiser, a big touring bike, or a powerful but agile dirtbike; the thrill of the ride is what draws you out again and again. Whatever emotional baggage you may have accumulated, you leave behind on the open road. When you're participating in a dance with your bike and the road, it doesn't matter that your boss is a pointy-headed sociopath, that your spouse shouts at you, or that your kids act like juvenile delinquents. There's no room for such worries on a bike, because the activity at hand requires your total, undivided attention.

Bikes Are Beautiful

Most of us find motorcycles themselves gratifying—objects of art with an innate beauty that fills some need within us.

Motorcyclists tend to be *gearheads*. We love looking at our motorcycles almost as much as we love riding them. (In fact, some folks seem to be more enamored with viewing their machines than they are with riding them; legions of people trailer their motorcycles to different events around the country instead of riding them.)

CYCLE BABBLE

Gearhead refers to a person with a strong interest in all things mechanical. While it's not exactly a technical term, often you will hear the word *gearhead* used when describing a motorcyclist.

Motorcycles possess a functional beauty, more so than any other motorized vehicle. The reason is simple; there just isn't room on a bike for anything unnecessary. You'll see all kinds of beautiful bikes throughout this book, but for starters check out this Ducati 1198. It epitomizes modern motorcycle design; the bike was initially created to be a lean, fast race winner, yet it's also widely regarded as one of the coolest-looking street machines ever made.

Ducati's Superbikes, such as this 1198, feature highly tuned engines, race-bred chassis, and gorgeous bodywork enveloping the mechanics. The 1198 epitomizes the purpose-driven beauty found on a modern motorcycle.
(Photo courtesy of Ducati North America)

It's hard to believe now, but when Ducati unveiled the 1198's predecessor, the 916, in 1993, it had a completely groundbreaking style, though much of its design was primarily functional. Its exhaust pipes were tucked under the seat for high-speed streamlining, and the back wheel was completely exposed on one side to aid in super-quick wheel changes during a race. Ducati immediately put the bike to work in the World Superbike Championships, and in its first season, it won. The 916 and its descendants won a total of 13 world championships, and elements of its design are still being copied by everyone from large-scale manufacturers to custom builders creating one-off show bikes.

The exotic superbike is just one type of drool-inducing motorcycle; some folks dig the essential V-twin look. Harley-Davidson—the king of the V-twin—has been selling big, brawny American muscle for many years, and to many eyes its products have been elevated to near art status. To most cruiser aficionados, the only thing better than a Harley is one of the customized machines of such chopper builders as Arlen Ness and Dave Perewitz. These bikes often resemble metallic sculptures more than motorcycles. A visit to any custom-bike show can take on the trappings of a visit to a museum.

All of this provides a good example of how important the look of a motorcycle is. That's as true of a Yamaha, Triumph, Laverda, or BMW as it is of a Harley or a Ducati. Motorcyclists love the way bikes look, and for every bike, there is someone who loves its appearance.

I learned this the hard way. A while back, in an article on motorcycle style, I poked fun at a bike that was generally accepted as being one of the uglier machines to have been produced during the past 20 years. I wrote that these motorcycles were probably very nice bikes, but they were so butt-ugly that no one ever found out because no one would be seen on one. I thought this was a fair assessment, since the bike had been a sales disaster.

MOTORCYCOLOGY

The demise of an entire motorcycle company can partly be traced to its producing one motorcycle that the public found visually unappealing. BSA attempted to enter the modern motorcycle market by producing a three-cylinder motorcycle, the BSA Rocket 3. The bike showed promise, but its styling, created by an industrial design firm with no experience in the motorcycle market, received such a dismal public reception that the resulting low sales caused BSA to implode.

Fair or not, at least one reader took issue with my critique and wrote in suggesting that my head was deeply embedded in a place that defied all laws of physics. The man owned one such "ugly motorcycle," and it had given him more than 100,000 miles of enjoyment. I felt bad about that situation, not because the reader questioned my hygienic habits and insulted my ancestors, but because I had belittled a motorcycle that obviously meant a great deal to him.

The Tao of Two Wheels

Some time ago, a colleague of mine, a reporter who covered religious topics at a newspaper, asked me why I didn't go to church. I told her I did go to church every day I went out riding my motorcycle.

For many motorcyclists, the ceremony of going for a ride provides the same spiritual sustenance other people find through the ceremonies conducted by organized religions. The similarities are striking. We wear our leathers and riding suits as vestments, we have a prescribed ritual for starting our engines, and our favorite roads compose our liturgy.

The very nature of riding a motorcycle forces the rider into a spiritual state. Think of it this way: most religious systems encourage some form of meditative technique. Christians have prayer. Some Native Americans meditate inside sweat lodges, and Eastern spiritual systems advocate elaborate chanting techniques. All these methods have as their common general goal the transcendence of the self or ego in order to get in touch with some greater force.

Motorcycling forces riders to transcend their egos—to empty themselves and exist in the world around them. The consequences of not being totally aware of their actions and environment, of becoming distracted by the baggage of their everyday lives, are too great. When you're out in the world on a bike, you must be completely in the moment, completely aware of your surroundings, or you may find yourself meeting your concept of God earlier than you might have hoped.

But when everything is working, when you and your bike are totally in sync and the road rushing under your feet feels like an extension of your body—at those times, you get in touch with divinity.

Biker Chic

Not all that long ago, motorcycles were considered the domain of leather-clad hoodlums—guys you didn't want your daughter to be seen with. But such a stereotype has always been inaccurate, and most people now realize that.

Motorcycling began to gain social acceptance in the 1960s, when the Japanese began exporting small, unintimidating motorcycles to the United States, but only in recent years has motorcycling been elevated to the status of high fashion.

Celebrities have always ridden motorcycles. Clark Gable terrorized Los Angeles on his Ariel Square Four. Marlon Brando used his own personal motorcycle in the film *The Wild One*. James Dean rode bikes from the time he was in high school. Steve McQueen's real-life racing antics made the jump scene in *The Great Escape* look feeble.

But these were Hollywood's bad boys—sexy rebels who knew no fear. You wouldn't find a nice woman like Donna Reed or a respectable fellow like Jimmy Stewart straddling a motorcycle.

Sometime during the 1980s, that changed. This shift in our collective perception began slowly. Photos of celebrity CEO Malcolm Forbes touring the world on his Harley-Davidson appeared in mainstream magazines, and Juan Carlos, the King of Spain, could be found touring his domain on a Harley. And, of course, Hollywood's latest string of bad boys—people such as Mickey Rourke, Sylvester Stallone, Bruce Willis, and Arnold Schwarzenegger—came out of the closet and proclaimed themselves bikers.

But it didn't stop there. Nice, respectable folks such as Jay Leno and Mary Hart let the world know they were motorcyclists. Country boy Lyle Lovett began appearing on magazine covers aboard his hot-rod Ducati. Rosie O'Donnell seldom appeared in the tabloids without her Suzuki Intruder. Ewan "Obi-Wan" McGregor took months off from his lucrative film career to take the trip-of-a-lifetime adventure tour. Mark-Paul Gosselaar of *NYPD Blue* likes to ride motocross. And Anthony Quinn's son Francesco has been riding since the tender age of four.

Now, motorcycles are must-have fashion accessories for celebrities and celebrity wannabes, much like nipple rings were *de rigueur* for Seattle grunge rockers in the early 1990s.

The Art of Motorcycles

Although the motorcycle-as-nipple-ring is a fairly recent development, bikes have always had a strong influence on popular culture. In turn, popular culture has played a strong role in developing the motorcycle community. The appeal of motorcycles to actors is no coincidence. Because riding a bike is a high-profile activity, motorcycles have always been an excellent method for studios to showcase and draw attention to their stars.

The history of motorcycles in film is as old as the history of motion pictures itself. Motorcycles appeared in some of the earliest silent films, including *Mabel at the Wheel* (1914), in which Charlie Chaplin drops Mabel off the back of his motorcycle and into a mud puddle.

Films about motorcycle riders appeared early on, including in *No Limit* (1935), in which English actor George Formby played a motorcycle-riding hero battling a gang of biker toughs.

While motorcycles played many roles in Hollywood films, the medium of film played an even more influential role in shaping motorcycle culture. As motorcycle films became more popular, increasing numbers of riders tried to emulate their screen heroes. When Marlon Brando portrayed Johnny in *The Wild One*, he portrayed a very atypical motorcyclist. After a generation of bikers grew up with Brando's Johnny as a role model, though, the image of the leather-clad, motorcycle-riding hood, while still an aberration, became much more common. Because of the influence of films, portrayals of motorcyclists became self-fulfilling prophecies. The myriad outlaw-biker B-movies Hollywood cranked out during the 1960s and 1970s spawned a subculture of motorcyclists who modeled themselves on the bikers in those films. When Peter Fonda portrayed the philosophical Wyatt in *Easy Rider*, he gave birth to the real-life hippie poet-biker stereotype. When Arnold Schwarzenegger came back as promised in *Terminator 2: Judgment Day*, he did so on a Harley Fat Boy. Soon a Harley and a cigar were the macho man's must-have accessories.

Motorcycles have only gotten better since then, with the newest crop of bikes more adept at almost everything, from luxury touring to hair-raising back-roads dancing, from local dirt riding to around-the-world adventuring, and from showboating down Main Street on a chopper to putting silently to the local coffeehouse on an electric commuter. In short, the breadth and scope of bikes has continued to widen until there is now definitely, as the old saying goes, something for everyone in motorcycling.

From Wild Ones to Biker Boyz

For many years films like *The Wild One* and *Easy Rider* seemed to mark the beginning and end of Hollywood's most influential period on motorcycling. Even now they're two of the most important motorcycle films ever made, and classics that every bike rider should see.

The Wild One became the archetypal biker flick because it was the first to portray the unique breed of bikers that sprang up in post–World War II America.

This film initiated a decades-long period of mistrust between motorcyclists and the general public. Johnny and his buddies seem pretty tame by today's standards; compared to bikers portrayed in later flicks, they're about as nice a bunch of boys as you'll ever meet. But back in 1953, Johnny represented the antichrist to Middle America.

MOTORCYCOLOGY

The event that inspired the film *The Wild One,* the so-called Hollister Invasion, was actually more of a nonevent. On the Fourth of July of 1947, about 3,500 motorcyclists rode to Hollister, California (a town of about 4,500), to attend a race meeting. Another 500 or so riders showed up just to have a little fun. A few of these bikers got a bit out of hand, and by noon the next day, 29 of them had been cited for drunkenness, indecent exposure, and traffic violations. Unfortunately, newspapers ran hyperbolic tales of anarchy and debauchery as thousands of bikers ran amuck, and *Life* magazine printed an infamous photo of a beer-guzzling rider stretched out on his customized Harley amid a pile of beer bottles. (The photo was staged by the *Life* photographer.) The myth of the outlaw biker was born.

The Wild One gave birth to a new genre: the biker B-movie. In the 1950s and 1960s, Hollywood cranked out a pile of low-budget biker flicks. Each of these films tried to outdo the others in portraying the wild outlaw biker. *Easy Rider,* starring Peter Fonda, Dennis Hopper, and Jack Nicholson (in his first major film role), finally shattered that stereotype. Directed by the late Dennis Hopper, the movie changed everything. No longer was the antihero biker a confused Neanderthal, mindlessly lashing out at whatever got in his way. Instead, *Easy Rider* presented the biker as a sensitive, thoughtful enigma.

Fast-forward to the current day, and after years of silence on the biker movie front, it's happening all over again. Hollywood has realized that the bike world has been rejuvenated with younger riders and new attitudes, and they've started putting out movies like *Torque* and *Biker Boyz.* Do these new flicks finally improve the bike riders' image? Yeah, right, apparently we're still trouble with a capital T!

With the film Easy Rider, actors Dennis Hopper and Peter Fonda turned the Hollywood biker image upside down.
(Photo courtesy of *Motorcyclist* magazine)

MOTORCYCLE MOMENTS

Although Peter Fonda was an accomplished motorcyclist before he filmed *Easy Rider*, co-star Dennis Hopper was anything but. Before he made the film, Hopper's motorcycle experience was confined to a scooter he had owned in the 1950s—and he had crashed that machine in a rather spectacular fashion. After finishing the film, Hopper admitted to having been scared silly by his Harley.

Easy Rider: The Convenience of Bikes

Given the influence motorcycles have had on film and on our general culture, it's easy to argue the more esoteric appeal of motorcycling, but the sport has some practical benefits as well.

The relatively low price of motorcycles makes them attractive as practical transportation. While prices have risen dramatically during the past few decades, for the most part bikes are still much less expensive than cars. You can buy a used motorcycle in "like-new" condition in the $4,000 price range. For that money, you can pick up a bike that will deliver years or even decades of trouble-free transportation. Try finding a car for the same amount that isn't ready for the crusher.

In congested urban areas, the small size and mobility of a motorcycle provide real advantages over a car. An experienced rider can zip through traffic, and in places where the practice is legal (such as California), you can ride between lanes on the freeways (a practice known as *lane splitting*).

CYCLE BABBLE

Lane splitting (or filtering) refers to the practice of riding between lanes of traffic on a freeway. While this practice may sound dangerous, studies indicate that it might actually be safer than idling along in a traffic jam.

And with a motorcycle, you will never have to worry about a parking spot. You can always find a space to back into because you'll require only a fraction of the space a car requires—and some pay-to-park lots even set aside free motorcycle parking areas.

Another practical benefit of motorcycles is their fuel efficiency. Even the biggest touring bike or fastest sportbike gets as many miles to the gallon as most econocars, and when ridden prudently, a smaller motorcycle can go for a couple of weeks without visiting the gas pump. Some bikes manage a frugal 80 mpg.

If global climate change is caused by the burning of fossil fuels, as the majority of scientists believe, then we may soon be facing the prospect of dramatically increased fuel prices. In a world filled with gridlocked cities, the fuel- and space-efficient nature of motorcycles could create a new boom of motorcycles as a serious form of transportation. This has been the case for several years in Europe, where many people have completely given up on owning a car.

The Least You Need to Know

- You get from motorcycling what you put into it.
- Like meditation, motorcycling requires your undivided attention.
- Biker flicks have shaped motorcycle culture as much as motorcycle culture has shaped biker flicks.
- Motorcycles can be practical as well as fun.

A Brief History of Bikes

In This Chapter

- How motorcycling developed from cheap transportation into a passionate hobby
- The myth of the outlaw biker
- How the baby boomers changed the face of motorcycling
- Harley-Davidson's role in today's motorcycle market

Motorcycling offers more pleasure than any other activity a person can engage in (well, okay, not *any* other activity, but almost). It also extracts a high penalty for making mistakes. If you're going to be a motorcyclist, you'll need as much knowledge as you can get to survive out there, and a solid understanding of the history of the sport is part of that knowledge.

But knowing how we got here from there serves as an ego boost as well. Motorcyclists are gearheads, people with an almost unnatural attraction to things mechanical. Like every other group, we have our inside secrets, status symbols that tell whether a person is a hardcore rider or just another dork with a motorcycle. Few of these clues scream "Dork!" as loudly as a rider poorly versed in the history of motorcycles. In this chapter, I'll give you the inside info you'll need to become a true motorcyclist.

Humble Beginnings

Almost as soon as the modern bicycle appeared toward the end of the nineteenth century, some inspired individual (my hero) decided to strap an internal-combustion motor to the contraption. By the turn of the century, a variety of motorized bicycles were available to the general public.

The motorized-bicycle experiments of two young men, William S. Harley and Arthur Davidson, proved to be more influential to American motorcycling than all the rest combined. The pair realized their experiments had commercial potential, and along with Arthur's brothers, Walter and William, they formed the Harley-Davidson Motor Company in 1903 to manufacture motorized bicycles. From this humble beginning sprang the longest continuously running motorcycle-manufacturing firm in the world, affectionately known as The Motor Company.

But Mr. Harley and the Davidson boys weren't the only people conducting such experiments.

MOTORCYCLE MOMENTS

Gottlieb Daimler, the German inventor who produced the first functional four-stroke engine, may well have created the first gasoline-powered motorcycle. After his early experiments using an engine to power a four-wheeled horseless carriage produced less than satisfactory results (probably due to the whopping 0.5 horsepower the motor cranked out), Daimler built his Einspur, or single-tracked test vehicle, in 1885. Although crude, this vehicle incorporated many features still found on motorcycles today, such as a cradle frame and twist-grip controls on the handlebars.

In 1902, one year before the formation of The Motor Company, a German engineer named Maurice (Mauritz) Johann Schulte designed a motorcycle, the first to be produced by Triumph Cycle Co., Ltd., of England. This machine was still very much a motorized bicycle with a Belgian-produced engine fitted to its frame.

The early years of the twentieth century saw hundreds of similar companies form. The low power output of the engines available at the time made them better suited to power small, two-wheeled vehicles than larger, carriage-type machines, and motorcycles thrived as forms of personal transportation. Plus, cars were still too expensive for most people to own; motorcycles were cheaper and more plentiful.

Like all technology of that time, motorcycle development proceeded at a frantic pace. Soon the early motorized bicycles were supplanted by machines designed from the start to be operated by some form of engine. By the end of World War I, most of the technical innovations we see today had been tried with varying degrees of success. Because other technologies, such as metallurgy—the study of metals—hadn't kept pace with such innovations, by the 1920s motorcycle designers had settled on relatively simple designs. The brilliant ideas of those early designers proved to be ahead of their time, and many would have to wait until the 1970s or 1980s to finally find acceptance.

Although the sport of motorcycling thrived initially, the same technological advances that drove its success led to the first of the sport's many crises. As internal-combustion engines became more powerful and efficient, they became more practical as power sources for horseless carriages. And with the advent of affordable automobiles such as Henry Ford's Model T in 1913, average people could afford to buy cars. Clearly, it was easier to haul the entire family to church in an automobile; you could only haul three or four family members on a motorcycle, and then only if it was equipped with a *sidecar.* By the end of World War I, many of the companies manufacturing motorcycles had either gone out of business or switched to the manufacture of some other product. Motorcycles might have become extinct, except for some clever marketing moves on the part of the remaining manufacturers.

 CYCLE BABBLE

Sidecars are small carriages attached to the side of a motorcycle to provide extra carrying capacity and extra stability in low-speed, low-traction conditions. Sidecars usually consist of a tubelike cockpit area resting on a frame that attaches to the motorcycle on one side and is held aloft by a wheel on the opposite side.

Motorcycling survived by positioning itself as a sport, a leisure activity, rather than trying to compete with automobiles as practical transportation. The move made sense. People had been racing motorcycles all along; promoting riding in general as a sport was a logical extension of that activity.

This market positioning helped motorcycling survive its second great crisis: the Great Depression. This worldwide economic disaster finished off many of the remaining motorcycle-manufacturing firms that had survived the advent of the inexpensive, reliable automobile, and, again, those companies that survived did so by promoting motorcycling as a sport.

The Wild Ones: The Outlaws' Conveyance

Motorcycling in America entered the modern era following World War II. Important technological advances had been made before the war, but most people were too busy struggling to survive the Depression to pay much attention.

World War II changed all that. After the war, a lot of restless people came back from Europe and Asia, people not content to go back to the way things were. They could afford transportation, and they had an elaborate new highway system to explore. Many of them decided to explore those new roads via motorcycles.

As you saw in the previous chapter, the film *The Wild One* played an important role in the formation of the postwar motorcycling community. It was a difficult time for many Americans. We'd won the war, but afterward, nothing seemed quite the same. To the general public, Johnny, Marlon Brando's character in the film, represented everything that was wrong with the country. Like Communism, the stereotype of the outlaw biker became a focal point for their fears.

When Marlon Brando roared into small-town America in The Wild One, *he used his own motorcycle, a 650cc Triumph Thunderbird very much like this 1953 example.*
(Photo © 1998 Timothy Remus)

But not everyone feared Johnny. Some people wanted more out of life than the latest automatic appliances in the kitchen and a new Plymouth sedan parked in the driveway. For them, Johnny represented an escape from the mind-numbing conformity of McCarthy-era America. In Johnny, Brando created a role model for these disaffected young people—a figure who jelled in America's psyche as the archetypal outlaw biker.

The Japanese Invasion

Throughout the 1950s, motorcycling remained the domain of extreme gearheads and onepercenters (outlaws). Nice people didn't ride a bike. Nice people didn't even associate with those who did ride, whether they were upstanding members of the American Motorcycle Association (AMA) or hardcore outlaws.

The reason for this involved more than just the perceived danger of the sport or of motorcyclists' outlaw image. There were practical reasons for the marginality of motorcycling as well.

Part of the problem was that the machines themselves demanded a great deal from their owners. The technological advancements of motorcycling hadn't kept pace with those of automobiles. By the 1950s, cars were relatively reliable, easily maintained devices, and the experience of owning one wasn't all that different than it is today.

Bikes were another story.

The reason only gearheads owned motorcycles back then was that you *had* to be a gearhead to own one. There was nothing easy about riding a bike. Even starting the beast was a traumatic experience in those pre-electric-start days. Glance at the starting procedure of a mid-1950s Triumph as outlined in its owner's manual, and you'll be instructed to tickle the carburetors (ooh, Missus), retard the spark (an instruction, not an insult), and align the piston according to the phase of the moon. Once you'd accomplished all this, it was time to *kick-start* the bike. If your bike was in a good mood that day, it would start without backfiring and smashing your ankle into hundreds of tiny bone shards (now that would ruin a Monday morning).

 CYCLE BABBLE

Kick-starting is a method of starting up a bike engine on a machine without an electric starter. A lever sticks out of the side of the engine, which you "kick." In reality this translates into putting all of the momentum you can gather throughout your whole body and directing it down toward your foot in a massive lunge. Mind you don't kick over that shiny bike by accident!

And all this just to *start* the bike. Keeping it running was just as difficult. Riders who put a lot of miles on their machines knew the inner workings of their bikes intimately. They saw them frequently, sometimes even when they hadn't intended to: more than one rider saw pistons, valves, and connecting rods flying from their engines as they exploded like oily grenades just below their baby-making equipment.

You Meet the Nicest People on a Honda

Part of the reason for the stagnation in motorcycle design at this time was lack of competition. The Indian Motorcycle Company (the first American motorcycle company, preceding Harley-Davidson by two years) had quit building motorcycles by the mid-1950s; even before it gave up the ghost, it had long ceased being competitive with Harley-Davidson. The British manufacturers had to keep up with only one another, and as long as none of them raised the stakes too high, none of them had to try too hard. There were interesting developments taking place in other European countries, but those countries were still in such turmoil from the war that manufacturers there concentrated on producing cheap transportation for their own people and weren't interested in exporting motorcycles to the rest of the world.

That was soon to change. In only a few years, these complacent manufacturers found themselves up against some very serious competition from a most unlikely source: Japan.

Like Italy and Germany, Japan was in ruins following World War II. Japan's manufacturing infrastructure had been even more severely devastated. After the war, Japan had to start from scratch. The Japanese rose to the challenge, and rather than rebuilding the past, they looked to the future for their inspiration.

MOTORCYCLE MOMENTS

While most early Japanese motorcycles were small bikes, the bikes manufactured by the Rikuo Company were big exceptions. That company manufactured large V-twin Harley-Davidson replicas, built under a licensing agreement with The Motor Company. Soon Rikuo was improving on the Harley design, introducing telescopic forks in 1948, a year before Harley introduced the innovation. This was followed by the introduction of a foot-operated gearshift (Harley still used a cumbersome, hand-operated system) and automatic spark advance (for easier starting). By this time, Rikuo believed it had modified its design to the point that it no longer had to pay for the license agreement. Harley disagreed and made its displeasure known to the Japanese government, which, in turn, withdrew its orders for police bikes from Rikuo, forcing the company out of business.

As in European countries, Japan's postwar motorcycle industry emerged to service society's need for cheap transportation. That industry had a humble beginning, with many manufacturers building clones of bikes from other countries.

Americans had little use for the more or less overgrown mopeds coming out of Japan, nor did any other country for quite a few years. But by the late 1950s, Japanese motorcycles began to make their way into Europe and then into the United States. By this time, Japanese bikes had evolved into distinctive, original machines with innovations that made riders take note. These were elegant, reliable, nimble, and fast bikes—and cheap, to boot.

The innovation people most took note of was the inclusion of electric starters on many of these machines. No longer did riders need the legs of mules to kick-start their bikes; they simply pushed a button and rode off.

Unlike other manufacturers, the Japanese realized the sales potential of motorcycles that were convenient to use, and no Japanese company capitalized on convenience as a selling point as well as Honda. In an ad campaign designed to highlight the utility of its machines, Honda set the sport of motorcycling on the path toward respectability.

MOTORCYCOLOGY

Before becoming a manufacturer of motorcycles, Soichiro Honda, the founder of Honda, operated a series of businesses that were less than successful. In fact, he once described his life as "nothing but mistakes, a series of failures, a series of regrets." But he credited those failures for his success. "Success can be achieved only through repeated failure and introspection. In fact, success represents 1 percent of your work and results from the 99 percent that is called failure."

That campaign was the famous "You meet the nicest people on a Honda" series of ads, and it single-handedly undid much of the damage done to the image of motorcycling by films such as *The Wild One*. The ads, which featured "normal" people doing non-outlaw-type things on Honda motorcycles, appeared in 1961 and were so effective that they made the sport of motorcycling seem acceptable to society as a whole. The ads had such a powerful effect that for years afterward, the word *Honda* became synonymous with small motorcycles, much like the name *Xerox* is used as a verb meaning "to photocopy."

The Japanese Hit the Big Time

Because the Japanese were producing only small motorcycles and not "real" bikes, the other major manufacturers didn't consider them a serious threat and paid little attention to them. That proved to be a mistake—a fatal mistake for many of the more marginal manufacturers—because the Japanese were deadly serious.

As the 1960s progressed, the bikes coming from Japan increased in size and capabilities, but the other manufacturers still paid them little heed. By 1965, when Honda introduced its CB450 Super Sport, the competition had wised up. This bike, known as the Black Bomber for its racy black bodywork, handled like a European machine and could outrun a stock Harley-Davidson with more than twice its engine displacement.

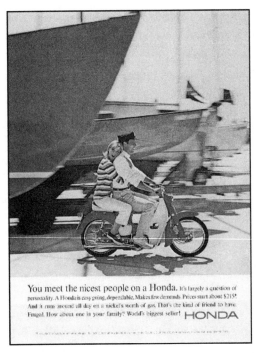

This Honda ad proved so effective at getting people to buy motorcycles that it's still studied in advertising classes today.
(Photo courtesy of Vreeke & Associates)

Finally, Japan's competitors realized what they were up against and found the motivation to respond to the threat. The British manufacturers BSA and Triumph began to jointly develop a large-displacement multicylinder machine in an attempt to preserve their advantage in sporting bikes, and Harley grafted an electric starter onto its big-twin engine in an attempt to provide Japanese-style convenience.

Both these projects proved to be too little too late. By the time the British unveiled their triples, which were flawed machines with styling only a mother or designer could love, Honda had unveiled its big gun: the four-cylinder CB750 Four.

It's impossible to overstate the impact this bike had on the motorcycling world.

What Honda did by introducing the CB750 was the equivalent of a car company producing a high-quality sports car equal to or better than the best machines produced by Porsche or Mercedes, and then selling it for the price of a Kia. Here was a machine capable of outrunning any mass-produced motorcycle on the road and able to do so all day long without any mechanical problems. Plus, people could afford it.

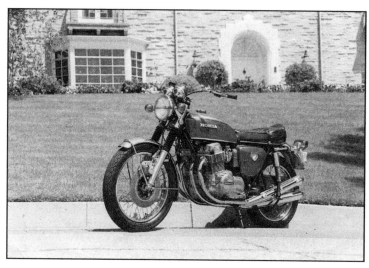

Perhaps the most significant motorcycle in history, the 1969 Honda CB750 Four changed the face of motorcycling.
(Photo courtesy of Vreeke & Associates)

Given the success of the big Honda, it was only a matter of time before other Japanese manufacturers followed suit and produced big bikes of their own. Kawasaki jumped into the four-cylinder arena with its mighty Z1, and after a couple of false starts, Suzuki also joined the fray, followed by Yamaha.

These big-bore motorcycles devastated the competition. For the British, hampered by management unable to let go of pre–World War II motorcycle designs, the competition proved to be too much. Harley-Davidson managed to survive, partly due to the fanatical loyalty of its customers, but entered into a long period of decline. For a while in the 1970s, it looked like the Japanese would be the only people left in the motorcycling business.

Baby Boomers on (Two) Wheels

The success of the Japanese manufacturers in the United States provides one of history's best examples of being in the right place at the right time. The Japanese caught a wave caused by the baby boom generation, and this massive influx of young people provided the fuel to propel the Japanese invasion.

Although some restless individuals returning from the war spent their newfound wealth on motorcycles and raising hell, most used that money to pursue the American dream—a dream that included raising a family. And raise families they did, prolifi-cally, creating a new generation so large that their whims would dictate trends for the rest of their lives and shape our culture for generations to come. The impact of the so-called baby boom generation will be felt long after the last baby boomer has moved on to that great salvage yard in the sky.

The Boomer Boom

Just as the first small Japanese motorcycles began to appear on the West Coast, the first wave of baby boomers was getting its collective driver's license. It didn't take an advanced degree in economics to see the profit potential of providing these kids, products of unprecedented affluence, with fun, affordable, and reliable motorcycles.

The maturation of the Japanese motorcycle industry mirrors the maturation of the baby boom generation. As these kids grew in size, so grew the Japanese bikes. By the 1970s, most baby boomers were entering adulthood. They roamed farther, rode faster, and were physically larger than when Mr. Honda started importing his small Super Cub and Dream motorcycles into the country. They no longer needed small, inexpensive motorcycles to ride to football practice or down to the beach. What they needed were full-size motorcycles with enough power to satisfy their adventurous spirits, bikes comfortable enough for cross-country trips. And the Japanese were happy to oblige.

MOTORCYCOLOGY

While the Italians produced mechanically brilliant motorcycles during the 1960s and 1970s, cosmetically they left much to be desired. The bikes were beautiful from a distance, but upon closer inspection, the quality of paint and bodywork was abysmal. One well-known example of this was *Cycle* magazine's preproduction 1974 Ducati 750 Super Sport test bike, which came with an actual fly embedded in the fiberglass of the fuel tank—perfecto, a free fossil!

By this time, these young people had become accustomed to the convenience and reliability of Japanese motorcycles. Harley-Davidsons of the 1970s were only incre-mentally improved over those built during the 1930s. Compounding these problems, American Machine and Foundry (AMF), Harley's parent company at that time, was more interested in turning a quick buck than in doing long-term development. Even Willie G. Davidson, a direct descendant of one of the company's founders, Arthur Davidson, admits that their bikes suffered quality-control problems during this period as a result of AMF's desire to get as many bikes as possible to the market.

Problems were even worse over in England. During the 1950s and 1960s, the British bike industry was mostly run by the same people who had brought the industry to prominence in the 1930s and 1940s. These people tended to oppose even the slightest change, often ignoring the specific requests of their American distributors.

The result was that the British motorcycle industry was in complete disarray and unable to cash in on the demographic trends taking place in the United States. It couldn't even develop a reliable electric-starting system that didn't explode through the engine cases on every ninth or tenth starting attempt.

For the bulk of this massive new generation of Americans, British or American motorcycles were not an option. The German firm BMW produced spectacular bikes that were as reliable and convenient as Japanese machines, but they cost more and weren't as widely marketed in the United States. The Italians also produced motorcycles that were in many ways equal to or superior to the Japanese bikes, but these, too, came at a premium price. Add to this the peculiar Italian penchant for designing and developing spectacular machinery but then showing near-total disinterest in producing or marketing those same bikes, and the Italians were an even smaller blip than the Germans on the radar of most motorcyclists. For most riders, the only real option was to buy Japanese.

The Bust

Whenever something is going well, those profiting from it convince themselves that it will go well forever. That's just human nature. The Japanese manufacturers imagined that their lock on the American motorcycle market was secure. But they were wrong.

In hindsight, it makes sense. As the baby boomers grew older, many of them lost interest in the adventuresome activities they engaged in during their youth. Even if they were still interested in pursuing sports such as motorcycling, their lives were changing in ways that limited the available time they had to do so. After they graduated from college, their careers began demanding ever-increasing amounts of their time. And when they started families, those families cut into both the free time they had to ride and the amount of cash available to spend on adult toys such as motorcycles.

You would think the motorcycle manufacturers would have seen this trend coming, but they didn't. By the time the tail end of the baby boom generation entered the workforce in the early to mid-1980s, a time when the manufacturers could have logically expected a market downturn, the Japanese had increased production to record levels. And when the bust hit, American distributors found themselves with warehouses filled with unsold Japanese motorcycles.

Throughout most of the 1980s, the American distributors concentrated on eliminating this surplus, selling three-, four-, and even five-year-old carryover bikes at a fraction of their original cost. The cost of carrying these machines for nearly half a decade drove many dealers out of business, and the lost profits from having to sell the motorcycles below cost almost bankrupted at least one of the Japanese manufacturers.

Manufacturers are still feeling the effects of this debacle. Those few people who had bought motorcycles at list price during the early 1980s were not too pleased to come back to trade those machines a year or two down the road and see the exact same bikes sitting on showroom floors priced at less than half of what they had paid. Not only was this insulting, but it made it extraordinarily difficult for them to sell their own used bikes.

MOTORCYCLE MOMENTS

While the 1980s surplus of unsold motorcycles proved an expensive mistake for the sellers of those bikes, bargain hunters had a field day. In 1985, I purchased a brand-new carryover 1982 Yamaha Seca 650, a bike that listed for $3,200 new in 1982, for $1,399 right out of the crate. Many riders still use those bargain bikes on a daily basis, racking up hundreds of thousands of miles on them.

The Risen Hog: The Resurrected Motorcycle Market

Once again, the future of the sport of motorcycling appeared uncertain, but help was coming. The cavalry was on its way, but this time it had chosen a most unlikely mount: Harley-Davidson motorcycles.

In 1981, a group of 13 senior Harley-Davidson executives purchased Harley-Davidson from owners AMF. Work commenced on a new engine, and the introduction of that engine, known as the Evolution, opened up an entirely new market for Harley-Davidson.

Before 1981, Harleys were still motorcycles of the old school, meaning that to own one, you had to have the mechanical acumen to overhaul the beast on the side of the road in the middle of the night with nothing but a Zippo lighter, an adjustable wrench, and an intimate familiarity with the motorcycle's internals to guide you. Harleys were just not practical, reliable machines for the majority of riders.

The Evolution, or Evo, engine ended that sorry state of affairs and proved to be a reliable, long-life engine. For the first time, an owner didn't have to be a grease monkey to ride a Harley.

Harley's image as an unreliable Stone Age artifact prevented the new machine from gaining immediate marketplace acceptance. To get a bit of breathing room, Harley petitioned the Reagan administration to impose a temporary tariff on imported motorcycles with engine displacements over 700cc.

In the end, Harley's successful comeback proved to be a blessing for everyone and contributed much to the rebounding of the industry as a whole. So successful was the new Evo engine that Harley asked the federal government to remove the tariff a year before it was originally scheduled to be lifted. By the early 1990s, Harley was selling every motorcycle it could make, with people waiting months and even years to be able to purchase one. By the summer of 2001, Harley surpassed Honda in total U.S. sales for the first time since the 1960s.

As you saw in Chapter 1, Harley's newfound success permeated every aspect of American culture. Soon you could buy everything from official Harley-Davidson underwear to Harley-Davidson toilet-seat covers and Harley-Davidson cigarettes.

Ironically, the one thing that was tough to find was an actual Harley-Davidson motorcycle. Weary of the quality-control problems it had during the AMF days, Harley was careful not to expand its production beyond its capabilities.

As Harley's increasing popularity fueled a new interest in motorcycles, the lack of available Harley-Davidsons created a vacuum. Once again, the Japanese stepped up to fill this void.

And once again, the baby boomers were the driving force behind this new interest in motorcycling. These were the same people who had bought all those little Hondas in the 1960s, who had terrorized the highways on shrieking Kawasakis in the 1970s, and who had spent the 1980s raising kids and making money.

Now their kids were grown up, and they once again found themselves with some free time and money on their hands. They missed the fun they used to have on their motorcycles, so they got back into the sport.

For some time, motorcycling's popularity flared spectacularly. Sales for the four Japanese manufacturers—Honda, Yamaha, Kawasaki, and Suzuki—rose steadily since 1992, Harley-Davidson was selling every bike it could build, and more European manufacturers were experiencing success in the U.S. market. Germany's BMW; Italy's Aprilia, Ducati, Moto-Guzzi, and MV Agusta; and the Austrian company KTM became a larger part of the American scene than they ever were in the past.

A rekindled Triumph even began producing bikes in 1991, after being out of action for nearly a decade.

Royal Enfield, another storied English brand, now operating in India, likewise developed a new fuel-injected model for export, while Russia's Ural made its likeable classic sidecar rig available in the States. And then there were the Taiwanese and Koreans, bringing sportbikes and cruisers to battle the Japanese at their own historic game—price. There was even some homegrown competition for Harley-Davidson, for the first time since the first demise of Indian. Polaris, an American manufacturer of snowmobiles and all-terrain vehicles, introduced a large cruiser-type bike called the Victory in 1998 and quickly built an impressive model lineup.

But like most every other market sector, motorcycle retail sales crashed once again when the economic downturn of 2008 threw a large shovelful of sand on the fire. While many motorcyclists kept right on riding (after all, bikes are cheap to operate), they did so on existing bikes rather than new ones. So the companies all hunkered down to weather the economic storm, reducing the number of bikes imported and offering incentives or fire-sale pricing on leftover models.

Despite the recessionary sales lull, one thing is certain: motorcyclists have never had a larger variety of outstanding motorcycles from which to choose, and every one of these machines provides levels of reliability and performance that were unimaginable 30 years ago. All things considered, there has never been a better time to be a motorcyclist.

The Least You Need to Know

- Motorcycles have been around nearly as long as the modern bicycle.
- The Japanese took the sport of motorcycling to new heights of popularity with their small, unintimidating, reliable, and fun machines.
- The fate of motorcycling since World War II has mirrored the fate of the baby boom generation.
- The rebirth of Harley-Davidson following the introduction of the Evolution engine proved so strong that it helped pull the entire motorcycle industry out of an economic slump.
- Today's motorcycle buyers have more choices than at any other time since the first part of the twentieth century.

Types of Motorcycles

In This Chapter

- Doing it in the dirt: types of dirtbikes and dual-sport bikes
- Which street standards are endangered species
- Cruisers: the ultimate American bikes
- Touring machines

Back in the olden days, one bike pretty much served every purpose. You could buy a BSA Gold Star, for example, and use it as everyday transportation on public roads. That bike could be adapted to dirt use, too—just remove the front fender, change the tires, and bolt on a higher pipe. And should you want to go racing, with a little work on the engine, your Gold Star could be competitive on any track in the world.

Now, though, there's not only a bewildering choice of bikes for a new rider, there's also an overwhelming amount of peer pressure. If your buddies ride Harleys, they'll burn your ears off if you tell them you want a Honda. If your friends all tear it up on sportbikes, they'll give you a million reasons not to ride a cruiser. Just like when you were growing up, you'll have to take your own road.

Split Personalities: Dual-Sports

Many riders want to travel off the beaten path, but at the same time, they need a motorcycle they can legally ride on public roads to get to that unbeaten path. Motorcycle manufacturers have long recognized this need; that's why they make *dual-sports*.

CYCLE BABBLE

Dual-sport motorcycles (sometimes called *dual-purpose* bikes) are street-legal motorcycles with varying degrees of off-road capabilities.

Each of the big-four Japanese companies, as well as several European firms, manufacture some form of dual-sport. Some examples are as follows:

- Honda makes the XR650L, maybe the most off-road-worthy of all the big Japanese dual-sports, and a perennial favorite for all sorts of riders seeking a versatile and reliable mount. The smaller CRF230L is also available.

- Kawasaki builds its KLR650, a big single-cylinder dual-sport bike, but also the smaller and lighter KLX250S and Super Sherpa.

- Suzuki's big DR650SE is generally a better streetbike than the Honda and a better dirtbike than the Kawasaki and it, too, is joined in the lineup by the DR-Z400S and DR200SE.

- BMW's prime entry in the dual-sport market is its gigantic R1200GS. But BMW also builds the energetic parallel-twin F800GS, along with single-cylinder G650X Country and G450X models.

- KTM, an Austrian manufacturer best known for its off-road racing success, makes the big 990 Adventure and 950 Super Enduro R V-twins, as well as three single-cylinder models, the 690 Enduro R, 530 EXC, and 450 EXC. All are great (but pricey) entries into this category.

- Yamaha offers a trio of lightweight dual-sport entries—the WR250R, XT250, and fat-tired TW200. All feature economical single-cylinder engines.

A big engine in a dual-sport will mean a big bike, and a big bike can weigh a lot. If you're off-road and you drop it, you'll start to hate picking up that big bike pretty quickly. So when you're buying a dual-sport you should try to decide what your ratio is going to be for on-road riding versus off-road riding. If you're into doing more roadwork, then buy a bigger bike; if you prefer the idea of exploring unpaved roads or trails, then buy a smaller, lighter one, or maybe even go for a more focused road-legal dirtbike.

Any of the bikes listed will make an ideal first motorcycle. In addition to having varying degrees of dirt-worthiness, each makes a very nimble and forgiving streetbike. They're all fantastic city bikes. Their easy handling makes them excellent bikes for a learner, but their all-around capability means a rider won't outgrow them after learning to ride. (If you want to check out these and other dual-sports, see Appendix A.)

The only drawback these bikes have is that they're tall machines. Part of the reason they work so well both on and off the road is that they have long-travel suspensions, which place the seat high off the pavement. While this lets riders see traffic, it also presents some challenges for those with shorter inseams. A word to the wise: test-ride one; the height isn't for everybody.

There's another type of dual-sport: the *leviathan*. These are large-displacement machines based on streetbikes. In a way, they're throwbacks to earlier times, when a single machine was used for all purposes.

 CYCLE BABBLE

The term **leviathan** originally referred to a biblical sea monster, but has come to mean something of immense size and power, a good description of these big, multicylinder dual-sports, which can weigh almost twice as much as the largest single-cylinder dual-sports.

BMW introduced the first of the leviathans in 1980, when it brought out the R80GS, an 800cc twin-cylinder bike with high fenders and an upswept muffler. This versatile bike proved popular, especially in Europe, but it might have remained an anomaly had it not been for one event: the Dakar rally.

The Dakar rally (previously called the Paris-Dakar rally) is an off-road endurance race across thousands of miles of Argentina and Chile, and it is here the leviathans really shine. The event's popularity during its early years in Europe and Africa generated the production of Dakar-style replicas from many motorcycle manufacturers.

First up was the BMW R80GS, which was basically a streetbike with a bit of off-road equipment and bodywork resembling the Dakar racebikes. Other examples imported to the United States for a period of time included the Cagiva/Ducati Elefant and Honda Transalp V-twins, and the Triumph Tiger triple. While some of the latest single-cylinder dual-sport machines have very good off-road skills, these earlier twin- and triple-cylinder machines were significantly more limited. They were just too heavy for true off-road work, and were thus best suited to graded dirt roads. In fact, you'd need mad skills to take them up a demanding mountain trail. But today's versions of these big buggers, such as BMW's R1200GS and KTM's 990 Adventure, make really good streetbikes, in part because of their long-travel (therefore comfortable) suspension, lofty visibility, and nimble handling. If you're a tall rider, you could do a lot worse than to buy one. If you're of shorter stature, a good tip is to slide your butt almost off the edge of your seat just before stopping. This can help you find good foot contact with the floor.

Finally, there's a newer kid on the dual-sport block: the *supermotard*. Supermotards (also known as supermoto) were created as a halfway house between a true off-road race bike and a streetbike. The result is a smaller and lighter machine that looks like a dirtbike fitted with road-going wheels and a larger front disc brake. You'll notice I say wheels and not just tires. Motards (a common abbreviation) don't run on the typical tall off-road-type wheels; they wear much shorter and wider road-going wheels—complete with supersticky road tires and road-based gearing.

CYCLE BABBLE

Supermotards are lightweight dirtbikes fitted with road-race wheels and tires. They're raced all around Europe and now stateside, too. Several bike companies make sanitized versions for public sale.

Motards have their own race series, which predictably takes place half on paved sections and half on dirt; the series attracts professional riders from both sides of the coin. Go to a race and watch the motocrossers banging arms with the road racers. It's amazing to watch.

Believe me, motards are about as much fun as you can have on two wheels; they're forgiving motorcycles, which you can throw around with wild abandon—all the while feeling like a race hero. For experienced riders, I highly recommend one as a second bike.

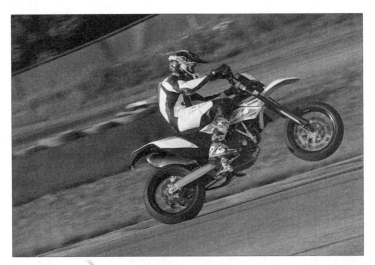

KTM was one of the first manufacturers to launch a supermotard for sale stateside. This 690 SMC is about as much fun as you can have on two wheels while staying legal!
(Photo courtesy of KTM-North America Inc.)

Cruisers: The All-American Bikes

Choppers, customs, cruisers—whichever term you use, you are referring to a distinctly American style of motorcycle. The American landscape, both social and geographical, shaped this style of motorcycle into its present form.

Many of the restless soldiers returning from Europe and Asia after World War II chose to explore the United States on motorcycles, but the motorcycles that were widely available didn't suit them. Outlaw bikers called the big Harley-Davidson touring bikes of that time "garbage wagons" because they considered all the accessories and extras mounted on them garbage. In fact, Bylaw Number 11 of the original Hell's Angels charter states, "An Angel cannot wear the colors (club insignia) while riding on a garbage wagon." The first thing most outlaws did was chop off all superfluous parts, which to them was anything that didn't help the bike go faster: fenders, lights, front brakes, whatever. Hence the term *chopper*.

CYCLE BABBLE

A **chopper** once referred to a custom motorcycle that had all superfluous parts "chopped" off in order to make the bike faster. Today it refers to a type of custom bike that usually has an extended fork, no rear suspension, and high handlebars.

Choppers came to symbolize the outlaw motorcycle contingent, the infamous one-percenters. By the 1960s, these bikes had evolved into radical machines far removed from the intent of the original customized bikes, which was improved straight-line performance. Anyone seeking outright performance rode a Japanese or British bike. Harley had long since given up the pretense of producing sporting motorcycles.

People rode Harleys to look cool, and nothing looked cooler than a Harley chopper. The extended forks and modified frames of these motorcycles made them nearly impossible to ride, but the owners didn't seem to mind. Riding a motorcycle with unsafe handling characteristics seemed to be another way of letting society know the rider didn't care if he or she lived or died.

Over the years, such machines gained in popularity—even as they declined in practicality—but manufacturers seemed not to notice. It wasn't until the 1970s, after decades of watching American riders customize their bikes, that the manufacturers got into the act and began offering custom-styled bikes.

The birth of the factory custom can in large part be attributed to one man: Willie G. Davidson. Willie G., as he is known, worked in Harley's styling department, but he was also an avid motorcyclist who knew what people were doing to their bikes. One popular customizing technique was to take the fork off of a Sportster and graft it onto a stripped-down Big Twin frame, so Willie G. did just that at the factory. The result was the original Super Glide.

Choppers sure are cool looking, but they can be a pain in the butt to ride, literally. It can also take a grocery store–size parking lot to turn one around with their extra long wheelbase.
(Photo courtesy of Simon Green)

The Super Glide model, offered in 1971, wasn't a screaming success, due in part to a funky boatlike rear fender (known as the Night Train fender). The next year, Harley gave the bike a more conventional rear fender and sold thousands of Super Glides.

Harley wasn't the only company working on a custom-styled bike. The British manufacturer Norton also developed a cruiser in the early 1970s. Unfortunately, its cruiser, the ungainly High Rider, was based on Norton's hot-selling Commando sportbike, and the odd marriage wasn't well received. The bike only contributed to the company's eventual demise.

Kawasaki was the first Japanese company to test the factory-chopper waters, introducing its KZ900LTD in 1976. The bike featured pull-back buckhorn handlebars, a teardrop-shape gas tank, a seat with a pronounced step between the rider and passenger portions, and a liberal dousing of chrome plating. These bikes forced the rider into a backward-leaning riding position (raising unbridled hell with his or her lower back), but otherwise, they were still functional, useful machines.

As the decade progressed, the Japanese stuck to this formula. This approach had a limited future; the real future of cruisers was being forged elsewhere, by Willie G.

Two of Willie G.'s creations, in particular, proved to be the models for today's cruisers: the Low Rider, introduced in 1977, and the Wide Glide of 1980. Study these bikes, and you'll see elements of most every cruiser now produced. The bobbed fender of the Wide Glide can be found on cruisers from Honda, Kawasaki, Suzuki, and Yamaha. The kicked-out front end and sculpted fenders of the Low Rider hint at the shape of Yamaha's Road Stars. These two bikes are arguably the most influential factory customs of all time.

What of the Japanese? As the 1980s progressed, Japanese manufacturers got closer and closer to building motorcycles that looked like Harley-Davidsons. But they have taken cruiser styling in new directions, too. Honda now builds the Fury, an aggressive factory chopper, as does Yamaha with the Star Raider. For the traditionalist, Yamaha also builds the Road Star, which looks much like a classic Indian or Harley-Davidson. While Suzuki offers both classic and modern-looking versions of its V-twin Boulevard series. (See Appendix A to get a good look at these bikes.)

This segment of the market has thrived for many years, and for good reason: cruisers are easy bikes to live with. Many of them are nearly maintenance free. To many people they look good and, when outfitted with a windshield, are comfortable out on the road. They may not handle as well as sportbikes, or haul as much gear as touring bikes, but in many ways, they fulfill the role of a standard, all-around motorcycle. Many riders don't ride a motorcycle to get from point A to point B as quickly as possible. They just like to ride. If that describes you, you might be cruiser material.

Power Cruisers

An interesting thing happened as the twentieth century wound to a close. People began demanding more performance from all types of motorcycles. Sportbikes began to increase in popularity, and not just among younger riders. Longtime riders and those who had returned to the sport after an extended absence from riding began to appreciate the tremendous performance offered by modern sportbikes. Even cruiser buyers began wanting more power and better handling. In response, manufacturers resurrected the "power cruiser" category.

The original batch of power cruisers in the early 1980s tended to be multicylinder machines, usually V-4s. Honda started this trend with its Magnas, and Suzuki joined in with its ill-fated Madura series. Yamaha's V-4 power cruiser proved so popular that a new version of the mighty V-Max is still with us in the twenty-first century. Kawasaki also got in the act, but it used an inline-four engine to power the Eliminator series, its combatant in the 1980s power cruiser wars.

Today's crop of power cruisers uses V-twin engines almost exclusively. Honda brought out the original member of the current class with its mighty VTX1800, which cranks out over 100 horsepower.

Yamaha and Kawasaki also jumped on the power cruiser bandwagon. Yamaha at first chose to go the traditional route, using the air-cooled pushrod engine from its Road Star series to power its Star Warrior power cruiser. But it later added the audacious new VMAX, a V-4 power cruiser that follows the style of the original 1985 V-Max.

In a turn of events that hasn't occurred since the introduction of the Knucklehead in 1936, Harley now ranks among the undisputed technological leaders in this class. The liquid-cooled V-Rod Muscle engine cranks out a reported 86 pound-feet of torque. Triumph, on the other hand, wants to trump everyone with its enormous 2.3-liter three-cylinder Rocket III Roadster.

Harley's Wide Glide was one of the most influential cruisers ever built. Just about every cruiser now being produced displays some elements of Wide Glide styling.
(Photo courtesy of *Motorcyclist* magazine)

Sportbikes

If you aren't the *Easy Rider* type, or just find the stereotypical cruiser-riders image unattractive, then you might be interested in something with a little more sporting capability. Well, you are definitely in the right place at the right time: the range of sporting motorcycles available has never been better.

Sportbikes are designed to handle well at high speeds. When British bikes began to appear in the United States in appreciable numbers following World War II, it became obvious that while Harleys may be faster in a straight line, the British models could run circles around a Harley when the road began to wind. This gave the British a reputation as the producers of the original sporting motorcycles. The British managed to maintain this reputation until the early 1970s, with bikes such as the awesome Norton 850 Commando and Triumph T160 Trident.

When the Japanese began producing large four-cylinder motorcycles, these became the new leaders in straight-line performance. The term *Universal Japanese Motorcycle (UJM)* was coined to describe them.

 CYCLE BABBLE

During the 1970s, the Japanese became so identified with four-cylinder, standard-style motorcycles that the term **Universal Japanese Motorcycle (UJM)** was coined to describe them.

While they were wicked fast, most UJMs of the 1970s didn't handle all that well, mostly because of inferior suspension components and flimsy frames. They outhandled Harleys (which tended to be about as nimble as a freight train), but they couldn't keep up with a properly functioning Norton Commando.

The real breakthrough in the development of sportbikes from Japan was Honda's 750cc Interceptor, introduced for the 1983 model year. With its revolutionary V-4 engine, this bike was Japan's best purpose-built sporting motorcycle yet.

The Interceptor revolutionized sportbikes. It started off a technology war between the Japanese manufacturers that continues to this day. Kawasaki brought out its original 900 Ninja, a bike in many ways as groundbreaking as the Interceptor. Yamaha introduced its five-valve FZ750, a bike so influential that Ferrari adopted some of its technology for its cars. And Suzuki blew the world away by introducing its GSX-R series, the first generation of the true modern sportbikes, bikes that are little more than racers with headlights.

The Italians are another prominent force in the sportbike scene. When they started building large-displacement sportbikes in the 1970s, such as Moto Guzzi's V7 Sport and Ducati's 750 Super Sport, the Italians raised the ceiling on riders' expectations from their machines. While they weren't initially exported in numbers large enough to become a real presence in the U.S. market, recently they've become a benchmark for performance bikes. In fact, America has since become Ducati's number one export market.

Today's sportbikes have a wider appeal than ever before. You can speed around a racetrack, which is arguably what they do best, in *track days*. You can use a sportbike as a potentially superfast modern road machine (watch out, though, or you'll be mourning the loss of your driver's license), or you can use it as the basis for a custom bike as innovative and wild looking as any chopper ever created. Because there are now so many niche scenes, the sportbike world experienced unprecedented growth in recent years.

 CYCLE BABBLE

Track days are organized riding events held at a racetrack. Professional instructors will teach you how to ride either your own bike or a rental bike, and speed around a racetrack in relative safety.

Despite their growth in popularity, though, sportbikes are neither the easiest to ride nor the most comfortable bikes on the planet. This is due to their racy engines and quick handling, which require smooth, precise control inputs to manage safely; and their crouched-over riding position, designed to get the rider out of the air stream while maximizing the use of arms, legs, and body to control the machine at high speeds.

Pure-Dirt

The motorcycles manufactured for purely off-road use today tend toward the extreme end of the motorcycle spectrum. These are machines such as the screaming race bikes leaping through the air in arenas around the country during Supercross and Arenacross races. True off-road bikes fall into two distinct categories, two-stroke or four-stroke.

Two-Strokes: The Screamers

Two-stroke *dirtbikes* usually don't make good beginner bikes. In fact, many of them are intended strictly as racing machines. With some two-stroke engines you have to mix oil into your gas before you fill your tank, which is a potentially messy, time-consuming process (and inconvenient if you find yourself miles from home without a can in which to mix fuel). While a few manufacturers still build "premix" models that require mixing oil and gas, these bikes are pure racers that are better left for experienced riders.

CYCLE BABBLE

Dirtbikes are machines intended for off-road use and aren't legal to ride on public roads. Sometimes the term *pure-dirt* is used to distinguish a dirtbike from a dual-sport motorcycle.

More civilized two-stroke models feature a separate reservoir for the two-stroke oil, almost like a smaller second gas tank. The advantage to this setup is the bike mixes the oil and gas on its own. However, virtually all of these so-called "oil injection" models are now used bikes, because emissions regulations basically caused all but a few pure-racing two-strokes to go extinct.

Since most of the currently available two-strokes were built for off-road competition, they aren't legal to ride on public roads. This means that even if you bought one, you'd have to transport the machine from your garage to the place you intend to ride in a pickup truck or a trailer.

Finally, two-strokes tend to have extremely abrupt power delivery, unleashing a whole bunch of horsepower in a trouser-soiling instant. When the engine is at lower rpms, the bike feels powerless; once it hits a certain point, the acceleration is suddenly overwhelming. This is great for racing, but unwelcome for a novice. Often you'll end up on your butt as the lightweight bike flips you off its back. That's not to say they can't be a lot of fun—but they're better off in experienced hands.

Four-Strokes: The New Power Elites

Alternatives to two-stroke racing dirtbikes are available for those who want to do serious off-road riding: four-stroke trailbikes.

First we must clear up a big misconception: four-stroke power, the same type of motor you'll find in any car or truck, never went out of style. However, until the late 1990s, these bikes have been disadvantaged by weight and starting, compared to the two-strokes. Today's four-stroke pure-dirt bikes start just as easily (some now boast electric starting), produce a smoother and more useable power, and, in some cases, weigh less than their two-stroke siblings. Case in point: the 450cc racing four-strokes now produce horsepower numbers in the realm of the old race-ready two-stroke 500s—in a less violent manner, while weighing the same.

The big breakthrough for trailbikes was when the high-performance production four-strokes got their weight under 250 pounds. This wrapped the smooth power into a lightweight, easy-to-start package that really pushed the four-stroke ahead of the two-strokes for casual riders. Honda has long been a proponent of such motorcycles, and its CRF series offers a terrific alternative to the old two-strokes. However, Honda is not alone—there's also Yamaha with its TT-R trailbikes, Kawasaki with its KLXs, and Suzuki has had its tough DR-Zs for many years.

Before we move on, bear in mind that while any pure-dirt motorcycle (four-stroke or two) won't usually be legal to drive on public roads (they'll often be missing necessary electrical equipment, such as lights, turn signals, and horns), it is usually possible to make them road legal, but that is missing the point—it's not really what these specialist bikes are all about.

Street Standards: A Renaissance

Because the British and Japanese motorcycles were so influential to motorcyclists who entered the sport in the 1960s and 1970s, the look of these bikes became imprinted in our psyches as the way a motorcycle *should* look.

These were pretty basic bikes: back then, function dictated form. The gas tank sat above the engine to allow the gas to run down into the carburetors without the need for a fuel pump. The need to place the engine between the two wheels, and the way the human body bends, pretty much dictated the placement of the rest of the parts.

As motorcycles became more specialized in the 1980s, the look of motorcycles changed. Motorcyclists were so excited by new developments that we didn't realize we were losing something in the process. Then one day in the late 1980s, we realized that the basic bike no longer existed. Motorcyclists began complaining about this situation, and soon the Japanese designed bikes that embodied the virtues of those older models.

Unfortunately, while the inclusion of the older styling features contributed to a retro look for these new machines, it also detracted from their overall versatility. Suzuki and Kawasaki were the first to come back to the market with standard motorcycles. Kawasaki's entrance into this new/old market segment was the Zephyr 550, a good-looking four-cylinder UJM-type bike introduced for the 1990 model year. It sold well in Europe, but not in the United States. Very few of these machines found their way to the public highways, and they were soon dropped from Kawasaki's lineup.

The VX800, Suzuki's entrant that the same year, did slightly better in the market. It was a competent, full-size machine that fulfilled the promise of the versatile standard. But it was never a sales dynamo and was imported to U.S. shores for only four years.

Neither Kawasaki nor Suzuki gave up on the concept of standard bikes after the lukewarm reception of their initial efforts. Kawasaki imported increasingly larger Zephyrs, but they came with increasingly larger price tags. None of the Zephyr series offered anything a rider couldn't find in a used GPz900 Ninja—and for a fraction of the Zephyr's price.

Honda was the first Japanese manufacturer to find relative success in the standard bike market, with its Nighthawk 750. Here was a bike that offered the versatility UJMs were known for, and looked okay doing it. Perhaps the factor that contributed most to the bike's success was its low price. In this case, you really did get your money's worth.

While the Nighthawk was the first modern Japanese standard to hold its own in the marketplace, it never set any kind of sales records. Looking back, all of these bikes mixed the *naked bike* look with a subtle touch of the cruiser, which was pretty odd considering that many riders of the 1960s and 1970s bought naked British and Japanese bikes to set themselves apart from the cruiser crowd. Luckily, a couple of manufacturers rethought the concept.

First, Yamaha introduced the Seca II XJ600. At first glance, this nimble, fun bike might not be considered a standard, since it included a small, frame-mounted *fairing*, but in retrospect maybe that was the point.

The riders were finally happy; the fairing actually added to the bike's practicality. It seemed that being *naked* wasn't a prerequisite for a standard. Suzuki also realized this and brought out its Bandit series. These bikes are comfortable motorcycles that incorporate some of the best technology available, have a useful fairing, and sell for a reasonable price.

CYCLE BABBLE

The devices mounted at the front of a motorcycle to protect the rider from the elements are called **fairings.** These range from small plastic windshields mounted to the handlebars, to complex, encompassing body panels that enshroud the entire front half of the bike. Bikes without any type of fairing are known as **naked bikes.**

The success of the Bandit finally spawned a resurgence in the standard motorcycle. Suzuki still makes the Bandit 1250S, plus the SV650 and newer Gladius, a pair of smaller naked bikes. Straightforward, no-nonsense bikes like these are so practical and fun that many veteran riders choose them over flashier and more sophisticated models.

Currently, the standard bike category has a more exciting selection of models to choose from than any other, partly because there aren't really any rules. Every manufacturer has taken a slightly different direction with their contributions. Some companies like Yamaha make bikes that are essentially their sportbikes without the plastic bodywork: check out the FZ1 and FZ6. With tongue placed firmly in cheek, Kawasaki even recycled the name of their original naked streetbike, the supercool 1973 Z1, when naming their latest naked bike, the Z1000. Even decades later, this shows how powerful the original Z1's reputation was.

Then there are those Italians again. You can choose from the Ducati Monster and the Hypermotard, an aggressively styled naked bike with supermotard cues. Rival Aprilia makes the manic Tuono, Benelli offers the seductive-sounding TNT, boutique manufacturer Bimota has the Ducati-powered DB6, and MV Agusta has the avant-garde Brutale.

Finally, in an almost perfect circle, Triumph is back in the big standard streetbike game. Back in the 1960s the ultimate British streetbike was the Triumph Bonneville; it's the bike the Japanese copied, and the bike that stole enough Harley sales to keep Willie G. awake at night. It was the motorcycle that just did everything right, and looked so hot doing it. After a few years out of business, it's so appropriate that Triumph is back in this category with its radical three-cylinder engine Speed Triple and Street Triple, plus a fun version of the original Bonneville.

The fierce competition in this category indicates that there is a really strong market for standard-style streetbikes. If you're a fan of these types of bikes and you like to be different, then this is a pretty cool time to be a motorcyclist.

In 2001, a revived Triumph launched an all-new version of the classic parallel-twin Bonneville model to much fanfare. Smooth, plenty fast, and consummately comfortable, the new bike more than deserved its praise—and Triumph still makes it today.
(Photo courtesy of Triumph Motorcycles)

The Ultimate Behemoths: Touring Bikes

Another category of specialized motorcycle to appear over the last several decades is the purpose-built *touring bike*, a bike equipped for longer rides on the road.

Harley started this trend by offering a fairing and luggage as optional equipment on its Electra Glide back in the 1960s, but other companies were slow to pick up on the trend.

In the late 1970s, BMW introduced its first factory *dresser*, the R100RT, a bike that met with market success.

CYCLE BABBLE

A **touring bike** is a bike equipped for longer rides, with fairings and lockable saddlebags. While early bikers looked on motorcycles equipped for touring with scorn, calling them *garbage wagons,* over time they began to see their appeal. They began to refer to garbage wagons as **baggers** and finally **dressers,** the term many Harley riders use today.

Honda had been producing a bike specifically for touring: the Gold Wing. In time, Honda began offering fairings and luggage as accessories, but these were still add-on parts, equipment for which the machines hadn't been specifically designed.

Other companies offered touring packages for their standard bikes, too, but there's a problem with this approach: accessories affect the handling of a machine, often adversely. Large fairings and luggage can really make a bike get squirrelly.

So Honda took up the challenge, producing its 1980 GL1100 Gold Wing Interstate, Japan's first turn-key touring bike designed from the ground up to have an integrated fairing and luggage.

Of course, the other Japanese manufacturers responded with purpose-built touring rigs of their own, but it seemed as if every effort they made only sent Honda back to the drawing board with a vengeance. This one-upmanship led to the Gold Wing GL1200 in 1984. This bike set new standards in function and comfort. The Gold Wing 1500, a six-cylinder behemoth introduced in 1988, blew away even its predecessor. The Gold Wing proved to be such a perfect touring machine that, for a time at least, the other Japanese manufacturers simply gave up trying to compete in that market segment.

The success of the Gold Wing meant that the ultimate behemoth class of touring bikes saw relatively little change for more than a decade, but eventually things began moving on the touring front again. All it took was a little competition, this time from BMW. In 1999, BMW introduced its K1200LT, and for the first time in more than 10 years, Honda's mighty six-cylinder Gold Wing began losing magazine comparison tests against its heavy-touring market competition. Honda responded by introducing the 1832cc Gold Wing, a bike that was much better in every way than its predecessor. Likewise, BMW has kept upping the ante with its K1200LT. But so has Harley-Davidson, with its Electra Glide (a model that has been around seemingly forever, but which technologically was bypassed by Honda eons ago). Kawasaki has a full-boat tourer in the Vulcan 1700 Voyager, as does Yamaha with its V-4–powered Royal Star Venture. A fairly new American company, Victory, also offers a swoopy-looking Vision Tour. Like the others in its class, it's a huge motorcycle weighing in at some 852 pounds—definitely not for the novice rider.

While the luxury-touring segment was rekindling and growing, there were also some exciting developments in other types of touring motorcycles, such as the *sport-touring* segment of the market. Sport-tourers combine the comfort and carrying capacity of a touring bike with the handling and excitement of a sportbike. You can think of these machines as sportbikes with larger fairings and hard, lockable luggage.

CYCLE BABBLE

Sport-tourers are hybrids, combining the performance of sportbikes with the practicality of tourers. To many, they're the best of both worlds.

This class existed for a long time without having a proper name. In fact, almost every BMW built in the last quarter of the century falls into this group.

Although the term sport-touring is fairly new, BMW has been building such bikes for decades.

Kawasaki produced the first purpose-built Japanese sport-tourer with its Concours, introduced in 1986, while Honda followed suit in 1991, bringing out its ST1100. So you can see that there have been a couple of decades of development in this market segment already, and the current crop of machines is astonishingly good. Kawasaki still makes the Concours, now upgraded to 1352cc and featuring an aluminum chassis and many other sportbike-derived features. Honda's current ST1300 was joined recently by an all-new VFR1200F, and Yamaha offers the FJ1300A. Over on the other side of the world, manufacturers such as Moto Guzzi and Triumph also offer BMW competition in the sport-touring arena.

As a group, these bikes represent a compromise, giving up a bit of sporting capability to the smaller, more agile sportbikes, while sacrificing some luggage-carrying capability and cockpit roominess when compared to the ultimate behemoths. It seems a compromise many riders are willing to make. If you like to crank up the throttle in corners and cover huge expanses of geography in a single sitting, but you don't need to carry everything you own with you on a trip, these bikes may be a good compromise for you, too.

Manufacturers have also developed the touring cruiser, another subcategory of the touring bike. The touring-cruiser bikes combine the looks of cruisers with the functionality of touring bikes. With their windshields and hard luggage, they are more comfortable and convenient than basic cruisers, yet they retain the American look that makes cruisers so popular. Yamaha's Royal Star Venture and Victory's Vision Cross Roads are two of the larger and more recent entries in this class. A bit down the food chain in overall bulk (but not overall capability) is Kawasaki's Vulcan 900 Classic LT. And, of course, Harley has several types of cruisers because it invented the category.

The Least You Need to Know

- Dual-sport motorcycles make excellent all-around bikes, especially for beginners.
- Cruiser styling reflects the unique tastes and needs of traditional American motorcyclists.
- Sportbikes are high-performance motorcycles designed to go fast and handle well. They usually have full-coverage bodywork and crouched riding positions, although there are some exceptions.
- Pure-dirt bikes look like dual-sports but are designed strictly for off-road use—and many are illegal to ride on the street.
- Standard-style motorcycles are characterized by comfortable riding positions and minimal bodywork.
- Touring bikes are usually large motorcycles with fairings; hard, lockable luggage; and other touring amenities.

So You Want to Buy a Bike?

Now comes the most exciting part of your entire adventure: getting your first bike. It's fun just to go out and look at it, and admire its combination of form and function. You'll soon be able to visualize its details, the curves in its bodywork, and the way it smells when you park it after a ride on a warm summer day. The machine will become a part of you.

But your first bike will be as demanding as it is exciting. To keep your bike in the condition you brought it home in, you'll need to have a basic understanding of its mechanical nature. And just buying a bike in the first place can be a traumatic event. As with any form of commerce, people sell motorcycles to make money, and if you walk into a dealership unprepared, you will be their cash cow.

In this part of the book, you'll learn what kind of bike is right for you, what that bike is made of, how different bikes work, how to buy your first motorcycle without getting ripped off, and what extra gear you'll need after you buy the bike.

Choosing the Right Bike

In This Chapter

- Deciding which type of motorcycle best meets your needs
- Why a smaller bike may be a good choice
- New bike or used bike? How to decide
- The hidden costs of motorcycling

You are about to enter into a relationship with a mechanical object unlike any you have had before. Owning a motorcycle is a much more intimate experience than owning a car or pickup truck, perhaps because you meld into the machine when you ride, your body encasing the mechanical heart of the bike. You become part of the machine. You ride just inches away from the engine, the source of your bike's power, and you feel and hear the internal-combustion event more directly than is possible in an enclosed vehicle. (Unless, of course, you're on an electric motorcycle like those found in Chapter 21.)

And you use your body to control the direction in which you travel, leading the bike down the road with your own subtle movements just as you would lead a dance partner. This provides a much more immediate experience than sitting inside a glass bubble, turning a steering wheel vaguely connected to some invisible mechanism.

Given the nature of this intimate relationship, it is vital that you choose the right partner. With the dizzying array of motorcycles available, choosing that partner might seem daunting at this stage, but it's really not as confusing as it might seem. You don't have to know every detail of every bike ever made; you only need to know yourself and your own needs.

What Do You Want to Do?

Before you select a type of bike, you first need to determine what kind of riding you want to do (as discussed in Chapter 3). If you have no interest in riding on public roads and you just want a bike to ride through the backcountry, woods, or desert, you should probably consider getting a strictly off-road dirtbike.

But you will probably want something you can ride on the road. Riding off-road is great fun, but by getting a bike that isn't street legal, you cut off a lot of your future options. Unless you already have friends who are into serious off-road riding, you'll probably want a machine you can legally ride to the local hangout to visit old friends and make new ones.

Or maybe you don't give a rip about riding off-road. You might have visions of riding through corners on a high-performance sportbike, leaning over so far your knees skim the surface of the asphalt. Or perhaps you envision yourself making epic road trips aboard the biggest touring rig available. Maybe you dream of conquering far-off jungles on a dual-sport machine.

On the other hand, you may not even know what you want out of a bike just yet.

Whether you know exactly what you want out of the sport or you're still trying to figure that out, it's best to keep your options open. Just because you want to see the world doesn't mean you have to buy an ultimate-behemoth luxo-tourer. And just because you want to be the next speed racer doesn't mean you have to buy the bike that won at Daytona this year.

Although bikes have grown increasingly specialized over the last 15 years, they remain remarkably versatile machines.

Any bike can be a tourer if you take it on a trip. I've put in 1,000-mile days on a hard-edged sportbike. I've traveled the entire United States on a big V-twin cruiser. My wife once rode a 500cc thumper from the Canadian border to Mexico and back.

And in the right hands, any bike can be a sportbike. While riding an 18-year-old, 650cc Japanese bike, I've shown my tail to testosterone-crazed squids (sportbike riders with more enthusiasm than talent) on the latest sporting hardware. And while riding a modern sportbike, I've been embarrassed on a twisty road by an old dude on a Harley that was older than I was.

While any bike can be used for nearly any purpose, there is a reason certain types of motorcycles are used for certain tasks more frequently than others. I still suffer from wrist problems from touring on a sportbike, and my wife bought a larger bike within weeks of returning from her trip on the thumper. And that guy who smoked me on his old Harley would probably love riding a modern sportbike, if he ever tried one.

Choosing a Versatile Motorcycle

You might think you know what you want to do before you start riding, but after you've been at it a while, you might discover an interest in an entirely different form of riding. You might get a Harley Sportster thinking you'll use it only to ride to the lake on the weekends, for example, and then develop an itch to ride to the farthest corners of North America.

That's why it's a good idea to get as versatile a motorcycle as possible for your first bike. As I said in Chapter 3, the big dual-sports are about as versatile as a bike can get. They can handle unpaved roads and worse, they can be set up for touring, and they sure as heck can get you to school or work or the computer store and back.

However, you might not be interested in this type of bike. You might be turned off by the looks of the machine. Another disadvantage of the dual-sport bikes is their height: they are tall machines, thanks largely to long-travel suspension that's designed to tame bad roads. While sitting up high is an advantage because it lets you see over traffic (and, more important, helps other drivers see you), it presents some challenges to those with shorter inseams. To fit on one, you need to be of at least average height, or you may find these bikes a bit of a handful in stop-and-go traffic.

Honda's perennial XR650L is a good example of a dual-sport. These bikes are about as tough and durable as they come, making them willing and able both on-road and off.
(Photo courtesy of American Honda Motor Co., Inc.)

If dual-sports aren't your thing, that doesn't mean you're out of luck. There are many versatile pure-street bikes to choose from, too.

Browse the buying guide to new bikes in Appendix A to learn more about the many types of dual-sport or pure-street bikes that might be right for you.

Getting a Good Fit

A big factor in versatility is comfort. If you are comfortable on a bike, you can ride it longer and farther. And different bodies fit on different bikes. You can't really tell by looking at it if a bike is going to fit you, either. For example, I fit nicely on Yamaha's YZF-R6S and could ride one from coast to coast without needing wrist surgery. But Honda's CBR600RR puts my hands to sleep within minutes. Yet a new rider would be hard-pressed to see a noticeable difference between the two bikes if they were parked side by side, and many other riders find the Honda just as comfortable as the Yamaha.

Motorcycle *ergonomics*—the science of designing motorcycles that conform to the human body—receives a lot of attention in the motorcycling press these days. Ergonomic considerations influence all aspects of motorcycle design, from the riding position to the placement of the controls, which, in turn, contribute to the overall versatility of a motorcycle. The better a motorcycle fits you, the more comfortable you will be. The more comfortable you are, the more useful your motorcycle will be, though be aware—things change at speed.

CYCLE BABBLE

The science of **ergonomics,** or human engineering, is used to design devices (including everything from cars to chairs) that conform to the human body. Ergonomics is a prime consideration when designing motorcycles; the idea is to provide maximum efficiency while keeping operator fatigue to a minimum.

The cruiser that feels so comfortable while stationary, with your legs pointed forward and your body dead upright, will be very different at 70 mph with the windblast catching your exposed body like a sailboat. The flip side is that on a sportbike, which puts the weight of your whole upper body on your wrists at low speeds, the windblast will support your body weight at high speeds. That's why a test ride is so important. I talk more about trying out and buying bikes in Chapter 7.

Starting Out Small

Probably the most common mistake new riders make when choosing their first bike is buying a bike that's way too large for them. All of the best riders I know worked their way up in size, only getting rid of a bike when they were actually riding it to its full potential. The people I know who just learned to ride and went straight out and bought a 1000cc sportbike … well, let's be brutally honest, they're terrifying! They're often a danger to others.

I discuss the basics of riding in Chapter 11, but it's important to explain a little about how motorcycles work here so you'll understand this point. Just like bicycles, motorcycles are unstable vehicles: if you don't hold them up, they'll fall over, though unlike a bicycle they're very heavy to pick up. When you ride, your bike is held up by its own inertia, as well as by the gyroscopic and centrifugal forces of its spinning wheels.

But any time your motorcycle is not traveling in a perfectly straight line, its weight shifts around in a manner you may be totally unused to. When traveling, a motorcycle doesn't follow its front wheels around a corner like a car does; instead, the bike leans around corners, rotating around a central axis, much like an airplane.

Because of this, you don't steer a motorcycle the way you drive a car. Instead, you *countersteer* it, using the handlebar to lever the motorcycle into a lean and initiate a turn.

 CYCLE BABBLE

Countersteering is the only way a bike will go around a corner above 10 or 15 mph. For a right-hand corner, push the handlebars away from you very slightly with your right hand. The bike will go right, even though this actually steers the bike left (hence the term *countersteer*). For a left-hand corner, push the handlebars with your left hand.

The point I'm trying to make here is that, on the road, motorcycles move around a lot in weird ways. This takes some getting used to, even on a lightweight motorcycle. On a heavier bike, this can be so disconcerting that it scares a new rider into never learning to steer the motorcycle properly.

The people who seem to run into the most trouble are those who choose a heavyweight cruiser, a big touring motorcycle, or a liter-class sportbike for their first bike. It's comparable to having a Lamborghini Gallardo or a Mack truck as your first car.

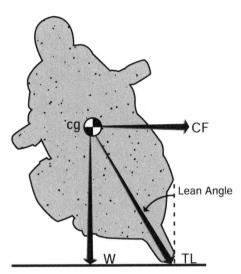

Instead of turning like a car, motorcycles lean into a turn, rotating on the machine's central axis like an airplane.

Perhaps it's a Freudian thing, but size seems to be some sort of a status symbol for cruiser riders. As a popular T-shirt slogan says, "Size does matter." Unfortunately, for a new rider, it matters in a negative way.

For one thing, the heavy weight makes the motorcycle tend to ride in a straight line, even when you attempt to negotiate a turn. The more bike weight you have, the more you have to wrestle the machine through every turn. In addition, excessive weight can be especially problematic in cruisers because of certain handling characteristics common to the breed. Because of the steering geometry required to give cruisers their chopperlike look, they tend not to be the best-handling bikes on the road. To many novice riders, the bikes feel as if they are going to flop over.

Trying to master a large touring bike is usually a mistake for a novice. I've seen the enthusiasm of a lot of new riders nipped in the bud after they bought an ultimate behemoth-type touring bike before they were ready. When you get in over your head on one of these machines, their heavy weight is going to hurt you. When things start to go wrong on an 800-pound motorcycle, they go wrong fast.

In the worst-case scenario, selecting a motorcycle that's too large can ruin your enthusiasm for the sport and get you seriously hurt; by contrast, if you select one that is too small, you may outgrow the bike sooner, but you'll hone your riding skills much faster.

Starting Out Slow

New sportbike riders tend not to have weight-related problems because sportbikes generally are light, maneuverable motorcycles.

Although they are not physically large machines, the problem with sportbikes has to do with power—specifically, the fact that they might have too much of it for a novice rider. Grab a handful of throttle on one of the larger machines, and you'll be traveling more than 100 mph before your brain even has a chance to register your change in speed. The slowest of these bikes can be overwhelmingly quick. Before you buy one for your first bike, you should honestly assess your self-control and your riding ability. These bikes, which are often little more than race machines made road legal, present a challenge for even the most experienced rider.

Best Bets for New Bikers

The trick is to find the right compromise: a bike small enough and safe enough to learn to ride, but competent enough to keep up with you as your skills grow. There are machines in each bike category that fulfill these requirements. As I mentioned earlier, any of the dual-sports makes a great first bike if you physically fit it and like its style. And most of the standard-style motorcycles are easy to learn to ride, and you can live with them for a very long time. Most of these bikes have high sporting capabilities, too, if you find yourself drawn to sportbikes.

The middleweight cruiser class teems with good choices for a first bike if your taste runs toward custom-style motorcycles. Just about any of the 500cc to 900cc cruisers are bikes you will enjoy riding for a long time.

If you're adamant about getting a Harley-Davidson for your first bike, you've got choices there, too, although the Big Twins are physically large bikes and will probably be uncomfortable for most novice riders. They also cost as much as most new cars.

But Harley makes its Sportster series for people looking for a bike smaller than a Big Twin. These attractive motorcycles represent good values for the money. And because Harley addressed the Sportster's biggest problem—vibration—several years back, the Sportster has become an excellent choice for the beginning rider.

If you hanker to see the world on your bike, you're in luck, even if you're a beginner. Any bike that fits you and has enough power to keep up with traffic can be outfitted for touring. You can tour on a dual-sport, standard, cruiser, or sporty bike; you don't need an ultimate behemoth. Don't get me wrong: the big touring bikes are fantastic machines. I've owned one myself and used it more than any other bike. These bikes are just too heavy for a novice rider.

Yamaha's premium tourer, the 869-pound Royal Star Venture S ($19,690; top photo), dwarfs the company's entry-level cruiser, the 324-pound V Star 250 ($3,990; bottom photo).

(Photos courtesy of Yamaha Motor Corporation, USA)

New or Used?

When you've selected a type of motorcycle, you need to decide whether you want to buy a new bike or a used one.

Price is probably the prime determining factor in this decision. If money is no object, you can just waltz into a dealership and buy any bike that strikes your fancy. But most of us have to make prudent decisions when it comes to expenditures, especially when it comes to spending money on recreational activities such as motorcycling. If you're on a budget, buying a used bike can be a wise decision.

We will go into the details of buying a used bike in Chapter 7. In general, though, modern motorcycles are pretty tough to destroy. One exception to this rule is sportbikes: there's been a trend for younger guys to *stunt ride* on sportbikes. They are, in effect, buying their bike to destroy it, so at all costs steer clear of buying a bike that's previously been used for stunt riding. Once they've finished with them, these bikes are usually just fit for the recycling center.

CYCLE BABBLE

Stunt riding is common with younger riders who are often new to motorcycling. They will use their bikes to pull tricks like wheelies, often causing a lot of damage to their motorcycle and themselves. It has been made popular by the underground video scene.

Generally, though, most lightly used bikes are in fairly good condition. This is especially true of motorcycles that appeal to more mature riders, such as touring bikes, cruisers, and standards. Dual-sports are usually in fair condition, unless the owner has attempted to do serious off-road riding on them.

One disadvantage of buying a used bike is that you are never quite certain what you are getting. Another disadvantage of buying used is that you don't usually get a warranty. I show you how to minimize your risks in Chapter 7.

MOTORCYCOLOGY

We won't discuss buying used off-road motorcycles because these are often highly tuned racebikes, or else less powerful playbikes that may still have been ridden by expert riders under stressful conditions. If you choose to purchase a used off-road motorcycle, you should be prepared to conduct a major servicing or even to rebuild it.

But given the reliable nature of modern bikes, these disadvantages are fairly insignificant. The advantage of buying used is that used bikes are less expensive than new ones. This is especially true of Japanese motorcycles, which historically have had fairly poor resale value. For example, Kawasaki's long-running 2010 Ninja 500R model retails for $5,499. At that price, the little Ninja represents one of the best values in motorcycling. Nice, clean, used models can be found for as little as $1,500 to $2,000. These bikes may be 15 years old or more, but they are the same basic motorcycle as the new model.

Harley-Davidsons used to prove the exception. A few years back people had to wait months to buy new Harleys, so the used market went insane. I once saw a 1998 Sportster 1200 Custom, a bike that listed for $8,700, advertised in a newspaper for $13,000. A premium of $4,300 is quite a price to pay for being impatient. Fortunately for buyers (and unfortunately for those looking to turn a quick buck), that climate has changed. You can now find new Harleys sitting for sale on showroom floors, a situation unheard of a few years ago. When supply and demand equalize, only a fool would pay more for a used bike than a new bike.

While buying a used bike may make the most sense from a pure dollars-and-cents point of view, buying a new bike has its advantages, too. When you buy a new bike, you get a warranty. While the odds of a modern bike breaking down are slim, it does happen, and when it does, that warranty is nice to have.

Another benefit of buying a new bike is that it can be easier to finance. Often the dealer will be able to finance the machine, saving you the hassle of procuring your own loan. And many manufacturers offer attractive low-interest financing packages.

Buying a new bike frees you from some of the worries of buying a used bike. Knowing the machine's complete history has certain benefits. When you are a bike's only owner, you can break it in properly yourself, and you know the bike has been properly maintained.

Plus, there's the intangible benefit of riding a brand-new motorcycle. There's nothing quite like the feeling of riding away from a dealership on your brand-new bike.

The Costs of Cycling

The most obvious (and largest) cost of motorcycling is the cost of the bike itself. New streetbikes range from a low of around $3,000 for a Kymco Quannon 150 to a high of nearly $44,000 for a Ducati 1098R Bayliss LE. Most new bikes fall into the range of $6,000 to $16,000.

Used-bike prices can vary even more than new-bike prices. I tell you where to find price references for specific bikes in Chapter 7, but expect to spend at least $2,500 to $5,000 for a good used motorcycle (unless you're a skilled bargain hunter).

No matter what type of bike you buy, or whether you buy new or used, you will find some unexpected costs. Some of these costs, such as buying insurance, will become apparent soon after you write the check for the bike. Others, such as the cost of basic maintenance, will rear their ugly heads only after you've racked up a few miles.

These costs aren't obvious to a new rider, and a little knowledge ahead of time can influence your choice of a bike. As you will learn, that choice will, in turn, influence those hidden costs.

Insurance Costs

Some insurance companies simply will not insure a motorcycle. Those that do usually use a completely arbitrary method of determining insurance premiums based on engine displacement. Basically, the smaller your engine is, the lower your insurance costs are likely to be, and any bodywork will add to your premium. This may seem logical to someone who knows absolutely nothing about bikes, but once you understand more about engines (which I discuss in Chapter 6), you'll realize that engine size means little.

But that's the way things are, so it's a good idea to take insurance costs into account when selecting a motorcycle. Check insurance prices in your area before buying a bike. Rates for the same bike from the same company can double from one location to the next. For example, my wife, who has a spotless driving record, paid about $260 per year for full-coverage insurance on her Honda ST1100 when she lived in North Dakota. When she moved to Minneapolis, her insurance premiums (using the same policy) doubled, shooting up to nearly $600 per year.

Maintenance Costs

Even less obvious than insurance costs are maintenance costs. While modern bikes don't usually require the same level of servicing and rebuilding that many older models do, they still require more maintenance than most cars. This is partly because motorcycles are more highly stressed.

Motorcycle designers have to use sophisticated techniques—such as high-revving engine designs—to get relatively small engines to generate so much power. Thus, these engines require more routine maintenance than less highly stressed car engines. Add in the other procedures your bike will require, such as carburetion adjustments and drive-chain, sprocket, and tire replacements (which I discuss in Chapter 17), and you can expect to fork out some serious cash for tune-ups over the years.

And if you don't do your own basic maintenance and instead take your bike in for things such as oil and tire changes, you can add a significant amount to your overall total. But there are some things you can do to minimize these expenses. The less you abuse your motorcycle in general, the less money you will have to spend maintaining it.

The Least You Need to Know

- The perfect bike for one rider may be ill suited for the next rider.
- When choosing a bike, consider the type of riding you want to do, the versatility of the bike, and the comfort of the bike.
- While a big bike might impress your buddies, it may also seriously hamper your growth as a skilled motorcyclist.
- There are valid reasons for choosing to buy either a new bike or a used bike. Used bikes are generally cheaper than new bikes and can be in good enough condition to ride. However, new bikes often come with financing and warranties, and are in perfect condition when you buy them.
- Different types and sizes of motorcycles have different hidden costs, such as insurance and maintenance.

Anatomy of a Motorcycle

In This Chapter

* Understanding the mechanical bits that make your bike tick
* How the top and bottom ends of the engine make your motorcycle go
* How carburetors, fuel injection, and the induction system work
* The importance of the frame, wheels, and tires
* The uses of bodywork

Many riders love motorcycles for their elegant lines, disrupted by the least possible number of mechanical components. Yet the simple appearance of the motorcycle belies a complex mechanical system—or, rather, set of systems.

In *Zen and the Art of Motorcycle Maintenance*, author Robert M. Persig writes that it is a mistake to see the motorcycle as simply a collection of parts. Rather, he describes motorcycles as a collection of ideas, and he describes working on bikes as "working on concepts." He writes, "That's all a motorcycle is, a system of concepts worked out in steel."

To get a complete understanding of a motorcycle, you'll need a little mechanical background, a basic understanding of Persig's "system of concepts." In this chapter, I give you a guided tour of the inner workings of a bike.

The Nature of the Beast

Motorcycles are mechanical devices, and in the early decades of the sport, bikes that tried to hide their mechanical nature usually failed to win over the motorcycling public. Philip Vincent, founder of the Vincent motorcycle company, discovered this in 1954 when he tried to sell versions of his magnificent Vincent motorcycles cloaked in fiberglass bodywork, then a revolutionary new material. The failure of the Black Prince and Black Knight helped seal Vincent's fate, and the last Vincent motorcycle was constructed at Vincent's Stevenage factory in 1955.

Subsequent fully enclosed motorcycles fared little better than the Vincent. Ducati marketed a fully enclosed series of bikes, including the Paso and 907 I.E., in the late 1980s and early 1990s, but these never set motorcycle buyers on fire either. As a result, most Ducati models now have partial or no fairings at all, to better showcase their engines. Honda likewise tested the market for shrink-wrapped bikes when it introduced the Pacific Coast in 1989. This model did so poorly that it was withdrawn from the market; it was such a competent all-around motorcycle, though, that it rose from the dead and returned to production.

MOTORCYCLE MOMENTS

Two important exceptions to the minimalist bodywork rule is the current crop of big tourers, where luxury trumps all else, and pureblooded sportbikes from Japan, Italy, England, Germany, and Austria. As in car racing, winning in motorcycle roadracing is all about gaining tenths or even hundredths of a second per lap on the competition. That's why modern sportbikes are more likely to be completely enveloped in bodywork, with even the tiniest aerodynamic details focused on getting the motorcycle through the air with the least resistance.

Manufacturers have learned that motorcyclists appreciate a bike's mechanical nature, and any biker worth his or her leather jacket will probably want to see the engine. That's why cruisers, in particular, feature their engines prominently. For them, it's not about going fast, it's about the image.

Meeting the Motor

The motor seems a logical place to start when dissecting a bike. After all, motorcycles are named for their engines. The engine, more than anything else, gives a motorcycle its character and personality. Looks may stir you to buy a bike, but the characteristics of the engine keep you riding it year after year. As Philip Vincent said, "Motorcycles are supposed to be ridden, and one cannot see the model when one is riding it."

In the next chapter, you'll examine the different types of engines and how the type of engine and its state of tune affect the character of the motorcycle. In this chapter, you just focus on the different parts of the engine and what each one does.

The engine proper is usually divided into two parts: the lower portion, called the *bottom end*, which includes the parts that transmit power to the rear wheel; and the upper portion, called the *top end*, which is where the internal-combustion process takes place. The engine also includes a system to introduce an air-fuel charge into the chambers where combustion takes place. This is called the *induction system* and consists of either a carburetor or carburetors, or fuel injectors. It works in conjunction with a series of valves that are part of the engine's top end.

CYCLE BABBLE

The **bottom end** of a bike refers to the bottom part of the engine, where the crankshaft and (usually) the transmission reside. The **top end** refers to the upper part of the engine, which contains the pistons, cylinders, and valve gear. The **induction system** consists of the apparatus that mixes an air-and-fuel charge that goes into the combustion chamber, located in the top end.

The Belly of the Beast: The Bottom End

I like to compare motorcycle components to the human body, to make it easier to envision. The bottom end is the entrails of a bike. This is where all the commotion in the engine is converted into forward motion.

The two clamshell-like metal halves that surround the bottom end are called cases. All motorcycle engine bottom ends contain a crankshaft (on a very few designs, two crankshafts occupy the space within the engine cases, but these are rare).

The crankshaft is connected via connecting rods to the pistons, which are the slugs moving up and down within the cylinders (the hollow shafts in the top end inside which internal combustion occurs). The connecting rods attach to the crankshaft on eccentric journals (sections of the crankshaft offset from the crank's longitudinal centerline), and their up-and-down movement is converted into a circular motion through the design of these journals.

As you'll see in the next chapter, the design of the crankshaft, together with the arrangement of the cylinders, largely gives the engine its character. For example, the design of the crankshaft and the engine's firing order give Harley-Davidsons their characteristic rumbling sound (it's what also contributes to Harley engines vibrating like washing machines with unbalanced loads).

The Transmission

On most modern motorcycles, the circular motion created by the crankshaft setup is transmitted to the transmission through a series of gears or by a chain.

For all practical purposes, you can think of the transmission of a modern motorcycle as part of the bottom end. The crankshaft and the gearset usually reside inside the same cavity within the cases. This is called a *unitized transmission*. Since the 1950s and 1960s, it has been a part of just about every motorcycle engine designed.

One notable exception is Harley-Davidson, the only company still manufacturing motorcycles that use separate engines and transmissions, connected by a *primary drive*. The primary, as it is called, consists of a sprocket attached to the crankshaft that rides outside the engine cases in a case of its own (called the primary case). This case is connected to the transmission, which is located behind the engine via a primary chain.

Harley's primary drive system presents added maintenance chores: the primary chain must be periodically adjusted, a rather difficult process that creates more opportunities for things to go wrong. No one knows for certain why Harley continues to use this archaic setup, but if I had to guess, I'd say it's purely for looks.

The transmission is an integral part of the bottom end on most motorcycles, but it is really a separate system. *Manual transmission* design varies from bike to bike, but most share some basic characteristics. Each transmission contains a gearset, which, as you might have guessed from the name, is a set of gears. Designers use mathematical equations incorporating the diameter of these gears and other parts on the motorcycle (including the primary drive, final drive, and rear tire diameter) to give a bike certain operating characteristics.

These gears are engaged by shifting a lever with your left foot, which moves *shifting forks* inside the transmission, which, in turn, move the gears within. If you have any trouble with the transmission, odds are it will involve those forks or else the selector mechanism that operates them.

CYCLE BABBLE

A **unitized transmission** (often referred to as a unit transmission) is a transmission that is an integral part of the engine's bottom end.

A **primary drive** is a drive chain, belt, or gears connecting the engine's crankshaft to its transmission.

A **manual transmission** is a device consisting of a set of gears (the gearset) that enable an operator to get up to speed. Most motorcycles now being produced have manual transmissions. In a motorcycle, the gears within the gearset are moved around with devices called **shifting forks.**

Harley-Davidson is the last major manufacturer still using an external primary drive on its motorcycle engines.
(Photo © 1998 Darwin Holmstrom)

Valve Clatter: The Top End

The top end of a four-stroke motorcycle is where the internal-combustion process takes place. The top end consists of the pistons, the cylinder block, and the head, which contains the valve train. As mentioned earlier, pistons are metal slugs that move up and down in the cylinders. The energy created by burning the air-fuel charge (a mixture of gasoline and air) pushes on the tops of the pistons (known as the crowns) to make your bike move. Pistons are both simple and complex devices, but for the sake of this discussion, I'll stick with this simple definition.

The cylinder block is a rather simple device, too: an aluminum casting with holes through it, inside of which the pistons move up and down. This component serves two purposes:

- It channels the pistons' energy and forces them to move up and down (rather than flying all over the place, which would not help make your motorcycle move).

- It dissipates the intense heat created by the burning air-fuel charge and the friction caused by the motion of the pistons. This is done by some sort of coolant circulating throughout the block, by cooling oil being sprayed on the hot spots on the piston, or by air flowing over the outside of the block (the reason for the fins visible on your engine). Usually, some combination of the three methods effectively cools the engine.

The *valve train* is the most convoluted and confusing system in the top end. It consists of a cam, which is a rod with eccentric lobes on it that opens the valves. Valves are devices consisting of metal stems with flat disks on one end. They ride in metal tubes, called valve guides, and open and close at precise moments to let air-fuel charges into the *combustion chambers* and to let the waste gases created during the combustion process exit.

There are two basic types of valve trains: overhead cam systems and pushrod systems. Each system has several varieties, but they all share some common traits.

Most modern bikes use overhead cams. In this type of valve train, the cams are located above the valves and act on them through a system of rocker arms, or the cam lobe acts directly on the valve through a tappet and shim. Rocker arms are metal levers that rotate on a small shaft like an upside-down teeter-totter; the cam lobes push one side of the rocker up, causing the other side of the rocker to push the valves down, opening them.

The pushrod system has cams located below the combustion chambers, usually in the engine cases, that act on pushrods—long, metal rods connected to the rocker arms located above the valves. While old, this is hardly a dead technology. These days, Harley-Davidson, Yamaha, Kawasaki, and Moto Guzzi all still use this traditional method of valve actuation in some of their engines. BMW uses a hybrid cam-in-head system, which locates the cam in the cylinder head but below the valves. BMW's system uses short pushrods to open the valves.

Overhead cams have a more positive action (less slop in the system) and allow the engine to operate at a higher rate of *revolutions per minute (rpm)* than can pushrod engines, which have more reciprocating mass (parts that move up and down or back and forth, instead of around and around). The term *rpm* refers to the number of times a crankshaft spins around each minute. Being able to run at higher rpm means an engine will put out more overall power.

CYCLE BABBLE

The head sits atop the cylinder block and houses the **valve train,** the system of valves that let the air-fuel charges in and let the exhaust gases out. The area at the top of the cylinder where the air-fuel charge burns and pushes the pistons down is called the **combustion chamber.**

Revolutions per minute (rpm) refers to the number of times the crankshaft spins per minute, essentially how fast an engine can spin. Often the term *revs* is used, especially in conversation.

One advantage of Harley's—and some Japanese cruisers'—pushrod system is easy maintenance. Harleys and some competitors use hydraulically adjusted tappets (small metal slugs between the cams and the pushrods) that eliminate the need for periodic valve adjustments. Some overhead cam designs also use hydraulic valve adjustments, but most require periodic manual adjustments.

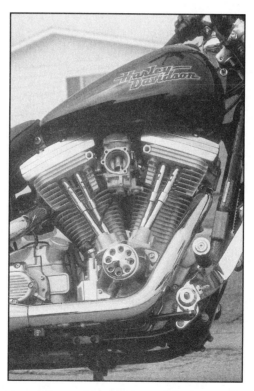

Harley-Davidson is one of several motorcycle manufacturers still using a pushrod-operated valve system.

(Photo © 1998 Darwin Holmstrom)

In a surprising move, Yamaha chose a pushrod-operated overhead valve system for its entry into the big-inch V-twin cruiser class, the Road Star. This was the first time a new Japanese motorcycle engine had used pushrods in some time. But this seemingly antiquated system hasn't hurt the Road Star's popularity one bit.

To Inject or Not to Inject? Induction Systems

Since Gottlieb Daimler constructed the first gasoline-powered motorcycle back in 1885, motorcycles have had carburetors—complex devices that mix gas and air into the fuel charge, which is then sucked into the combustion chamber. Carburetors—or carbs, as they are often called—rely on suction to deliver the air-fuel charge to the combustion chamber. Although modern carbs are remarkably efficient devices, they share the same physics with the crude device old Gottlieb bolted onto his half-horsepower engine way back when.

Today most motorcycles have one carburetor for each cylinder, with a few exceptions.

The carburetor's century-long supremacy as the ultimate form of motorcycle induction system has been challenged in the last decade by *fuel injection*. Fuel injection refers to a system that forces the fuel charge into the intake port with a high-pressure pump.

 CYCLE BABBLE

Fuel-injection systems use a high-pressure pump to inject a precise amount of fuel into the engine. Unlike carburetors, they automatically adjust for atmospheric conditions such as temperature and altitude.

The first reliable motorcycle fuel-injection system appeared on the 1980 Kawasaki Z-1 Classic. Since then, every other manufacturer has been working to fit fuel injection on every model they offer.

With the universal acceptance of fuel injection in the automotive world, it might seem odd that motorcycles have been slower to adopt the technology. Fuel injection offers certain benefits, such as greater control over the ratio of the air-fuel charge and better performance in a wide range of atmospheric conditions such as heat and altitude. But the problem is usually a matter of cost, as in what the customer will pay for the privilege of the technology. The cost of development time to fit fuel injection throughout a model lineup isn't cheap; even so, more bikes are using such systems. Modern technology has finally made fuel injection a viable option on motorcycles.

The Clutch

One of the major obstacles designers of early motorcycles faced was creating a system for engaging and disengaging the power transmitted to the back wheel. This wasn't a problem as long as you were moving, but once you decided to stop, it quickly became important.

Most early motorcycles used a leather belt to transmit power from the engine to the rear wheel! This belt connected directly to the crankshaft. To give the rider some control over the flow of power, a pulley mounted on a lever was used to loosen and tighten the belt.

Unsurprisingly, this system proved to be only marginally effective, even on the underpowered machines of the time, and it soon became clear that a better system was needed. That system was the *clutch*. The clutch is a series of spring-loaded plates that, when pressed together, transmit power from the crankshaft to the transmission.

CYCLE BABBLE

A **clutch** is a device that engages and disengages power from the crankshaft to the transmission, allowing a rider to change gears.

Early clutches were operated by a foot pedal, like on an automobile, with levers mounted to the gas tank to shift gears in the transmission. It's still sometimes fitted on custom choppers as an old-school engineering touch.

When the British began exporting motorcycles to the United States with hand-operated clutches and foot-operated shifters, stateside riders soon realized the benefits of such an ergonomic system, forcing Harley-Davidson to adopt hand clutches and foot shifts for its motorcycles.

Nearly every full-size motorcycle built since World War I uses a clutch, with a few interesting exceptions. Honda experimented with a clutchless, or automatic, transmission on its CB750A Hondamatic in the mid-1970s, and Moto Guzzi and Rokon also marketed automatic bikes at about the same time.

More recently, racing-style quick shifters have become available on some sportbikes, such as BMW's HP2 Sport. This setup momentarily kills the fuel injection when you nudge the shift lever up, reducing the power flow through the transmission just long enough to allow full-throttle upshifts without using the clutch.

As well, electronic shifting is now an option on the Yamaha FJ1300AE sport-touring bike. With this system, all you need to do to shift gears is press a paddle on the left handlebar or else toe the gearshift lever with your foot—there's no clutch lever.

Honda has gone one better with the dual-clutch transmission option on the VR1200. Such technology has been used in racecars for years, but the VFR1200 represents its first use on a streetbike. The system uses two coaxial transmission input shafts (one for the odd-numbered gears and one for the even-numbered gears) and two separate clutches. Basically, it's like having two separate gearboxes in one, and the electronic system that controls it allows shifting to occur nearly at lightning speed. It can also be used in either manual or fully automatic mode. Such systems add weight, cost, and complexity to the motorcycle equation, but they're certain to become popular on high-end machines.

Rotating the Rubber: Drive Systems

You now have a fair idea about what all that commotion taking place down below your legs is all about, but really, it means nothing if you have no way of transmitting that commotion to the back wheel of your bike.

As with many other aspects of motorcycle technology, the three final-drive systems most commonly used today—chain, shaft, and belt—had all been tried before the European squabbling that started World War I got out of hand.

In Chains

In the early years of the sport, the crude belt system mentioned earlier was employed, but by the end of World War I, most manufacturers had settled on a *chain final-drive system* (although a few opted for drive shafts). The simplicity and ease of repair of a chain-driven system made it a logical choice back then.

CYCLE BABBLE

Chain final-drive systems transmit the power to the rear wheel via a chain.

In this system, a small sprocket mounted to an output shaft in the transmission is connected to a larger sprocket attached to the rear wheel of the motorcycle by the drive chain. Although such a setup requires periodic maintenance (the chain gradually stretches, so the rear wheel needs to be adjusted to take up the slack), the benefits of this system make it popular to this day.

Just as with bicycles, chains are the accepted standard for delivering power to the rear wheel of a motorcycle. Proven decade after decade in all manner of circumstances, chains are highly efficient, affordable, and reliable. They are also relatively easy to repair and change, and you can even raise or lower your bike's final-drive ratio (i.e., the overall gearing) by selecting front or rear sprockets with a different number of teeth.

The four drawbacks of chain drives are that they are a bit on the noisy side (if the engine wasn't running you could hear the chain whirring over the sprockets while you're rolling down the road); they tend to fling chain lube everywhere; they need to be adjusted regularly; and they need to be lubricated on a regular basis. The chemicals and lubes used to do this are sometimes noxious or sticky.

MOTORCYCOLOGY

Although they're messy, the chain lubes and solvents now available are much cleaner and easier to use than ever before. While we may get some oil on our boot, the motorcycle pioneers were covered in the nasty, sticky stuff.

Getting the Shaft

Although this is not the case for the most modern type of shaft-drive bikes, older types of *shaft final-drive systems* affected handling by causing the motorcycle to rise on its suspension during acceleration and to drop during deceleration. When you open the throttle, the rotation of the driveshaft causes the rear suspension to extend, raising the motorcycle. Still, shaft drives are popular because they are so clean, quiet, convenient, and low maintenance, especially when traveling. It's hard enough packing a motorcycle for an extended trip without having to put cans of lube in your duffel bag next to your shirts and underwear. Because of this, the most popular touring and sport-touring bikes have shaft drives.

CYCLE BABBLE

Shaft final-drive systems transmit the power to the rear wheel via a driveshaft. Think of them as a shorter version of the drive shaft from a car.

Fortunately, several clever companies (including BMW, Kawasaki, Moto Guzzi, and Yamaha) have all but eliminated the antics associated with shaft systems by using creative rear-suspension geometry. By arranging suspension components in a parallelogram-type position, the rear suspensions on these bikes feed the shaft-jacking motion into the frame along a horizontal axis rather than a vertical axis, converting the up-and-down motion into a forward-and-backward motion. The rider hardly notices this sort of movement.

Whereas clever designers can overcome the shaft's acrobatics, another drawback of shaft systems cannot be overcome so easily: their weight. Shaft drives are heavy, and that weight is unsprung, meaning that it is not supported by the suspension. Unsprung weight tends to reduce ride quality and road-holding capability, while also working a bike's suspension harder.

The drawbacks of both shaft and chain systems led some companies to explore an old alternative: belt drives.

Belt It Out

Although belt drives were abandoned early on, by the beginning of the 1980s advances in materials (now rubber belts are reinforced with steel thread) had once again made them a viable alternative. Harley-Davidson was the first to reintroduce the concept, equipping special-edition bikes (such as its original Sturgis model) with both primary- and final-drive belts. The primary-drive belt system never caught on, but the final-drive belt did, and today every Harley and Victory cruiser comes standard with such a belt.

Kawasaki, Suzuki, and Yamaha also use belts on some of their cruiser-style bikes.

The advantage of *belt final-drive systems* over chains is that belts are much cleaner, requiring neither messy lube nor cleaning solvents. Also, while they do need periodic adjustments, they need such attention less frequently than chains.

The advantage of a belt system over traditional shaft drive is that belts, like chains, do not transmit unwanted motion into the *chassis*. They also do not come with the unsprung weight penalty of a shaft system.

 CYCLE BABBLE

Belt final-drive systems transmit the power to the rear wheel via a toothed drive belt. The **chassis** refers to the combined frame and suspension on a motorcycle.

The disadvantages of belt systems are that accurate adjustment is critical and they can be true buggers to replace when they do go bad. For instance, except for certain models, most Harley Big Twins require that you partially disassemble the frame in order to replace a belt. And to replace a belt on all Big Twins, you must remove the primary drive and clutch assembly, which is no small job.

This disadvantage has been negated on many of the newer bikes using belts. Victory uses a removable subframe to ease belt replacement. Such convenient features make a belt drive increasingly attractive. Even BMW uses a belt on its F800ST twin.

Putting It All Together

The frame, suspension, wheels, and tires on a motorcycle are basically the things that hold a bike together. In the past, that was pretty much all they did, but modern designers use them for much more.

The frames on early motorcycles were just a collection of tubes holding all the parts together. In the 1970s, however, streetbike designers began to realize that the stiffness of the frame affected overall handling characteristics and began experimenting with stiffer designs.

Motorcycle frames looked more or less the same from the time Harley and the Davidson boys built their first motorcycle until the mid-1980s. As a result of developments over the past 25 years, the twin-spar aluminum frames found on most modern sportbikes resemble the single- or double-cradle designs of the past about as much as an F-117 fighter jet resembles the Wright brothers' Flyer.

Suspension—which refers to the combination of forks, shocks, and, to a degree, tires—also has come a long way over the same time period. Just having a suspension was quite an innovation at one time. Early bikes relied on sprung girder forks up front and a soft saddle in back. It wasn't until the 1940s and 1950s that most motorcycle manufacturers began offering the hydraulic front forks and swinging-arm rear suspensions we now accept as the industry standard.

Once accepted, this setup became engraved in stone. It didn't change for the better part of 30 years.

During the 1970s, dirtbike manufacturers developed a variation of the swinging-arm rear suspension that used a single shock (Monoshock), and that system found its way onto streetbikes in the 1980s. The advantage of these systems was their longer travel—in other words, they allowed the wheel to travel farther up and down when the bike strikes a bump or other surface irregularity, improving stability and reducing the amount of jarring transmitted to the rider. The next step was incorporating variable-rate linkage into the system, allowing a soft ride over modest surface irregularities, and a firm ride when the going got truly rough. This type of system is the most common in use today.

Cruisers often use the older dual-shock setup because it gives these bikes the retro look cruiser buyers want. However, the ride quality on some cruisers tends to be a bit harsh because they often forfeit wheel travel to get a low seat height.

A few manufacturers have attempted to market alternatives to the hydraulic fork front suspension, most dramatically Bimota, with its hub-center-steered Tesi model, and Yamaha, with its GTS1000. Neither bike ever sold well, however.

BMW has produced the most successful alternate front suspension, the Telelever system. Modeled after the British Saxon-Motodd concept, the Telelever system replaces the conventional hydraulic fork with a swingarm and single shock absorber. This setup eliminates much of the brake dive (the tendency of the chassis to pitch forward during hard braking) associated with a traditional fork, but I believe that part of its success can be attributed to the fact that it still looks like a traditional fork.

Wheels and tires have also seen a surge of development since the early 1970s. The first technological advancement was the advent of cast wheels in the 1970s. These allowed bikes to use automotive-type tubeless tires, which provide a tremendous safety advantage because they are less likely to blow out than a tube-type tire. If you have ever had a tire blow out on a car, you know you don't want it to happen to you when you're riding a bike as it will only leave one functioning wheel, not three.

Tires themselves have come a long way, too. Today's touring tires can last 10,000 to 15,000 miles. And today's radial street tires provide phenomenal grip, though at the expense of high mileage. A really *sticky* tire can be worn out in 3,000 miles.

    CYCLE BABBLE

Sticky is a term used to describe sporting tires that provide incredible grip.

What all this means is that you have access to motorcycles that ride better, handle better, last longer, and are safer than anything a motorcyclist could have imagined possible just a few years ago.

It's Electric

The system least likely to cause trouble in your motorcycle is the electrical system. But if you do encounter an electrical failure of some sort, it will most likely occur early in the bike's life, well within the warranty period.

The function of the electrical system is to …

- Provide current to the ignition to burn the fuel charge.
- Power all the electrical devices on your bike, such as the headlight.

The electrical system consists of a battery, some form of electrical-generation device, and an ignition system to provide spark to the combustion chamber. I discuss this system in greater detail in Chapter 16.

Bodywork

Bodywork, a major component on most motorcycles today, didn't even exist on most motorcycles 30 years ago. For the first 95 years of motorcycling, bodywork just meant some sort of container mounted to the frame to store the gasoline.

The Europeans deserve much of the credit (or blame, depending on your own preferences) for making bodywork such a pervasive part of motorcycle design. BMW, Ducati, Laverda, Moto Guzzi, and Norton all marketed motorcycles with fairings in the 1970s. (As you learned in Chapter 3, fairings are the devices mounted at the front of a motorcycle to protect the rider from the elements.) By the end of the 1970s, the Japanese manufacturers were starting to do the same.

The only really surprising thing about this development was that it took the manufacturers so long to get in on the act. Perhaps the manufacturers were still haunted by the relative failure of the Vincent enclosed motorcycles discussed at the beginning of this chapter.

As the 1980s progressed, bodywork became more encompassing. Soon many street-bikes came with not only fairings, but also cowlings, a piece of bodywork that covered the engine. These items were designed to integrate with the rear portions of the bike, resulting in clean-looking bikes that have no visible engine components, creating an almost automotive appearance. Cowlings can protect you from the heat coming off the engine, and also help to shield you from rain working its way up through the nooks and crannies of a regular fairing.

As long as the bike still looks like a motorcycle, riders often appreciate such body-work, as well as the additional weather protection it provides.

Like everything, though, those benefits come at a price. As I mentioned in Chapter 4, the price of bodywork is higher insurance premiums and higher repair costs. Even routine maintenance becomes more expensive on a bike that must have its bodywork removed.

Yamaha's YZF-R1 features such attractive bodywork that at first glance, some observers mistake it for an Italian motorcycle.
(Photo courtesy of Yamaha Motor Corporation, USA)

The Least You Need to Know

- The engine gives a motorcycle its character and personality.
- The bottom end of the engine is where all the commotion in the engine is converted into forward motion.
- The top end of the engine is where the internal-combustion process takes place.
- The drive systems used today are chain, shaft, and belt.
- Bodywork, such as fairings and cowlings, helps protect motorcycle riders from the elements.

Start Your Engines

In This Chapter

- Why different types of engines give motorcycles different characteristics
- The difference between two-stroke and four-stroke engines
- The types of four-stroke engines: singles, V-twins, and more

In the previous chapter, you took an in-depth technical look at the parts of a motorcycle. Now you're going to venture into a more esoteric, subjective area: the engine, the soul of a motorcycle.

You might wince at this bit of anthropomorphism, thinking a motorcycle has as much of a soul as a toaster or an electric screwdriver. But motorcyclists who have ridden for a while know the truth: motorcycles possess a distinct, essential spirit, and while the word *soul* doesn't exactly describe it, it comes closer than any other word in the English language. If bikes don't have souls, someone forgot to tell that to my motorcycles.

A variety of characteristics give each bike its unique identity, but none so clearly defines a bike's personality as its engine. And each type of engine has different characteristics, which is why certain types are used for specific motorcycles.

Many of the internal differences that give an engine its character are technical details beyond the scope of this book. But knowing the basic types of engines and what you can expect from each will help you select the bike best suited for you.

Engineering

All engine types get their characteristics from a combination of *horsepower* and *torque*. While closely related, horsepower and torque are not the same thing: each is a measure of a different characteristic of an engine's power. Here is a simple way to think of it: horsepower is a measure of how fast you can go, and torque is a measure of an engine's snap, or how fast it can get to its maximum speed.

CYCLE BABBLE

Horsepower is a measure of an engine's strength. It is called horsepower because it was originally calculated by measuring how much weight a horse could lift in a certain period of time. **Torque** is a twisting force, and in a motorcycle, it is a measure of the leverage the engine exerts on the rear wheel.

In the real world, torque is usually more useful than prodigious amounts of peak horsepower. The benefits of lots of horsepower tend to be most apparent at speeds well beyond what local law-enforcement officials will allow; you can use torque at speeds that won't land you in jail.

Two basic types of motorcycle engines are in use today: the two-stroke and the four-stroke. Over the following pages, you'll look at each one.

The Four-Stroke

Anyone who has ever added oil to a car has experience with *four-stroke engines;* the vast majority of road-going vehicles ever to turn a wheel on streets in the United States have four-stroke engines.

CYCLE BABBLE

The **four-stroke engine** is sometimes called the *Otto cycle,* in honor of its inventor, Nikolaus August Otto. It's called a four-stroke because the piston makes four strokes, or movements along the length of the cylinder, per cycle.

The four-stroke gets its name from the number of strokes the piston makes during each power cycle (each series of events that produces power). The piston first moves down, drawing in the air-fuel charge (intake stroke), and then moves up (compression stroke), at which time the air-fuel charge ignites and burns, pushing the piston down (power stroke). The fourth stroke occurs when the piston moves back up, forcing out the burned gases (exhaust stroke).

The Single

The single, so called because it only has one piston and cylinder, is the most basic of engines—it once powered most motorcycles on the road. In the old days, motorcycles were such problematic beasts that the general philosophy held that the fewer moving parts you had, the less chance there was that those parts would break. If there was a way of having zero-cylinder motorcycles, without having to pedal, they'd have done it.

As designs and materials advanced, along with production techniques, manufacturers were able to create ever more complex motorcycles, with two, three, four, six, and even eight cylinders. Generally, the more cylinders you have, the smoother the engine runs. But with a counterbalancer (rotating weights inside the engine) to cancel out some of the vibration, plus rubber motor-mounts, today's big singles will no longer blur your vision as they vibrate you off your seat.

Yamaha's WR250X represents a modern interpretation of the sporting single-cylinder motorcycle, once the most common type of bike.
(Photo courtesy of Yamaha Motor Corporation, USA)

The primary drawback of single-cylinder engines, though, is that they don't have a lot of horsepower, which has contributed to their waning popularity.

But singles have advantages, too. Because they have few parts, they tend to be light powerplants (engines), which is why they are so popular in dirtbikes and the big dual-sports. And although they might not generate a lot of power, they still provide satisfying amounts of grunty torque.

Suppose you are riding a BMW G650GS single. Beside you, your companion rides a Suzuki GSX-R600, a four-cylinder bike that makes more than twice as much horsepower as your Beemer, but roughly the same torque. You pass the city limits, and the speed limit rises to 65. Say, for the sake of argument, that you're both running at roughly 2,500 rpm. You both whack open the throttle at the same time. You'll pull away first—even though the Suzuki has twice as much horsepower—because at 2,500 rpm you have about 34 pound-feet of torque available to you, while the Suzuki has only about 22 pound-feet of torque available (torque, the force the engine exerts on the rear wheel, is measured in pound-feet).

Of course, within a few seconds, the Suzuki will have rocketed away from you when all that horsepower kicks in, but by then you are both going faster than the powers that be will allow anyway. And if the Suzuki rider drops the shifter down a few gears, she will have left you behind from the moment you hit the throttle. Either way, she will have accelerated to go-to-jail speeds quicker than you can process the sound of the sirens on Officer Bob's police cruiser as he begins a high-speed pursuit.

The point of this hypothetical scenario is that while single-cylinder bikes offer less overall power than multicylinder bikes, the power they do offer is often more usable in the real world, a world populated by traffic lights, stray dogs, pedestrians, senior citizens, and law-enforcement officials. The same is true of many twin-cylinder motorcycles.

The V-Twin

The V-twin design found widespread support even in the early days of motorcycle development, largely because it fit the shape of the bicycle-style frames used on motorcycles at the time. A V-twin engine is a two-cylinder engine with its cylinders splayed out in a V shape.

By 1907, Harley and those Davidson boys displayed a prototype V-twin engine for their motorcycles. When Englishman Philip Vincent decided to add another cylinder to his Comet and create the first Rapide, the two cylinders together formed a traditional V. And when the Japanese got serious about building American-style cruisers, their engine of choice was the V-twin, too.

Modern manufacturers build V-twin motorcycles for a variety of reasons; some are practical and objective, while others, such as tradition and style, are purely subjective.

V-twin engines vary widely in their characteristics. Some designs, such as Harley-Davidson's 45-degree big V-twins, vibrate excessively. But Harley has taken the Twin Cam 96A/96B Big Twin engines and either rubber-mounted them (Dyna models) or fitted them with counterbalancers (Softail models). Likewise, Harley rubber-mounted its 883/1200 Evolution engines in its Sportsters.

Other V-twin cruisers use narrow-angle V engines but also use some sort of system for reducing vibration. Honda uses a staggered crankshaft, which fools the engine into thinking the V angle is a wider 90 degrees. Other manufacturers, such as Kawasaki, use heavy counterbalancers.

One characteristic common to most V-twin engines (and all successful ones) is ample torque, especially in the larger models. Riders of high-revving sportbikes often comment on the lack of peak horsepower that V-twin bikes usually display, but they're missing the point. While V-twins usually give away a lot of power up at the top of the rpm band (which, in the real world, means at triple-digit speeds), they make up for it by offering tremendous usable power at lower rpm.

On a cruiser with a large V-twin engine, you can probably forget about riding all day at 145 mph, but when you whack open the throttle at lower speeds (such as the 65 to 70 mph you'll usually find yourself riding), you are rewarded with satisfying thrust that sets you back in the saddle.

Different types of high-performance V-twin engines have become popular for sportbikes. Their narrow crankcases improve ground clearance while cornering, they are simpler and lighter than comparably sized four-cylinder engines, and they can be tuned to produce a combination of useful torque and peak horsepower. Moto Guzzi and Ducati popularized different V-twin designs in the 1970s, and more recently other sportbike companies such as Aprilia, KTM, and Suzuki have followed suit.

The Boxer

In 1923, Max Friz, an engineer working for BMW, built a motorcycle engine, the R32. It was a 500cc opposed twin, using basic principles still in use today. This engine earned the nickname Boxer because the pistons thrust outward, away from each other, like fists.

This wasn't the first opposed engine, but Friz's execution was unique, and the effectiveness of his design makes BMW's Boxer engines popular to this day. By opposing each other, the pistons cancel out primary vibration, creating a remarkably smooth twin-cylinder engine. And by locating the pistons on the side of the engine, Friz placed them in the cooling airstream, leading to a cool-running—and, thus, long-lasting—engine. It's not uncommon to find BMWs with 200,000 or more miles showing on the odometer.

The success of Friz's design wasn't lost on manufacturers from other countries. During World War II, Harley-Davidson used his Boxer design for a military motorcycle; in 1941, Ural began manufacturing a Beemer clone in Russia. Harley ditched this idea soon after World War II, but Ural is still at it.

Many people find that the Boxer design offers an ideal compromise between twin-cylinder torque and multicylinder smoothness. Like the V-twin, a Boxer's primary characteristic is abundant torque rather than massive peak horsepower. This torque is usually found a bit higher in the rpm range than a V-twin's, but it still comes on early enough to be useful in the real world. In return, Boxers tend to have more top speed than V-twins. Combine that with the engine design's inherent smoothness and the result is Boxer riders who can cruise for extended periods at elevated speeds.

Edward Turner's Speed Twin

In 1927, a young man in Britain named Edward Turner, working alone in his own shop, designed and built a 350cc single-cylinder motorcycle. The British motorcycle industry took note of this achievement, and he soon landed a job designing bikes. By 1936, he'd worked his way up to general manager and chief designer at Triumph Engineering Co.

In July 1937, Turner introduced the 500cc Speed Twin, which featured a 27-horsepower *parallel-twin engine* that formed the basis of most Triumph motorcycle engines until the 1980s. This engine, and its imitators from companies such as BSA and Norton, became the powerplant of choice for sporting motorcycles for decades to come.

 CYCLE BABBLE

A **parallel-twin engine** is a two-cylinder engine with its cylinders placed side by side in an upright position. From the side it can be mistaken for a single-cylinder engine.

Because of the design of its crankshaft, along with certain dynamic problems inherent in the parallel-twin design, these engines vibrated much more than a Boxer engine, but they vibrated less than a V-twin. Plus, they were light and powerful for their day. Their compact size enabled engineers to create compact motorcycles that could run circles around the big Harleys and Indians of that era, and the power output of a 650 nearly equaled that of the big V-twins, which displaced as much as 1200cc. For a long time, it was the most commonly used sportbike engine.

Although the parallel twin has long since ceased being the powerplant of choice for superbikes, the design still has enough appeal to keep it in production. Modern versions, with redesigned crankshafts and counterbalancers to tame vibration, power a variety of midsize bikes from manufacturers such as BMW, Suzuki, and Kawasaki. For instance, Kawasaki produces parallel twins in both cruiser and sportbike form. The company's Vulcan 500 LTD cruiser and Ninja 500R sportbike are comfortable, good-handling, nimble motorcycles with enough power to keep a rider amused for decades.

The British Triple

Eventually, the British responded to the Japanese invasion and introduced a new engine design, the *inline-triple*. In many respects, this was just a parallel twin with an extra cylinder grafted on, but it featured some unique characteristics—notably, its compactness. British twins gained their reputation for being fine-handling motorcycles in large part because their compact engines allowed designers to tuck everything in, leaving very few hard parts to scrape the pavement during high-speed antics. With the triples, designers went to great lengths to retain that compactness.

Although promising, these bikes initially had too many problems to save the British motorcycle industry. Anyone who wants to learn how not to conduct business would do well to study the development of the Triumph T150 Trident and BSA Rocket 3. A design firm with no experience in motorcycles was hired to style the bikes, resulting in controversial styling. Mechanically, the new bikes also failed. Although the engines were powerful, they proved unreliable in service, victims of underdevelopment.

 CYCLE BABBLE

An **inline-triple** is an engine with three cylinders placed in a row.

An **inline-four** is an engine with four cylinders in a row.

After the appearance of the new bikes was universally rejected by motorcycle buyers, Triumph successfully restyled the Trident (BSA had gone out of business by that time) and gradually worked out the mechanical bugs, but it was just too late. By then, Honda had already introduced its CB750 *inline-four*-cylinder bike and, in doing so, effectively stripped the British of any useful influence in the new-motorcycle market.

Honda CB750: A Four for the Masses

The effect Honda's CB750 Four had on the motorcycling world can be compared to the effect the introduction of Microsoft's Windows operating platform had on the personal computer industry. Sure, the old DOS system retained a few die-hard adherents, as did the British motorcycle industry, but just as the vast majority of computer users preferred Windows to DOS, the vast majority of the motorcycling public wanted inline-four-cylinder bikes.

Although twin-cylinder bikes have experienced a resurgence in popularity of late, many riders still want four-cylinder motorcycles, which makes sense: the benefits of four-cylinder bikes can't be denied.

The primary benefits of a four-cylinder engine in a motorcycle are smoothness and a capability to run at higher rpm than a comparable twin. Sportbike fours generally are tuned to make their power higher up in the powerband than twins, and they produce less torque at lower rpm. All but the most highly tuned fours make adequate torque down low. Some inline-fours aimed at a more general audience, such as Suzuki's 1250S Bandit, make more torque than many twins.

A strike against four-cylinder motorcycles in the past was that the engines were rather bulky, although designers have since rectified this situation. For example, most manufacturers of inline-fours have moved ancillary items—ignition distributors, water pumps, and alternators, for example—to make the engine narrower. They've also stacked the transmission shafts to reduce the engine's length.

Still, inline-four engines remain more complex than twins and singles. More parts mean more expensive maintenance.

Honda's groundbreaking CB750, introduced in 1969, was perhaps the most influential motorcycle in history.

(Photo courtesy of Vreeke and Associates)

Odds are, you'll end up with a four-cylinder engine, not because it's better (or worse) than any other type, but because it is such a common design. This is especially true if you buy a used bike.

The Inline-Six

For a few years in the mid-1970s and early 1980s, a handful of manufacturers experimented with inline-six-cylinder motorcycle engines, featuring six cylinders in a row. The parallel twin had grown to a triple, then progressed to the inline-fours (the same thing with yet another cylinder tacked on), so a six probably seemed logical. But these proved to be oddities, footnotes in the motorcycle history books. The odds of you stumbling across one of these beasties by chance are slim (unlike the bikes themselves, which are as wide as a Peterbilt), and now most of these machines are the property of collectors.

The Italian company Benelli produced 750cc and 900cc six-cylinder bikes, but like many old Italian bikes, these are machines you'll probably see only in pictures. More common were the big sixes produced by Honda and Kawasaki. These were functional motorcycles, but both were victims of their own excess. The width and weight of those six-cylinders just proved to be too much, so handling suffered horribly. And if four-cylinder engines are complex to maintain, then sixes can be absolute nightmares.

The V-4s

When Honda introduced its water-cooled *V-4 engine* bikes for the 1982 model year, pundits predicted the demise of the inline-four. It seemed reasonable at the time. These engines have exceptional power characteristics, providing good torque figures and more than adequate horsepower. Plus, they are one of the smoothest engine designs in existence.

 CYCLE BABBLE

A **V-4 engine** is an engine of four cylinders arranged in a V-shape configuration, with two cylinders on each side of the V.

This engine design became something of a standard—powering a variety of sport-bikes, cruisers, and touring bikes—for a time, but it never came close to replacing the inline-four. That was probably due to the expense of manufacturing such a complex engine design rather than any inherent flaws with the concept. In service, these have proven to be remarkably reliable motorcycles.

If you are in the market for a used motorcycle, a bike with a V-4 engine is a safe bet. These bikes have been nearly indestructible.

The Gold Wing

The engine Honda uses in its Gold Wing touring bikes is unique—it doesn't really fit into any other category. The only thing comparable to the four-cylinder version is the engine Subaru uses in its cars. This is a flat, Boxer-type engine, with four or six liquid-cooled cylinders instead of two air-cooled cylinders, like BMW uses. The flat-four- and flat-six-cylinder engines used in Honda's Gold Wings are called flat because their cylinders are arranged in a flat, opposing configuration.

These are the smoothest engines used in motorcycles, period, and are a major part of the Gold Wing's appeal to the touring crowd. They also have a fairly centralized mass, which makes the entire motorcycle easier to maneuver. I've seen Gold Wing riders whip their bikes around as if they were riding sportbikes instead of ultimate behemoths weighing almost twice what the average sportbike weighs.

When Honda introduced its Gold Wing in 1975, it created a new class of motorcycle: the luxury tourer.

(Photo courtesy of Simon Green)

The L-Twin

Italian manufacturers have developed a unique take on the V-twin concept. By widening the angle of the V to 90 degrees (changing the shape from a V to an L, thus giving the configuration its name), they have created a smoother, more balanced twin-cylinder engine. Ducati's engines, which are longitudinal (they are positioned lengthwise in the frame), most obviously display the L configuration. Moto Guzzi's engines, which are transverse (arranged crosswise in the frame), are also angled at 90 degrees. These are incredibly well-designed engines, as proven by their multiple successes on the world racing circuit.

The Two-Stroke

The other common type of motorcycle engine is the two-stroke; we briefly touched on it earlier. It's called two-stroke because its cycle consists of only two strokes (yes, really): the piston moves down, drawing in the air-fuel charge, and then moves up, at which point the charge ignites, forcing the piston back down and starting the process all over again. To provide lubrication for such an engine, oil must be mixed in with the fuel charge. This is what gives some two-strokes their characteristic smoky exhaust.

While this type of combustion cycle creates a high-revving, powerful little motor, it does so at a price: air pollution. And that is the reason Environmental Protection Agency standards essentially banished two-strokes from U.S. roads. Today two-strokes are found mainly on off-road bikes and Grand Prix racing bikes in the 125cc and 250cc classes. But two-strokes aren't secure even there; off-road four-strokes have made serious inroads on what was previously exclusively two-stroke territory.

With the exception of Honda, Japanese manufacturers originally invaded the U.S. market with small two-stroke motorcycles.

Japanese two-strokes ranged from small 50cc mopeds to Suzuki's GT750 and Kawasaki's infamous three-cylinder 750cc H2. Although some of these bikes contin-ued in production until the late 1970s, it was already clear that increasingly stringent air-quality rules would make two-strokes extinct, at least in the United States. Other than Yamaha, which continued to develop its popular RD series throughout the decade, most manufacturers quit developing two-strokes for the U.S. market, other than for scooters and bikes such as Aprilia's RS50 repliracer.

Many of us grew up riding these fast, lightweight, cheap machines, and our memories of them are probably clouded by all the fun we had on them (and perhaps all that exhaust smoke has damaged our memories). Two-strokes are still out there, although they become tougher to find every year.

Even if you can find one intact, they tend not to be practical motorcycles. They generate a lot of power for their size, but that power usually comes on suddenly at the very top of the rpm range. I've found it takes a special type of lunatic to make good use of a two-stroke, a somewhat crazed motorcyclist who rides with the throttle wide open and controls speed with the shifter. Every ride, even a simple trip to the local convenience store, is a Grand Prix event for these folks. While you may be just the sort of lunatic I'm describing, this is not the best way to learn to ride.

The Least You Need to Know

- The engine is where you'll find a motorcycle's soul.
- The combination of torque and peak horsepower shapes an engine's personality.
- The shape and design of an engine contribute to its power-delivery characteristics.
- Four-stroke engines have broader ranges of power than two-stroke engines and make better bikes for beginners. The number of cylinders also influences power-delivery characteristics.
- Two-strokes tend to have power-delivery characteristics best suited for experienced, slightly insane motorcyclists.

Buying Your First Bike

In This Chapter

- Where to find a bike
- What to look for in a bike
- What's it worth?
- Wheeling and dealing

By now, you're so familiar with the workings of engines that you can tell a BMW from a Honda just by the sound. And you know exactly what kind of bike you want. What's next? Getting your first bike. The time has come to lose your moto-virginity.

Like your first lover, you will remember your first bike as long as you live. Although you will always enjoy the freedom motorcycling brings you, nothing quite compares to the heady exhilaration of those first rides. At this point, the best way to ensure that those rides are as pleasurable as possible is to get a good, dependable motorcycle.

Where to Buy Your Bike

Shopping for a motorcycle differs from shopping for a car in every aspect. For the most part, cars are appliances, like washing machines (some even look like them), which are bought and sold by staid, sensible people.

Motorcycles are expressions of passion, and the people buying and selling them tend to be passionate people, some are just plain nuts. (Should you doubt this, ask yourself when you last saw someone covered with Chevrolet tattoos, wearing a T-shirt stating he'd rather see his sister in a brothel than his brother in a Toyota.)

MOTORCYCOLOGY

Finding a good motorcycle shop is a challenge in itself, but if you find a truly great one, you may have found a fun place to hang out, drink coffee, and absorb moto-culture. A good dealer knows that hardcore motorcyclists tend to spend every cent they have on bikes and accessories, and will go to great lengths to make you feel at home in his or her shop.

Just finding a motorcycle differs from finding a car. You can find motorcycles in several places, some obvious and others less so.

Dealerships

The most obvious—and perhaps the easiest—place to find a bike is at a dealership. If you're buying a new bike, you'll have no choice but to buy from a dealer. But even if you're buying used, buying from a reputable shop can be the best way to get your first bike.

Physically locating a motorcycle dealership can present a challenge if you're not familiar with the area you're living in. People selling motorcycles don't have the kind of cash flow car dealers have, so usually you won't find motorcycle shops amid the endless car lots, strip malls, and office buildings in the sprawl suburban America has become. Motorcycle dealerships can be hidden in out-of-the-way locations where leases are lower. Check the Yellow Pages under "Motorcycles" to find dealers and repair shops in your area.

Choosing a Dealer

Not all dealerships are created equal. The quality of the staff makes or breaks a shop.

When you're buying your first motorcycle, it's tough to know whether you are being taken advantage of. My first experience with a dealer turned out badly. I wanted to buy a 100cc Kawasaki dirtbike, but my father distrusted Japanese products (this was the early 1970s in rural Minnesota), so he took me to a shop selling American-made minibikes. He liked the minibikes because they were powered by snowmobile engines, which he believed to have been built right there in Minnesota. Actually, these engines were manufactured in Japan and were wholly unsuited for summertime operation. The second day I owned the bike, I seized a piston.

The dealer fully expected us to be back the next day; he knew these bikes were unfit, but he had a plan. He traded me the trashed minibike for a new 80cc Yamaha motorcycle. It ended up costing about 20 percent more than the 100cc Kawasaki would have cost, but it was either that or keep the blown-up minibike.

If that wasn't bad enough, the dealer lied to me about the model year of the bike. I was too naïve to know where to check the date of manufacture (see bullets below) and ended up buying a two-year-old carryover motorcycle for more than the price of a new one.

But I was only 11 years old, and I didn't have this book. Here are some tips to keep this from happening to you:

- Learn as much about the motorcycle as possible. Check the buying guides to new (Appendix A) and used (Appendix B) bikes to see if it's listed there. Go to the library and read back issues of motorcycle magazines that have tested the bike.

- Make sure your salesperson knows motorcycles. Ask good questions. By the answers, you can tell whether the person is uninformed, unscrupulous, or both. (See Chapter 8 for examples of questions you should ask.)

- Check the mileage on the odometer against the mileage on the title, and check the model year on the title against the date of manufacture on the frame, usually located on a plate riveted to either the steering head or the lower frame tube or beam. If something's not kosher, chances are, neither is the shop selling the bike.

Buying a motorcycle from a salesperson who knows bikes and whom you can trust can be fun, the beginning of a productive relationship. But getting ripped off can poison you for life. Generally, you're more likely to have a bad experience at a shop where motorcycles are just a sideline, such as a car dealership that also carries a line of bikes, or a dealership devoted primarily to snowmobiles, watercraft, or some other type of recreational vehicle and just carries motorcycles because its franchise requires it. Your best bet is to find a shop that lives and breathes motorcycles.

But like any generalization, there are exceptions. The best salesperson I've ever dealt with worked at a Chrysler shop that carried Honda motorcycles. If you can find just one person at a shop who knows and cares about motorcycles, that's good enough.

The date of manufacture is usually stamped either on the steering head or on the frame of a motorcycle.

(Photos © 1998 Darwin Holmstrom)

How's Their Service Department?

Finding the right dealership with a salesperson you trust means little if the mechanic working in the service department is a lazy, clumsy fool.

This is more of an issue when buying a new bike under warranty than it is when buying a used bike. With a used motorcycle, if you get a good deal, you can always take it to a mechanic you trust somewhere else. When you buy new, you may be forced to go back to the same dealership for warranty work; many shops balk at covering warranty work on motorcycles bought at other dealerships.

An unskilled mechanic actually wrecked the top end on one of my bikes once. This was at a shop where I'd developed a relationship with one of the salespeople, a nice guy and a dedicated motorcyclist. I made the mistake of assuming that the personnel in the service department were as competent as my friend in sales.

I was leaving on a solo motorcycle trip to the Ozark Mountains in a couple of days, so I brought my motorcycle in for a complete tune-up. I wanted to make certain my bike was running well.

When I picked up my bike, it wouldn't idle. In fact, it never idled again. The mechanic, who I later learned had been hired because his father owned the shop, had overtightened the valves. Before I left the parking lot, I'd bent a valve stem. You guessed it ... that's not good.

I was still somewhat of a novice and didn't know what had happened. I took the bike back to the service department, and even though they knew exactly what they had done, they blamed the problem on dirt in the carburetors. They kept the bike overnight to clean the carbs, but there was nothing they could do, short of a valve job.

Shops like this usually develop reputations in the motorcycling community. Within two years of trashing my bike, this shop went out of business.

So how can you find out which shops offer reliable service? Wherever motorcyclists hang out, they talk about mechanical things. And they love to gossip. If you can find a coffee shop, a bike night, or a bar where motorcyclists congregate, ask them about the reputation of a shop's service department. If several people agree on a shop to avoid, avoid it. If you have no local hangout, check with independent repair shops. These are often staffed by mechanics who cut their teeth in local dealerships and who usually know the scoop on other shops.

The Classified Ads

The other obvious place to hunt for a used bike is in the classifieds section of a newspaper. I enjoy this form of shopping because it puts me in direct contact with the local motorcycling community. When I go to look at bikes I've found in classified ads, I meet all kinds of motorcyclists, from people who bought a bike on a whim years ago but never rode it much, to hardcore riders who are moving on to a different bike.

Shopping the classifieds requires you to bring even more knowledge to the transaction than buying from a dealership. The range of conditions you will find classified bikes in varies as widely as the personalities of the owners selling them. Even the most unscrupulous dealer fears lawsuits enough to make certain the wheels are correctly bolted on. (At least, they usually do—I once tested a bike that handled so squirrelly, I stopped and discovered the dealer had mounted the wheel backward!)

You never know what to expect on a machine you found through the want ads. Frames can be bent from accident damage. Chain alignment may be wonky from adjustment by cruel people who should be banned from owning a wrench. Seats may be attached with duct tape. Remember, your life depends on the condition of your machine, and any one of these conditions, as well as a host of other possible problems, could have you hanging out with the other roadkill.

Many people will let you test ride a bike, but check it out carefully to make certain it's safe before taking it on the road. Some people will want the money up front before even allowing a test ride. Before judging them too harshly, would you let a total stranger ride your pride and joy? What if they were a novice? Later in this chapter, I'll show you what to look for when you examine a bike.

MOTORCYCOLOGY

Another source of motorcycle ads are the newsprint magazines that contain nothing but photos of vehicles that are for sale. In many metropolitan areas, these magazines either have large motorcycle sections or are entirely devoted to recreational vehicles. While it's possible to find good buys through such magazines, more often than not, you'll find yourself chasing down overpriced bikes in much worse condition than they appear in the photos. Still, these magazines are worth checking out. If nothing else, they're fun to read. Fortunately, many of them are now available online as well, which makes browsing easier because you can search for a specific year, make, model, and even certain features.

When buying a bike from a private party, obtaining a clear title is absolutely critical. As with buying from a dealer, make certain the information on the title matches the information on the bike. This is especially important on motorcycles with high theft rates, such as Japanese sportbikes and Harley-Davidsons, but it's important with all bikes. A friend of mine once replaced the frame on his Suzuki after a crash without changing the title to reflect that change. One morning, he went out to the street to find that his motorcycle had been carted off by the police. They wouldn't release the bike to him because of the irregular title. He ended up forfeiting the bike because it would have cost him more to get it back than it was worth.

If you buy a motorcycle that turns out to be stolen, you will not only lose the bike, but you may well end up in legal trouble for receiving stolen merchandise. Generally, this is a problem only when buying from private parties, but dealerships have sold stolen motorcycles, too. One clue that something may be less than above board is if the bike has a replacement title from another state.

Buying a motorcycle through the classifieds requires you to bring more to the table yourself, but it's often worth the effort. Private sellers don't have to build the overhead costs of running a dealership into the price, so you have a better chance of getting a bargain. The best advice I've got is to take a friend (or trusted mechanic) who does know what to look for, then thank them with a beer later or a meal on the way home.

I read the classified motorcycle ads every day, even though I'm usually not in the market to buy a bike. I find it's a good way to keep up on the motorcycle market, as well as the motorcycling community. I like to see who's selling what and how much they're asking. Sometimes I find even more information than I expected. My all-time favorite ad, written by a guy selling his Harley Electra Glide, ended with the following phrase: "She caught me cheating, and now it's the big D for me: make offer."

Bulletin Boards

If you are lucky enough to have a local hangout for motorcyclists, chances are the place has a bulletin board with ads and snapshots of bikes pinned on three deep. (If you don't have such a place, you will probably find a similar bulletin board at the shop of an independent mechanic.)

These bulletin boards contain some of the best deals available. Usually, the seller knows what he has and what it's worth, and is offering the bike at a fair price.

My all-time best motorcycle buy, a Suzuki GS650G, came off of one such board. I went to look at the bike, not expecting to buy it because I had only $500 to spend, and the bike appeared to be in pristine condition—which it was (and still is).

The young man selling it was asking $800—a fair price, given the condition of the bike. When I told him I had only $500, he was ready to take it on the spot. I told him the bike was worth more and to think it over and call me the next day if he still wanted to sell it.

The next day he called, and I found myself the proud owner of what turned out to be one of the most reliable and rugged motorcycles I've ever owned.

Motorcycle Clubs

Motorcycle clubs are another rich source of used motorcycles. Members of clubs tend to buy and sell a lot of motorcycles. They trade bikes the way some kids trade baseball cards and comic books.

Again, check with other motorcyclists at local hangouts and shops to find out what kind of clubs operate in your community. I discuss clubs at greater length in Chapter 19, but for now, I want to point out the advantages of clubs when shopping for a motorcycle.

Members of motorcycle clubs tend to be longtime motorcyclists, people who love to talk about bikes, sometimes too much! But be patient as you can learn a great deal about every subject in this book from these people, and they are an especially valuable resource when it comes to buying motorcycles.

The bikes these folks sell tend to gravitate toward the higher end of the price scale, usually with good cause. The following is a list of reasons a motorcycle bought from a club member will likely be worth the money:

- Club members' bikes are usually in excellent condition. They take pride in their equipment, partly because they know their fellow members will judge them by the quality of their bikes, and partly because they bond with their machines even more closely than a "normal" motorcyclist (if there is such a thing) does. They treat their bikes like members of the family; that's why they joined a club.

- People in clubs have enough motorcycle savvy to buy bikes that are worth something, motorcycles with decent resale value.

- They know the value of their machines and usually won't ask more than they're worth, if for no other reason than other club members will doubt their intelligence if they get greedy.

- Motorcycle clubs are an especially tight subcommunity within the general motorcycling community. If one club member ripped off another club member, he or she would be ostracized from the group.

Garages

An astounding number of perfectly good motorcycles rest in people's garages. As pointed out in Chapter 2, Japanese manufacturers sold shiploads of motorcycles in the 1980s. A lot of these bikes eventually found their way to corners of garages, where they've sat unlicensed for years.

Finding bikes this way can be problematic. For starters, if you snoop around in people's garages, you could find yourself staring down the wrong end of a shotgun. The best way to find out about these lost treasures is through word of mouth, which, in itself, presents a problem. These bikes aren't at the forefront of their owners' consciousness. Owners don't spend much time thinking about these machines and probably spend even less time talking about them.

If you do see a bike sitting in someone's garage, the trick is to figure out (a) whose garage it is and (b) how to tell the owner you're interested in the bike without letting him or her know that you regularly peep through people's open garage doors.

STEER CLEAR

Even if you get a good price on a garage bike, it might not be worth the trouble. Sitting idle causes problems, such as dried seals: when rubber seals in the engine, suspension, and brakes sit in disuse for an extended time, they dry and crack, causing leaks and a host of other problems. Equally problematic is when carburetors are left full of gas, which will eventually dry up, leaving deposits that clog the tiny jets and orifices inside, making the engine hard or even impossible to start. Unless you're prepared to undertake major mechanical repairs, make certain a bike has been stored properly; that most of the fluids have stayed inside the engine, suspension, and brakes; and that the carburetors were properly drained.

Once you've cleared that hurdle, the trick is to negotiate a price. Most likely, such owners have no idea what the real value of their bikes are, so you never know how much they will ask for them. The owner could throw out a number that is ridiculously low or high, or else guess something in the ballpark of reality.

If it's low, I go for it without regret. The owner has no use for the bike, other than as a place to store stuff on. I consider it my duty to liberate the neglected machine and make it a productive member of the motorcycling community. And I don't worry that I'm ripping the owners off. Obviously, they don't need the money, or they would have sold the bike long ago.

If the number is ridiculously high, my advice is to walk away. The owner believes that price to be the bike's true value, and if you try to barter, the person will probably be insulted.

The Internet

Although you might be a novice to motorcycles, I'm going to assume that you are not unaware of computers or the Internet, or of the ease in finding things online to buy, such as motorcycles. Some of these websites make prime hunting grounds for the bike of your dreams: www.ebaymotors.com, www.craigslist.org, www.cycletrader.com, and www.powersportsnetwork.com.

But be advised that there are a ridiculous number of scam artists on the web who will fleece the unwary as part of a day's work. Here are a few tips: avoid buying long-distance and sight-unseen; be wary of complicated deals or oddball stories about missing paperwork; likewise, be wary of large down payments to hold the merchandise; and insist on a face-to-face sale. Finally, remember this: if a deal seems too good to be true, it almost certainly is.

The web can also be a prime research source if you're somewhat undecided about which motorcycle is right for you. *Motorcyclist* and *Motorcycle Cruiser* magazines both have archives of past road tests on their websites—www.motorcyclistonline.com and www.motorcyclecruiser.com, respectively—so you can get the editors' lowdown on bikes you're considering.

What to Look For

Buying a used motorcycle seems something of a crapshoot to the uninitiated. Judging a dependable bike from a pile of junk may appear difficult to the first-time buyer, but a couple of basic motorcycle characteristics make it easier than you might think.

First, motorcycles have nothing to hide. If a frame has been repaired, you will see welds or cracks in the paint. If the bike leaks fluids, those fluids will ooze out before your eyes. Second, there's just not that much to a motorcycle. Compared to cars, they are relatively simple devices.

Further simplifying the buying process is the fact that what you need to check is limited to just a few basic items; luckily, you won't need to worry about all the parts of a motorcycle covered in Chapter 5 (at least on Japanese bikes—European and American machines present a few more challenges).

The things to look for when buying can be broken down into two broad categories: condition and completeness.

Critical: Condition

You need to ascertain the mechanical and cosmetic condition of a motorcycle before you make an offer.

Judging a bike's cosmetic condition is easy: just ask yourself how it looks. By looking at the bodywork and such items as mirrors, turn signals, and mufflers, and examining those items for scratches, dents, and other deformities, you can usually tell whether a bike is in good shape. Pay particular attention to the outside edges of those items, the edges likely to contact pavement in even the most minor tip-over.

Usually you will find some evidence of a tip-over, even if it's just microscopic scratches. Finding a machine that hasn't fallen over at least once is rare. If the scratches are so minor they are difficult to see, you needn't worry. Often they can be minimized with some chrome polish and some elbow grease. (Be aware, however, that a dealer will also find these scratches if you someday decide to trade in the bike.)

Even if you find more major evidence of a low-speed spill, that shouldn't dissuade you from buying the bike; just reflect the costs of cosmetic restoration in your offer. Often the owner will have already taken such things into consideration when setting a price.

MOTORCYCOLOGY

Some motorcycles have built-in odd noises. Suzuki's two-valve GS series, for example, had a cam-chain guide that allowed the chain to slap while idling at low speeds. This causes no damage whatsoever, but the mechanical knocking sound has caused many unnecessary top-end rebuilds because owners didn't know about the defect and thought something was wrong.

With any kind of accident damage on a motorcycle, it's essential to check the frame alignment. First, make sure the front wheel is steered dead ahead; then, kneeling on the floor directly behind the bike, look at how the front and back wheels align. Do the same thing kneeling in front of the bike, too. If they don't appear to be straight in relation to each other, it's easier to go on to the next bike.

When purchasing European or American motorcycles, there are a few other things to watch for. Cosmetically, Harleys will more often than not be immaculate as Harley owners typically spend more time than most cleaning their bikes, but you need to check things such as the belt-drive system (discussed in Chapter 5). Fraying or missing belt teeth indicate future problems that are expensive to correct.

The level of finish on older European bikes tends to be lower than that of Japanese motorcycles, and corrosion can be a problem. This is especially true of Italian bikes, but it can be a problem even on BMWs. For example, BMW didn't apply a clear finish to exposed aluminum on items such as the fork legs. While this finish tends to yellow with exposure to sunlight, giving the forks on older Japanese motorcycles a dingy appearance, it protects the metal from corrosion. This corrosion becomes more pronounced in coastal areas because of the salt in sea air. It's also a problem for machines used during the winter because of the salt placed on roads in snowy climes.

The outside condition of a bike can help give clues to the condition of internal parts. If a bike looks good and runs well (if it starts easily when both cold and hot, if it idles smoothly without making horrible noises, and if it accelerates adequately for a bike of its size), odds are, it's okay inside. The owner has more than likely lavished as much care on the motorcycle's internals as he or she has on the bike's appearance.

I once went shopping for a Harley-Davidson with a friend of mine who was looking for an Electra Glide. At one dealership, we found two of them. Both bikes were the same model year, both were similarly equipped, and both had around 57,000 miles on them. The price on each bike was identical. One bike was black, and the other a hideous dusty-rose color. My friend was partial to black motorcycles.

> **MOTORCYCOLOGY**
>
> If you have a high degree of mechanical skill, as well as access to tools and a decent workshop, rebuilding bikes that have been crashed can be an inexpensive way to get a decent motorcycle. But be forewarned: this is not an undertaking for mechanical novices.

Unfortunately, the black bike was in much worse shape cosmetically. It had spent much of its life sitting outside in the elements, judging by the corrosion on the engine and other aluminum parts. This was a red flag to me: if the previous owner had taken such abysmal care of the outside of the bike, what sort of care had he given the inside?

I advised my friend to buy the rose-colored bike, if he was determined to buy either. But he bought the black one with the pitted aluminum.

The bike was nothing but trouble, right from the start. He'd had it less than a week when the clutch went out and left him stranded on the freeway. The next week, the drive belt went out. After we fixed that, he started having trouble with the carburetor. We took it apart and discovered that someone had tried to repair it using what looked like rubber cement. My friend had that bike for several years, and he never did get it to run right, even after he overhauled the engine. He spent so much money fixing the thing that he could have painted the rose-colored bike several times over.

Completeness

Along with the condition of a bike, make certain that all the pieces are there. Items such as missing side covers or other body panels can cost as much as a cheap motorcycle.

Check a motorcycle to make certain it has the following items:

- Side covers, the plastic covers that cover components located behind the engine, under the seat, can often break and come off the motorcycle. They are very expensive (and, in some cases, impossible) to replace.

- Emblems and insignias are often glued or screwed to the tank or side cover. They are also difficult to find for older motorcycles.

- If a bike has an aftermarket fairing, make certain that all the original lighting and turn-signal brackets and components come with the bike. If you decide to restore the motorcycle to its original condition, you'll need these pieces; on some bikes, they can cost as much as the motorcycle itself.

- Fenders will probably be an issue only if someone has tried to build a chopper out of a motorcycle. Generally, such bikes make poor candidates for restoration and should be avoided.

STEER CLEAR

Before upping your offer because the seller assures you that a bike has had a recent tune-up, make sure that he or she can provide documented proof that the tune-up has been performed.

Be especially concerned with completeness when buying an older motorcycle. You may find items such as side covers and seat covers unavailable for an older bike. These parts usually can be found with a little legwork. (I discuss alternative sources for parts, such as salvage yards, in Chapter 17.) Just because a bike isn't complete is no reason to reject it outright: just reflect the potential cost of replacing parts in your offer.

Some motorcycles, like this classic Honda, are obviously not complete. Unfortunately, it's not always this easy to spot when something is missing. Make sure you know exactly what you're getting—or not, as the case may be.
(Photo courtesy of Simon Green)

What's It Worth?

You've found the bike of your dreams. It's mechanically and cosmetically perfect, and you already have visions of roaming the highways on it. Now you have to figure out how much the bike is worth.

There's not much to negotiating the price of a new bike. Your best bet is to call every dealer within reasonable driving distance (remember, you will probably have to return to that dealer for warranty work) and find out what each one is charging for the model you're interested in. Once you have the best price, you might want to go to the nearest dealer you trust and give them an opportunity to match it. Even if they can't match it exactly, if they can even come close, it might be worth a few extra dollars to buy from someone you trust who is located nearby.

When shopping for a new motorcycle, you can save a lot of money by remaining flexible about which make and model to buy. Say you've decided to purchase a midsize cruiser, such as Kawasaki's Vulcan 900 Classic. While searching for such a bike, you find a decade-old Honda Shadow in mint condition at one third the price of the Kawasaki. While the Kawasaki is a fine motorcycle, the Shadow is capable of providing every bit as much enjoyment, and with its shaft drive and hydraulically adjusted valves, the Honda will save you hundreds of dollars per year in maintenance costs over the Kawasaki. You can pocket the money saved and use it to finance a cross-country motorcycle trip.

You can also save a lot of money by watching for carryover models. While shopping for the best deal on a Honda Shadow Phantom, you might run across a brand-new last year's model Suzuki Boulevard C50 for $1,500 less. In this case, maintenance costs will be roughly equal because both bikes have a V-twin engine, shaft drive, and spoke wheels; if you keep an open mind, that will be an extra $1,500 in your pocket.

Buying a used bike is where the process most diverges from buying a car. Because motorcycle prices can fluctuate widely from region to region, depending on how large a market an area has, accurate price guides are difficult to compile.

Further complicating the creation of useful price guides is the wide variation in the condition of each motorcycle. One seller's V Star 950 can be in mint condition at 60,000 miles, while the next guy's can be a hunk of junk at 10,000 miles.

When deciding how much a bike is worth, a guidebook's value assessment is only part of the equation. In addition to things such as condition and completeness, you have to look at routine wear and tear. Keeping a motorcycle in tip-top running condition is an expensive proposition. A bike with a fresh tune-up is definitely worth more than a bike that needs a tune-up.

Another item that increases a bike's value is fresh tires. You should be able to tell by looking whether the tires have low miles: check the depth of the tread at the edges of the tire compared to the depth of the tread at the center. A good pair of sticky tires can run you over $500, with mounting and balancing, so factor that into your price determination.

On the other hand, new tires of low quality actually detract from the value of a bike, at least in my personal equation. If a bike has a pair of bargain-brand tires, I have to decide whether to ride on tires that I consider undesirable or to toss out a nearly new set of tires and spend $300 or more on another pair. If a bike is wearing a pair of budget-brand tires, I automatically deduct $300 from my offer.

It's a good idea to speak with as many other owners of a certain model as you can before making a purchase. Here again, belonging to a club can be beneficial. The Internet is also your friend, because a bit of browsing will probably get you to a bulletin board where owners compare notes on their experiences with the exact model you're considering. Also check any service bulletins that may have been issued to your dealer on a certain model before buying that model.

These rough guidelines may help, but in the end, it's just going to be you and the seller. The entire process may boil down to how badly you want to buy the bike or how much the owner wants to sell it. One thing I can guarantee: if you buy the motorcycle that's right for you, one or two years from now, as you're riding down the road enjoying your machine, you will not be thinking, *Damn, I paid too much for this thing.*

Making the Deal

Now comes the most crucial (and most nerve-wracking) part of the entire process: negotiating the deal. You've decided what the motorcycle is worth to you, and the seller knows what the bike is worth to him or her. Now the two of you have to see if those figures jibe.

For me, negotiating the price of a motorcycle isn't the same as negotiating the price of anything else. People have more of an emotional attachment to motorcycles than they do to other goods: you're buying someone's passion. Whereas I have no moral qualms telling someone they're insane if they think a car or a radio is worth a ridiculous sum of money, I'll politely decline purchasing a motorcycle if the owner has an unrealistic opinion of its value. Its emotional value to that person may be such that the bike actually is worth the price to the owner (but not to many other human beings).

In such situations, you'll have to use your own judgment of the seller. If he or she seems reasonable, bring out the source you're using to arrive at your price and explain that their price is a bit steep. If the seller seems like a lunatic (and they're out there), extricate yourself from the situation as quickly as possible.

On the other hand, if the price is in the ballpark, I'll haggle until I get it in my acceptable window. If I can't, I'll usually leave them my number. It's amazing how many people will call you back: once given the lure of real money, it's generally a buyer's market.

In the end, this is a decision only you can make. I've provided you with the basics, but when you're face to face with the seller, trying to make a decision that will affect your life for years to come, you have to be the final judge.

The Least You Need to Know

- The quality of a dealership and of its service department is almost as important as the quality of the motorcycle itself.
- Clubs are a great source of motorcycles and information about motorcycles.
- Before taking a motorcycle out for a test ride, inspect it as if your life depends on it—because it does.
- Be flexible when choosing a motorcycle.

Insider Tips on Buying a Bike

In This Chapter

- Keeping costs down by selecting a low-maintenance bike
- Getting the best price from a dealership
- Financing a bike at the lowest interest rate
- Saving money on insurance

In Chapter 7, I told you how to buy your first bike. Now let me give you a few hints on other costs and responsibilities associated with buying a motorcycle, such as maintaining, financing, and insuring that bike. I'll also give you advice on trading bikes and some more tips on getting the best prices.

The purchase price of a motorcycle is just the tip of the iceberg when it comes to expenses you'll incur when owning a bike. Maintenance will also be an expense, but I'm going to give you some hints on how to minimize those costs.

A smart shopper can also minimize the costs of financing and insuring a bike. I'm going to show you some ways to save money when you finance and insure a bike. I'm also going to offer some tips on trading in a bike, if you ever decide to do so.

Minimizing Maintenance Costs

Your choice of a bike can determine how much maintenance you'll need to do. Sometimes engineers design motorcycles with certain high-maintenance features to increase the performance of a bike.

So if you're after extremely high performance, you'll have to accept the fact that you'll have to spend more money on maintenance. But if you're willing to accept a slightly lower level of performance, you can look for simpler features and practice certain riding habits that will help you keep maintenance costs down.

Three elements, in particular, will affect your maintenance costs: the shaft drive, the centerstand, and the valves. (See Chapters 16 and 17 for a description of these parts.)

Getting Shafted

Select a bike with a shaft drive. As you'll see in Chapters 16 and 17, chain maintenance is one of the most frequent procedures you'll need to perform on your bike. It can also be among the dirtiest.

Performance bikes will usually have a chain drive because chains tend to disrupt handling less than shafts. Chain-drive systems are also lightweight and an efficient way to transfer power to the rear wheel. If you want such a bike, you'll usually have to accept a chain as part of the package.

So if you want to buy a midsize Japanese cruiser, my advice is to get an older, used one because these usually have shaft drives. BMW boxers of all years, and almost all Moto Guzzi twins, likewise use shaft drive.

Another option is to select a bike with a belt-drive system. These can be a good compromise between the handling benefits of a chain and the low-maintenance benefits of a shaft. Belt-drive systems, such as those used by numerous Japanese and American cruisers, require less maintenance than chains, but only slightly more than shafts.

Getting Centered: The Benefits of a Centerstand

Make certain that your bike comes equipped with a centerstand. Without one, it's a major hassle to raise the rear end of the bike off the ground to remove the rear wheel or replace the sprocket. All Japanese bikes used to come with centerstands—it was one of the things that set them apart from Harley-Davidsons, which have never been equipped with modern centerstands.

In the 1980s, Japanese manufacturers began excluding centerstands from ultra-high-performance sportbikes because the designs of the exhaust systems used on those bikes prohibited the mounting of centerstands and also because centerstands hindered cornering clearance.

But in the past few years, manufacturers have also begun excluding them from bikes that already have limited cornering clearance, such as cruisers. Combine the lack of a centerstand with a chain drive, and I guarantee that you will create new expletives while maintaining your bike. Understand, though, that the reality of modern motorcycling is that many owners purchase aftermarket service stands. (Service stands generally support one end of the bike or the other and are separate from the motorcycle, whereas centerstands bolt to the motorcycle's frame.) These days, it's simply the price of being a motorcyclist.

Hydraulically Adjusted Valves

One of the costliest aspects of maintaining a motorcycle is adjusting the valve lash, or the clearance between each valve stem and the camshaft or rocker arm that activates it.

This is a crucial, time-consuming, and expensive (therefore, often neglected) part of motorcycle maintenance. On most modern motorcycles, valve adjustment is too complex a job for an inexperienced mechanic to tackle alone. Most riders take their bikes into shops to have the procedure performed.

If the motorcycle has any bodywork that the mechanic has to remove to gain access to the valves, or if the motorcycle is constructed in a way that requires the mechanic to go to heroic lengths to gain access to the valves, labor costs will be even higher.

Fortunately, modern metallurgy and manufacturing techniques mean that valve adjustments on new motorcycles don't have to be done nearly as often as on old bikes. Keep that in mind when you're trying to choose between an older bike and a brand-new one.

There is another way to avoid this expensive bit of maintenance. Back in the early 1980s, Honda introduced several motorcycle models that had overhead-cam engines with hydraulically adjusted valves. Kawasaki, Suzuki, and Yamaha's Star motorcycles followed suit, introducing cruisers with similar systems. New Harleys also come with hydraulically adjusted valves. Such systems completely eliminate the costs of valve adjustments.

Getting the Best Deal

To get the best deal on a bike, you're best off dealing directly with a sales manager. As I said in Chapter 7, call all the dealerships within the distance you are willing to drive (both to buy the bike and to get it serviced), and have the sales manager quote you an *out-the-door price*. This will be the amount you'll actually pay and will include the price of the motorcycle as well as taxes, licensing, and other fees.

CYCLE BABBLE

The **out-the-door price** is the amount you'll actually pay for a bike, factoring in all costs such as taxes, licensing, and other miscellaneous fees.

If the manager beats around the bush and won't give you a straight out-the-door price, he or she could be planning to stick you with some hidden costs. This may give you some insight into how the dealer will handle any warranty work or other issues that might come up later, so you might want to shop elsewhere if the dealer is evasive.

You might already know that you'll find the best buys on leftover bikes in the off season—in the fall and winter. What you might not know is that you may also find great buys on the last day of a month because, at that time, dealers are anxious to meet their monthly sales goals.

To Your Credit: Financing

Lacking the cash to buy a new motorcycle outright, and with automotive-style leasing plans typically unavailable, many riders are forced to finance their new bike. The interest paid in finance charges can represent a significant amount of the overall cost of owning a motorcycle, so before you even go looking for a bike, you should arrange the lowest-priced financing you can find.

First, call at least three banks to get the following information:

- The interest rates for unsecured personal loans with payments spread out over both a 36-month period and a 48-month period.

- The same information about a loan if it is secured by the title to your bike.

- The monthly payment for a $10,000 loan in each instance.

You use the amount of $10,000 so that you can calculate your payments based on the amount you borrow. For example, if a bank quotes you a monthly payment of $320 for an unsecured, 36-month loan of $10,000, you can divide $320 by 10, and you'll know that you're being charged $32 a month for every $1,000 you borrow. The good thing about this little formula is that it works for whatever purchase price you're considering.

For instance, let's say you choose to borrow only $6,000 to buy a Suzuki SV650. To determine your monthly payment, just multiply 32 (representing the payment for every $1,000 borrowed) by 6 (representing the $6,000 the Suzuki costs). The answer, in this case, is $192 per month.

I agree that calculating the payment per $1,000 borrowed per month is a different way of looking at motorcycle financing, but as I said, this method is flexible and useful, and I promise that after you practice the math a few times it will begin to make sense. Either that, or it might give you a dandy migraine. In either event, here are a few more tips on how to make it easier to finance your new bike at a dealership—and more:

- Have personal information ready and in order. The dealer or loan officer will want to see a payroll check stub, will want to know how long you've been at the job, and will pull your credit report. You should also get a credit report on your own to make sure everything is accurate.

- Even if you have less than stellar credit, you might be able to get financing. What a dealer/loan officer wants to see is that you've got a good, solid job to handle your outstanding debt.

- Make the biggest down payment you can afford. It will significantly reduce your monthly loan payments. A good starting point is 25 percent.

- Know that there are alternatives to getting a loan from the dealership. For instance, check out financing the bike through motorcycle-manufacturer lending institutions. Or check the local credit unions and independent lenders, such as HSBC, used by many dealers. And don't forget resources on the web. Check out www.bestloandeals.com, www.cyclebytel.com, www.motorcyclelender.com, and www.123motorcycleloans.com on the Internet.

Getting Insured

Most states require you to at least have liability insurance before you can operate a vehicle on public roads. If you finance your bike and use its title as security, you need to have full coverage. Full coverage isn't a bad idea anyway if your bike is worth a significant amount of money, but be prepared: full-coverage insurance on a bike is expensive, especially if you live in a major metropolitan area. However, you can do some things to minimize your expenses.

As I said in Chapter 4, most companies base insurance rates on several factors, such as the type of bike, the size of its engine, and the amount of expensive bodywork on the bike. They also take your driving record into account.

There's nothing you can do about your driving history (you can't change the past), but you can minimize your insurance costs by choosing a bike that is under 600cc and has minimal bodywork. The list of new bikes under 600cc without plastic fairings is short:

Aprilia SXV 4.5 and 5.5

BMW G 450 X

Honda CRF230L and
  CRF230M
Honda Rebel

Hyosung GT250
Hyosung GV250

Kawasaki Eliminator 125
Kawasaki KLX250S and SF
Kawasaki Super Sherpa
Kawasaki Vulcan 500 LTD

KTM 450 EXC and 530 EXC

Royal Enfield Bullet 500
  Classic and G5

Suzuki DR200SE
Suzuki DR-Z400S and SM
Suzuki GZ250
Suzuki TU250

Yamaha FZ6
Yamaha TW200
Yamaha WR250R and
  WR250X
Yamaha XT250
Yamaha V Star 250

The list of used bikes that meet this criteria isn't much longer. In addition to used models of the bikes in the preceding list, it includes a few more choices:

Honda CB650SC/CB700SC
  Nighthawk
Honda FT500/VT500 Ascot
Honda VF500C V30 Magna
Honda VT500/VT600/
  VT700 Shadow
Honda XL350R/XL500R/
  XL600R

Kawasaki EN450 454 LTD/
  EN500 Vulcan 500
Kawasaki KLR600
Kawasaki KZ550/KZ550
  LTD/KZ550 Spectre
Kawasaki ZL600 Eliminator
Kawasaki ZR550 Zephyr

KTM 400/XCe

Suzuki DR350SE
Suzuki GS550E/L
Suzuki GSF400 Bandit

Triumph Speed Four

Yamaha XJ550 Seca/Maxim
  (although some Secas came
  with a small bikini fairing)
Yamaha XT550/XT600
Yamaha YX600 Radian

All of these will work as a first bike. Some will work better than others, and some will be better buys than others (see Appendixes A and B for lists of which are the best first bikes and which are the best buys). All will be relatively inexpensive to insure, especially the older, less expensive models.

Another trick for getting lower rates on your full-coverage insurance is to get a policy with a high deductible. Purchasing a policy with a $500 deductible instead of a $250 deductible means that you'll pay the first $500 to repair the bike if something happens to it. This might seem like a lot of money to shell out in case of an accident, but it won't take you long to save that much on your premiums.

Besides, if you do file a claim, your insurer may raise your rates an exorbitant amount (possibly as much as you'll spend just to fix the bike yourself if you have a higher deductible). If you do make a claim, most of the time, you will pay for it one way or another. Usually, it costs less to fix it yourself in the long run.

Trading Bikes

If your first bike isn't what you had hoped, or if you're ready to move up to a different bike, you may face the decision of whether to sell it, or else trade it in at the dealership to get money toward your new bike.

Usually, you will get more money selling your bike straight out. In a couple of cases, I've made more by trading a bike, but the vast majority of times I've traded, I've lost money. In both cases where I came out ahead, I had an unusual motorcycle—one the dealer already had a buyer lined up for. If I had been able to find such a buyer on my own, I would have made more money than I did when I traded.

The only advantage of trading is convenience. When trading bikes, convenience is usually expensive. You will almost always get more money selling your old bike yourself, and you will always get a better price if you buy your new bike without a trade.

The Least You Need to Know

- You'll save a lot of money over time by choosing a low-maintenance motorcycle.
- Make certain you know the out-the-door price before buying a bike.
- Interest can be a significant part of the overall cost of buying a bike, so shop around for your loan.
- In the long run, you can save a lot of money on insurance by having a policy with a fairly high deductible.

Getting the Gear

In This Chapter

- The facts of helmet use
- Which type of helmet provides the most protection
- Essential protective gear
- Gear that will help you beat the elements
- Where to find the best deals on accessories

There's no doubt that many motorcyclists live for a therapeutic solo ride on the open road, soaking up riding in its simplest form. Others, however, have a different set of priorities: they just like to be seen by as big a crowd as possible.

Whatever camp you fall into, you'll need gear, lots of gear. Well, you're in luck—enough motorcycling gear is discussed in this chapter to make us the envy of scuba divers. While some of the items are optional, maybe even frivolous, others are absolutely essential.

Helmets: Keeping What You've Already Got

Have you ever banged your head on a doorway, or the edge of a desk? Did it hurt? It did? Okay, what speed were you traveling at when you hit that doorpost? Walking pace, huh? Do you want to find out how much it would hurt at 7 mph (twice as fast as walking pace)? Okay then, run down the street and aim the top of your head at a good solid post (not really, I'm just trying to remind you about pain). Am I making the point well enough? Can you imagine the pain at 35 mph?

Here's another twist on it. Have you ever been hit in the face by a little piece of debris while riding a bicycle? What about getting a fly in your eye? Fancy that happening at 70 mph? Do you think it'd be okay, or would you get permanent damage? Are you really willing to find out?

Just in case you're one of those people who don't feel pain, I'll give you another reason. Have you ever been in a convertible car at speed, trying to hold a cell phone conversation? It's impossible, right? Way too loud. Well, again, use your imagination and remove the car's windshield; you already know it won't be any quieter. Finally, for authenticity, we can add the noise of your own motorcycle engine. I wonder how long it will be before you're lying in bed at night with your ears ringing.

Maybe for now we'll assume that you don't feel pain, you have skin like tanned leather, and your ears are immune to constant loud noise … pardon? Let's consider accidental impact, or road abrasion. Almost all of us fell off a bicycle as a kid. I remember bailing, then getting up and crying my eyes out with my knees bleeding and my head throbbing. I would guess it happened at 15 mph. I don't know about you, but I don't ever want to hit the ground at 45 mph, or 75 mph, without a helmet. I can't imagine what would happen to my skull, or to my brain.

Maybe the guy saying you don't need a helmet doesn't have a brain worth protecting. It's a logical conclusion. I'm sorry to be so blunt on this one, but look at what we're dealing with. If you've got a brain, you protect it with a helmet. Period.

How Helmets Are Made

Helmets help keep the contents of your head on the inside rather than the outside by using four basic components in their construction:

- **The outer shell.** The outside of a helmet can be constructed of fiberglass, *polycarbonate*, or *TriComposite* material. Either way, it spreads the energy from an impact across a wide area, reducing the chances of head injury in the exact spot where the impact occurred.

- **The impact-absorbing lining.** This is sandwiched between the outer shell and the inner comfort padding and is usually made of a dense layer of expanded polystyrene. It crumples to absorb the impact.

- **The comfort padding.** This innermost layer of soft foam and cloth conforms to your head and is primarily responsible for how comfortable the helmet is.

- **The retention system.** This consists of the strap—connected to the bottom of the helmet—that goes under your chin and holds the thing on your melon.

CYCLE BABBLE

Polycarbonate is a posh word for plastic, the cheapest outer-shell material used in helmet production. **TriComposite** is a mix of three woven materials: Kevlar, carbon fiber, and fiberglass. This mix creates the most expensive outer shell for a motorcycle helmet.

Helmets come in a variety of styles, from small, bowl-shape half-helmets that may protect your brainstem (if the helmet manages to stay in place) to sleek, fully enclosed helmets that protect everything above your neck. In between are the three-quarter, or open-face helmets, which cover most of your head but leave your face unprotected. These give much better cranial protection than half-helmets, but if your face contacts the pavement at speed, an open-face helmet will provide you with a one-way ticket on the ugly train.

Neither half-helmets nor open-face helmets offer the comfort or protection full-face helmets provide by shielding the wearer from the elements—and the ground, too, in a serious crash. Whichever type of helmet you choose, the important thing is to wear it. It is the single most crucial piece of motorcycle gear.

This helmet from Bell is one of only a few open faces offering serious protection and good soundproofing.
(Photo courtesy of Bell Powersports, Inc.)

Choosing the Right Helmet

The main considerations in choosing the right helmet for your head are fit, fit, and umm, oh yeah, fit. It's so important I've given "fit" its own section. First, though, here are some other things worth knowing.

Helmets come in a wide variety of styles and prices. You can probably still find a $10 helmet, if it's what you think your head's worth, but good helmets run up to $800.

Why do some helmets cost more than others? There are a variety of reasons. The material used in the outer shell makes a big difference. Polycarbonate helmets are typically the cheapest, followed by more expensive fiberglass and then by the most expensive, lightweight TriComposite.

Paint schemes add to the price of a helmet; expect to pay more for a helmet with graphics than for a solid-color helmet. (If the paint scheme replicates the helmet of a top racer, expect to pay even more.) Wearing a brightly colored helmet isn't a bad idea, though; at least the car drivers will see you.

Another factor in helmet price is ventilation system. A good helmet will channel air all around your noggin on even the hottest days, and will also have efficient visor design, for good visibility and eye protection.

Developed in MotoGP racing, this high-end AGV GP-Tech helmet costs as much as a handful of cheap helmets, but it protects something irreplaceable—your head.
(Photo courtesy of AGV USA, Inc.)

Safety First

All helmets have to meet minimum safety standards set by the federal Department of Transportation (DOT); look for a sticker on the outside and a permanent label on the inside. Two other private organizations, the American National Standards Institute (ANSI) and the Snell Memorial Foundation, also certify helmets. Type "helmet" into the search window at www.motorcyclistonline.com to find impact test results of different models.

Getting a Good Fit

Once you get used to wearing a helmet, you won't feel comfortable riding without one. Of course, that assumes you've picked a helmet that fits you correctly. A helmet that is too loose will move around in an accident, potentially causing neck injury, and a helmet that is too tight will give you a splitting headache every day you wear it.

STEER CLEAR

Don't buy your first helmet online. It's vital that your helmet fits you perfectly, and the only way to achieve this is to try on as many as possible.

A helmet should be comfortably tight, though that's harder to find than you'd expect. You can't afford to have your heart set on a specific brand, as often you'll find that certain brands fit a particular head shape better than others. What you're looking for is a helmet that won't slide around your head and is hard to pull off with the strap undone, but one that doesn't create a pressure spot anywhere on your head.

When you try on a helmet, wear it around the store for a while, and when you take it off, note any soreness or red spots. Wearing a helmet that exerts pressure on your head can turn into a brutal form of torture after an extended period; improperly fitted helmets have permanently turned many riders against helmet use. The right helmet is a revelation, something you can wear for hours on end, and something you'll learn to love wearing. Just remember, it won't work if you don't do the strap up.

STEER CLEAR

Never buy or wear a used motorcycle helmet. Helmets protect your head in an accident by destroying themselves. In a spill the outer shell will flex and the inner shell will crumple, often leaving no visible damage to the exterior. Hitting the damaged area a second time will result in little head protection.

In Style: What to Wear

In a car you're surrounded by a steel shell; on a bike your only protection is what you wear. I'll give you enough information here to make an informed decision about what that protection should consist of. The following list describes the bare-minimum amount of protective gear you need to wear when riding:

- Leather boots, with at least ankle coverage

- Leather, full-fingered riding gloves

- Long pants

- A riding jacket

This list defines the absolute minimal amount of clothing you can wear to ride safely. You may have seen people riding in shorts, tennis shoes, and nothing else. What are they thinking?! My advice is to not become attached to these people because, should they survive even the most minor spill, they will not emerge from the experience as people you'd want to look at on a regular basis.

If you're unfortunate enough to be involved in a bike accident, good gear can make the difference between a quick recovery and a new lifestyle. Take a look at motorcycle racers: they're looking for the ultimate protection, and we can all learn a lot from their hard-earned experience.

In the worst-case scenario, you could hit something, or slide along the concrete. So you need two different kinds of protection—*body armor* that will absorb impact (from anything you may hit), and the material that your clothing is constructed from to provide you with excellent abrasion resistance.

CYCLE BABBLE

Body armor is found within good-quality motorcycle clothing. It is often made from an impact-absorbing closed-cell foam or plastic, and nests inside special pockets located within the garments. That way, the armor is in the correct position and ready to protect you every time you ride.

In Europe there is a test standard for motorcycle clothing called the CE approval mark. It is akin to the approval system for helmets in the United States. The CE approval process rigorously checks all aspects of bike clothing—things like armor effectiveness, the outer materials abrasion resistance, seam strength, and so on. If you see a CE-approved garment that you like, then you can buy it with complete confidence.

Body armor like this will give you very good protection, should you come off your bike and land hard.

(Photo courtesy of Simon Green)

Looking Good in Leather

Competition-weight cowhide leather (leather from a cow that is at least 1.3mm thick) provides the best crash protection of any material, period. That's why it's still the material of choice for racing suits. I can guarantee you (from personal experience) that buying a new jacket is much less painful than getting road rash, which is what riders call the abrasions from a crash. Having grit picked from an open wound is an unforgettable experience.

Racers wear a one-piece suit made from leather, which is precured for comfort while positioned on their bike. The suit will have double-thickness leather reinforcing the areas on which they'll typically slide. This means the butt, back, knees, elbows, and shoulders. The guys with the top-of-the-line race suits will have a total thickness of 3mm of hide in those prone areas, and if you've ever watched bike racing, then you'll have seen them slide at 100 mph, get up, and walk away. That's how good cowhide is.

Most Europeans wear race suits on the road for that exact same reason, but not in America. I see people ride every day in shorts, jeans, or chaps. When you consider that race suits have double-thickness leather in the butt, and chaps have none ... well, you can see the downside to chaps.

If you can't bear to wear a full suit, then at least wear a cowhide jacket with the same reinforced areas as a race suit. Unfortunately, fashion leather is usually made from cheaper hide, often sheepskin, and while this may initially look the same, it offers next to no abrasion protection.

If you can't even bring yourself to wear a leather jacket, then there are some other good options.

The plain black leather biker jacket comes in many styles now; you don't have to look like something from an old biker movie.
(Photo courtesy of Alpinestars)

Synthetic Riding Suits: Ties Optional

While leather is still the optimum material for crash protection, an increasing number of riders choose synthetic riding suits made from materials such as Cordura and Kevlar. The advantages of leather are most apparent at extremely high speeds (which is why racers choose leather), but at speeds under triple-digit velocities, synthetic jackets and pants can provide enough protection.

Synthetics have certain advantages over leather. Most of them are machine washable, unlike leather, which must be sent to a cleaner. And many of them are waterproof or water resistant, eliminating the need for special rain gear. Plus, these synthetic suits can easily be worn over regular clothing, a tremendous advantage for people who use their motorcycles to commute to work. Many synthetic suits are constructed with removable liners, allowing the rider to use them over a broad range of weather conditions. In hot weather, riders can wear light clothing beneath their suits, and as the temperatures drop, riders can put in the thermal liners and wear extra layers of clothing. A company called Aerostich even offers an electrically heated liner for its Darien jacket.

Aerostich's Darien jacket and pants, which feature Gore-Tex outer fabric and body armor in all of the right places, combine safety and outstanding protection from the elements.

(Photo courtesy of Aerostich)

Gloves

Whenever I fall off anything, my first instinct is to put my hands out to ease my fall. It is one thing to fall off a bicycle, but fall off a motorcycle traveling at highway speed and you will lose some skin. Always wearing a pair of leather riding gloves, prefer-ably a pair that extend over your wrist bones, will make a difference. A good pair of motorcycle gloves will have extra leather on the palms, knuckles, and fingers. This provides additional protection against abrasion in case of an accident.

A good pair of gloves also will have some small amount of armor built inside the palm and knuckle areas. Your hands will often stick out further than the rest of your bike, so having some impact protection is a good idea. Good gloves will even stop your hands from going numb on a long ride.

Riders trying to look tough often wear fingerless gloves. While these will provide some palm protection in the event of a crash, they don't really offer anything else. If you aren't getting enough "feel" through a regular pair of bike gloves, then search out a pair of kangaroo skin gloves. These will offer you phenomenal protection from an ultrathin hide, giving you the ultimate feedback from your fingertips.

A good pair of riding gloves, like these kangaroo skin race gloves, will provide com-fort, feedback, and protection.
(Photo courtesy of Simon Green)

Fancy Footwear

Even choosing footwear for riding requires some thoughtful consideration. You need to wear a pair of tall leather boots to protect your ankles from being burned by the exhaust pipes and from stones and other debris. You also need to take other factors into account when selecting a pair of boots.

On a motorcycle, your feet are an important part of your motorcycle's chassis: they are what hold up the motorcycle when you are at rest. In effect, when you aren't moving, the soles of your shoes are like an extra set of tires. Because of this, you'll want to wear a pair of boots with grippy soles. While fashion boots or cowboy boots may provide adequate ankle protection, their leather soles are far too slippery for them to be useful riding shoes. If you wear fashion boots, make certain they are work-style boots, with grippy rubber soles.

I prefer a boot with Velcro or latches to a lace-up boot, and not just because they take less time to put on. Laces come loose and get caught in moving parts, like your drive chain. It really doesn't look good rolling to a stop, trying to put your left foot down, then realizing your lace is caught in the chain, as the whole bike slowly falls over and takes you with it. Not cool.

Extreme Riding Gear

Nothing surpasses the pleasure of seeing the world on a motorcycle because, on a bike, you are right there, in the thick of it. That means you get to smell the freshly cut hay alongside the road you're riding down. The morning sun recharges you, just as it recharges the flora.

The downside of all this nature worship is that you will experience the world in its entirety, and you must take the bad with the good. That means being prepared for any kind of weather.

Rain Gear

Ride long enough, and your rain suit will become as much of a part of your everyday riding gear as your helmet: you won't leave home without it. A good rain suit can turn a miserable, wet ride into a tolerable or even fun one.

Rain suits are either one- or two-piece suits, made of polyvinyl chloride (PVC) or coated nylon. I prefer the one-piece suits because rain always manages to seep in between the pants and the jacket on two-piece suits.

PVC provides better rain protection than most coated nylon suits, but PVC doesn't breathe so it makes you sweat. Because it can get so sticky to the touch, it can be difficult to get on and off. To get around this, the best PVC suits have a nylon mesh lining that slides against your leather riding gear. Look for a suit that has such lining in both the upper and lower portions.

In my experience, the best rain gear is a waterproof riding suit, such as the Aerostich Darien jacket and pants, which are made of Gore-Tex Cordura material. With these, you don't have to bother putting a rain suit on when foul weather approaches and taking it off when it passes. Even the best rain suits are a hassle to put on by the side of the road on a windy day, and when they get wet, they can be real buggers to get off over leather.

You can get a bare-bones two-piece rain suit for around $50. Expect to spend $150 or more for a top-quality one-piece suit.

As backward as it may seem, I've encountered a lot of bikers who refuse to wear rain gear. This strikes me as so odd. I know from long years of experience that few things in this world are as miserable as spending an entire day in drenched leather waiting for hypothermia to set in.

Are you starting to realize how many posers there are in motorcycling?

Ride long enough, and your rain suit will become part of your everyday riding gear: you won't leave home without it.
(Photo © 1998 Darwin Holmstrom)

Freezing to Death: Beating the Cold

Motorcyclists tend to get cold more often than they get hot. Even on a relatively mild day—say, 65°F—the wind-chill on a motorcycle traveling at 65 mph can approach freezing. Hypothermia (a condition in which your body temperature drops to dangerously low levels) is a very real danger on a bike. As I said earlier, in cold weather, a synthetic motorcycle suit can be a real lifesaver, but even those who can't afford such a suit can throw together the proper gear for riding on a cool day.

On really cold days, I wear jeans and a turtleneck sweater over my thermal underwear. I like to wear a sweatshirt over that, along with riding pants, and of course a good jacket. When the temperatures get too cold, the summer leather riding suits usually go into hibernation.

Even if you can't afford a Darien jacket with an electric liner, you can still benefit from electrically heated clothing on a budget. Widder and several other companies make electrically heated vests that you can wear under your jacket. These vests can keep you toasty on even the coldest ride. On supercold days, I've worn an electric vest under my rain gear, even though it wasn't raining. The vest warmed up the entire inside of the suit and kept me as warm as if I'd been driving a car.

MOTORCYCOLOGY

I've found that a one-piece pair of thermal underwear (a union suit) is preferable to the traditional two-piece set. When you dress in bulky layers, your clothes tend to ride up, creating a gap of bare skin between the top and bottom pieces of a two-piece suit. You can avoid this with a union suit.

Keeping your hands warm can go a long way toward keeping your whole body warm. Several companies offer electrically heated handgrip kits, and BMW offers them as an option on its bikes. You can also purchase something called Hippo Hands, sheaths that attach to your handlebars and surround your controls. These devices may look odd, but they provide exceptional protection against the elements.

Baked, Boiled, or Fried: Beating the Heat

All motorcyclists have to deal with the heat. Riding all day under the hot sun takes a lot out of your body. You can become dangerously dehydrated and even suffer heatstroke. At the very least, you may become tired, and your judgment and riding skills will suffer.

One of my most dangerous riding experiences occurred because of dehydration. I got a mild case of food poisoning in Las Vegas, but I didn't realize it until I was headed across the Arizona desert. At the worst possible moment I could imagine, I realized I couldn't keep down water. I spent a difficult (and dangerous) day making my way from gas station to gas station, until I finally had the sense to call it quits and get a motel room.

Since that episode, I've learned a lot about riding in heat. The most important thing to remember is to keep hydrated. Always drink plenty of fluids, and on really hot days, drink fluids especially designed to rehydrate your cells, such as sports drinks. Remember that caffeine is a diuretic and will deplete your body's store of water rather than replenish it. If you feel thirsty, you have already gone too long without a drink. If you ride much in hot climates, you should really invest in a CamelBak or some other brand of hydration system. Fill these with ice, and in addition to providing you with refreshing water to drink, they will keep you cool during the day.

The right gear is crucial for hot-weather riding. Most leather makers now offer perforated leather riding gear, which lets air flow through the garment. A few companies even offer mesh jackets with protective armor, sort of like the gear worn by off-road riders. These help you keep cool but still provide reasonable abrasion protection. Alpinestar's Scout Drystar jacket is a very popular jacket of this type.

Another method for keeping cool is to soak your shirt under your riding gear. This works especially well with a heavily ventilated jacket, such as Vanson's ProPerf gear, which is made from fully perforated leather.

Lightweight, ventilated jackets like this one offer excellent, controllable ventilation, which can be closed up when the temperature drops. Any good jacket should also provide you with some serious accident protection.

(Photo courtesy of Simon Green)

Again, synthetic riding suits make excellent hot-weather riding gear. You can remove the lining from most of these and just use the outer shell, which retains all the armor and protective qualities. The suits themselves have many zippered vents, allowing you to control airflow. Aerostich recommends wearing long pants and a long-sleeve shirt under its suits because, theoretically, its Cordura can melt under extremely high temperatures (but in all the years of manufacturing, examining, and repairing suits that have been through crashes, they have yet to find a single case of this happening). While I can't condone this practice, your risks would probably be minimal if you chose to wear just shorts and a T-shirt under your Aerostich suit on an extremely hot day. You would still have far more abrasion protection than someone riding in jeans and a light jacket.

Accessories: All the Extras

A good part of the fun of owning a motorcycle is getting all the accessories that go along with it. Motorcyclists may try to convince you otherwise, but they lie. They love modifying their bikes and collecting gadgets.

A huge array of accessories is available for every type of bike and every type of biker, from cruiser windshields to travel trailers, to global positioning units (computers that use satellites to tell you where you are) and bike-to-bike communicators. Some are mere novelties, things mainly used to amuse your friends when you stop for a cup of coffee. Other accessories come closer to necessities.

On the more frivolous side are the purely cosmetic items, things that serve no purpose except to alter a bike's looks.

Most accessories available today are harmless. That wasn't always true, especially during the chopper craze of the 1960s and 1970s. Some of the popular accessories of the day, such as high handlebars and forward-mounted highway pegs, could induce high-speed wobbles in some bikes' handling. Some accessories, such as extended forks and aftermarket frames with steep rakes, actually made a motorcycle downright dangerous to ride.

Today's accessories can still have unintended side effects. A while back, I bought a Yamaha Venture, an ultimate behemoth type of touring bike, on which the previous owner had installed a pair of chrome covers over the vents in the side panel. While he probably found these covers attractive, they trapped heat in the engine compartment and made the bike run hot, so I removed them.

The owner had also installed a strange set of 1950s-era taillights around the license plate frame. At first, I didn't care for the way these Elvis lights, as I call them, looked; but after a while they grew on me, so I kept them. Besides, anything that makes you more visible to traffic is a functional accessory.

Windshields

On the closer-to-necessity side are windshields. While a bike with a sporty, forward-leaning riding position can get by without a windshield because the rider is naturally braced against the wind, on more laid-back bikes (such as cruisers), an effective windshield can make the difference between a comfortable ride and a trip to the chiropractor.

Saddlebags

Saddlebags are probably the most useful accessory you can add to your bike, turning it from a pretty plaything into a practical form of transportation. Hard bags, which are more or less suitcases mounted to the bike, are the most useful because they offer better weather protection, plus most of them can be locked. Unfortunately, relatively few motorcycles offer them as options (although the number is growing). You can purchase them for many bikes from aftermarket manufacturers, such as GIVI. These tend to be expensive, but if you can afford a set, it is money well spent.

You'll probably end up buying a pair of soft saddlebags that you mount over your seat. These are usually made of vinyl, leather, or Cordura.

Tankbags

Tankbags also add much to a motorcycle's usefulness. These are similar to soft saddlebags, usually constructed of nylon, but they mount on top of the fuel tank. These can be mounted by adjustable straps or held in place by strong magnets in the base of the bags that stick to the tank. Of course, this requires that your tank be constructed of steel; such a system won't work on plastic tanks or tank covers.

Tankbags are great for traveling, not only because they offer extra storage, but because most of them also have a clear map pocket on top. If you've ever tried to unfold a map and read it at the side of a road on a windy day, you'll appreciate this feature.

The major drawback of using a tankbag is that the straps can scratch the paint on your gas tank.

The variety of accessories available could fill its own book, and since they reflect an owner's individual taste, only you can decide which ones are right for your bike.

Magazines

Some of the most useful accessories are things that you neither wear nor mount on your motorcycles. Magazines—or, more precisely, the valuable information contained in magazines—can help you become a much better motorcyclist. That information might even save your life some day. This is as true of online magazines as it is of print magazines.

Not that I'm biased or anything, but the magazines in Source Interlink Media's Motorcycle Group, titles such as *Motorcyclist*, *Motorcycle Cruiser*, *Sport Rider*, *Hot Bike*, and *Dirt Rider*, contain some of the best information found anywhere.

Where to Buy Accessories

Where you buy those accessories is up to you, too. You can buy your gear from a local dealer, or you can buy from one of several mail-order firms that sell just about every accessory available, usually at discount prices. Both methods have drawbacks, and both have benefits.

When you buy from a local dealer, you see what you're getting: you can try on a helmet or a garment, or see if a windshield fits your bike without obstructing your view. And if you do buy something that won't fit you or your bike (although the chances of that happening are slim because the staff can help you select the correct item in the first place), you can always bring it back. Another advantage of buying local is that you don't have to wait for it to be shipped.

On the other hand, the mail-order places usually have a much wider variety of items than any local shop could afford to carry. Plus, they usually sell those items for less than the shops. The drawbacks are that you don't get to check the fit of the items before purchasing them, and returning them can be a hassle.

One other drawback of buying from a mail-order company is that you won't be supporting your local shops. A lot of smaller shops operate on a slim profit margin, and it wouldn't take much to put many of them out of business. When you buy from some company in a distant location, you could help put your local dealer out of business.

This might not seem like it would concern you in any practical way, but it does. If an emergency arises and you need to repair your bike right now, that local dealer is awfully nice to have.

For a comprehensive list of companies that provide motorcycle accessories, see Appendix C.

The Least You Need to Know

- Although some states allow you to choose whether you wear a helmet, if you have a functioning brain, there is no real choice.
- Wear competition-weight leather to protect your body from the elements and in case of a crash.
- Not wearing gloves can turn a minor mishap into a visit to the emergency room.
- Rain suits can take the misery out of riding in the rain.
- Although mail-order companies may offer a wide range of motorcycle accessories, your local dealer can help you choose the right accessories and avoid the hassle of returning items.

On the Road

Starting up your bike and hitting the road: this is what motorcycling is all about. All the rest of the motorcycling experience pales when compared to actually riding.

Riding is fun, but it's also serious business, with grave consequences if you make a mistake. Because of the serious nature of riding, you need to be prepared.

This part of the book covers a variety of survival strategies for the street, as well as the basics of how to ride. I also discuss hazards that you might encounter and what to do in case of an emergency. So get your helmet and riding gear, and make sure your bike is ready to roll, because we're going riding.

Preparing to Hit the Road

In This Chapter

- How to get in the right frame of mind for riding
- Understanding the licensing procedure
- How the Motorcycle Safety Foundation can help you learn to ride
- What switches and levers do
- Mastering the preride inspection

You're just about ready to hit the road (hopefully not literally), but first you need to learn how to ride. You need to learn what the controls on a bike do and how you make them do that. You need to learn how to prepare your motorcycle for the road, and you also need to prepare yourself mentally.

Before you can even ride a bike, you have to get an instructional (learner's) permit. After you learn to ride, you'll want to get your motorcycle endorsement. Not only will this keep you out of trouble with the law, but it will also statistically lower your chances of getting taken out on your bike.

If you haven't ridden before, you'll need to start from scratch. Unfortunately, most of the things you learned when you started to drive a car don't apply to motorcycles—you're a newbie!

Every day you ride, you will encounter unexpected challenges, such as all kinds of distracted car drivers. In any encounter between a car and a motorcycle, the car has the advantage.

In this chapter, I explain what you need to do to get your permit and motorcycle endorsement. I also show you how to use the controls on your bike, how to prepare your bike for each ride, and how to mentally prepare yourself for each ride.

Getting in Your Right Mind: Mental Motorcycling

Riding a bike requires your undivided attention. If you preoccupy yourself thinking about polishing the silverware on the way home, then you probably won't make it home. Before you head out onto the public roads, you have to make sure your mind is right. As Strother Martin (the overseer in the film *Cool Hand Luke*) might have said, motorcyclists whose minds ain't right get to spend the rest of eternity in the box.

STEER CLEAR

Nothing gets your mind less right for riding than messing it up with alcohol or drugs. You have to be able to balance to ride, and just one beer can upset your balance in ways you can't perceive, and that can have fatal consequences. According to the National Highway Traffic Safety Administration, 30 percent of all fatally injured motorcycle riders had blood-alcohol levels of .08 g/dL (meaning they were legally drunk). An additional 7 percent had lower levels of alcohol (.01–.07 g/dL) in their systems.

You need to clear your mind of distractions before you get on your bike. Do whatever it takes to get your mind cleared (including going to the bathroom—you'd be surprised at how your concentration can suffer when you're twitching around with your legs crossed).

Another great distraction is anger at other drivers. Anger on the road is dangerous; it will cloud your judgment, and you need that to make the split-second decisions required to survive in traffic. You need to remain calm and collected in every situation, regardless of whether you are right or wrong. While you may have the right of way, the person in the car has your life in his or her hands. Don't develop road rage against someone who can hurt you simply by turning a steering wheel. Instead, calmly remove yourself from such situations. Use your bike to get as far away from the other vehicle as possible.

Getting Licensed

Every state in the union requires riders to obtain a special endorsement on their driver's license before operating a motorcycle. While this may seem like just another hoop to jump through, these states are probably doing you a favor. According to the Motorcycle Safety Foundation, unlicensed riders account for the majority of accident victims; by getting a license, you vastly increase your odds of not becoming a statistic. Licensing programs help get a safer, more knowledgeable population of motorcyclists out on the street.

Motorcycle tests, both written and riding, have improved a great deal since I first got my license. I'd have to say my first experience with the licensing procedure was useless. Whoever compiled the test obviously didn't ride a bike, and the questions had no relevance to the knowledge needed to survive on a motorcycle.

I had a nice surprise when I retook the written test some years later; it actually asked useful questions. You had to know things about real-world motorcycling to pass.

Each state has a different written test with different questions. The most useful tests are those devised in conjunction with the Motorcycle Safety Foundation. To obtain a study guide for your state's test, call your local Department of Motor Vehicles.

Getting Your Learner's Permit

The first step in getting licensed is to get your permit, which you receive upon successfully completing your written test. The purpose of the permit is to allow you to get out and practice in the real world before taking your driving test. You should get your permit even before you actually learn to ride so that you can legally practice your riding.

In most states, getting your permit will allow you to ride during daylight hours without a passenger. Most states have extra requirements for permitted riders, such as not allowing them to ride after dark or allowing them to ride on limited-access highways only. You will be required to wear a helmet if you have just a permit—but that shouldn't matter to you because you're reading this book, therefore you have a brain, so you want to wear your helmet all the time anyway. Right?

Getting Your Endorsement

You'll get your endorsement, the notation on your driver's license officially designating you as a motorcyclist, after you complete the riding portion of your test. For this, you'll be required to demonstrate your riding skills on either a closed course or public streets.

When I took my test, I just rode around a city block, did a U-turn in the street without putting my foot down, and basically didn't kill myself (or anyone else, if I remember correctly). A tester watched from the sidewalk, and when I returned, he gave me my license, along with a speech informing me of the reasons why I should become an organ donor. This portion of the test has improved somewhat since then, but it still teaches you very little about the skills you'll need to survive on the mean streets. In contrast, getting a motorcycle license in Europe requires you to participate in three to five long days of training, most of which takes place on congested public roads. Currently in the United States, your best bet is to take a Motorcycle Safety Foundation RiderCourse.

The Motorcycle Safety Foundation

A nationwide not-for-profit organization established in March 1973, the Motorcycle Safety Foundation (MSF) works to make motorcycling a safer activity and has developed programs recognized around the world for their excellence and effectiveness. The MSF does the following:

- It works to make high-quality rider-training programs, designed for both new and experienced riders, available to as wide a population as possible.

- It works with state and national governments and organizations to promote motorcycle safety and to help adopt effective motorcycle-operator licensing practices.

- It collects data and information on motorcycle safety and works to get that information out to the public.

MOTORCYCOLOGY

Another advantage of successfully completing an MSF RiderCourse is that many insurance companies give you a break on your premiums. It is the single best thing you can do to ensure that you have a long and healthy career as a motorcyclist.

There is nothing better you can do to prepare yourself for the challenges of motorcycling than to take an MSF RiderCourse. That applies to experienced riders as well as novices. The MSF has worked to make such courses available across the entire United States. Even if you have to drive a few miles to reach the RiderCourse nearest you, you can find no better use of your time if you're serious about motorcycling. To find the RiderCourse nearest you, call the Motorcycle Safety Foundation at 1-800-446-9227 or check out www.msf-usa.org on the web.

In addition to possibly saving your butt somewhere down the line, taking an MSF RiderCourse has practical value. That's because the Department of Motor Vehicles may waive either your written and/or riding tests if you present them with appropriate evidence that you've successfully completed an accredited RiderCourse.

And for off-road enthusiasts, the MSF even offers a DirtBike School. It's a pair of one-day courses (one focusing on basics and the other on trail riding) that emphasizes the mental and physical skills required for dirtbike riding, and, of course, safety is paramount. Class sizes are kept small to ensure plenty of individual attention from the MSF-certified coaches, and students can be assured of getting the proper fundamentals to have big fun off-road. For more information, check out www.dirtbikeschool.com on the web; you also can enroll with a phone call to 1-877-288-7093.

Control Freaks: How to Ride a Motorcycle

Driving a car is downright clumsy compared to riding a motorcycle. In a car you're moving your arms all over the place, steering and using the gear shifter. By contrast, a motorcycle is all about finesse, every movement small and precise. The controls are all immediately at hand, so no big movements are necessary. The bike reacts to every tiny thing you do; even an accidental shuffle will make the bike quickly change course.

Primary Controls

You use six major controls to operate just about every motorcycle made since World War II (with the exception of a few bikes that use automatic transmissions). The location of these controls has been standardized on all motorcycles manufactured after the mid-1970s (although the location of the shifter and rear brake may be reversed on vintage European and American motorcycles). The following figures illustrate the standard places where you'll find controls on all but a few rare, classic bikes.

The six primary controls you'll use to ride your bike.

1. The handlebars are the bars attached to the top of the front-suspension forks that you use to control the bike's direction. (Note that I didn't say steer the bike: remember, at anything higher than parking-lot speeds, you countersteer the bike, using the handlebars to lever the bike over, not steer it.)

2. The throttle is a twist grip located on the right end of the handlebar. This controls your speed. You twist the grip toward you to speed the engine up, and twist it away to slow the engine down. All properly functioning modern throttles have springs that automatically return them to the closed position.

3. The front brake lever is the lever mounted to the right side of the handlebar, in front of the throttle, that controls the front brake.

4. The rear brake lever is the lever in front of the right footpeg that controls the rear brake (some models have a linked braking system, so it would partially apply the front brake, too).

5. The clutch lever is located on the left end of the handlebar (mirror image of the front brake lever). It controls the clutch and is used to disengage the drive from the engine to help shift gears.

6. The shift lever (or gear lever) is located in front of the left footpeg. You operate it with the front of your foot, from above or below to shift the transmission's gears up or down.

By using these controls with your hands and feet, you can make the motorcycle stop and go, and you can control the bike's direction. While you are riding, you constantly use these controls—often using all of them at the same time. Driving a car will never be the same.

Secondary Controls

In addition to the six primary controls, you'll need to use a variety of other controls to ride a bike effectively. The most important of these are illustrated in the following figure.

MOTORCYCOLOGY

Fuel petcocks are much less important on modern bikes than on older bikes; many modern bikes with fuel pumps don't even use traditional petcocks. Even on those that do have one, you'll seldom need to bother with it. On older bikes, you'll need to turn this valve off each time you park the bike and remember to turn it on when you restart it. The one big advantage of petcocks is their Reserve feature, which saves a small amount of fuel in the bottom of the tank, in case you run out.

The secondary controls you'll use to ride your bike.

1. The ignition switch is similar to the ignition switch in cars, except that it usually locks the forks in place (thus disabling the steering as a theft deterrent). It may also operate a parking light, and it is separate from the starter. You don't turn the key to start a bike like you do a car.

2. The electric-starter button is on the right end of the handlebar near the throttle. Nearly every street-legal motorcycle made today comes with an electric starter, which you operate by pressing this button.

3. The kick-start lever is rare on most bikes made today, except for some smaller dual-sports and off-road bikes, but you may encounter it on certain used bikes. It's usually located near the right footpeg (although it's located on the left side on certain European bikes). To work this device, you need to fold it out, kick the lever in a downward motion with your foot, and then fold it back out of the way.

4. The choke (or enrichment control) is a lever or a knob that is located in various positions but is usually found on the handlebars; you use it to help start your bike when the engine is cold.

5. The fuel petcock (or fuel tap) is a valve that controls the flow of fuel from the gas tank to the induction system; it usually has positions for on, off, reserve, and perhaps prime. Prime is used only after the engine has not been run for an extended period of time; it fills the float bowls with fuel before starting the engine.

6. The engine cut-off switch (or kill switch) turns off the engine. If you can't start your bike, the first thing you should check is whether the kill switch was accidentally left in the off position.

7. All street-legal motorcycles manufactured since the 1970s are equipped with turn signals. Unlike cars, many bikes don't have a self-canceling feature built into their turn-signal switches. On most modern bikes, you operate the turn signals by pushing the switch left or right for your turn, and then you push it straight in to cancel the turn signal.

8. Your horn can save your life, so don't be timid about using it. You operate most horns by pushing a button located next to the turn-signal switch.

9. The headlight dimmer switch switches the headlight between high- and low-beam modes. On most modern bikes, you can't turn off the lights, so this switch just changes beams.

10. The speedometer helps you avoid getting speeding tickets.

11. The tachometer indicates the number of revolutions your engine is turning each minute (rpms).

12. The indicator lights (sometimes known as idiot lights) are primarily the same as the indicator lights on your car, with the addition of a neutral indicator light (usually green) that indicates when the transmission is in neutral (i.e., not in gear).

> **MOTORCYCOLOGY**
>
> You'll use your idiot lights more on a bike than you do on a car, especially the neutral light and the turn-signal indicator. Because many bikes don't have self-canceling turn signals, it's easy to forget that they're on.

Although these are all peripheral system controls used to augment riding rather than directly to ride the bike, you will need to use most of them every time you ride.

The Preride Inspection

Motorcycles require more upkeep than cars. This has always been the case, and it is still a fact of motorcycling life, even with the technological advances you learned about in earlier chapters. The consequences of a systems failure on a bike are much more severe than they are if something goes wrong with your car. Take a flat tire, for example. When a tire goes flat on your car, you can have difficulty controlling it. When the same thing happens on a bike, it's like a fairground ride from hell.

The best way to avoid a catastrophic failure is to inspect your motorcycle on a regular basis. Some items need to be checked more often than others; some should be checked each time you go out for a ride.

The Motorcycle Safety Foundation uses the T-CLOCS method to help remember what to check during the preride inspection:

T	Tires and wheels
C	Controls
L	Lights
O	Oil
C	Chassis
S	Stands

This method is useful, but I'm going to present a simpler one because I've found that if the preride inspection is too complicated, most riders just ignore the whole thing.

I try to check all the items on the T-CLOCS list fairly regularly, but to be honest, I don't check them all every time I ride. A lot depends on the bike I'm riding; for example, if I know that a bike doesn't use oil, I might check the oil only once a week. If the bike is a nasty oil burner, I might check it in the morning and then check it a couple more times as the day progresses.

I've found that the cables and other controls on modern bikes seem to need less attention than those on older bikes; I might go a couple of weeks without attending to my cables and controls, depending on the conditions I've been riding under. As for the drive chain, it'll need regular attention. You need to lubricate your drive chain for every ride, and make sure it's adjusted right, too; that way when it's finally stretched too much, it'll be the only thing you replace. If you neglect it, once loose it'll distort the teeth on both sprockets (especially the rear one), making the chain replacement four times as expensive. We'll cover chain maintenance fully in Chapter 16.

While I'm looking around my bike, I also check for loose bolts in the chassis and make certain the spring is attached to the kickstand each time I ride. The main things I consider absolutely essential to check before each ride are the tires, lights, and chain.

Checking the Tires

I check the air pressure in my tires each morning before I start my bike. I keep an air-pressure gauge in my jacket pocket, and I check the tires when they are cold (when you ride, the air inside them warms up, and the pressure reads higher). Not only is riding with the proper air pressure in your tires safer, but it also makes your tires last longer. Check your owner's manual to find the proper air-pressure level for your motorcycle.

Whenever I check my tire pressures, I also look over the tires themselves to check their wear and to look for any abnormalities, such as bulges, damage to the carcass, and cracking in the sidewalls. I also make sure they haven't picked up a nail, screw, or chunk of glass. I will not ride on a tire I have any questions about. Neither should you.

The best way to avoid a flat is to keep a close eye on your tires and to make certain they are free of debris, such as nails or other objects that could puncture the tire. Change your tires as soon as they wear down to an unacceptable level. Some tires feature "wear bars" that make this easier to judge.

While I'm on the floor checking my tires, I make certain that the bolts holding the axles in place are tight. Probably the one thing worse than having a flat tire would be having a wheel assembly fall off completely. I'm not good enough on a unicycle to get through that mess.

Keep a plastic air-pressure gauge in your jacket (any metal objects in your pocket have injury potential in an accident) or on your bike so you can check the air pressure each morning.

MOTORCYCLE MOMENTS

A friend of mine once lost the front tire on his Harley chopper while we were riding to a rally together because his axle bolts vibrated loose. He went end over end and landed in a ditch about 50 feet from his bike. Although he wasn't wearing a helmet, he seemed to be unhurt, except for a few cuts and bruises. We loaded his bike into a friend's truck and continued to the rally. My friend appeared to be none the worse for wear and tear, but later we learned he'd suffered a severe concussion, and to this day he doesn't remember a thing about that rally.

Looking at Lights

Your lighting system is fairly easy to overlook, but it can get you into a lot of trouble.

If your brake lights aren't working, you can end up with an unwelcome Chevy enema before you even get out of town. Motorcycles have awesome stopping power, and most car drivers don't give themselves enough room to stop when they're following you. Brake lights are not much protection to keep tailgaters from embedding themselves into your privates, but they are all you have (at least until someone designs an anti-tailgating device that uses a 70mm cannon mounted on your tail section).

Motorcycle headlights and taillights seem to fail more frequently than their automotive counterparts, because there's increased vibration. Many motorcycles have only one headlight, so if both of its beams burn out, you will be up the creek when the sun goes down. So it's a good idea to check both the high beam and low beam of your headlight when you check your taillight and brake light.

MOTORCYCOLOGY

Motorcycle headlights usually have two elements: one for high beam and one for low beam. Only one element burns out at a time in a properly functioning system, so you should still have a low-beam element if your high beam burns out, and vice versa. However, be warned that the remaining element may burn out soon after the first, leaving you in the dark. It's a good idea to always pack a spare headlight bulb and tail lamp bulb in your gear.

This might seem like a lot of preparation before you can ride, and it is. But the consequences of being unprepared on a bike are just too great.

Learn the controls of your motorcycle. Memorize them and test yourself on them. In an emergency situation, your life can depend on your split-second reactions. You can't afford to lose any time in reacting because you had to think about where a control was: that microsecond can cost you your life.

Try to internalize the habit of giving your bike a preride inspection. You might feel tempted to skip it when you're late for work or are trying to get to a movie on time, but the possible consequences of some sort of failure of your motorcycle could be so severe that you might never see a movie or be able to work again. Take a few minutes to check over your machine before you take your life in your hands. Those minutes may add years to your life.

The Least You Need to Know

- Unlicensed riders account for the majority of all motorcycle fatalities.
- There is no better way to learn to ride than to take a RiderCourse from the Motorcycle Safety Foundation.
- The controls on a bike are completely different from the controls on a car.
- You'll need to use both your hands and both your feet, often all at the same time, to ride a motorcycle.
- Because the consequences of equipment failure on a bike are so much greater than on a car, you need to take a few minutes before each ride to inspect certain key components.

Learning to Ride

In This Chapter

- How to control your bike
- The basic skills you need to start and stop a motorcycle
- Applying the brakes or throttle
- How to turn and change lanes

Back when I was instructing, the first question I would ask a new student was, "Have you ever ridden before?" If the answer was no, then I knew exactly what I needed to teach them. If the answer was yes, then my follow-up was, "What model of bike was it, and when did you ride last?" Years of experience taught me that if I was given a vague, nonspecific answer about their grandpa's uncle's son who had a dirtbike, then it was a lie coming from someone who couldn't bear to admit he or she'd never ridden. These were always the worst students; they knew it all already. As a result, they would always be overtaken by the others (in terms of skill) very quickly.

I've found that people who have to put more thought into learning to ride a bike eventually become safer and more skilled motorcyclists. Having to think about all the things they need to do seems to make them mentally more involved in riding, thus helping them develop good habits from the beginning.

In this chapter, I provide you with the basic skills you need to ride a motorcycle. Be a sponge and soak it all up; you'll be all the better for it. In Chapters 12 and 13, I go into more advanced techniques. You should read all three chapters before doing any serious riding.

Steering Clear

Some people seem to intuitively understand how to operate a motorcycle, while others need to consciously learn to do so. Neither group has any kind of initial advantage. The latter group simply has to put a bit more mental energy into learning to ride.

While instructing, I saw many people from both groups, but every one of them loved to learn about *countersteering*. I've read so many overcomplicated explanations on countersteering that confuse the reader, sometimes the only effect they have is to turn a novice rider into a rigid, petrified mess.

CYCLE BABBLE

Countersteering refers to turning the handlebars on a motorcycle in the opposite direction than the direction in which you want to turn. Countersteering is the only way to get a motorcycle to change directions at speeds of more than 10 to 15 mph.

Let's make it easy. You can ride a bike around slowly, sitting dead upright and turning the handlebars to point you in whatever direction you're heading. Once you start going faster on a bike, you lean. I'm sure you've watched people on bikes and seen it happen.

When you're riding your bike at higher speeds and you lean, you're putting some of your upper body weight on the handlebars. Those handlebars will move a bit with the weight of your torso. Try this: sit on your bike in the garage and lean it slightly to the right—watch the handlebars. They actually turned a little to the left, didn't they? That's countersteering.

I used to find that many of the riders who took to motorcycling in an intuitive way just knew to lean. The ones who didn't needed to be taught. But don't worry, it's easy. Let's say you're riding down a nice straight street on your shiny new bike, the sun's out, and the world's a great place, but ahead you see a right-hand curve; don't think about countersteering, just chill out and put a bit of pressure onto the palm of your right hand, and the bike will do the rest.

That's all there is to it. Push right to go right, push left to go left. Leaning the bike will have exactly the same effect; the benefit to using your hands to do this is razor-sharp accuracy. If you don't instinctively lean, then don't worry, you'll actually take to countersteering more easily using this simple technique. Countersteering leans the bike for you.

For practice you can ride down a straight, wide, empty street and experiment by ever-so-gently nudging your handlebars with the palms of your left hand and then right hand, one at a time.

Now that I've hammered that point into your head, it's time to crank up your bike's engine and go riding.

STEER CLEAR

Before you begin learning to ride, you need to find a safe place to practice where there are no other vehicles or hazards, such as an empty parking lot. Practice basic starting, turning, and stopping procedures until you are comfortable with your ability before venturing out into traffic. Just mastering the basics of riding a motorcycle will prove challenging enough; you don't need to compound these challenges by adding the risks posed by other drivers. Better yet, take a Motorcycle Safety Foundation RiderCourse, in which you'll learn these skills in a controlled environment under the guidance of a trained instructor (see Chapter 10 for details).

Starting the Beast

Just getting on a bike requires a little knowledge. To begin, you mount a motorcycle from the left side because the kickstand is nearly always located on that side, so it already will be leaning in that direction (provided it is not on the *centerstand*). Hold both handgrips on the handlebar to prevent the bike from moving, squeeze the front brake lever with the fingers of your right hand, and swing your leg over the seat. When you're standing securely over the bike, straighten it with the handlebars. After you've comfortably balanced the bike, rest your weight on the seat.

CYCLE BABBLE

A **centerstand** is a supporting stand located just in front of a motorcycle's rear wheel that supports the bike in an upright position.

Never forget to raise the kickstand when you get on a bike. If you ride off with it still down, it'll dig into the ground and take you off the bike at the first left-hand corner—hysterical for spectators, not for you. To do this, use your left heel to kick the kickstand into the up position after you have balanced the bike.

If the bike is supported on the centerstand, the technique is a little different and requires some practice, ideally with a friend standing on the opposite side of the bike.

The most common problem new riders experience when taking their bikes off their centerstand happens when the bike falls away from the rider onto the ground (hence the friend to catch it on the other side).

When a big, heavy motorcycle is rolled off its centerstand, it's an unstable rolling lump, so here's a foolproof removal technique. Stand on the left side of your bike and take a look at the centerstand. It has an arm (or operating lever) sticking out toward you. This is to give you leverage and control. Don't ever take your bike off its stand without your foot firmly in place on that arm—we'll call it your centerstand *tang*.

Now it's time to practice. Put your left hand on the left handlebar grip, and your right hand on the passenger *grab rail* (some motorcycles even have a special handle mounted under the passenger seat for this job). Put your right foot on the centerstand tang. Now rock the bike forward using your right hand, and as the bike rolls off the stand, make sure you maintain firm pressure on the tang with your right foot. The bike cannot fall over, as the centerstand's feet are now pressed to the floor (if your foot is doing its job). Next, transfer your right hand to the front brake lever so the bike can't roll, and lean the bike toward your body while simultaneously lifting your foot off the tang. Finally, mount the motorcycle just like before, holding the brake all the time.

 CYCLE BABBLE

The **tang** is an arm or lever welded onto a motorcycle's centerstand. It allows the rider to use his or her body weight for leverage in order to make it easy to put the bike on, or to take it off, its centerstand.

Grab rails are mounted to the back of a motorcycle. They are the handles that a motorcycle passenger holds while on the bike, so as to not accidentally fall off.

There are thousands of people out there who don't use the centerstand on their bike, as it "doesn't feel safe." Don't become one of them; practice, and I guarantee it'll become easy-peezy lemon-squeezy.

The starting procedure varies with each motorcycle. For example, if you have a dirtbike or an older motorcycle (anything manufactured before the late 1970s), you'll probably have to turn on the fuel petcock before starting the bike (see Chapter 10). Otherwise, the bike won't start. Or if it does, it will begin to sputter and then die, as float bowls empty. This inevitably happens at precisely the wrong moment. Most modern bikes have vacuum-operated petcocks that open as soon as the starter button is pushed and close when the engine is shut down.

Ignition On

The next step is to turn on the ignition switch and make sure that the kill switch is not in the off position. Even the most experienced motorcyclist sometimes bumps the kill switch into the off position and then wears his or her battery down trying to start the beast. You can save yourself a lot of grief by getting into the habit of automatically turning the switch to the on position each time you turn on the ignition switch.

The ignition switch is usually located on or near the instrument panel, but a recent trend is to locate the switch in some odd position under the seat or fuel tank (where the switches were located on motorcycles manufactured before about 1970). This retro touch, which emulates the switch location on some Harley-Davidson models, appears on many of the newer Japanese cruisers.

Finding Neutral

Next, make certain your transmission is in neutral. Even though most current bikes won't start if you're in gear, there are some old ones that might start and then head off down the street on their own (I wonder how the cops would write that one up). This is why the neutral light is so important on a motorcycle. But you can't always trust the light; they can be funky from time to time.

To be sure you're in neutral, rock the bike back and forth. If the bike is in gear, you won't be able to move it more than a few inches before the rear wheel refuses to turn. If this happens, gently move the shift lever up or down until you can roll the motorcycle freely.

Setting the Choke

After you've switched on the ignition and found neutral, you'll more than likely need to set your choke, especially if the engine is cold. How much choke you have to use varies from bike to bike. This is almost a mystical procedure, and you'll need to use every one of your senses to learn the exact combination of choke and throttle required. You'll need to listen to the engine turning over, feel it catch and begin

to fire, smell the exhaust to see if you are giving it too much throttle and flooding the carburetors, watch the tachometer once the engine starts, and adjust the choke accordingly. A properly running motorcycle with perfectly adjusted controls usually needs very little throttle to start when cold, although it may need a bit more when warm. Unfortunately, we seldom achieve absolute perfection in tuning our engines, causing the procedure to vary widely.

If you're lucky enough to have a new fuel-injected motorcycle, you don't have a choke to worry about; just turn on the ignition key and hit the starter button with the throttle closed. The digitized fuel injection will do the rest, including adjusting the mixture and the idle speed.

Electric Starting Your Bike

On electric-start bikes, you start the engine with the press of a button. With the clutch lever pulled in, push the starter button; the bike should fire up. It will make a brief grinding sound as the starter spins the flywheel in the engine. Then when the engine starts running, release the starter button immediately.

MOTORCYCOLOGY

Different manufacturers use a variety of safety devices to ensure that you don't start a bike while it is in gear, such as starters that operate only when the clutch lever is pulled in, when the transmission is in neutral, or when the sidestand is retracted. Unfortunately, there is no standard, agreed-upon procedure.

If the engine doesn't fire immediately, don't hold the button down for an extended period of time because this may drain the battery, overheat the starter, and cause other damage. Usually, if the engine doesn't fire immediately, the problem is something as simple as you forgetting to turn on the fuel petcock or accidentally bumping the kill switch to the off position.

Kick-Starting Your Bike

Kick-starting is pretty much the same, except that instead of just pushing a button, you'll need to use the kick-starting lever.

First, fold out the lever, or the peg at the top of the lever. If the lever is located on the right side of the bike (as it will be on all but a few European bikes), lean the bike slightly to the left to give your hands more leverage against the force of your kick. This supports the bike during the starting procedure.

Quickly and forcefully kick the lever kick downward. The inertia of the engine will want to make the lever slam back up again on many bikes, slapping it against your shin or ankle with tremendous force if your foot slips off the peg; make certain that you have a firm footing on the peg before kicking. Repeat this procedure until the bike starts. You'll soon understand the appeal of electric starters.

If all this sounds like a lot of bother, just be glad you're riding a modern bike. This procedure is simple compared to starting a tuned old BSA Gold Star.

Taking Off: The Biting Point

Taking off on a motorcycle is a lot like taking off in a car with a manual transmission, except that you have to balance the bike at the same time.

It's possible that you've never driven a car with a manual transmission; maybe you've never driven anything motorized at all. Either way, don't worry—we can still make it easy.

Think of a motorcycle as a bicycle that won't stop pedaling. You can slow it down by using the brakes, but it'll just keep going as soon as you let go of the brake lever, because it never stops pedaling. Now think of the clutch as the lever that stops it from pedaling.

Let's talk about taking off, while sitting on your bike: you need to use the ball of your right foot to click the gear lever down into first gear (although confusingly, some older bikes had shift levers on the right side that needed to be clicked *up* for first gear). You should lean the bike ever so slightly to the left before you pick up your right foot, as you don't want to lose your balance. So lean left, pull the clutch lever in with the fingers on your left hand (remember, we've gotta stop that thing from pedaling), and then click it down into gear with your right foot.

Now that you're sitting on the bike with the engine running, in gear, the only thing stopping you from moving is the clutch. We're in no rush here. I've learned that good clutch control is one of the most important skills in motorcycling. Clutches are not just in or out, they're not like a light switch with just an on or off position; a clutch delivers the engine's power gradually. Unlike some riders ....

At this point you can't just let go of the clutch lever like it's hot, you need to use some finesse. Bad clutch control will make the engine accidentally stall, or make the bike wheelie—you don't want either.

So here's the trick: don't twist the throttle. Instead, you are going to let all this happen while the engine is just ticking over on its own. Now gradually release the clutch lever with your fingers, all the while listening to the engine note. When you hear the engine note change, that's called the biting point. It means something is finally happening; motorcycle movement is next. A good practice technique is to pull the clutch lever straight back in and then find the biting point all over again. If you can find the biting point easily, then you're getting really good at this, so pat yourself on the back—with your right hand.

You want to get going? Okay, sorry, so now you're at the biting point, you need to give the bike a bit more gas by twisting the throttle toward you. The problem is that as a novice it's really easy to be clumsy and use too much gas, or to let go of the clutch too quickly, have the bike lunge forward, and then accidentally twist the throttle wide open—while you try to hold on to a runaway bike.

So position your hand carefully. You have to hold the throttle with your right hand. If you hold it ready to twist it and give it loads of gas, you'll notice it positions the wrist on your right hand very high. So we're going to intentionally position your wrist low. It's harder to give it loads of gas, but that's what we're after, at least until you're used to taking off.

Now feed the clutch out to the biting point one more time, and this time look up, as you'll need to watch where you're going. Listen to the engine and continue feeding the clutch out (what you're doing now is called *slipping the clutch*). If the engine noise drops, then twist the throttle carefully, just enough to get the engine humming again. Continue feeding out the clutch and you'll find yourself moving. At this point many novices think all the hard work is done, and let the clutch straight out in a millisecond. Don't—you'll stall the engine; you need to keep slipping the clutch. On a little bike you might need to gradually feed out that clutch for the first 20 or 30 feet; on a big bike you might need to slip it for 60 feet for an impressively smooth takeoff.

CYCLE BABBLE

Slipping the clutch is the term used to describe the slow release of the clutch lever on a bike, essential for a smooth takeoff. Unlike a car, most motorcycles have multiple clutch plates running in engine oil, preventing them from overheating or burning.

Don't actually start this practice until you've read at least the next section: how to stop!

Although the biting point varies slightly from bike to bike, depending on such factors as clutch wear and adjustment, it falls near the middle of a clutch lever's travel on a properly functioning bike.

Stopping What You've Started

I've noticed one common mistake people tend to make when they teach others how to ride: they show their students how to start without showing them how to stop. You'll see these people running around parking lots, chasing their students, shrieking, "Pull in the clutch! Pull in the clutch!" It's easy to forget that stopping is as important as starting, and for the beginner, it can be nearly as difficult a skill to master.

For the first few times, keep it as simple as possible and pretend you're on a bicycle. Just pull in both handlebar levers smoothly and put both feet down. In fact, for the first half hour I would strongly recommend that you do nothing more than take off and stop this way, again and again until it's second nature.

When you've got that down, then you'll want to come to a complete stop using all of the controls. You'll need to operate your hands and your feet all at the same time. In one motion, you pull in the clutch lever with your left hand and squeeze the front brake lever with your right, while shifting down to first gear with your left foot and pressing down on the rear brake pedal with your right. Remember, just before you come to a stop, lower your left foot to the floor to take the weight of the bike.

Using the brakes on a bike is much more challenging than using the brakes on a car. For starters, you'll have to use both your right hand and your right foot to brake (or perhaps left foot, if you're aboard a classic machine), rather than just using your right foot as in a car. Plus, riding a two-wheeled vehicle introduces all kinds of weird chassis dynamics into the situation.

Your front brake is the most important of the two brakes. An average motorcycle relies on the front brake for 70 to 80 percent of its stopping power. Unfortunately, as most new riders have been driving cars for many years before they learn to ride a bike, they're in the habit of braking only with their foot, a habit that must be changed to stop a bike safely.

You don't want to hit either of the brakes hard, or you'll lock up your tires and skid, especially the rear tire, which locks up more easily than the front tire. According to the California Highway Patrol, a rider locking up his or her rear brake is a factor in the majority of crashes. If your rear tire starts to skid, there's a good chance you'll either *low-side* or *high-side*. When you high-side, you cause it by inadvertently releasing the brake while skidding, thereby allowing the rear tire to regain traction and jerking the motorcycle in the opposite direction.

> 📖 **CYCLE BABBLE**
>
> There are two basic types of motorcycle crashes: **low-siding,** when you slide down, falling toward the inside of the corner, and **high-siding,** which happens when you start to slide in one direction and then as your tires regain their grip, you flip over in the opposite direction.

Braking Practice

To know how to brake effectively on your motorcycle, you need to get your head around weight distribution.

When you're riding along normally on your motorcycle, you've got pretty even weight distribution between the two wheels. In fact, most bike manufacturers try to design a 50/50 (or close to it) weight distribution into their machines.

When you accelerate very hard, the weight distribution is thrown off center to the back of the bike, making the front-end light. If you watch motorcycle racing on TV you can see it happen; it's also what makes a bike wheelie.

The flip side is that when you brake hard, a lot of the weight is thrown forward, onto the front wheel and tire. If there's a lot of weight pressing down on the front tire, it

means the back tire is barely carrying any load. And if it doesn't have much weight on it, then it doesn't have much grip.

This is why under heavy braking you cannot rely on your back brake to stop you. It's far too likely to slide considering all of the weight (and therefore grip) is on the front one. I hope you now understand why your front brake is your best friend when you need to shave off some speed.

Now you can probably also understand why motorcycle manufacturers put the big brakes up front and the itty-bitty little ones in the back.

Practically, it comes down to this: good braking technique requires you to start by squeezing the front brake lever (never, ever grab), then follow with a little less rear brake as you continue squeezing the front one. Practice this, a lot. If you ever feel a tire start to slide, then release that brake and reapply.

It's a lot to take in, which is why it's smarter to practice it before it's a real emergency. The plan is that when it finally happens for real, you'll be confident and relaxed as you deal with it.

Parking the Bike

Once your bike is stopped, turn the engine off (use the key; that way you won't forget the kill switch was left in the off position), extend the kickstand to the down position, and then gently lean the bike to the left until it rests securely on the stand. If your bike has a centerstand, it's a good idea to park the bike on it if the ground is fairly level. A centerstand provides a more secure perch than the kickstand.

If you've ever watched someone struggle to put a bike on its centerstand, you've probably watched him or her doing it wrong. Just like taking them off, there's a trick to putting most bikes on their centerstands:

1. First, get off the bike on the left-hand side, keeping a hold on the front brake, and leaning the bike slightly onto your leg.

2. Take your right foot and, using the centerstand tang, lower the stand until you feel both of its feet touching the ground.

3. Next, while keeping a hold on the left handgrip with your left hand, move your right hand down and grasp the motorcycle frame under the rider's portion of the saddle (this gives you more leverage).

Shifting Gears

As with any manual transmission, you'll need to shift your motorcycle's gears as its engine speed increases and decreases. Shifting up allows you to ride faster, and shifting down allows you to ride slower.

You shift up when your rpms increase to a certain point: upshift too late, and you'll rev your engine excessively; upshift too early, and you'll lug your engine (lugging refers to the chugging sound an engine makes when it is in danger of stalling). The

Make certain that the ball of your foot is firmly planted on the centerstand tang before you lift the bike up on its centerstand.
(Photo courtesy of Simon Green)

4. Position the ball of your foot on the centerstand tang, and keep your heel up in the air, so that you don't waste any of the energy coming down from your leg. Then, in one final movement, put all of your weight down through your leg onto your foot and lift upward with your right hand. The bike will make the backward movement all on its own.

Some bikes require more strength than others to lift onto their centerstands, but if you practice and do it right, you should be able to make it look easy, as you raise any bike up onto the centerstand by yourself.

idea is to keep the engine in its powerband (the rpm range in which the engine happily generates most of its power).

You want to keep the engine in its powerband for safety reasons as well as mechanical and performance reasons. Technically, when an engine is in its powerband, it is operating at its peak efficiency, which is good for the mechanical components in the engine and allows the motorcycle to accelerate quickly. If the engine is not in its powerband because it is running at too many rpms, it causes excessive wear on its mechanical parts; if it is not in the powerband because the revs are too low, it can cause detonation in the cylinders (tiny, uncontrolled explosions that can damage components), buildup of unburned hydrocarbons, and lack of power.

It's the lack of power that poses a safety problem. In the real world, you will regularly encounter situations in which you'll need to accelerate quickly to avoid an accident. If you don't have the engine in its powerband, you'll need to waste precious split seconds downshifting, and a split second can mean the difference between a near miss and a tragic accident.

To shift up, roll off the throttle at the same time that you squeeze in the clutch lever. When the throttle is fully closed and the clutch lever is in, move the shift lever up with your toe in a firm, smooth movement until the lever stops. Don't worry, the gearbox operates sequentially and can only move up one gear at a time; you're not going to accidentally go up too far.

You're more likely to cause a problem by not changing up firmly; you might not get it into the next gear. This is called finding a *false neutral* and can be potentially dangerous (because you're free-wheeling). When you have engaged the next gear (you can hear this happen and feel it with your foot), ease the clutch lever back out and slowly roll the throttle back up to speed. You change up through the gears one at a time as you feel necessary while speeding up.

CYCLE BABBLE

The transmission's inability to engage gears is called finding a **false neutral,** because although the transmission is not in neutral, it behaves as though it is.

When you start to slow down, you'll need to downshift. You need to do this with the same finesse as when you upshift because, by downshifting when the engine speed has dropped to an idle, you can lock up your rear tire just as if you had applied too much brake, causing you to lose control and crash. So the key here is to change down one gear at a time, and only when the engine speed matches your road speed.

To downshift, roll off the throttle and squeeze the clutch. Firmly press down on the shift lever, and then apply a small amount of throttle (known as "blipping" the throttle) as you ease out the clutch lever. When coming to a complete stop, you may shift all the way down to neutral without releasing the clutch, but again, you'll want to do this gradually. Many motorcycle transmissions can be damaged by shifting to a lower gear at too high a speed, even if the clutch lever is pulled in.

The easiest way to remember the direction in which to move the shift lever is this: pull up to speed up, push down to slow down.

MOTORCYCOLOGY

You can slow your progress by carefully downshifting, a process that causes engine braking. To do this, you shift down one gear at a time, releasing the clutch after each downshift. But be careful not to do this too aggressively, or you can lock up the rear wheel and lose control. Engine braking is an especially useful technique when navigating mountain roads, helping you keep your brakes cooler so they remain near their peak efficiency.

Throttle Control

When you're first starting out, smooth use of the throttle can make the difference between successfully learning to ride and making a trip to the emergency room.

Depending on the drive system used (shaft versus belt or chain—see Chapter 5), motorcycles react differently to throttle input. The rear ends of shaft-driven bikes tend to move up when the throttle is applied, while chain-driven bikes tend to squat down a bit under acceleration. Either way, you're going to encounter some moving around back there when you ride. Jerky use of the throttle exacerbates whatever tendency a bike has to move around under acceleration, while smooth throttle use minimizes these effects.

And the more power a bike has, the more the rear end tends to jerk around under acceleration. That is one of the main reasons why smaller, less powerful bikes are easier to learn to ride—they jerk around less when you apply the throttle.

But even a smaller bike is going to have more than enough power to get you into serious trouble if you get ham-fisted with the throttle, especially when you consider that even a small bike has enough acceleration to leave a supercar sitting at a green stop light. Make certain you can accelerate and decelerate smoothly before venturing into traffic.

Taking Turns

As I mentioned earlier, you countersteer a bike, a process you'll just have to practice and learn. But turning a bike involves more than just countersteering. Because motorcyclists are less visible to other motorists while riding a bike, and because our potential for injury in an accident is so much greater, we need to take extra care when changing directions or changing lanes.

The first thing to remember is to reduce your speed before turning. Motorcycles can corner incredibly quickly, but a motorcyclist's balance can be upset by many more things than a car driver has to contend with. Also, overly hard and poorly coordinated braking can upset a motorcycle's chassis more than a car's, causing all sorts of strange dynamics. These antics can be especially dangerous while leaning over in a corner, so brake and reduce your speed before entering a curve in the road.

Before turning or changing lanes, you should check your mirrors and make a sideways check into your *blind spot*, to make sure the lane you want to occupy is clear. Never rely just on your mirrors, which on most bikes give you a better view of your elbows and shoulders than they do of the traffic behind you.

CYCLE BABBLE

Mirrors on a motorcycle never show the whole road behind and to the side of you. The area not covered by your mirror is known as your **blind spot**. The only way to check it is with a sideward glance.

On the other hand, you shouldn't look completely over your shoulder because many riders inadvertently turn their handlebars as they turn their head, changing their bike's course. Also, an over-the-shoulder observation takes too much of your attention away from the traffic in front of you. There is a fine line between looking too long behind you and insufficiently checking to make certain your lane is clear, but you will have to straddle that line every time you ride. Making certain a lane is clear every time you change lanes is a vital way to avoid having an accident.

When you are certain the coast is clear and you are ready to turn, apply your turn signal well in advance to let other drivers know what you intend to do. Then lean the motorcycle into the turn by applying slight pressure to the inside of the handlebar in the direction you want to turn. As I discussed earlier, this causes the motorcycle to lean in the direction you want to turn. The faster you are moving, the more you'll have to lean the motorcycle to negotiate the turn. At normal highway speeds, you

should lean with the bike. When negotiating tight turns that require you to ride more slowly, just lean the motorcycle while you remain in an upright position.

Once you have settled into a turn, roll on the throttle to maintain a steady speed or accelerate slightly. This helps keep the bike stable through the turn. Rapid accelera-tion or deceleration in a corner can cause you to lose control of the bike.

Taking the Test

When you have mastered these basic skills and feel confident in your ability, take your test and get your motorcycle license endorsement as soon as possible. This will allow you more freedom as a motorcyclist, as well as save you from potential legal hassles. Getting a license also lowers your odds of getting hurt on your bike. To find out what is required for you to obtain your motorcycle endorsement, contact your local Department of Motor Vehicles.

The Least You Need to Know

- Countersteering is the only way to turn a motorcycle traveling at speeds higher than about 10 to 15 mph.
- Before going out into traffic, find a deserted parking lot or some other place you can practice the basic skills of riding.
- The front brake provides 70 to 80 percent of a motorcycle's stopping power—use it.
- Practice being able to stop as quickly as possible, without locking up the tire. Most accidents involve locking the rear tire under emergency braking.
- Smoothness is the key to successful throttle and brake use.
- Always look to make certain a lane is clear before turning or changing lanes—don't trust your mirror.

Rules of the Road

In This Chapter

- The importance of awareness and visibility in motorcycle survival
- Avoiding other drivers' blind spots
- Why trucks and motorcycles don't mix
- Using other traffic to your advantage
- Creating a safety zone

You've practiced riding your bike until the procedures discussed in Chapter 11 are instinctive. Now that you have the hang of riding and have received your motorcycle endorsement, you're ready to venture out on public roads. You're about to move up to a higher level of fun, but you're also about to move up to a higher level of risk.

The key to surviving on your motorcycle is awareness. Not only do you need to be aware of what you are doing and what others are up to, you also have to try to make all of those other drivers aware of you. Much of it boils down to visibility. By being aware and making yourself visible, you are trying to accomplish two things:

- You are trying to avoid potentially dangerous situations. The best way to survive an accident is to not get into one in the first place.
- You are trying to give yourself time to react to an unexpected situation as quickly as possible. Being aware shortens your reaction time in an emergency, dramatically increasing your chances of avoiding an accident.

In this chapter, I show you different strategies to help you be more aware of what's going on around you, and how to make yourself more visible to others. I also show you how to avoid potentially dangerous situations and ways to use other vehicles to your advantage.

Driving in the U.S.A.

When riding a motorcycle, the safest attitude to adopt is to view every driver as unfit to be behind the wheel of a motor vehicle. Do this, and you'll be prepared for anything that might happen on the road.

Always treat other drivers like they are an overenthusiastic extra from the *Mad Max* movies. Many of them are too busy to notice something as small as a motorcycle. The number one thing car drivers who hit motorcyclists tell police officers is, "I didn't see the motorcycle."

Unfortunately, you can't control other drivers' habits. But you can control your own.

Be Aware

Always be conscious of what's going on around you. You need to focus on what's ahead of you because that is the direction in which a dangerous situation will most likely arise. But you also need to be aware of what's going on in your periphery and what's going on behind you.

In a study published at the University of Southern California (the Hurt Report, 1981), researchers studied 900 motorcycle accidents and identified the directions from which cars most often struck motorcyclists in collisions at intersections. According to the study, 77 percent of the collisions occurred from the front of the motorcycle, with nearly half (43.4 percent) occurring from the rider's front and left.

If the region around a motorcyclist were illustrated as the face of a clock, the area a rider needs to most focus on is the area from 10 o'clock to 2 o'clock, especially watching the area between 11 and 1.

But just because a scant 5.5 percent of accidents occur in a motorcyclist's 5- to 7-o'clock range doesn't mean you can ignore that area. Percentages mean nothing if another driver creams you from the rear.

Active Scanning

To be aware while you are riding, you need to constantly provide your brain with input. Because your surroundings are always changing while you ride, you need to continuously update the information you transmit to your brain.

Because your eyes are your primary brain-input devices, you acquire the vast majority of the information you need to survive by seeing. But surviving on a motorcycle requires a very active form of seeing. You need to actively scan your surroundings while you ride.

While keeping the area in front of you foremost in your mind, you need to constantly scan all other areas around you for possible danger. Don't let your eyes fix on any one object for more than a fraction of a second. Scan all aspects of your surroundings, and don't just focus on other traffic. Watch the condition of the road surface. Stay alert for potholes, loose gravel, or piles of wet leaves, which can be as slippery as ice. Watch for traffic entering the road, especially at intersections. Remember that driveways, parking lots, and crossings are small intersections, too.

This diagram shows the direction in which most motorcycle crashes occur. As you can see, 77 percent of a motorcyclist's danger comes from the front of a motorcycle, and 43.4 percent comes from the front/left.

77%

43.4%

16.8%

16.8%

6%

7.4%

2.7%

0.8%

0.4%

0.8%

3.4%

1.3%

0.3%

1
2
3
4
5
6
7
8
9
10
11
12

And watch for animals or pedestrians. If you hit a pedestrian or an animal on your motorcycle, you're both in trouble. Make certain to include the rearview mirror in your scanning, but also turn your head slightly to check your blind spots, especially when turning, changing lanes, or stopping. Remember not to turn your head any farther than you have to in order to make certain your lane is clear, so that you don't steer off course or lose focus on the action in front of you.

MOTORCYCOLOGY

A good way to become aware of potentially dangerous situations when you ride is to play the "What If?" game. While you ride and scan your surroundings, think about those elements that could quickly turn dangerous. Imagine what would happen if a piece of the sheet metal on the flat-bed truck up ahead came loose and flew off. What would you do? Do you have enough space to maneuver out of the way in a hurry? And what if the driver of that slow-moving car in the oncoming lane suddenly decided to make a left turn into a driveway right in front of you? Are you prepared? Imagining such situations is good preparation because, sooner or later, they will happen.

To aid the scanning process, you can develop some techniques for using your eyes that help you constantly monitor the most dangerous area in front of you but also let you scan your entire surroundings:

- Focus on your intended path. Because you are moving rapidly through your surroundings, you need to concentrate on an area about 12 to 14 seconds ahead of your bike—that will give you enough time to react to an emergency situation.

- Keep your eyes up because that will aim your vision ahead, where the greatest danger resides.

- Move your eyes around, forcing them to move frequently and not become fixed on any one thing. This will widen your field of perception.

- Learn to recognize potentially dangerous situations. A vague movement out of the corner of your eye may be a deer preparing to leap in front of your bike or a car backing out of a hidden driveway. That shadow on the road ahead may be oil, fresh tar, or some other slippery surface that could cause you to lose traction and crash.

- Constantly monitor your rearview mirrors. The region in front of your bike is the area you should primarily concern yourself with, but you constantly need to be aware of your entire surroundings, especially the area behind you.

You need to constantly scan your surroundings for potentially dangerous situations. That car in the oncoming lane making a left turn in front of you is most likely to get you in this scenario, but any of the other elements in this picture could end your motorcycling career, too—from that woman on the sidewalk to that oil spot in the lane ahead of you.

Make awareness a required condition for riding a motorcycle; like your helmet, don't leave home without it. This is the surest way to have a long, healthy motorcycling career. As you get into the habit of being aware, you'll notice that your ability to process information will speed up, and before you know it you'll also find your automobile-driving skills have improved.

Avoiding Blind Spots

When car drivers say they didn't see a motorcyclist, they are probably telling the truth. Motorcycles are much smaller than other vehicles and are harder to see. Often other drivers don't see a bike simply because they don't expect to see a bike. Or the bike was hidden in the driver's blind spot.

MOTORCYCOLOGY

One thing to keep in mind when scanning your surroundings and looking ahead is that your motorcycle goes where your eyes go. This is called *target fixation*. If you spot an object or some debris on the road, *don't look at it*. If you look at it, you will hit it because your bike will follow your eyes. Once you've detected something you want to avoid, look at where you want to go instead of at that object. A good way to practice this is to identify a spot on a road and make a conscious effort to avoid it.

To avoid riding in other drivers' blind spots, you need to know where those blind spots are. There's a simple way to figure this out. While you are following a car, take a look in their mirror. If you can see a pair of eyes in it, then they'll be able to see you. If all you can see is an ear, or the top of the driver's head, then you may as well be invisible to that driver.

Jockeying for Position: Lane Positioning

You need to monitor the road ahead for debris that can cause you to lose traction and crash. You especially need to watch for oncoming traffic turning left in front of you—the number one hazard a motorcyclist will encounter at an intersection. You can count on at least one car making a left turn in front of you every single time you ride your bike in a congested area. I'll discuss this scenario more specifically in the next chapter, but for now, the important thing for you to understand is that you need to be aware of other vehicles so that you can react as quickly as possible to any situation.

Your mind needs to be up there, ahead of the bike, processing every small bit of information available. The faster you ride, the farther ahead you'll need to look. You can maximize your forward visibility by properly positioning yourself in your lane of traffic.

Keep Your Forward View Clear

Always place your bike in a position that gives you the best view of what is ahead of you. You can see best when there is no traffic in front of you, blocking your view. If at all possible, you should choose a lane in which there are no cars in front of you. If traffic is too heavy and no clear lanes are available, try to stay to the left of your chosen lane so that you have a strong dominant road position and you can see past the vehicles in front.

Avoid riding in the center of the lane, down the *oil line*, because that's usually the most slippery part of the road. Car engines, transmissions, and radiators are located between the car's wheels, and most of the slippery goop that cars drip on the highway comes from these parts and lands splat in the center of the lane. Your best traction, and your best view of the road ahead, is from the tire tracks in a lane, so ride there.

CYCLE BABBLE

The **oil line** is a dark-colored area running down the very center of almost every lane of every road in the world. Any older car that leaks oil will drip this slippery stuff onto the center of its lane as it goes down the road. Over the years the oil line can build up considerably, becoming a slippery danger for anyone riding along it, especially when the road is wet.

Make certain that you don't follow any vehicle too closely. Stay back far enough that you can see any debris, such as a rock or a chunk of a tire, far enough in advance and can avoid it.

MOTORCYCLE MOMENTS

Following cars too closely is the surest way to end up hitting something. One day while riding to work on my bike, I came up behind a truck traveling slower than the speed limit. As the road was empty, I moved to overtake, but unfortunately the truck was braking. The truck wasn't in great working order and had a broken brake light switch, so it had no brake lights to warn me, and I hit the back of it. The truck left the scene of the accident and the police became involved. It would have been a lot easier if I had stayed back a good distance. Once you're hurt, it doesn't really matter who is right or wrong.

Tricks and Trucks

The worst position you can place your motorcycle in is behind a big commercial truck. Such trucks (along with large pickups, vans, sport-utility vehicles, and buses) completely block your forward vision and cause a variety of other problems as well. Because of their poor aerodynamics, trucks disrupt the air in ways that mess with your bike. The turbulent air coming off the back of a truck can move your motor-cycle all over the road. Not only do trucks leave a rough wake in the air behind them, but they also leave a lot of debris. Trucks are usually filled with stuff, which often gets blown out of the back or leaks out on the road. Many of you have probably had to replace a windshield on a car because a stone flew out of a truck and hit your car. Imagine what that stone could do to your face without a helmet on to protect it.

Other things fall out of trucks besides rocks. Many trucks haul petroleum products or other chemicals. This can be nasty if it gets on you or your bike. I've been sprayed with stuff that has ruined all of my expensive bike gear. Trucks and motorcycles do not mix. As a general rule, you should just stay away from trucks entirely.

Because of the turbulent air surrounding a truck, passing one is a dangerous and difficult procedure, but there will be times, especially on multilane highways, when passing a truck will be your safest course of action. The worst thing you can do when passing a truck is to tense up and try to fight the turbulent air. Instead relax, learn what to expect, and let the turbulence work for you.

When you pass through the initial turbulent air coming off the back of the truck, a steady stream of air will either try to pull you toward or push you away from it. This depends on the direction of the wind. If the wind is coming from the side of the truck opposite your motorcycle, it will create a vacuum alongside the truck, pulling you toward it. If the wind is from your side of the truck, it will bounce off the truck and blow you away from the truck.

Just relax and lean the truck toward if the wind is trying to push you away, or lean the bike away from the truck if a vacuum is trying to pull you toward the truck. You want to do this smoothly, leaning your bike just enough to make it go straight down the road. As you get toward the front of the truck, you will encounter a blast of wind, perhaps the most intense turbulence of the entire passing experience. You'll need to lean into this wind to keep going straight as you pass in front of the truck. The quicker you perform your overtaking maneuver, the easier it is, so don't be afraid to use your bike's power.

Use Other Traffic as Protection

After you become familiar with traffic patterns and get into the habit of automatically positioning your bike in the area that affords you the best visibility, you can begin to use other traffic as a shield. On multilane highways, you can position yourself so that other drivers going in your direction block you from being struck by left-turning drivers in the oncoming lane. This is a skill that requires you to instantly read and assess a situation, and no two situations will be exactly the same. But if you master it, you will be able to move through crowded streets much more safely.

Doing this effectively sometimes requires you to ride a bit aggressively to keep up with traffic. Sometimes riding a bit aggressively can be a good defensive strategy. Some studies indicate that riders who go just a bit faster than traffic have statistically better odds of avoiding an accident than motorcyclists who ride at the same speed as other drivers or ride slower than traffic. My own experience backs up these studies. By moving slightly faster than other vehicles, I seem to have less trouble with drivers

menacing me from behind, allowing me to concentrate more on what's going on ahead of me. This doesn't mean that if you go out and ride as fast as your motorcycle will go you will be safer than if you travel at the speed limit. The key words here are *slightly faster* than traffic. And if you ride beyond your ability, you are not doing yourself or anyone else any favors. If you are uncomfortable riding faster than traffic, you shouldn't do so.

Be Seen

Part of your job as a motorcyclist is to make yourself visible. It helps to wear brightly colored clothing and helmets, and to wear fluorescent vests or riding suits that incorporate reflective material. This will make you more visible, especially in low-light conditions.

Realistically, I'm aware that many of you are quite unlikely to wear a fluorescent vest. I had to wear one while instructing, but freely admit that I always took it off for my ride home. Thankfully there are other ways to be seen, ways that anybody should be happy to use. When you buy your bike helmet, pick a brightly colored one. No matter what bike you ride, your helmet is visible—it will even stick out above a touring bike's fairing, and a helmet is something you should automatically put on. I've known people who own brightly colored vests, then forget to wear them. It's much harder to forget to wear your helmet, so it may as well be visible.

Consider your other motorcycle gear, too. If you've bought a red bike, then buy a bike jacket with some bright red panels on the shoulders or arms, as this will help you to be spotted. You don't have to look like a dork to be visible!

Use the high beam on your headlight during the daytime, when you won't blind oncoming traffic. In some states, it may be legal to mount a modulator on your head-light so that it pulses during daylight hours. Some studies indicate that such devices may be effective.

Lane position is important enough to either help you be seen, or hurt you. Most car drivers will pull up to a stop sign and take a lightning-quick glance where they expect to see a car, then move on. If you're riding in a good dominant position within your lane, just to the left of the oil line, then chances are they'll spot you. If you're riding your bike to the right of your lane, bouncing through the potholes, well, you probably won't get noticed; it's simply not where people look.

STEER CLEAR

Never trust the turn signals of other vehicles. Often other drivers will drive down the road for miles with their turn signals flashing for no good reason, but usually they just turn whenever the mood strikes them, with no warning whatsoever.

Another problem with riding your bike over to the right of your lane is that you'll have less physical presence, subconsciously encouraging cars to overtake you, usually not very safely. Don't be a timid mouse on your bike, ride in a good strong position within your lane. You've got rights, too!

Always keep in your mind that when viewed from dead in front or directly behind, you are roughly a third or a quarter of the width of a car or truck. It's your responsibility to still be seen.

Signaling your intention to turn or change lanes early will give other drivers time to notice you and prepare for you to move. Once you've determined that the lane you want to enter is clear, activate your turn signal and check your mirrors to see if the vehicles behind you slow down to let you turn. Sometimes I've felt it necessary to accentuate my turn signal with a hand signal, just to get the attention of the dodgy driver behind me. Unfortunately, most drivers don't have a clue what hand signals mean, but at least it helps to alert them that I'm there.

If the driver in the car is still coming at you full speed after you've signaled, you may want to speed up and wait until the next turn. Always remember to cancel your turn signal, especially in a situation like this. Never leave your turn signal blinking away; it's very common for motorcyclists to do this (as our signals usually don't self-cancel). Unfortunately, car drivers will think you are turning, so they'll pull straight out in front of you.

Another trick to get the attention of other drivers is to tap your brake pedal (or lever) just enough to activate your brake light. Sometimes the flashing of your brake light can be enough to wake car drivers from whatever stupor they are in. And use your horn if you have to, but don't rely on it. The horns on most motorcycles are often quieter than squeaking polystyrene.

Even if you think you have a car driver's attention, don't assume that you do. You may think you've made eye contact with other drivers, but maybe they still don't notice you. Do what you can to make yourself more visible, but always act as if you are invisible.

The Three R's: Riding, Reading, and Reacting

Learn to read traffic while you are riding your motorcycle. After a while, certain clues will alert you to potentially dangerous situations. For example, when you are riding down a street lined with parked cars, if there are kids playing on the sidewalk you should watch for kids or dogs darting out from between cars. Look for people getting out of parked cars and opening their door in front of you. Even worse, a rushed driver could pull his or her car away from its parking spot and into your lane.

You can almost count on at least one driver doing something stupid in certain situations. For example, when you pull up in a lane alongside a line of cars stuck behind someone making a left turn, expect at least one of them to pull into your lane, right in front of you, to get around the turning vehicle. When you see this situation, slow down to give yourself time to react, move over to the far-right side of your lane to give yourself room to escape, and get ready, because it's going to happen.

Identify Hazards

To read potentially dangerous situations, you need to learn to identify the types of hazards you are most likely to encounter. These hazards can be divided into three main groups:

- **Cars, trucks, and other vehicles.** Other traffic has the most potential to do you bodily harm while you're riding a bike, and every driver on the road has the potential to be your executioner. Never trust any of them, but learn to identify those most likely to try to take you out.

- **Pedestrians and animals.** Although they are slower moving than vehicles, pedestrians (especially kids) and animals are more unpredictable because they can change direction much more quickly, and their movements don't follow the usual patterns of traffic.

- **Stationary objects.** These can be anything from a piece of junk on the road to potholes, signposts, trees, or guardrails. These won't cut you off like other vehicles or dart in front of you like an animal, but they do limit where you can move to avoid a dangerous situation.

STEER CLEAR

Watch out for the paint on the road, which can be quite slippery. This includes the bars marking the crosswalk, the directional arrows, and words such as "Stop Ahead" that are painted in the lane. Never stop on the paint, and make certain that you put your feet down on unpainted pavement when you stop.

The most dangerous places to ride are intersections, partly because they often contain all of the hazards mentioned here. Any place where other traffic may cross your path poses a potentially dangerous situation.

Watch the Front Tires

Watching the front tires of a car will give you some clue about what that car will do next. The front tire of a car has to turn before the car turns. When I'm riding in heavy traffic, I constantly monitor the front tires of cars around me. Seeing the front tire turn will give you an extra split second to react in an emergency situation. So will watching drivers' heads. If they're planning on pulling away from a curb or changing lanes on a freeway, they'll most likely be turning their heads to look for oncoming traffic.

Watching the front tire can alert you to a left-turning driver about to cross your path. If someone in an oncoming lane slows down, be aware of what his front tire is doing and prepare to react accordingly. Even if you're not in an intersection, the person could be preparing to turn in front of you to enter a driveway or a parking lot, or even just to make an illegal U-turn. It can happen anywhere—and often does. Watch for people who appear to be pulling into a parking space and then do a U-turn right in front of you.

Learning to read traffic helps a great deal, but it doesn't make you invulnerable. You could become the world's foremost traffic-reading expert and still be taken by surprise. Always expect the unexpected. Look both ways, even when crossing a one-way street, because fools can come from anywhere, and the world is filled with fools.

The Safety Zone

When you are on a bike, your fenders are your own flesh and blood, and you don't want to challenge thousands of pounds of metal with them. Because of your vulnerability, you want to keep as much free space around your motorcycle as possible. This means not getting boxed in, not following traffic too closely, and trying to ride in lanes with no traffic in front of you. But there's more you can do to increase the safety zone around you and your bike.

When you're riding, always try to find a spot in traffic that provides you with the most room possible. Sometimes that will mean moving over into a safer lane. Always try to be in the lane that gives you the most free space to ride in.

How you change lanes can increase your margin of safety. Make certain that you don't change lanes while you are in another driver's blind spot. And make certain that a driver from the lane on the other side of the one you intend to occupy doesn't have the same intention. If the people right next to you have a hard time seeing you, imagine how hard it is for the person two lanes over.

Do whatever you have to in order to get out of a situation in which another motorist is following you too closely. Unfortunately, you'll have to rely on evasive actions, such as changing lanes or speeding up, to extricate yourself from this very dangerous situation.

Again, never follow other vehicles too closely. At the very least, give yourself two seconds of space between you and the car ahead of you (about 44 feet of space at 30 mph and 88 feet of space at 60 mph). This will give you the minimum space you'll need to swerve, brake, or perform a combination of both actions if an emergency situation arises.

Poor road conditions will increase the space you'll need to have in order to stop. If there is oil, gravel, wet leaves, or any other debris on the road, that will increase your stopping distance, too. Factor the condition of the road into the equation, and allow extra space between you and the vehicle in front of you.

MOTORCYCOLOGY

Being prepared to brake at any time is essential on a motorcycle, though even being ready on your brakes can be problematic. If you accidentally rest your foot (even lightly) on your rear brake, you'll activate your brake light. The problem comes when you actually brake and the driver behind you gets no warning as your brake light was already on. Most people who rest their foot on their brake pedal never realize that it's the reason why they have so many near-miss situations.

Following too closely can get you killed even when doing something that seems relatively safe, such as turning across the road to pull into a parking lot. The person in front of you may suddenly stop or slow way down as he or she enters the parking lot, leaving you stuck and unable to get out of the way of oncoming traffic.

STEER CLEAR

Many riders will operate their front brake with just one or two fingers. For most nonemergency situations, this is fine. However, when you need to brake in a real emergency, using two fingers on the lever means that the other two fingers are behind the lever and may get pinched during heavy braking. Those two stray fingers can also prevent the brake lever from being able to travel its full distance. For these reasons, develop the good habit of always braking with all four fingers.

You even need to be aware of your safety zone in the parking lot itself. Parking lots are especially dangerous places because people are looking for parking spaces and are not watching where they are going. As well, in a relatively small area you may encounter different cars simultaneously turning, backing up, accelerating, and braking—a veritable potpourri of chaos. And you can bet none of the drivers are looking out for someone on a motorcycle at that moment.

It's difficult to discuss all the dangerous situations you may encounter without sounding like an alarmist or giving you a negative view of the sport of motorcycling, but it's not as bad as it sounds. Practice the procedures I've outlined in this chapter, and soon they'll be as much a part of your routine as countersteering and shifting gears. You always need to remain conscious of these dangerous situations, because that is the best way to avoid them. As you practice and internalize these procedures, you'll become more at ease with your ability to cope with any situation that comes your way.

The Least You Need to Know

- Awareness is the key to surviving on a motorcycle. Always be aware of your surroundings, and actively scan your surroundings at all times.
- Do everything in your power to make yourself visible to other drivers, but never assume that they see you. Avoid riding in other drivers' blind spots.
- Stay as far away from trucks as possible.
- Use other traffic to shield you from left-turning drivers.
- Always leave yourself room to get out of a dangerous situation. Keep as much free space around you and your motorcycle as possible.

In This Chapter

- Riding safely through intersections
- Techniques for freeway riding
- Controlling your motorcycle around corners
- The importance of remaining calm

In Chapter 12, I stressed how important it is for you to constantly scan your surroundings so that you can identify potentially dangerous situations. Now it's time for you to learn more about those dangers and how to deal with them. In this chapter, I'm going to explain how to ride in specific situations.

The problem with discussing specific situations is that every situation differs. For every bit of advice I provide in this chapter, I can think of possible situations in which that advice doesn't apply. So keep in mind that the principles in this chapter are general templates. In the end, you have to rely on the information you gather through your own diligent observations to ultimately guide your actions.

Intersection Encounters

As I said in Chapter 12, the most dangerous situation you'll encounter on a bike is a driver turning left in front of you, and most often that happens in some sort of intersection. That makes intersections the most dangerous places to ride. You can do a lot to minimize that danger by following certain procedures when approaching and passing through an intersection.

When you ride through any intersection—that is, any area where traffic can possibly cross your lane of traffic—always consider the following:

- **Slow down.** This puts you in control of the situation. It gives you more time to scan the intersection for potential dangers. The earlier you can detect a dangerous situation, the quicker you can react to avoid it. Slowing by just 10 mph reduces your necessary stopping distance by almost half.

- **Cover both your front-brake lever and your rear-brake pedal when riding through an intersection.** This reduces your reaction time.

- **Position your bike away from other cars.** This gives you room to maneuver out of the way if an errant car jockey fails to see you and moves toward you.

- **Watch the front tires of other vehicles.** I discussed this in Chapter 12, but it's doubly important at an intersection. An oncoming vehicle with its tires turned toward your lane can pull in front of you nearly half a second quicker than a vehicle with its wheels pointing straight ahead. In this situation, half a second is literally worth a lifetime.

- **Make absolutely certain that an intersection is clear of other traffic before you proceed.** Watch for drivers stopped in other lanes waiting to turn—they may not see you and may turn in front of you. Slow down enough to allow yourself room to stop.

Memorize the preceding rules, internalize them, and make them part of your riding technique. By doing this, you'll significantly reduce your chances of getting in an accident.

Types of Intersections

When riding, consider any area where something might cross your path an intersection. This includes the usual places, like crossings and where two roads meet, but it includes a lot of places you might not think of as intersections.

For example, turnouts are intersections. Turnouts are often located at scenic points, and people pulling into and out of them tend to pay more attention to the scenery than to traffic. This applies to any spot where people congregate alongside a road, like a beach, a bridge where people fish, or a park-and-ride parking lot (parking lots along roads where commuters leave their cars and get on buses). Always slow down when passing such a place, and move away from the side of the road the turnout is located on, giving yourself more room to maneuver.

STEER CLEAR

In some ways, alleys are similar to intersections because you have to watch for traffic crossing your path in an alley. Alleys are filled with blind driveways, and people often back out their cars without looking. Even a diligent driver who looks before backing up might not be able to see you because of some obstruction, such as a fence or a dumpster. And kids and animals like to hang out in alleys, too. Slow down when you ride through an alley, and watch for kids, dogs, cats, and cars.

The most dangerous intersections are the intricate ones, where several roads converge at once. Traffic doesn't follow usual patterns at such intersections, and vehicles enter the road at unexpected angles. Often there are frontage roads (roads running parallel to main roads) merging at such intersections, too, further confusing everybody. When riding through these intersections, slow down even more than you normally do because you have more activity to monitor.

Moving Through Intersections

When passing through an intersection while you're following a vehicle that blocks your view, such as a bus, watch for left-turning vehicles that are unable to see you behind the bus. Again, leave plenty of space between you and the vehicle in front of you so that you have room to get out of the way. And position yourself in the part of the lane that allows you to see and be seen.

When you are following large vehicles in traffic, you might not be able to decide where to position your bike. If you can see oncoming vehicles clearly, it's best to ride on the far-right side of the lane, positioning yourself as far away as possible from a left-turning driver. But if you're following a bus or a truck, you may be better off riding in the far-left part of the lane, where you can best be seen, and where you can scan for possible left-turning drivers.

Stopping at an Intersection

When approaching an intersection where you need to stop, pay extra attention to the vehicles behind you. Be especially careful when stopping on a yellow light, in case the driver behind you thinks yellow means *put the accelerator to the floor and drive like crazy*.

Because of the danger of drivers rear-ending you at intersections, you need to scan for a possible escape route whenever you approach an intersection. Always position

yourself toward one edge of the lane or the other, to provide the quickest escape route if you need one. Choose the side of the lane that gives you the most free space to maneuver out of the way, which will usually be the side of the lane farthest away from oncoming traffic.

When you stop behind a vehicle, don't pull up close behind it. If you do so, you'll block yourself in. You won't have room to move out of the way if the vehicle in front backs up or rolls back accidentally, and you won't have room to get around the vehicle in front if the vehicle behind you doesn't stop. Remember that even a slow-speed nudge will be enough to knock you and your bike over. Always leave enough room between you and the vehicle in front of you so that you can move around it in an emergency situation.

Leaving yourself enough room to maneuver is important any time you have to stop, whether or not you're at an intersection. The main advantage of a motorcycle is its nimble nature, so be ready to use this to your advantage to escape any situation that turns bad. Even on the freeway, expect trouble from behind and monitor the traffic behind you. If you see a vehicle behind you that's not stopping, look for a clear spot and rapidly accelerate toward it.

To do this, your bike will have to be ready to go. When you sit at an intersection, or anytime you have to stop when there is traffic around, keep your bike in first gear, with the clutch lever pulled in. That way, if you need to get out of someone's way in a hurry, you won't have to waste time putting the bike in gear.

When you stop at an intersection, look for the best traction for putting your feet down. Avoid putting your feet down on any damp, shiny, or dark spot. The spot may be oil, antifreeze, or diesel—the latter is one of the most slippery fluids you'll encounter.

Also be careful not to put your feet down on any painted lines or marks in an intersection. Painted spots will be slippery, and just a small slip of your foot when you are stopping can cause you to fall over. And remember, if you fall down because of something slippery on the road, there's a pretty good chance that whoever is following you will also hit the slippery stuff and possibly lose traction, too.

STEER CLEAR

Some people consider the first part of a red light just an extension of the yellow. The only way to protect yourself from red-light runners is to slow down when you ride through an intersection. Always make certain the path is clear before entering an intersection, even if you have the right-of-way.

The safest part of the lane to put your foot down in is the tire track. As I said in Chapter 12, the slippery goop that drips off cars builds up in the center of the lane, creating an oil line. When you put your foot down, place it at the edge of the tire track farthest away from this oil line.

Leaving an Intersection

When leaving an intersection, the number one thing to remember is to not proceed until you're absolutely certain that the path is clear.

When the light turns green, wait until things settle before entering the intersection. Most car drivers see green and go; years of riding has made me paranoid enough to flick my eyes each way searching for unwanted movement before I take off on my bike.

When starting through an intersection from a standing stop, it is especially important not to trust eye contact as a means of determining whether another driver has seen you. Even if other drivers do see you, they might not register your motorcycle as traffic.

Turning in Intersections

The same rules that apply to passing through an intersection apply to turning at an intersection. Make certain that all lanes are clear before making a turn.

Often other traffic will block your view at an intersection, especially if a turning lane is present. If you find your view blocked, slowly ease ahead until you can see past the offending vehicle. Remember, when you do this, your tire will enter traffic before your view clears, so be extra cautious. Lean forward and stretch your neck ahead as far as is comfortable, being careful to remain stable and in control of the bike, to see around the vehicle blocking your view. This will help make certain that you don't roll your bike out in front of an oncoming vehicle when you ease ahead to clear your view.

When making a turn at an intersection, be extra careful when trucks are present. Trucks with long trailers make wide turns, and they often need more than one lane to negotiate a turn in an intersection. If you pull up beside a truck, thinking the truck is going straight, and the truck turns in your direction, you could be trapped.

You may be able to power ahead and get out of the situation, but then you run the risk of being struck by an oncoming vehicle hidden from your view by the truck. If you're lucky, there will be a shoulder instead of a curb at the side of the road, allowing you space to get away from the trailer. Personally, I'd carefully take my bike onto the sidewalk (and risk a ticket) rather than risk an injury, but then again I wouldn't let myself get into that situation in the first place.

Your best course of action is to avoid squeezing between a truck and something else at all costs, even if it means not entering a turning lane and having to use a different route.

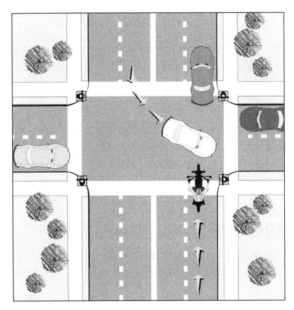

Drivers turning left in front of you are the number one hazard you will encounter on a bike.

Avoiding Dangerous Intersections

Some intersections are death traps for motorcyclists. You will encounter intersections with electromagnetic stoplight sensors (which trigger a change in the traffic light by detecting large masses of iron or steel over them) that might not be able to detect an object as small as your motorcycle—especially if it's one of the newer models with a nonmagnetic aluminum frame and wheels. At such intersections, you can find yourself faced with the choice of running a red light or waiting until a car pulls up behind you, neither of which is an acceptable option.

MOTORCYCOLOGY

If you stop at an intersection with an electromagnetic sensor, the placement of your motorcycle can determine whether the sensor will recognize your bike. Electromagnetic sensors are usually located under the pavement toward the end of a lane. You can often see them by looking for a cut in the pavement, usually square in shape, that extends from nearly one side of the lane to the other. The sensor itself is located beneath this cut, and if you stop your motorcycle directly over the part of the cut that runs parallel with your lane, you can sometimes trigger the light to change.

Other intersections may have too many obstructions—such as signs, light posts, and buildings—for you to make certain all lanes are clear before you enter them.

If you know of an intersection like this, one that makes you uncomfortable, just avoid it. Even if you have to ride a few extra miles, if you can select a safer route, your chances of arriving are improved by avoiding dangerous intersections.

STEER CLEAR

Watch for cars trying to pass you when you are negotiating an on-ramp. This may seem insane, but some drivers actually do it. The combination of a slippery surface and a tight curve may limit your speed on an on-ramp, but that won't matter to some car jockeys. If a driver does try to pass you on an on-ramp, all you can do is move over and let the driver by.

The Lifesaver

We've talked a lot about how people can put you at risk by turning across your path at an intersection. There is another very common intersection danger, which we'll cover here in some more detail. It is the danger posed by people you haven't seen while you are making your turn.

The Blind Spot

The first thing you need to understand is where your *blind spot* is located, and the easiest way to do this is to enlist the help of a friend or loved one.

CYCLE BABBLE

The **blind spot** is an area located somewhere between the edge of your mirrors and the beginning of your peripheral (sideward) vision. It's a gap in your visibility that is big enough to easily hide a car.

You need to roll your bike out of the garage or storage shed, and take a seat on it. It's better to wear your helmet, too, as we're going to be taking a look at your peripheral vision. Ask your friend to stand behind you and stay about a car length away. Position her in a location where you can easily see her in your mirror.

Now she needs to start slowly moving around your motorcycle, in a circle, while maintaining the same distance from you. You need to keep your main focus ahead of you, where it usually is while you're riding (no turning your head around). You'll notice that she soon disappears from your mirror but she doesn't immediately re-appear in your peripheral vision.

She just walked right through your blind spot. Ask her to do it once more, only this time you need to stop her once she's in your blind spot. Now that she is standing in your blind spot, slowly turn your head until you can see her.

Once you can see her there, freeze your position. That's how far you need to turn your head in order to see your blind spot, no farther. Remember that, as you don't want to turn it any farther than necessary.

There is a risk to turning your head too far; actually, there are a couple of risks. The first one is that you're spending a long time looking behind you when everything is still happening in front. The other risk has to do with how this glance affects your machine control.

Let's do another fun experiment. Put your arms out in front of you now, nice and straight as if they're holding your handlebars. You're now going to turn your head all the way around to look behind you, and as you do it, concentrate on what your arms just did. Do it a few times, and you'll start to notice that they move as you crane your neck. If you can't see it, get your friend to watch, or even watch your friend while she does it. Most people will move their hands about 4 or 5 inches while they look backward.

If you're riding your bike at 40 mph and you turn around like that, inadvertently moving the steering 4 inches, you'll probably become a leather-encased bug on some Mack truck's windshield.

That's why after checking my mirror, I only look to my blind spot, rather than perform a full rearward observation. I call this blind-spot check the *lifesaver*, quite simply because that's exactly what it is.

CYCLE BABBLE

The **lifesaver** is the observation you make just before committing yourself to making a left- or right-hand turn. It is the final check into your blind spot, which isn't otherwise covered by your mirrors.

Take note, it's also worth relaxing your elbows as you ride; you'll have much finer control over your motorcycle than you would with rigid outstretched arms.

Turning Left

Making a left-hand turn is more dangerous than making a right-hand turn, because you must cross the lane (or lanes) of oncoming traffic.

I've been making a lifesaver glance over my shoulder for as many years as I can remember. It doesn't upset my balance, it doesn't change the direction of my bike, and it takes just a split second to do, but I've lost count of how many times I've seen something surprising while doing it.

I've had nut jobs in cars trying to pass me, or merge in (on the wrong side of the road) while I'm about to make a left-hand turn. I've seen emergency vehicles passing lines of traffic, and even other bikes racing past me while I'm signaling left. In every one of those situations, I would have turned my handlebars and hit those other vehicles if I hadn't done the lifesaver over my left shoulder first.

The idea is to check, have time to react, and then make your turn *if* the coast is clear. The point is to have reaction time. It's common, but useless, for people to look *as* they turn—all you will see is what you hit. To be effective, it needs to be lifesaver, pause, maneuver.

Turning Right

While turning right typically poses less danger than turning left (in any left-hand-drive country, at least), there are still reasons to make a lifesaver. The perfect right-hand turn would involve checking your mirrors, using your turn signal, moving your bike over to the right side of your lane, and then slowing down, making your lifesaver over your right shoulder, then finally making the turn.

Moving to the right side of your lane will get you out of the way of the following cars before you start braking; it will make it very obvious to them that you're turning right; and, finally, it shouldn't leave room for anybody to pass you on the inside—in theory.

Using that logic, lifesavers before turning right won't show you anything. In practice, I've still been surprised to see bicycles come flying up the inside. Considering the minimal amount of effort required to perform a lifesaver, it's something you should never skip. Make it a part of every turning maneuver.

Freeway Riding

Although it might not seem likely, limited-access multilane freeways are statistically much safer than city streets and highways with intersections. There are two reasons for this:

- Traffic moves in only one direction on freeways.

- Freeways remove your number one hazard: vehicles in oncoming lanes turning left in front of you.

But riding on a freeway presents a new set of challenges. Traffic moves faster on freeways, meaning that things happen faster. You have to look even farther ahead on a freeway to give yourself more time to react to an emergency. The faster traffic moves, the farther ahead you need to look.

On a freeway, you have to be careful not to ride too fast. Motorcycles can cut through freeway traffic more quickly than cars, making it easier to speed on a bike. But riding much faster than traffic puts you at risk because, if you're riding too fast, you won't be able to react if a car moves into your lane.

And even though you don't have intersections on a freeway, you have on-ramps and off-ramps, both of which create challenges for a motorcyclist.

On-ramps are especially tricky on a bike. These often consist of tight turns, forcing you to lean hard to turn your motorcycle. This in itself wouldn't be that problematic, but if a given on-ramp has a slippery surface—such as one that's soaked with rain—it forces you to negotiate the ramp more slowly than you would in a car. The cars, of course, won't slow down for you and will tailgate you or even try to pass you.

Having to negotiate the curve on an on-ramp is the first challenge. The second one is adjusting your speed once you have negotiated the curve so that you can enter traffic safely. This is where a motorcycle's capability to accelerate quickly comes into play.

As you round the curve of an on-ramp, monitor the traffic in the lane you will merge into and locate a safe space to enter that lane. Once you have finished negotiating the curve and the motorcycle is upright, accelerate toward the safe spot you've identified, adjusting your speed and then signaling so that you can safely merge with traffic.

When passing an on-ramp where other traffic is merging onto the freeway, move over to a lane as far away from the on-ramp as possible. Drivers merging into your lane may not see your motorcycle and may mistake the space you're occupying as a free spot to enter traffic. And other nearby drivers may also be watching the merging traffic and thus may not see you. If they move over to let the merging traffic enter, they may hit you.

This is also a problem at off-ramps. If you are riding in the lane closest to the off-ramp, you risk getting cut off by a driver who doesn't see you and thinks he or she has a clear shot at the off-ramp. As with an on-ramp, your safest location is as far away from the ramp as possible.

Watch for drivers who don't see you as they cut across traffic to get on an off-ramp.

Lane Positioning

You can do a lot to increase your safety on crowded multilane roads by always being conscious of your lane positioning. Always think of where your bike is in relation to the other vehicles on the road. Try not to ride in people's blind spots, and try not to ride beside vehicles. If you position yourself so that there are no people driving next to you, no one can make a sudden lane change and hit you.

It's especially important to keep a safe distance between your motorcycle and trucks. Remember, the larger the vehicle, the larger its blind spot. Sport-utility vehicles are especially bad. If you find yourself beside any vehicle, especially a truck, speed up, if you have room, until you are well in front of the vehicle. If you don't have room to speed up, you are probably following the vehicle in front of you too closely. If that is the case, you should slow down just a bit, until the vehicle in the lane beside you is clearly in your field of vision; then wait until there is adequate room ahead of you to pass.

Changing Lanes

Because traffic moves so quickly on a freeway, changing lanes requires extra caution on your part, especially on freeways with more than two lanes of traffic. On such multiple-lane freeways, not only do you need to make certain that the lane is clear before you enter it, but you also need to check to see if someone from another lane is moving into the free spot you have identified.

 STEER CLEAR

Getting cut off by the vehicle behind you while you change lanes on a freeway illustrates the importance of avoiding tailgaters. When other vehicles follow you too closely, carefully get out of their way and let them pass. Remember to signal early and make definite moves so that the driver behind you is aware of what you are doing.

The speed of traffic also makes the vehicles behind you more of a threat when changing lanes on a freeway. You always need to let the vehicles behind you know what you intend to do. Once you have made certain that a lane is clear, slow down and use your turn signal early. Do everything possible to communicate your intentions to other drivers. Watch to make certain the car behind you is slowing down.

And remember not to trust that other drivers see you just because they slow down. Even if they see you slow down, they might not see your turn signal. Motorcycle turn signals are smaller than those on cars, so they can be hard for other drivers to see, especially in bright sunlight. Before you change lanes, make certain that the driver behind you isn't planning to change lanes, too.

As I said in Chapter 12, when you change lanes, don't do so in other drivers' blind spots. This is another situation in which the speed of your motorcycle comes in handy. You can use that speed to accelerate out of other drivers' blind spots, moving into a position where they can see you.

Always make sure you're riding in the correct gear for a given speed. To accelerate quickly, you need to keep your engine operating in the powerband. Remember, your motorcycle was designed to operate most efficiently at certain rpm; when you ride with your tachometer in the most efficient rev zone, you can instantly accelerate if you need to.

Make certain that the vehicle beside you doesn't attempt to change lanes at the same time you do.

Rain Grooves

Some roads have grooves cut into their surface to facilitate water runoff in a rain-storm. These rain grooves are especially common on freeways. They can cause your bike to feel unstable—a disconcerting experience, even for expert motorcyclists. But don't worry; even though your bike may feel like it is moving all over the place, it is a relatively harmless situation—that is, unless you panic.

When you hit rain grooves, the best thing to do is relax your grip on the bars and just ride it out. If you tense up and try to fight it, your bike will only move around more.

Splitting Lanes

In some American states and most European countries, it is legal for a motorcycle to ride between lanes of traffic. This is known as *splitting lanes* or *filtering*. Doing this when traffic is moving at normal speeds is, of course, a bad idea. When traffic is moving fast, remain in your normal lane of traffic.

Lane splitting is not a task for a beginning rider. But for an experienced motorcyclist, splitting lanes when traffic is moving very slowly or is stopped can be as safe as or safer than just sitting there, if for no other reason than it gets you out of traffic more quickly and reduces the amount of time you're exposed to danger.

The ability to filter through traffic is actually one of the biggest advantages to being a motorcyclist. Personally, if I couldn't filter through city traffic, I would stop riding a bike; it's really something you should learn to do well. Some general rules help make lane splitting safer:

- Ride only about 10 or 15 mph faster than traffic is moving. If traffic is moving at 15 mph, ride no faster than 25 or 30 mph between lanes. If traffic is stopped, keep your speed under 15 mph. If you ride any faster, you won't have time to react if someone pulls out in front of you.

- If traffic slows, don't immediately hop between lanes and start lane splitting. Traffic may be slowing for just a moment and will speed up again. Make certain that traffic is slowing or stopping before lane splitting.

- Watch for other motorcyclists who might be lane splitting before pulling between the lanes. If traffic is stopping, odds are some other motorcyclist has the same idea that you do. Focus primarily on what's in front of you, but always be aware of what's behind you.

- Watch for people changing lanes. If you see an open spot in traffic, you can almost count on someone crossing from another lane to take that spot. It's best to try to keep a car on either side of you, which will block other vehicles from crossing your lane.

- If freeway traffic is stopped or moving very slowly, it's best to move over to the fastest (farthest left) lane before lane splitting. This decreases your odds of encountering merging traffic or drivers making sudden lane changes.

- When traffic stops, watch for people opening their car doors. It happens more often than you might think. Some drivers are mad at us for being able to move when they're stationary, so instead of buying a bike and joining us, it's been known for them to try and take us out with their car door. Nice, huh?

Riding in the Twisties

Although motorcycles are more maneuverable than cars, not all bikes can go around corners as quickly. Most motorcycles are capable of cornering quite rapidly if you ride them correctly—though as you learned earlier, certain types of bikes are built for higher-speed cornering, while some others are not. Hopefully you will have chosen the right type of bike for your riding style.

Traction: A Sticky Matter

A variety of factors contribute to your bike's traction. The material your tire is made of plays a role. Softer, stickier rubber grips better than harder rubber. Tire temperature affects traction, too: the colder the tire, the harder the rubber. A tire that has been heated up through use has more gripping power than a cold tire. The shape and depth of your tread contribute to traction. The surface of the road also plays a role. When cornering, the contact patch of your tire is crucial to traction. The contact patch is the part of the tire that actually touches the road. A big, wide sportbike tire will have a larger contact patch than a classic motorcycle with skinny tires.

The relatively small amount of rubber in the contact patch is the main reason motorcycle tires can't corner as effortlessly as cars. Plus, unlike cars, motorcycles lean when they turn. As your motorcycle leans, the contact patch of its tires decreases, meaning that you have less traction available in a turn.

To further complicate matters, if you don't accelerate, decelerate, and brake smoothly, you'll upset the chassis, causing the motorcycle to move around. Such gyrations can cause the size of the tires' contact patches to vary, which affects traction and handling.

A final note on tire traction: brand-new tires have very little grip. After fitting a new front or rear tire to your motorcycle, you will need to scrub it in. This means riding a little more smoothly and carefully than normal for the first few miles, until the tire loses its new polished appearance.

MOTORCYCOLOGY

Smooth throttle control is one of the primary reasons for choosing a smaller, less powerful motorcycle for your first bike. The more power that is available when you twist the throttle, the harder it will be for you to develop smooth throttle control. Motorcycles that have abrupt throttle response, a characteristic of bikes with narrow powerbands, are more difficult to control; bikes with broader powerbands deliver smoother, more controllable power.

Gravity Is Your Friend

I've made taking a curve on a motorcycle sound like going on a ride at a carnival, and there are similarities. But on a bike, you're in control. By practicing proper cornering techniques, you can actually make all this commotion work for you instead of against you.

Get your braking done before you turn. Apply the brakes when the motorcycle is upright, before you lean over to turn. If you brake when you're leaning over, you're much more likely to slide off than you are if you brake when the motorcycle is upright. Remember, when you're leaning over, you already have less traction available.

Because of that lack of traction, you must use the throttle smoothly in a corner. Maintaining a steady engine speed keeps your bike settled in a curve, while jerky use of the throttle upsets your bike. The smoother you are with your throttle, the more control you have over your bike.

Don't accelerate or shift during a corner, because this will upset your chassis. Wait until you've finished the turn and your bike is once again upright to accelerate. As you develop your technique and become more proficient at taking curves, you will be able to apply power slightly earlier as you exit a corner. When you do this, you make the motorcycle's dynamics work for you: when you accelerate, you place more weight on the rear of the motorcycle, thus increasing your traction. As you become more familiar with your bike's reactions to throttle input, you can use that increased traction as you exit a corner.

Dangerous Debris

You always need to scan the surface of the road for debris, such as leaves, sand, fluids, and gravel buildup, but the situation in which these conditions will most often lead to a crash is when you encounter them in a curve. These materials tend to accumulate on the outside edge of a curve, so pay close attention to that part of the road when scanning a corner.

If there is debris on a curve, slow down to give yourself time to maneuver around the debris. If you are unable to avoid it, don't panic and hit the brakes; that will make you more likely to lose traction and crash than if you maintain a steady speed through the corner. If you've slowed down to a safe speed before entering the corner, you should be all right.

STEER CLEAR

Approach areas where shade covers the road with extra caution, especially in the morning, when shaded areas can be slippery from dew or frost. You may not be able to see debris like sand or oil in a shaded area. When you are unsure of the condition of the road, slow down.

If you are going too fast and need to slow down in a corner, stand up the bike for a brief moment, brake, and then immediately lean back into the curve. If you do this for more than a split second, you will run off the road, which sort of defeats your purpose.

Don't Panic

If you find yourself going into a curve too fast on dry pavement, don't panic. Just countersteer more to lean harder into the curve. The more you lean, the sharper you turn. You need to trust the capability of your tires (remember this when you're next considering buying cheap and nasty tires). Although motorcycles have less traction than cars, they have more traction than you might imagine. Just watch a MotoGP racer go through a curve leaned over so far that it looks like he's riding sideways. That should give you an idea of just how much traction a motorcycle can have.

The funniest part is that while leaning we all think we are being more heroic than we really are. Usually you'll feel like the bike is nearly touching the floor, when you're only actually a few degrees from vertical; so again, don't panic. Even if you feel the toe of your boot drag the ground, it's okay; most bikes still have the capability to go even lower.

Leaning harder actually slows you down. By leaning harder, you can scrub off excess speed with your tires. The most important thing is to keep a cool head. Unless you are going at a ridiculous speed, if you don't panic you should be able to make just about any corner—that is, as long as you have sufficient cornering clearance, a quantity many cruisers and tourers do not have in abundance.

Your safest bet is to make certain you're not going too fast when you enter the corner in the first place. If you're in doubt, slow down even more. You can get in a lot less trouble by going too slow through a corner than you can by going too fast. If you're riding within your abilities, you should be able to stop a bike at any time, as well as maneuver around any obstacle, whether you are going straight or around a corner.

Cornering Lines

The path you take through a corner plays an important role in both safety and speed (the gentlest arc through a curve is also the fastest). By selecting the right route, you improve your view and make yourself more obvious to oncoming traffic.

The most important thing is to stay in your lane. One of the leading causes of fatalities among people who treat public highways like racetracks—hotshots who ride at unsafe speeds on twisting public roads—is straying over the centerline and getting hit by oncoming traffic.

When going around a corner, treat your lane like it's the only part of the road that exists. The oncoming lane might as well be a cliff or a solid wall of rock, because under no circumstance should you ride there when going around a curve.

When approaching a corner, move to the outside of the lane before entering the turn. This lets you see farther around the corner, and it also makes you visible to oncoming traffic earlier. As you enter the corner, countersteer the bike to the turn's apex—the point in the corner where you can begin straightening up the bike—and start smoothly accelerating. Racers take this line through a curve because it is the fastest way to do so, but you do it on the street because it affords you the best visibility of oncoming traffic and any hazards that might be on the road ahead.

The Vanishing Point

A great way to learn how to ride corners efficiently is to use the *vanishing point*. Using this technique will encourage you to position your bike safely; it will help you to use appropriate speed; and, finally, it will force you to keep looking where you want to go.

CYCLE BABBLE

The **vanishing point** is the furthest point around a curve that our eyes can see. It will appear to close in on us or pull away from us, depending on how appropriate our speed is within that corner.

If you look at any curve in the road, there is a point where the curb for your side of the road visually meets the curb from the opposite side of the road. On a tight corner that point will appear close; on a long sweeping curve that point will appear farther away. That farthest point where your eyes see the two sides (or edges) of the road "meet" is your vanishing point.

You can use the vanishing point to gauge your speed as you ride through the twisties. Riding toward a curve, the vanishing point will look like it's coming flying toward you, so you bring the bike down in speed. As you ride around the curve, the vanishing point will appear to maintain the same distance ahead of you. Once the vanishing point starts to disappear off into the distance, the curve has opened up once more and you can gradually accelerate away.

Good road position will allow you to see further around a curve, giving you earlier warning of any potential danger.
(Photos courtesy of Simon Green)

When I was instructing advanced classes, I would teach my experienced students to position themselves to the left-hand side of their lane when approaching a right-hand curve. This would give them the best view of what was around that corner. They would then use the vanishing point to control their speed (in fact, they weren't even allowed to look at their speedometers while under tuition; that was my concern). If the vanishing point was coming toward them, they were going in too fast. If it was getting farther away from them, they could safely use a little more speed. If their speed was perfect, then that vanishing point would look like it was matching their pace all the way around the curve. Though I must clarify, this was only ever taught to experienced riders on a quiet open road.

But even for you, the novice, by constantly looking at the vanishing point, you are looking as far ahead as visibility allows. This will give you the earliest possible warning of any danger around the corner, thus allowing you the maximum time to react.

Also by looking ahead, your eyes will guide the bike to where you want to go. Remember we talked about target fixation earlier? It's all too common for a novice rider to look at a tree on a curve, as the idea of hitting it worries them; but remember if you look there, you'll go there. The vanishing point forces your eyes to focus on the positive (the way out of the corner), not the negative (the tree or other obstacle).

As far as the use of speed goes, I would certainly stress the importance of slowing down if ever a vanishing point appears to be coming toward you. Once your skill levels are higher, you'll also find yourself accelerating out of corners as the vanishing point appears to move away; but let's wait until you've got some serious bike miles under your belt first.

Using the vanishing point demands total concentration, and is very, very rewarding. If this appeals to you, track days should be next on your motorcycling to-do list.

The Least You Need to Know

- Slowing down when going through an intersection or taking a turn puts you in control of the situation.
- When stopping at an intersection, always leave enough room between you and the vehicle in front of you to allow you to maneuver around it in an emergency.
- Never enter an intersection until you are absolutely certain that all lanes of traffic are clear.
- Riding too fast on a freeway puts you at risk because it decreases the time you have available to react if another vehicle moves into your lane.
- Never cross over into the oncoming lane of traffic while negotiating a curve.

Special Situations and Emergencies

In This Chapter

* Motorcycling in bad weather
* Riding at night
* Riding with a passenger or in a group
* What to do in an emergency
* Raising a fallen bike

In this chapter, I explain the techniques required to ride in emergencies and special situations that require you to modify your normal riding procedures. Regardless of how well you master safe-riding techniques, sooner or later you will be faced with an emergency situation. Like anything in life, some things are out of your control. There's always that one deer running out from behind a shrub just feet in front of your bike, or that one drunk driver who happens to fall asleep at the wheel and veer into your lane. If you go down, it may not be your fault, but you will be the one who feels the pain.

Riders on the Storm

Riding in the rain challenges your riding skills, because on wet pavement, you have less traction available than you normally do. Because of this, you can't …

* **Lean as hard.** As I said in Chapter 13, leaning decreases the size of the contact patch of your tire, which, in turn, decreases your available traction.

* **Stop as quickly.** You need to use your brakes with caution in the rain.

- **See (or be seen by other drivers) as well.** The rain is especially problematic for a motorcyclist because you have no windshield wipers on a bike. The rain covering your visor, goggles, glasses, or windshield can be removed only by you or the wind.

> **MOTORCYCOLOGY**
>
> You should always wear bright, reflective clothing when riding a motorcycle, but because of the reduced visibility during a rainstorm, brightly colored rain gear is crucial. Not only is visibility decreased during a rainstorm, but when it's raining, other drivers are even more unlikely to be watching for motorcycles than they normally are. You need to do everything you can to help other drivers see you.

Even though it is more challenging, riding in the rain can be relatively safe, provided that you use extra caution. The most important thing to do is slow down. The combination of decreased traction and decreased visibility drastically reduces your acceptable margin of error in the rain.

Smooth handling is even more important on wet pavement than on dry pavement. Jerky steering or throttle input that you wouldn't normally notice on dry pavement can cause you to lose traction and crash in the rain. This means any kind of aggressive riding is simply not an option.

You also need to take extra care to ride in the tire tracks in the rain because the oil line in the center of the lane rises to the surface during a rainstorm, especially just after the rain starts. This goop always limits traction, but just after rain begins to fall, the stuff is especially slippery. Plus, you can't see it as well because the pavement is covered with water.

You might not notice a worn tire in dry conditions, but when the road gets wet, a bald tire becomes extra deadly. Part of the reason tires have grooves cut into them is to help move water away from under the tire's contact patch. These grooves are too shallow on worn tires to allow the water to move, causing the tire to hydroplane—that is, to ride atop the surface of the water. As you might guess, a hydroplaning tire is an extremely low-traction (sometimes even no-traction) situation. This is one of the primary reasons you should always make certain that your tires are in good condition.

> **MOTORCYCOLOGY**
>
> Some motorcycle gloves have a chamois strip, or even a tiny rubber wiper blade on the back of the index finger, so that you can wipe the rain from your visor. It might be a good idea to buy such a pair.

Have you ever wondered where all of the rubber goes as your tires wear out? Well, as tires grip they're constantly shedding rubber particles. These particles sit on the road surface and when the rain finally comes, it creates a super slippery paste, until there's enough water to wash it all away. That means that if you're on your bike and it starts to spot with rain for the first time in a couple of weeks, prepare yourself for an evil road surface. The first rain in a while always creates a unique smell; now you know what that smell is caused by—all that discarded tire rubber.

Night Rider

Reduced visibility is your primary challenge when riding at night. And at night, there are even more dangers you need to see than during the day because many animals roam around at night. Plus, a higher percentage of other drivers are drunk at night than during the day. This is especially true on the weekends.

MOTORCYCOLOGY

Sometimes an animal's eyes will shine in your headlights like a glass reflector. Seeing them alongside the road should serve as a warning to you that an animal is present. Slow down upon seeing the slightest twinkle, and monitor the edges of the road with added diligence. Remember that many animals, such as deer, travel in groups—so if you see one, there are probably more in the immediate area.

Here's how to practice proper night-riding techniques:

- **Don't ride too fast.** When riding at night, always slow down compared to how you'd ride in the daytime.

- **Don't ride "out of your headlights."** The headlight (or sometimes headlights) on a motorcycle illuminate only a small part of the road, making some obstacles and debris invisible. If you can't see a hazard, you can't avoid it. When you do see an obstacle, you have much less time to avoid it than you do during daylight hours. Adjust your speed so that you are able to stop or swerve as soon as you spot any potentially dangerous situation.

Motorcycle headlights have improved immensely in recent years, but they still don't illuminate the road the way a car's headlights can—especially since many cars now have superbright high-intensity discharge (HID) lighting. Adding driving lights can help increase your field of vision.

To get the maximum visibility from your headlight, you need to make certain that it's properly adjusted. The high beam should touch the road at its maximum range, yet the low beam should be below the eye level of approaching motorists. The procedure for adjusting the headlight varies from bike to bike. Consult your owner's manual to find the procedure for your particular bike.

When riding at night, learn to read the headlights of the car in front of you. You may be able to follow another vehicle (remembering to allow even more space between you and that vehicle than you do during daylight hours) and use its headlights to help increase your field of vision. If the headlights of the vehicle ahead bounce, you can expect a bump in the road. If the vehicle swerves, the driver may be trying to avoid something.

Two for the Road

Part of the fun of motorcycling is sharing it with another person (or riding two-up). Bringing a passenger (also known as a pillion rider) along can make the experience of riding more rewarding, but it also requires extra care on your part.

Adding a passenger changes the weight distribution on your bike. It's obviously much heavier overall, but it's a weight that is unfortunately placed not only very high up, but right at the back of the bike, too. The most obvious difference will be a light-feeling front end and a much less stable bike than usual.

This dramatically changes the handling dynamics. The bike will turn differently with a passenger on board and will need more distance to stop. You can compensate for this somewhat by adjusting your suspension and increasing the air pressure of your tires. Suspension adjustments vary from bike to bike, but most modern motorcycles at least have a preload adjustment on the rear shocks that you can adjust to a firmer setting for carrying a passenger. Again, consult your owner's manual for the exact procedure for your bike.

It's not just the bike, though; you'll need to adjust your riding, too. If you accelerate flat out with 200 pounds of passenger perched over the back wheel, your front will start getting very light, very quickly—maybe even light enough to lift off the ground. If you don't want to ride a wheelie, or even more importantly don't know how to lower an accidental wheelie, then things can get ugly real quick, for both of you.

Before riding with a passenger, go over some rules of the road with him. Explain the following concepts:

- The passenger should not get on the bike until you have taken it off the stand and are secure in an upright position, using the front brake lever to prevent it from rolling.

- The passenger must wear the same protective clothing as the rest of us—a helmet is essential. If you don't have two helmets, then it looks like you're buying a second one.

- The passenger should hold on to you by the waist or hips while riding. Some riders prefer to grasp the passenger's grab rail (on bikes so equipped), but holding on to your waist or hips is a good idea as it will subconsciously encourage the passenger to lean into corners along with you.

- The passenger should keep her feet on the footpegs at all times, even while the bike is stopped.

- The passenger should keep his feet away from all hot parts, especially the exhaust pipes.

- The passenger must sit behind you, on the passenger portion of the seat. If there is no passenger seat, there should be no passenger. And never seat a child on the gas tank in front of you: basically, if a kid can't reach the pillion footpegs, she shouldn't be on the bike. Finally, the maximum capacity of a bike is two people.

While giving someone a ride, have him relax and lean with you. A passenger who has never ridden on the back of a bike before will often try and stay upright, even in corners. This greatly reduces your ability to negotiate a corner. You may find yourself leaning further and harder, wondering why the bike isn't doing what you expect of it, all because your pillion is sitting bolt upright, with an inane grin on her face, while you desperately struggle to not crash.

MOTORCYCOLOGY

Always go over the rules with your passenger before riding. The other person may not be aware of things that seem obvious to you. Once I gave a ride to a stranded motorist on the back of a sport-touring bike. I helped the young man put my spare helmet on and gave him an extra pair of gloves I had in my saddlebag, and then I took him to the nearest gas station for help. I thought I'd done a good job preparing the kid, but after I dropped him off, my wife, who had followed on her motorcycle, said he'd ridden the entire way with his feet sticking out in the air—I'd forgotten to tell him to put his feet on the footpegs.

Above all, don't try to impress your passenger with your riding ability. An old friend of mine swore he would never go on a bike again, because as a child he'd been taken on the ride from hell. The rider was actually just trying to impress my friend with the bike's power, but all he actually did was to scare him off a bike for seven years.

Eventually I persuaded my friend to ride on the back of my bike. I rode like a grandma for less than a mile and then let him off. He looked very confused, but a few days later asked to go on again. I never used the bike's power until he asked me to. The last time I heard from him, he was the proud owner of his very own sportbike.

Oddball Corners

In Chapter 13, I discussed cornering techniques. These techniques apply to normal turns with a *constant radius* (the curve follows a constant arc). Sometimes the shape of a curve can change in midcorner, forcing you to alter your technique.

A change in the shape of a road can take you by surprise, forcing you to change direction in midcorner. Like everything else in motorcycling, the key to dealing with these situations is awareness. If you are riding on an unfamiliar road, slow down and expect anything. What looks like a smooth, fast corner upon entry may be a sneaky *decreasing-radius* curve that will cause you to run off the road.

 CYCLE BABBLE

A **constant-radius** turn is a turn with a steady, unchanging arc. In a **decreasing-radius** curve, the arc gets sharper as you progress through the curve, while in an **increasing-radius** curve, the arc becomes less sharp.

Increasing-Radius Curves

An *increasing-radius* curve is a curve that gets less sharp as it progresses. In a way, these corners are less dangerous than a normal corner, but they may require you to alter your course in midcurve. If you are prepared, you can use the extra room you will have in an increasing-radius curve as bonus safe space.

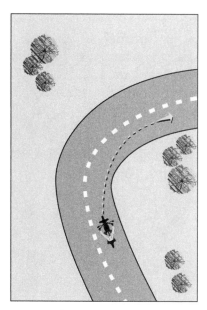

If you're prepared, you can pass through an increasing-radius curve more safely than you can a constant-radius curve.

Decreasing-Radius Curves

The most challenging type of corner you will encounter is the decreasing-radius curve—a curve that gets sharper as you progress through it, forcing you to turn more sharply as you go. And as I told you in Chapter 13, you don't want to make sudden movements in a corner.

Your best bet is to always expect a decreasing-radius curve: first, be prepared to lean a bit more to successfully negotiate a turn, and second, always be in the right gear. If you feel that it's absolutely essential, then it's a whole lot safer to throttle off very gently (letting the engine slow you down) than it is to brake halfway round a corner.

If you're doing everything right and the radius of the corner doesn't decrease, that just means you'll have more room to maneuver. If it does decrease, you'll be ready.

When riding on an unfamiliar road, always expect a curve to get sharper as you progress, and be prepared to lean harder to complete the turn.

Multiple Curves

The technique for riding through a single curve may not be the best technique for riding through multiple curves. By starting in the part of the lane away from the direction you are turning, as you do on a single curve, you may find it difficult to negotiate the second curve. When you get to a snaky section of road like this, first slow down more than you would for a single curve. Then position yourself in the first curve so that you'll be best able to negotiate the following curves. Always position yourself so that you have the maximum visibility of whatever's ahead.

Riding through multiple curves will test your ability to countersteer your bike. Successfully negotiating such curves will require you to get physical with your machine. You'll need to be able to go from leaning hard in one direction to leaning hard in another direction in an instant. If you remember to push the handlebars to guide you, it can actually be loads of fun.

Crowned Roads

Some roads are shaped with a pronounced peak in the middle, to facilitate water run-off. These roads change the angle of your tires' contact patches, limiting your lean angle and causing your bike to steer differently. When you are riding on irregularly shaped pavement, slow down.

Surface Hazards

In a perfect world, there would be nothing on our roads but good, grippy pavement or tarmac. But we live in a world that is far from perfect, and the conditions of some of our public roads are the polar opposite of perfect. In metro areas, the most common surface hazards you will come across are automotive fluids of some sort, whether that is condensation from air conditioners, expelled coolant, or petroleum products such as engine oil, transmission fluid, gasoline, or diesel fuel. Often you won't even see these fluids, but they are there, and you need to be aware of them because often they are as slippery as ice. Avoid any wet spot you do see, and try to ride in the tire tracks in your lane to help avoid those fluids you don't see.

Another common metro surface hazard is broken pavement. Often you will ride on stretches of road that are in atrocious condition. Be very careful when traveling through extremely rough stretches, because hitting a sharp pothole or bump can cause your tire to lose traction, leading to you getting tossed down for a close-up look at that broken pavement.

A type of hazard you're more likely to run across in rural areas than urban areas is gravel and other traction-breaking substances on the road. You can almost count on finding gravel in corners where there is a driveway or unpaved road meeting the pavement, and you'll find gravel in corners where you would never expect to find gravel. You'll find other things on the road in rural areas, too, such as hay, grain, and tire treads. Once a friend and I even hit a pool of milk left behind by a leaking milk truck. Be on the lookout for signs that you might encounter some sort of debris on the road. For example, if you are driving by a hay field where a farmer is loading hay onto a wagon or truck, your odds of finding a section of nearby road covered with hay are high. Sometimes there will even be literal signs, as in road signs that say, "Cattle Crossing." Even if you don't see cattle on the road, you may encounter a very slippery by-product because cattle tend to leave behind funky-smelling calling cards when they cross a road.

When you encounter such surface hazards, don't panic. If you are in a corner, slow down and weight the outside footpeg with your foot. This will put your motorcycle in a more upright position—giving you a larger tire contact patch and, thus, more traction—without significantly altering your line. Remember, if you stand it up too much, you may go off the road, causing a much worse accident than if you *low-sided* your bike because you lost traction in a corner. The most important thing to do in such situations is to ride in the tire track area within your lane. This is the area that is likely to be most clean, because tires push debris toward the outer edge of a curve.

CYCLE BABBLE

A **low-side** crash occurs when the front tire, rear tire, or both lose traction, and the motorcycle tips over toward the inside of the corner.

Group Riding

Motorcyclists tend to be social creatures and, as such, often ride in groups. For many people, riding with friends is the most enjoyable aspect of motorcycling. Sometimes it's fun to ride in a large group of bikes just to see the looks on people's faces as you ride by. Going out for a ride with your friends can be a blast, but it will require extra effort on everyone's part to do it safely. You'll be riding with people whose riding skills—along with their temperaments—vary.

Group Riding Techniques

When riding in a group, you can ride in one of three formations:

- **Staggered formation.** In this formation, the motorcycles line up on both sides of the lane, with one bike on the left side, the next bike a ways back on the right side, the following bike a ways back on the left side, and so on, with each bike maintaining a two-second interval between the next bike. This formation keeps the group close together while maintaining the maximum amount of safe space around each bike.

- **Single-file formation.** When you are out riding with your friends on a winding road, you will all need to use your entire lane to safely negotiate each corner. On such roads, ride in a single-file formation. Remember not to follow each other too closely, or if one person goes down, he or she might take down other riders, too.

- **Side-by-side formation.** When bikes ride side by side, they reduce the amount of safe space between each bike, so this type of formation should be discouraged. Sometimes an escort may require you to ride in such a formation to make the group as compact as possible, but otherwise, avoid riding two motorcycles abreast.

Avoiding Group Mentality

When riding with your friends, watch out for group mentality taking over. This is when everyone tries to outride everyone else. Many otherwise sane riders crash when group mentality takes over.

When riding in a group, ride for yourself and no one else. Be aware of who you're riding with, where they are, and how fast they're going. Above all, don't ride above your own ability. It's a lot more embarrassing to slide down the road in front of your friends than it is to arrive a few seconds later than them for coffee.

SOS: Emergency Situations

Nobody is perfect. Ride long enough, and you will go down, regardless of how careful you are, how diligent you are, or how skilled you are. Even if you always ride within your ability, not everything is under your control.

The types of emergency situations you can encounter are infinite, but they can be classified into two general categories: losing traction and impact.

STEER CLEAR

According to the Hurt Report (which I mentioned in Chapter 12), 94.5 percent of motorcycle accidents happen within the first hour after putting the kickstand up. Often when you first get on your bike, your mind isn't completely engaged in the business of riding. You may be wondering if you put your change in your wallet at the fast-food restaurant you just visited, or you may be thinking about work. Sometimes it just takes a few miles to get into a groove. Thinking about what could happen in that first hour of a ride is likely to help you avoid having an accident, because you may be more careful when you first get on your bike.

Losing Traction

The most common and usually least consequential emergency you will encounter is losing traction and falling down.

Remember, don't panic. If you remain calm and use smooth throttle control, you can often regain control after you have lost traction. If your back tire starts to slide at speed, don't snap shut the throttle: if you suddenly quit supplying power to the back tire, it will violently regain traction, jerking your motorcycle in the opposite direction. Your best bet is to ride the slide through. Go watch some flat-track or supermoto racing to see just how far a back wheel can slide without the rider crashing.

If it's too late and you know you're going down, just relax and let go of the bike. If you're wearing your protective gear—and you should *always* be wearing your gear—chances are, you're going to be okay. Try to slide on your back. Keep your arms and legs stretched out, and try not to let them dig into the ground, which can cause you to flip through the air. Stay relaxed. Stay low to the ground, and try to move away from the motorcycle. Don't stand up until you're sure you've stopped, then check out the cool battle scars on your bike leathers.

Impact: Hitting or Being Hit

If you strike a small object, it is possible to prevent yourself from crashing by following the proper technique.

If you find yourself in the position of being unable to avoid a small object or piece of debris, don't slam on the front brake. This will cause your motorcycle to pitch forward, forcing your front tire into the object rather than over it. It may even cause your front wheel to lock up, and if ever you needed traction from your front tire, now is the time.

MOTORCYCOLOGY

Many motorcyclists learn how to crash by riding dirtbikes. You are much more likely to fall down on the rough surfaces found off-road than you are on smooth pavement, so dirtbike riders crash much more often than streetbike riders. Learning how to react in a crash is probably the most important off-road skill that transfers to the street.

Try to hit the object as straight on as possible. Apply a bit of throttle to take some weight off the front tire, and as you strike the object, pull back on the handlebars. If you remain calm, you can ride over the object without crashing.

Being struck by another vehicle is probably the most serious type of accident you can have, followed by you striking another vehicle. Both situations are extremely dangerous, but if you strike another vehicle, at least you have a split second to react. When you are struck by another vehicle, you usually don't know what hit you.

The only way to deal with such situations is to avoid them—remember to be aware of your complete surroundings, ride at a speed that is slow enough to allow you time to react, and never, ever ride without a good helmet and the rest of your bike gear.

What to Do After an Emergency

If you do have a crash, you need to remain calm. If you are still on the road, you need to move off the road, if at all possible. No matter how badly you're hurt, you will be hurt worse if somebody then runs you over. It's wild to watch motorcycle racers crash, and then get up and run, but they know from experience that getting out of the way is vital.

Once you're out of harm's way, you need to take stock of your injuries, particularly to your spine. Check to see if you can move your fingers. Don't move any more than necessary until you're absolutely certain you haven't damaged your spine. Above all, don't remove your helmet until you have made certain that you have no spinal damage because that can cause even worse damage. Even if you have damaged your spine, you may be okay and suffer no paralysis if you don't further damage your spinal column.

If you are able to walk away from a crash, you can treat it like an automobile accident; exchange insurance information if other drivers are involved, and remove your motorcycle from the roadway, if it is safe to do so. If there is any chance of spinal injury, all you can do is wait for help.

How to Raise a Fallen Bike

Once you've determined you're all right, you need to turn your attention to your fallen bike. If you're lucky, it will be safe to ride. But be careful because incorrectly raising even a small bike can injure your back. You've just survived a crash; wouldn't it be embarrassing to injure yourself when you pick up your bike? "Okay, Doc, this is how it happened …."

When I was growing up, there was a strong belief among every one of my peers that if you couldn't pick the bike up, you shouldn't be riding it. It meant that if you were in the middle of nowhere, completely alone, you'd still be able to cope.

If, however, you own a bike that's way too big to pick up alone, then wherever possible, find someone to help you lift the bike. If you have to lift it by yourself, there are procedures to help prevent you from injuring your back.

When picking up your bike, the first thing is to stand on the side of the bike where you can most easily grab the handlebars. You want to try and lift the bike holding the handlebars and something at the back, like the grab rail. Don't even attempt to pull it from the other side—you'll never get enough leverage. Bend your knees and use your legs, not your back, to lift the machine upright. Get the bike back onto its stand as soon as you can. If your motorcycle is down on its right side, you might want to extend your sidestand before you even start lifting, in case you get the bike upright and it falls over in the opposite direction. Then you'd be really mad!

Don't smoke anywhere near the fallen bike because gas most likely will have dripped out. Battery acid might also be leaking. This can burn holes in your riding gear and even your skin, as well as corrode metal parts on your bike. You'll want to check the level of the fluid in your battery after a fall, if it's the older type of battery where you can top up the level.

Once you've gotten the bike upright, check for other damage, too. Brake, clutch, and shift levers can get bent or broken in a fall. Riding a bike with a broken clutch or brake lever is difficult and dangerous. You may be in a situation in which you have to ride away from your crash site with a broken or bent lever, but replace it as soon as possible.

Also check your wheels and tires after a crash. Make certain that a fender or chain guard isn't rubbing on your tire. Make certain that your handlebars are firmly attached to your fork. If your handlebars break loose, you're going to crash again.

The Least You Need to Know

- The oil line between the tire tracks on a highway lane is at its most slippery just after rain begins.
- Don't ride "out of your headlights" at night.
- You need more room to stop when riding with a passenger.
- The safest method of group riding is usually in a staggered formation.
- The most important thing to do in an emergency situation is to not panic.

Doing It in the Dirt: Riding Off-Road

In This Chapter

- Using off-road skills to improve your on-road performance
- Riding up and down hills
- Advanced techniques for riding over ledges and obstacles
- Riding on a variety of surfaces

Learning to ride off-road has some advantages. When you ride off-road, you remove the number one hazard you'll face on public highways and streets: other drivers. And the dirt generally is more forgiving than the pavement if you fall down, which you will do more often off-road, simply because you'll be riding over more rugged terrain than the relatively flat surfaces covering most roads. There are a lot more rocks, ruts, holes, and trees in most off-road riding areas than on your average city street.

Quite a few road racers practice riding off-road during their off seasons. They claim that riding off-road hones their skills and makes them better racers. Off-road riding is a fun way for all of us to sharpen our riding skills, whether we race or not. In this chapter, I give you a brief description of the challenges you'll encounter off-road and show you how to adapt to those challenges.

Form Is Function: Posture

Balance is crucial to successful dirt riding, and to achieve good balance, you need good posture—that is, correct body positioning on the motorcycle. Because most dirtbikes are so light, you use body movement to steer them more than you do on a streetbike. In the dirt, you need to get physical with your motorcycle.

A neutral, centered body position and proper throttle control are the two most important things to learn about riding off-road. They'll also make the difference between successfully climbing a hill and crashing. And the proper posture for going up a hill isn't the same as the proper posture for going down.

Generally, you want to keep your weight centered over the motorcycle. To accomplish this, you'll use one technique when going uphill and another when going downhill.

Going Uphill

Climbing a hill on a motorcycle can be one of the most fun aspects of off-road riding, but it can also be one of the scariest. That makes it scary fun, and believe me, that's good!

You need to use some common sense when deciding whether to climb any hill. You might not have the skill needed to climb some hills. Even if you do, your motorcycle might not be able to make it.

Make certain that you know what is on the other side of a hill before you climb it. If you are riding up a hill that you can't see over, slow down until you can see what's on the other side. Finding that the other side is a cliff face might not be as much fun as you'd think.

The problem with slowing down to see what's on the other side of a hill is that you need your momentum to carry you to the top. On a steep hill, if you lose momentum, you lose the battle, especially on a two-stroke. If you're unfamiliar with the terrain you're riding in, take some time to explore your surroundings, and check out the hills (and what's on the other side of those hills) before attempting to climb them.

When approaching a hill, keep both feet firmly on the pegs. Shift into a low gear and accelerate before ascending. If the hill isn't too challenging, you can remain seated. Just shift your weight forward by sliding forward on the seat. If the hill is steep, stand up on the footpegs and lean as far forward as you can while still remaining in control of the bike. The more weight you can put over the front wheel, the less your chance of flipping over backward—which, I'm guessing, you don't want to do. But, hey, I could be wrong ....

If the hill is too steep and your bike begins to stall, you'll have to downshift, if you can. Shift smoothly and quickly, being smooth on the throttle to avoid doing a wheelie and flipping over backward. That's really the key to getting up the hill: if you see a steep spot, immediately pick the smoothest path, and give the bike some

Recommended—Intermediate, Cruiser. *Born and bred in Milwaukee in the 1950s, the iconic Harley-Davidson Sportster lives on as the entry-level 883 Low. It's the easiest handling and least expensive way into the Harley experience.* (Photo courtesy of Harley-Davidson Motor Co.)

Recommended—Experienced, Touring. *Honda's venerable GL1800 Gold Wing is quite possibly the most competent, capable touring motorcycle in the world. It can be equipped with premium audio, a comfort package, cruise control, reverse, Sirius XM Radio, satellite navigation, and even an airbag.* (Photo courtesy of American Honda Motor Co., Inc.)

Recommended—Beginner, Cruiser. *You'd be hard pressed to find a more custom-looking lightweight cruiser than Honda's Shadow Phantom. It balances a sinister black finish and retro-style touches with a civilized fuel-injected engine and shaft drive.* (Photo courtesy of American Honda Motor Co., Inc.)

Recommended— Beginner, Cruiser. *The Honda Rebel is a staple at rider-training facilities for good reason. The 234cc air-cooled parallel twin provides decent power, while a super-low total curb weight of 331 pounds allows easy handling for beginners. (Photo courtesy of American Honda Motor Co., Inc.)*

Recommended— Intermediate, Cruiser. *Kawasaki's Vulcan 900 Classic is agile, friendly, and fun, and those on a budget will appreciate its affordable price and premium features. The LT model shown here adds light touring amenities. (Photo courtesy of Kawasaki Motors Corp., USA.)*

Recommended— Experienced, Cruiser. *When only the most audacious will do, try the big three-cylinder Triumph Rocket III Roadster on for size. This touring model includes a windshield, padded seats, front and rear floorboards, and hard bags. (Photo courtesy of Triumph Motorcycles [America] Ltd.)*

Recommended—Intermediate, Cruiser. *The V Star 950 features the "neostreamline" styling of Yamaha's larger Star Roadliner on a smaller, easier-handling, and more affordable platform. Niceties include a fuel-injected V-twin engine and belt final drive. (Photo courtesy of Yamaha Motor Corporation, USA.)*

Recommended—Beginner, Cruiser. *The smallest of Yamaha's V-twins, the V Star 250 (formerly the Virago) is powered by a 249cc, air-cooled V-twin. Weighing just 324 pounds, it's an attractive and affordable entry into cruiser motorcycles. (Photo courtesy of Yamaha Motor Corporation, USA.)*

Recommended—Experienced, Superbike. *With 177 horsepower at the crankshaft, the RSV4 R is Aprilia's ultimate sportbike. Upgrading to the 182.5-horsepower factory version pictured here adds Ohlins suspension, carbon-fiber bodywork, forged wheels, adjustable frame geometry, and more. (Photo courtesy of Piaggio Group Americas, Inc.)*

Recommended—Experienced, Dual-Sport. *Tourers worldwide cherish the BMW R1200 GS and the even more adventurous GS Adventure model. The reliable boxer engine, huge luggage capacity, and long-travel suspension can literally take you around the globe. (Photo courtesy of BMW Motorrad USA.)*

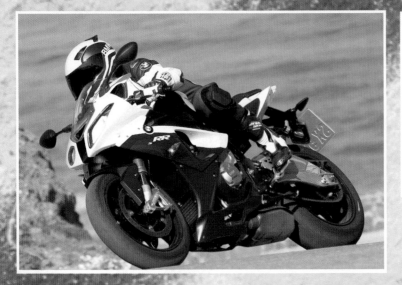

Recommended—Experienced, Superbike. *BMW finally entered the serious superbike ranks with the S1000 RR. Though conventional in concept, its execution is jaw dropping, with a claimed 193 horsepower, four riding modes, and available race ABS and dynamic traction control, including a unique lean angle sensor. (Photo courtesy of BMW Motorrad USA.)*

Recommended—Intermediate, Dual-Sport. *The F800 GS is the middleweight in BMW's dual-sport lineup—and the most off-road oriented. With an energetic 798cc parallel-twin engine, wide pegs, and a low center of gravity, it's both quick and maneuverable. (Photo courtesy of BMW Motorrad USA.)*

Recommended—Experienced, Superbike. *With a Testastretta Evoluzione engine producing a claimed 170 horsepower and nearly 100 pound-feet of torque, and a dry weight of just 377 pounds, the Ducati 1198 offers true hyperbike performance. (Photo courtesy of Ducati North America.)*

Recommended—Beginner, Standard/Naked. *This Monster 696 is Ducati's most affordable naked bike. With nearly 80 horsepower, invigorating styling, and a high-mounted exhaust system, it both looks and plays the part of the urban hooligan.* (Photo courtesy of Ducati North America.)

Recommended—Intermediate, Standard/Naked. *The XR1200 brings Harley-Davidson's legendary dirt track heritage to life, and puts it in your driveway. The XR1200X model shown here adds adjustable suspension, upgraded brakes, and special black-out treatment.* (Photo courtesy of Harley-Davidson Motor Co.)

Recommended—Experienced, Sport-Tourer. *Honda's latest tour de force is the VFR1200F. Powered by a lusty V4 that borrows from MotoGP technology, the ultimate VFR has throttle by wire, shaft final drive, and an available multimode dual-clutch transmission, which has manual paddle shifting and two fully automatic modes.* (Photo courtesy of American Honda Motor Co., Inc.)

Recommended—Beginner, Dual-Sport. *Honda's long-running XR650L is more than a decade old, but it's still a fantastic motorcycle, especially in the dirt. This big, tall single will go just about anywhere you point it. (Photo courtesy of American Honda Motor Co., Inc.)*

Recommended—Intermediate, Standard/Naked. *An energetic 649cc parallel-twin engine, six-speed gearbox, and semi-long-travel suspension help make the Kawasaki Versys a competent all-arounder. Its upright seating position and light weight make it highly effective around town. (Photo courtesy of Kawasaki Motors Corp., USA.)*

Recommended—Intermediate, Dual-Sport. *This competition-caliber enduro bike also happens to be street legal. Powered by a liquid-cooled 449cc single and weighing just 251 pounds, the KTM 450 EXC is all about off-road performance. (Photo courtesy of KTM North America.)*

Recommended—Intermediate, Standard/Naked. *The Gladius is a fresh branch on Suzuki's family tree. Sensible ergonomics provides livable comfort, instead of forcing the rider to adopt a hunched-over sportbike crouch or a slouched-back cruiser riding position. (Photo courtesy of American Suzuki Motor Corp.)*

Recommended—Experienced, Sport-Tourer. *Triumph's Sprint ST is powered by a potent 1050cc inline triple that makes one of the best sounds in motorcycling. Derived from superbikes, this machine definitely leans more toward sport than touring. (Photo courtesy of Triumph Motorcycles [America] Ltd.)*

Recommended—Beginner, Standard/Naked. *The Triumph Bonneville T100 is the latest version of one of history's most famous motorcycles. Handsome, comfortable, and relaxed on the highway, the modern Bonneville is also sophisticated with electronic fuel injection. (Photo courtesy of Triumph Motorcycles [America] Ltd.)*

Recommended—Experienced, Supersport. *The extremely racy Yamaha YZF-R6 features such technologies as an aluminum frame and swingarm, computerized throttle, intake and fuel-injection systems, a magnesium subframe, and even a built-in lap timer. Yes, it's fast! (Photo courtesy of Yamaha Motor Corporation, USA.)*

Recommended—Intermediate, Standard/Naked. *Powered by a Yamaha R6 supersport motor tuned for enhanced midrange punch, the FZ6 has an upright riding position that's comfortable for all types of riding. Less body-work can mean lower insurance premiums, too.* (Photo courtesy of Yamaha Motor Corporation, USA.)

Recommended—Beginner, Dual-Sport. *Yamaha's WR250R makes dual-sport adventure fun. Good power, a six-speed transmission, and long-travel suspension help out off-road—as well as when cruising on the highway. And it starts with the push of a button.* (Photo courtesy of Yamaha Motor Corporation, USA.)

Recommended—Beginner, Electric. *Zero Motorcycles offers two street-legal electric machines, the Supermoto-themed S and the dual-sport DS pictured here. Both offer a claimed 50-mile range, four-hour recharge time, and a max speed of 67 mph.* (Photo courtesy of Zero Motorcycles.)

more throttle before you reach this new challenge. It's about reading the changes and reacting as quickly as you can. It's mentally and physically draining, which is probably why it's so wonderfully addictive.

> **MOTORCYCLE MOMENTS**
>
> When I was growing up, my friends and I loved to climb hills on our dirtbikes. One friend could ride up hills the rest of us could never get over—he had a natural talent for hill climbing. Unfortunately, he was a bit short on common sense and often went riding over hills before he knew what was on the other side. Once, while I was following him through unfamiliar territory, he climbed a hill, but I went around it, preferring to see what was on the other side before attempting the climb. I rounded the hill just in time to see him and his motorcycle plunge into a 25-foot ravine. He was unhurt, but his motorcycle was toast.

When going over the crest of a steep hill, move as far back as possible to place as much weight over the rear wheel as you can.

If you don't have enough power to make it, but you're still moving ahead and have enough space to turn around, you can turn around and ride back down. If you stop, or if you can't continue and don't have enough room to turn around, you have a problem. If you have good enough footing to maneuver the bike once you've stopped, apply the front brake and remain stopped until you are stable.

If you don't have a solid footing, you're going to fall down. Usually this will hurt only your pride, but if you're on an extremely steep hill, you and your bike may fall back down the hill. If this happens, all you can do is try to get out of the way of the falling bike, and then chastise yourself for being foolish enough to try a hill so far beyond your ability.

If you've managed to avoid falling and you're sitting there squeezing the front brake, wondering what to do next, you can use gravity to help get you turned around. Turn your wheel toward whichever direction is most clear behind you, and then gently ease off the front brake—not enough to get yourself rolling, but just enough to slowly move to the side. Keep the bike leaning toward the top of the hill, because the upward side is the only side on which you'll have a firm footing. Lean away from the top, and you're going down the hill the hard way. When you're sideways, ease ahead and turn down the hill, following the trail you took up.

> **STEER CLEAR**
>
> Getting stuck on the side of a steep hill with your bike is both dangerous and hard physical work. Wrestling a bike around while trying not to fall down a hill is usually enough to make most sane people think twice the next time they're tempted to climb a hill that is too steep.

If you've fallen, follow this same procedure, except remain off the bike, standing on the downside of the machine as you turn it around. Remember to use the hand brake as you maneuver the bike, or you could run yourself over.

Going Downhill

You might not think so, but descending a hill can be just as challenging as climbing a hill. In fact, if you don't know what you are doing, you can fall even more spectacularly going downhill.

Point the motorcycle directly down the hill before descending. The more straight on you are when going down, the less your chances are of falling. Slide your butt back on the seat as far as you can, while still maintaining a firm grip on the handlebars, to transfer weight to the rear. Shift into a low gear, and don't open the throttle as you go down. Let the engine assist in your braking. Use the rear brake liberally, but be careful about locking up the tire. Be very cautious when using the front brake, especially in low-traction situations. When going downhill, your front end will want to dig into the ground if the terrain is soft or loose. Using your front brake will increase this tendency and can send you flying over your handlebars.

Just like ascending, the key to getting down a hill in one piece is reacting quickly to all the changes in the terrain. Bumps and ruts will pitch the bike sideways (as if downward momentum isn't enough to deal with). The trick is to think fast. If your bike starts going to the side, find something you can put your foot on temporarily to keep your balance. One dab of your foot onto something solid can save the bike from going over. A dropped bike will often stall, and being on a 40-degree incline trying to kick-start a stalled dirtbike is kind of tricky. Any way you can keep it upright is a very good thing.

 STEER CLEAR

Gravity can be your friend when going downhill, but it also makes crashes happen more quickly and more violently. When you fall down while climbing a hill, it seems to happen in slow motion because your momentum is carrying you up, away from the ground. When your bike pitches you off while going downhill, it happens pretty quickly because your momentum is already carrying you down, toward the ground.

Ledges and Embankments

As your hill-climbing skills improve, you may want to seek out more challenging terrain. Riding up and down sharp ledges and embankments can provide those challenges, but you really need to use your head here. There is a fine line between a ledge and a cliff, and if you purposely go plunging off a cliff, chances are you won't get much sympathy while you recuperate in the intensive-care ward.

Use the same basic technique for climbing ledges and embankments that you use to climb other hills, only more of it. You'll need to shift your weight farther forward, apply more throttle, and gain more momentum. Again, be aware of what's at the top of the embankment. If you successfully climb the embankment, you'll be going at a pretty good clip as you crest the top. As you get over the top, let off the throttle and prepare to deal with what you find at the top.

When going down a short, steep hill, you may need to give the bike a little gas as your front tire goes over the edge, to keep the bike from getting hung up on the ledge. Otherwise, follow the normal downhill procedure.

Things That Go Bump in the Road

Even on the worst paved road you can find, you won't encounter obstacles such as stumps, logs, boulders, and roots. When riding off-road, these obstacles are part of the package, and you'll need to know how to deal with them. If you hit such obstacles when you are unprepared, they can deflect your front tire, causing you to crash.

To avoid these obstacles, concentrate on the trail ahead of you, scanning for objects in your path. Adjust your speed for conditions. If you are riding through dense foliage, slow down until you can determine what's ahead of you.

Even if you avoid hitting an obstacle with your bike, if you don't maintain a proper riding position, you can hit it with your toes or feet, especially on a narrow trail. To avoid this, ride with the balls of your feet on the footpegs so that your toes don't hang below your motorcycle's frame. This prevents you from catching your toes on obstacles, which more often than not will lead to a bunch of broken bones in your feet. And having to ride 20 or 30 miles to the nearest emergency room with a bunch of broken bones in your feet is no fun. You'll have to trust me on that.

If you hit an obstacle that deflects your bike, resist the urge to stick out your leg. This will upset your center of gravity, making you more likely to go down, and it also creates the risk of knee injury. As bad as breaking a bunch of bones in your foot sounds, it's actually a pleasant experience compared to suffering a knee injury. Instead of sticking out your foot, keep your feet on the pegs and shift your weight around to correct your bike's course.

Riding over an obstacle is a maneuver best left only to an experienced rider. It requires precise throttle control, along with the ability to bring the front wheel up in the air at will. This is known as doing a wheelie, and when riding off-road, being able to do a wheelie can spare you many painful crashes.

If you have to ride over an obstacle, approach it as directly as possible, trying to hit it straight on (at a 90-degree angle). As your front wheel is about to strike the obstacle, apply some throttle to unload the front wheel and pull back on the handlebars, being careful not to give the bike too much gas so that you don't flip over backward. You are now doing a wheelie, with your back tire rapidly approaching the obstacle. If the obstacle is reasonably small, close the throttle before the rear wheel hits it. This will bring your front end down, and you can ride over the obstacle with your back wheel. Your front wheel is always the trickiest wheel, simply because it has the ability to steer.

If the obstacle is too large for your back wheel to go over without your bike getting hung up, you shouldn't be attempting to go over it in the first place. If you're in the middle of the attempt when you realize you're in trouble, that observation won't help you much. At the exact moment your rear tire catches the obstacle, apply a bit more throttle. This should launch you over the obstacle. To do this, you should be experienced at jumping and should be able to land on your back wheel, which is, theoretically, what should happen (either that, or you will fly into the brush). As I said, this is a procedure best left to an expert rider. Before attempting it, you should know your bike and your riding techniques so well that the entire procedure comes to you naturally.

Make certain that you know what you are doing before attempting to ride over an obstacle.

Surface Conditions

The defining characteristic of a road—even a lousy, decomposing road—is a relatively level surface. The surfaces found off-road vary as much as the flora and fauna, but they can be broken down into three general categories:

- Sand

- Water and mud

- Rocks

The one thing these surfaces have in common is that they're all low-traction situations. Learning to cope with low-traction riding can greatly improve your street-riding skills. When the rear tire loses traction at speed on the street, your greatest danger comes when you suddenly regain traction, because this violently pitches your motorcycle in the opposite direction (called a high-side). You need to learn how to control a slide by using smooth throttle control rather than abruptly releasing the throttle, which will cause you to regain traction too quickly.

Because the dirt is more forgiving (you won't regain traction so abruptly when you release the throttle), you can practice sliding off-road without as much danger of high-siding the bike. Sliding on the pavement will always require a more delicate use of the throttle, and your off-road skills won't translate directly to the street, but at least you'll know how to slide and control the bike in a slide. This knowledge can save your life in an emergency.

While the three categories of off-road surfaces all have low traction in common, each will require a slightly different riding technique.

MOTORCYCOLOGY

Learning to ride under the low-traction conditions encountered off-road is the most important skill you can transfer to street riding. Learning how a motorcycle reacts in low-traction conditions and how to control it in such conditions can be invaluable information on the street. But remember one important difference: on pavement, you generally have more grip, and the speeds are often higher. As a result, when you lose the rear end at street-riding speeds and then close the throttle, the rear tire tends to bite hard, and the bike tries to throw you over the high side much more violently and quickly than it does when riding off-road.

Sliding Through Sand

When riding in sand, the front end of your bike will feel as if it is moving through a thick fluid. You'll never quite feel like your front end is planted, yet the snaky movements it makes won't be as abrupt as in rocks, water, or mud.

The key to riding in sand is to remain relaxed. Keep your feet on the pegs and your head up, with your eyes focused ahead. Your bike will move around (undulate might be a better description), but this is normal.

Throughout this book, I've always told you to slow down when encountering a potentially dangerous situation. But that advice doesn't apply to riding in sand. Here, you'll want to speed up, going fast enough for your tires to rise to the top of the sand. When riding on sand, you want to re-create the condition of hydroplaning on water, as discussed in Chapter 14. There, you wanted to avoid hydroplaning. Here, it's a good thing. If you slow down in the sand, your bike will sink in, which could cause either your front wheel to knife in and veer to one side, or your back wheel to spin, losing valuable traction.

When turning in sand, you have to be especially careful to keep your front end from knifing in. You need to get as much weight as possible off the front tire. Shift your weight to the rear of the bike, and apply the throttle to unload some weight from the front end. When you master the technique, you'll find that you use your throttle to slide the rear end around to turn in sand more than you actually steer the bike.

A general tip to keep in mind when riding in sand is that you should accelerate sooner and brake later than you would when riding on surfaces that provide better traction. The drag created by pushing your wheels through sand means it takes your bike longer to accelerate and takes it less time to slow down than when you're riding on higher-traction surfaces.

Wheeling in Water

Riding in water and mud will provide you with skills that translate directly to street riding, because you may encounter such conditions on-road as well as off-road.

Surfaces underwater are especially slick. This applies to riding over low-water crossings on public roads as well as riding through streams and swamps. If there is debris present, such as fallen leaves or pine needles, the surfaces become even more slippery. Again, this is true of the water on a road as well as the water encountered while riding off-road.

STEER CLEAR

If you encounter a low-water bridge on a paved road (a place where the road descends into a creek or river), follow the procedures outlined here, and be extra cautious. If the water is moving quickly, it may actually pull your wheels downstream. You must remain calm when this happens. Keep your weight centered so that neither the front nor the rear wheel washes out from under you, and proceed at a slow but steady pace, keeping your eyes focused on the road ahead, where it rises out of the water.

When riding through water, ride slowly and be prepared for whatever your front tire may encounter because you won't be able to visually scan submerged surfaces. I've stressed the importance of using smooth throttle and brake control in all situations, but no other situation requires you to accelerate and brake more smoothly than riding in water.

When riding through water, you should ...

- Beware of surface irregularities, such as rocks and holes that are hidden by the water.

- Learn to read different water surfaces. You can get some idea about how deep the water is by the way it moves. If you see shallow ripples, the water is probably being disturbed by the surface underneath, meaning that it is not too deep. If the water is slow moving and calm, it is probably deeper.

- Maintain your momentum, and focus on the opposite bank or where the road emerges from the water at a low-water crossing.

- Keep speeds relatively low. In addition to minimizing the damage if you fall down, this keeps water from splashing up onto your engine.

After riding through water, your brakes may be wet and ineffective. Dry them by applying light braking pressure while riding until they return to normal power.

If you have submerged your bike's engine, you'll want to change your oil as soon as possible.

MOTORCYCOLOGY

Nothing has caused me to crash more often than ruts. Ruts that are hidden in tall grass are the worst because you can't see them. But trying to turn out of a rut I could see has to rank as the second most common cause of the crashes I've had. These usually have been quite spectacular, of the end-over-end variety. Moral of the story? Don't fight a rut.

Water and mud go together—where there's water, there's mud, and where there's mud, there's water. But riding in mud requires you to modify your technique a bit. The biggest difference is that, when riding in mud, you'll usually encounter ruts. When you do, stay relaxed and let your tires follow the ruts. Don't fight the front wheel or try to turn out of a rut. It is a fight the rut will win. Again, I know this from firsthand experience. Look ahead to where you want to go rather than down at the rut.

If you're riding through heavy mud and your bike begins to bog down, don't open the throttle abruptly. Doing so will only cause your tire to dig down deeper, getting you even more stuck in the mud. You wouldn't believe how heavy a 250-pound motorcycle can feel when it is stuck in the mud. Your best bet is to gradually open the throttle and try to keep your momentum.

Riding in Rocks

Riding in rocks differs from riding in mud or sand in many ways. The most important difference is that sand and mud are, by nature, very soft, while rocks tend to be very hard.

The technique for riding on a surface composed of small rocks is similar to the technique for riding on sand: maintain a steady speed, using smooth throttle and brake control. It differs in that you don't need to go as fast. Your tires won't plow in quite as deeply as in sand. You must still maintain a steady pace, but it just doesn't have to be as quick a pace.

Another difference between small rocks and sand is that the movements of your front end caused by the rocks will be jerkier and less fluid than the undulation caused by the sand. Again, your best way of dealing with this is to remain relaxed and ride at a moderate, steady pace. If you tense up and grip the handlebars too tightly, the front-end movements caused by the rocks will increase in intensity.

School

The Motorcycle Safety Foundation (MSF) offers a DirtBike School consisting of a pair of daylong courses. The first course, referred to as a Close Range Exercise (CRE), focuses on off-road safety and skill development in a controlled environment. The second course, Introduction to Trail Riding (ITR), builds on the CRE curriculum, and then adds skill development on actual trails. This fun, low-pressure coursework teaches the basics of off-road riding and then progresses to more advanced off-road riding techniques. The courses are offered in a variety of riding areas around the country, and though each area is different, the quality of the hands-on instruction provided by trained MSF staff doesn't vary. For more information, contact the MSF DirtBike School at 1-877-288-7093, or go to www.dirtbikeschool. com on the web.

Many riders go their entire lives without venturing off pavement. By doing so, they miss one of the most enjoyable aspects of motorcycling. If it is at all possible, I recommend that each of you pick up an inexpensive trailbike in addition to your streetbike, and hit the trails every chance you get. You won't regret it.

Just make sure that you do this kind of riding with a buddy. Dirt riding is like scuba diving; it's not really a solo thing. Imagine riding into the middle of nowhere and inadvertently dumping your bike while climbing some steep incline and cracking the engine case on a rock. Even with a buddy around, it's still a major problem, but if you're on your own … well, you could be vulture meat.

Preserving Your Off-Road Access

For those of you who *do* want to get down 'n' dirty, you'll learn something special about your sport right off the bat: access to your riding areas is under attack 24/7. Fortunately, you've got some superb organizations out there doing yeoman's service on your behalf, and they deserve your support. Of course, the American Motorcyclist Association (AMA) is in the thick of the fight, with the tireless efforts of its Government Relations Department. The department keeps a weather eye out for legislation—state or federal—that might discriminate against motorcyclists. Help them out by becoming an AMA member: just call 1-800-AMA-JOIN or go to www. ama-cycle.org on the web. (I'll talk more about the AMA in Chapter 19.)

Then there's the National Off-Highway Vehicle Conservation Council (NOHVCC), a corporate- and individual-funded educational foundation working "to further a positive future for responsible OHV recreation." The NOHVCC helps local OHV/ATV clubs become active in the land-closure battle with a host of resources. To find out more, go to www.nohvcc.org on the web. Similarly, the activist BlueRibbon Coalition (BRC) uses the voices of its members in ongoing land-use issues. The BRC's mission, in part, is to champion "responsible use of public lands and waters for the benefit of all recreationists," and they do so by promoting cooperation between off-road enthusiasts and other types of public land users. To find out how you can help, call 1-800-BLUE-RIB, or go online at www.sharetrails.org.

The Least You Need to Know

- Proper posture and careful throttle control are the two most important skills to learn when riding your bike off-road.
- The skills learned by riding off-road transfer to riding on-road indirectly, not directly.
- Riding off-road teaches you important techniques for dealing with low-traction situations.
- Taking an off-road training course, such as the MSF DirtBike School, can help you learn proper techniques.
- Dirtbike courses often provide both the bike and the safety gear so you can learn the skills without having to invest in off-road equipment of your own.

Living with a Motorcycle

In Part 1, I told you just how far motorcycle technology has advanced in the past few decades. Today's motorcycle requires a fraction of the effort needed to keep a pre-1970 model running.

But many motorcycles still need more maintenance than any modern car. You'll still need to perform routine procedures, not just to keep your bike in top condition, but to ensure your own safety. You can't afford an equipment failure on a bike.

By buying the simplest bike that meets your needs, performing routine maintenance, and not running the bike into the ground, you can get the most out of your motorcycle.

Zen and the Art of Motorcycle Maintenance

Chapter 16

In This Chapter

- Getting a handle on the tools you need to maintain your bike
- Spotting potentially dangerous tire and brake problems
- Changing oil and why you need to do it
- Maintaining your chain

People either love performing maintenance on their motorcycles or they hate it. In his book *Zen and the Art of Motorcycle Maintenance*, Robert M. Pirsig writes that the reason some people hate motorcycle maintenance is that it is part of the "inhuman language" of technology. "Anything to do with valves and shafts and wrenches is a part of that dehumanized world," he writes. Pirsig is from the other group, the tinkerers and fiddlers who think nothing of tearing apart their engines and adjusting their valves. He finds working on his bike a form of therapy, a communion with something greater than himself. "The Buddha, the Godhead, resides quite as comfortably in the circuits of a digital computer or the gears of a cycle transmission as he does at the top of a mountain or in the petals of a flower," he writes.

I didn't used to, but somewhere along the line I started to enjoy the mechanical aspect of owning a bike. Now I perform most of my own maintenance, and I've always managed to keep my bikes running. Believe me, if I can do it, you can do it. Whether you are a mechanical savant like Pirsig or a ham-fisted doofus, with a little patience, a little knowledge, a lot of practice, and, of course, some tools, you can do most of the things required to keep your bike on the road. In this chapter, I tell you how.

This chapter deals with routine maintenance, while Chapter 17 deals with repairing your bike if it breaks down. Many of the procedures used in routine maintenance are the same as those used to repair your bike, so use the two chapters together.

Tools of the Trade

Unless you own a Harley-Davidson, your bike will most likely come with a toolkit. This may be located under the seat, behind a side cover, or in a special compartment.

MOTORCYCOLOGY

The tips of screwdrivers are called *blades*. Like knife blades, they get dull and rounded off over time. When that happens, you're likely to strip screws. When the tips of your screwdrivers get dull, replace them.

Some bikes don't come with standard toolkits. Although BMW equips its bikes with high-quality toolkits, standard toolkits are usually poor, most often made of something that looks like metal, but is in fact more like cheese. These are best left for emergency situations, or left completely unused for resale value considerations. When you do maintenance at home, you'll want to equip yourself with a real set of tools. At the very least, you'll want to have these tools:

- **Air-pressure gauge.** Buy a gauge of good quality, and keep it clean so that it provides you with an accurate reading.

- **Wrench set.** Buy the highest-quality set of wrenches you can possibly afford—cheap ones will bend, crack, and break. The most versatile wrenches are combination wrenches. These have an open-end and a box-end (fully enclosed) spanner at either end. Harleys use SAE standard fasteners (the type of fasteners used by most American manufacturing firms, measured in inches rather than millimeters), so get a standard set of wrenches if you buy a Harley. Most other bikes use metric fasteners.

- **Allen wrench set.** Many fasteners on motorcycles use Allen-head bolts instead of traditional hex-head bolts. This means the bolts are turned by an Allen wrench—a wrench you insert in the center of the bolt instead of around the edges. As with regular wrenches, get a standard set for a Harley and a metric set for everything else.

- **Screwdrivers.** You will need flat-blade and Phillips screwdrivers in a variety of sizes. As with all your tools, you will find that your work goes much better if you buy high-quality screwdrivers.

- **Ratchet and sockets.** These will become your most used tools, so, once again, get the best set you can afford. For motorcycles, get a set with a ³⁄₈-inch drive ratchet, with as many different size sockets as you can. Again, Harley takes standard; most everything else takes metric. Make sure that your new socket set includes an appropriate spark plug socket.

- **Pliers.** It's useful to have several types of pliers. Basic pliers work in a variety of situations, but you'll also need to get a pair of needle-nose pliers—the kind that look like they're made from a hummingbird's beak. These are useful when working in tight places (motorcycles are covered in them) and with small objects (those, too). I also like to have a pair of Channellock or adjustable pliers. You can use these for everything from holding odd-size large bolts to removing oil filters when your filter wrench won't fit.

- **Oil-filter wrench.** These wrenches come in several varieties. Get one that best fits around your particular oil filter—that is, if your motorcycle *has* a spin-on filter.

- **Soft-face mallet.** You will sometimes need it to convince an obstinate part to move. The soft face will prevent you from damaging the obstinate part—even though you may want to damage it in the heat of the moment.

- **Lubricants.** You'll need to have some kind of penetrating spray lubricant on hand to loosen tight bolts. If you have a chain-driven motorcycle, you'll also need special lubricants and cleaners for your chain.

- **Funnels.** You're going to need at least a few different-size funnels on hand. Get one small funnel for filling awkwardly located hydraulic master cylinders, a larger one with a longer spout for filling oil, and a fairly large one with a screen in the spout for filling gasoline.

- **Containers.** You'll need to get a gas can and some sort of pan to catch oil in when you change your oil and filter. This container should be large enough to hold at least 5 quarts of oil, yet be shallow enough to fit under your bike when it is on its centerstand.

- **Stool.** More than one weekend mechanic has suffered debilitating nerve damage from squatting in one position for too long while working on a bike.

STEER CLEAR

Before you change your oil, make certain that you know where you can dispose of the used oil. It's illegal and unsafe to dump the oil or spread it on a road. Some areas provide certified oil-recycling stations. Usually, service stations or drive-in oil-change places have large waste-oil storage capabilities. If you ask nicely down at the local oil-change shop or auto-parts store, they may let you dump your waste oil in with theirs. Just remember not to make a mess and to clean up afterward, or you won't be welcome back.

The Essential Shop Manual

A new bike will come with an owner's manual; used bikes may or may not come with one.

But if you're serious about performing your own maintenance, your best bet is to buy an actual shop manual for your bike. These manuals, designed as guides for authorized dealer mechanics, are specific to your bike and generally tell you the best way to perform each procedure. These manuals are expensive, but they will save you money in the long run.

If you buy a used bike that is no longer in production, you might not be able to find a shop manual. In such cases, your best bet is to buy one of the aftermarket manuals from publishers such as Clymer or Haynes; these are readily available in bookstores or on the Internet. If you can't find a manual for your exact model, you should be able to find one for another bike using the same family of engine. This isn't an ideal solution, but it's better than nothing.

Keeping the Shiny Side Up: Supporting the Bike

Before doing any work on your bike, make certain it's securely positioned. If your bike has a centerstand, use it for procedures (such as changing oil and tightening the chain) that don't require you to remove any heavy parts from the bike.

If you need to remove heavy parts, such as wheels and tires, you'll need to find another method of supporting the bike because when you remove the parts, you'll change the weight distribution of the bike, upsetting the balance on the centerstand. You'll also need to use an alternative method of supporting the bike if it's not equipped with a centerstand.

I use a variety of materials to support my bikes, depending on the bike. I've created stable stands by using cinderblocks with two-by-fours as buffers to keep from damaging the parts under my bike. The key is to make certain that your blocking is stable.

STEER CLEAR

If your bike has a fairing that extends around the bottom of the engine, remove this before placing your bike on any kind of support. The plastic cowling isn't strong enough to support the bike and will break under the machine's weight.

Some companies sell special motorcycle lifts. While these are expensive, a good lift is your safest, most secure method of supporting your bike while you work on it. Some companies sell rear-end stands that prop a bike up by the swingarm, just like the racers use. These are great and fairly affordable.

Oil: Your Bike's Blood

Oil serves three purposes in your bike's engine:

- Oil reduces friction and wear, making all internal parts move more smoothly and efficiently.

- Oil dissipates heat. It carries heat away from the moving parts of an engine as it flows over them. On some bikes, oil is sprayed on the hottest parts of an engine, such as the underside of the piston domes, to enhance heat dissipation.

- Oil cleans the inside of your engine. The inside of your engine is filled with metal parts that rub together at tremendous speeds, causing microscopic particles of metal to shear off. These particles are suspended in the oil and then eventually trapped in your oil filter.

Two-stroke engines use oil differently than four-stroke engines (see Chapter 6). In a two-stroke, the oil enters the engine with the air/fuel charge and is burned up and eliminated with the exhaust, causing the characteristic blue smoke coming from the exhaust pipe. This is why the EPA isn't very fond of two-strokes.

Four-strokes circulate their oil, using either a dry-sump system, in which the oil is stored in an external container, or a wet-sump system, in which the oil is contained in the engine's crankcase. Most bikes use wet-sump systems.

Checking the Oil Level

On a two-stroke, you'll need to check the oil level every day because two-strokes are designed to burn oil. On a modern, properly running four-stroke, though, you need to check the oil level only two or three times a week. If you have a bike that uses lots of oil, check more often.

On two-strokes and dry-sump four-strokes, you'll check the oil level in the external tank, usually located either beneath the seat or within the frame itself (although on some late-model Harleys, the tank is down by the transmission). On a wet-sump four-stroke, you'll check the oil level at the bottom of the engine.

In all cases, you'll either check by looking at the level on the dipstick (a flat blade connected to the filler cap), by looking into a sight glass (a window into the tank), or by removing a small level plug and watching to see if oil drips out. The sight-glass method is much easier and less messy. Just make sure that the motorcycle is positioned properly before checking your oil. Most bikes need to be positioned vertically for an accurate oil level reading, so if you take your reading on the sidestand, you'll be miles off.

MOTORCYCOLOGY

When you are checking oil, your bike should be in an upright position (unless otherwise stated in the owner's manual). On bikes without centerstands, this means you need two people: one to support the bike and the other to check the oil.

Another thing to keep in mind is that most bikes require you to simply rest the cap in the hole to get an accurate reading on the dipstick, rather than requiring that you screw the cap down. Your owner's manual will tell you which method to use.

If the oil level gets down near the add mark, fill the tank back up to the full mark, but be careful. It usually takes much less oil than you might imagine to fill the tank to the full mark, and overfilling your tank can cause as many problems as running it too low. Pour in a small amount and then recheck the level. Keep doing this until you reach the full mark.

Changing Oil

The single most important thing you can do to ensure a long engine life for your motorcycle is to perform regular oil changes. As you ride your bike, two things happen to your oil:

- The molecules in the oil break apart, causing the oil to lose its lubricating properties.

- The oil gets contaminated with the microscopic particles that wear away from the parts inside your engine, causing the oil to become more abrasive.

MOTORCYCOLOGY

Recent friction-modifying additives used in some automotive oils may damage your clutch, so you should use motorcycle-specific oil. Most motorcycle clutches are referred to as "wet" clutches because, unlike car clutches, they are located inside the engine cases and are thus bathed in engine oil. While this constant oil bath helps your bike clutch run cool and last longer, oil containing friction modifiers may also make the clutch slip.

Here's how to change your oil:

1. **Drain the oil.** Locate the drain plug, which is somewhere on the bottom of the engine on wet-sump systems (the location varies with dry sumps), and place your pan-shape container under the plug. When you remove the plug (usually a hex-head bolt), the oil will come out with some force, so take that into account when placing the pan.

2. **Remove the filter.** Change the filter every time you change the oil. There are two basic types of modern filters—the cartridge type, which has a replaceable filter element located inside a recess in the engine case or inside a canister attached to the engine, and the spin-on type, which spins on and off like an automotive oil filter.

   When removing a canister-type filter, be extremely careful not to strip the fastener(s) holding the canister or cover plate on, and thoroughly clean the area around the canister or cover plate before removal. There will be a spring and perhaps also some metal washers inside the canister to hold the filter in place. Note their location for when you install the new filter, and be careful not to lose the spring or the washers. After you remove the old filter, wipe out the inside of the canister or recess with a clean rag. When choosing a rag for this purpose, be aware that any dirt or grit living on the rag may soon be living inside your engine, where it can do serious harm.

3. **Clean and replace the drain plug when the engine is done draining.** Some drain plugs have a magnetic tip to collect metal shavings from inside the engine. Thoroughly clean the tip before replacing the plug. Most drain

plugs have an aluminum or copper crush washer to enhance the plug's seal. Make certain that you don't lose this washer when removing the plug. Also make certain that the surface of the engine is clean before you replace the plug/washer combo.

Canister filter

Filter cover

Oil seal

Spin-on filter

A spin-on oil filter is much more convenient to change than a canister-type filter.

4. **Replace the filter.** With a spin-on filter, lightly smear a drop or two of clean oil around the rubber seal attached to the new filter before mounting it, to create an oil-tight seal between the filter and engine. Do not overtighten.

   A canister-type filter will come with a rubber O-ring seal for the canister or cover. Make certain to use a new O-ring with each change. When you have the seal in place, lightly smear it with a drop or two of clean oil, making sure you don't get any foreign material on the O-ring, before replacing the canister. Mount the new filter inside the canister or recess, making certain to assemble the spring and washers correctly. And when tightening the fastener(s), be extra careful not to strip the threads. Because of the spring holding the filter in place within the canister, it is easy to get the canister slightly askew when mounting it, which could lead to thread misalignment. If you encounter the slightest resistance when replacing the fastener(s), make certain that everything is aligned before proceeding.

5. **Fill with fresh, clean oil,** using the recommendations in your owner's manual for the type of oil and the amount. Next, restart your engine to pump oil into the filter. Be extra careful when doing this, and don't rev the throttle any more than is necessary because your engine will not be properly lubricated upon start-up. Let the engine idle for about a minute, then shut it off and recheck the oil level. It will have gone down because of the oil pumped into the filter, so refill to the full mark on the dipstick.

STEER CLEAR

Drain the oil when the engine is hot because then the oil will be less viscous and will drain completely. This creates a challenge because the oil will be scalding hot, as will the engine and other components. Wear disposable latex gloves and be especially careful to avoid touching the exhaust pipes, which can cause nasty burns.

After you have changed the oil, keep a close watch on the oil level, and visually check for leaks around the drain plug and filter. An oil leak on your motorcycle is much worse than an oil leak on a car. If you've got an oil drip, it'll be flung straight onto your back tire as you ride. Not surprisingly, oil does not improve a tire's traction, so nobody with any sense lets their bike continuously leak oil.

The most likely source for an oil leak is around the filter in a canister-type unit. If you get even a small particle of foreign material between the rubber seal and the engine, you might notice leakage from the canister. This will only get worse. If this happens, you need to get a new rubber seal and do the whole thing over again.

Air Filters: Clearing the Sinuses

Air filters prevent dust and dirt from getting sucked into your engine, but over time they become plugged up with all that dust and dirt. When this happens, your bike doesn't get enough air to properly mix with the fuel charge entering your engine, leading to poor performance and increased gas consumption. Air filters are made of paper or foam. Foam filters must be saturated with special oil. Filters are located in a bike's airbox, an air chamber connected to the carburetors. When a filter becomes clogged, you have to replace it (if it is a paper type) or clean it (if it is made of foam).

First, you need to remove the filter. On modern bikes, the airbox is usually located under the gas tank or under the seat. See your owner's manual for the removal procedure, because it varies with each model of bike.

Next, replace a paper filter, or clean and re-oil a foam filter according to your owner's manual's instructions. Afterward, replace the filter.

MOTORCYCOLOGY

Replacing a stock paper air filter with a quality aftermarket filter can noticeably improve your bike's performance if it has a fuel-injection system that can compensate for the increased airflow. If your bike has carburetors, though, a freer-flowing aftermarket filter can cause some problems. To meet EPA emissions requirements, many bikes have carburetors that mix more air with the fuel charge than is optimal for combustion. This reduces emissions, but it also decreases performance and causes the engine to run hotter than before. By using an aftermarket filter, you increase the airflow even more, which can raise engine temperatures to dangerous levels, especially on an air-cooled bike. Because of this, it might be a good idea to have a qualified mechanic rejet (insert new parts that increase the flow of gasoline) your carburetors if you want to install an aftermarket air filter. But make sure to verify that this is legal to do in your state first.

Batteries: An Electrifying Experience

Batteries are one area in which motorcycle technology has more than kept pace with automotive technology. Motorcycle batteries need far less attention. Indeed, most bikes these days come with sealed batteries that need no—as in none, zero—maintenance. Your manual should tell you what type of battery your bike has.

Now, locating the battery might very well be a problem. Batteries used to be located under a bike's seat, but now you can find them anywhere, from up by the headlight to back by the swingarm. Consult your manual.

If you have the old-style battery that requires periodic filling, check the electrolyte level by looking at the side of the battery. The battery case is made of translucent plastic, allowing you to see the level of the fluid inside. If the level is slightly low, add distilled water.

Several things can cause extremely low electrolyte levels. Your battery may have cracked or in some way come apart and is leaking, in which case you'll need to replace it immediately. Or you may have tipped the bike over or leaned it far enough for the electrolyte to drip out the overflow tube at the top of the battery. Or your charging system may be malfunctioning, overcharging your battery and evaporating the fluid. If you suspect charging-system problems and you're not a skilled mechanic, it's probably time to take the bike in for professional help.

Keeping Cool

Today most bikes use some sort of supplemental cooling system. Some bikes may have an external oil radiator. Others may use a liquid-cooling system similar to that found in most cars. The liquid-cooling system is the most common on today's street-bikes and requires some maintenance on your part.

STEER CLEAR

Be extra careful about what kind of antifreeze you use in your motorcycle. Automotive antifreeze contains silica, an abrasive designed to keep the cooling system polished inside. This abrasive can damage a motorcycle's water pump, leading to engine failure and expensive repairs.

At least once a week, you should check your coolant level. Usually, you do this by checking your overflow tank, a white plastic tank located in a position remote from the radiator. When you do this, you should also give your radiator hoses a visual inspection, looking for cracks and leaks. If you need to fill the system with coolant, use a mixture of motorcycle-specific antifreeze and distilled water, as recommended in your owner's manual. Every couple of years, you should replace the coolant.

Chain Maintenance

If you have a chain-driven motorcycle, maintaining your chain will become your most frequently performed chore. You'll probably need to adjust the tension of the chain, clean it, and lubricate it roughly twice a month (more often if you put a lot of miles on your bike).

Checking the Tension

To check the tension, grasp the lower run of the chain (not the upper one hidden by the chainguard) about halfway between the front and rear sprockets, and move the chain up and down. As they don't wear evenly, check several spots on the chain by rolling the bike ahead and rechecking the tension. If the amount the chain moves varies from spot to spot, the chain may have a tight spot. If the chain moves up and down more than about an inch in the tightest spot, it needs to be tightened. If the movement is severe enough, you may need to replace the chain. I'll tell you how to do that in Chapter 17.

Check the tension along the chain's lower run, about halfway between the front and rear sprockets.

Adjusting the Chain

To adjust the chain, place the bike on the centerstand (rest it on its sidestand if you have no centerstand) and recheck the chain's tension. Once on the centerstand, your chain's tension may vary from when you first checked it because the bike's weight is now off the suspension. Take this difference into account when adjusting the chain. If you adjust the chain to its proper tension on the centerstand, it may become too tight when off the centerstand, and a too-tight chain can break and shoot off your bike like a slinky missile.

Loosen the axle nut (or nuts, if there is more than one). You will have to remove a security pin on most bikes when undoing the axle nut. Once the nut is loose, you can adjust the chain. You do this by adjusting some bolts on the very end of the swingarm, one on either side of the wheel. Usually, there will be two hex-heads on each bolt—an inner nut to move the axle, and an outer nut to lock the other in place when finished. Loosen the outer nuts and then carefully adjust the inner nuts, moving the nuts on either side of the wheel an equal amount. It is vital that you adjust the adjuster nut on the left as much as the nut on the right side; otherwise you'll be making your back wheel sit completely wonky.

When you have tightened your chain by the desired amount, tighten down the outside nuts. Retighten the axle nut, and insert a new security pin.

Loosen but don't remove the axle bolt. Make certain to adjust the bolts on each side of the wheel the exact same amount. Don't overtighten the chain.

The procedure for adjusting your chain varies from bike to bike, but most bikes use something similar to this method. Some bikes have a bolt on the back of the swingarm, with the locking nut between the bolt and the swingarm. A few bikes, especially modern sportbikes with single-sided swingarms, use an eccentric cam on the axle to adjust chain tension. See your owner's manual for the procedure for adjusting these types of chains.

Cleaning and Lubricating Your Chain

To get the most use out of a chain, you'll need to keep it clean and lubricated. Most bikes now use longer-lasting O-ring chains (chains with internal lubricant kept in place by tiny rubber seals), but these still need surface lubrication. The problem with O-ring chains is that many substances degrade rubber O-rings, including common lubricants and cleaning solvents. Use only cleaners and lubricants approved for use on O-ring chains.

You might clean your chain every few rides, but you should be lubricating it after every single ride. It's best to lube it after a ride, not before, because after a ride the chain is nice and hot, meaning the lube will penetrate into the links more deeply.

To clean a chain, put on some old clothes, and place an O-ring-approved cleaner on a soft brush. Use that to clean the grime off the chain. When you've got all the crud off, wipe the chain dry before applying fresh lubricant. This is a messy, dirty, frustrating job, but it greatly increases chain life, and chains and sprockets are extremely expensive.

To lubricate your chain, aim the spray from the can of lubricant at the inside of the chain while rotating the wheel to evenly coat the chain's entire length. Like all motorcycle maintenance, this is infinitely easier if you have a centerstand. As lubricant and tires don't make a good combination (you could lube yourself right off the back of your bike) it's wise to protect the back tire while you spray on the chain lube. Holding a newspaper between the chain and the tire works fine.

Motorcycle drive chains last much longer than they did just a few years ago, but they also cost a lot more than they used to. And they still wear out. Add in the cost of replacing drive sprockets (which are usually replaced at the same time as the chain), and you're looking at spending $200 to $300.

With good chain adjustment and lubrication, I've regularly gone through two chains before my sprockets needed replacement. That's a good incentive to look after your chain! You can also minimize wear on your chain by not beating on your bike. The harder you accelerate, the more you stretch your chain.

Shaft Maintenance

Although shaft drive systems require much less maintenance than chain drives, you will need to change the oil in the rear gearcase assembly on the back wheel once or twice a year. This is a simple process. Drain the old oil by removing the drain plug at the bottom of the housing, replace the plug, and refill the housing back to the recommended level by removing a plug at the top of the housing and pouring the correct gear oil in there. Gear oil is extremely heavy oil (usually 80W) that you can buy at nearly all motorcycle dealerships. To check the oil level, remove the filler plug and visually check the level.

Filling oil in the gearcase a couple of times a year is far easier than cleaning, lubing, and adjusting your chain.

Cleaning Up

Some of us clean our bikes obsessively, while others prefer to let the grime accumulate. Sooner or later, though, even the grubbiest motorcycle needs a bath. Even if you like your bike grubby, it's a good idea to clean it once in a while, if for no other reason than that cleaning allows you to inspect the bike thoroughly, checking for fluid leaks, loose bolts, and other problems.

Don't use pressure washers on your bike, because many delicate parts are more exposed on a motorcycle than on a car. A pressure washer can force dirt and grime between seals, causing bearing failures and other problems. Instead, get a large bucket of warm, soapy water; a sponge; a soft brush; a chamois; and a bunch of soft towels and rags, and wash your bike by hand. It's not that hard if you follow the proper procedure:

1. **Degrease the bike.** Apply degreaser to the grimiest parts of the bike—such as the engine, wheels, and swingarm—with a soft brush. A hard brush may scratch painted surfaces.

2. **Wash the bike with soap and water.** Wash the bike from top to bottom with the sponge, making certain that you wash off all the degreaser. Use a small brush (such as a toothbrush) to get in those hard-to-reach places. Wipe the bike dry with the chamois cloth.

3. **Polish the bike.** Use chrome polish on chromed metal surfaces (but not chromed plastic surfaces because the polish may melt the plastic). Every so often, use a light polish to buff out the paint, but don't use this every time you wash because it takes off a thin layer of paint with every use.

4. **Wax the bike.** Apply a hard wax to the painted bodywork and buff it out until it shines. This is especially important after polishing the paint because the polish softens the paint and the wax protects it. Apply a light coat of lubricant, like WD-40 (though again, keep it away from your tires) to unpainted metal surfaces to prevent erosion.

On Ice: Storing Your Bike

Winter storage is the worst part of owning a bike. It's not difficult, but it means you won't be able to ride until spring. First, clean the bike so that it doesn't corrode over the winter. Make certain that the bike is dry before storing it. Change the engine oil and replace the oil filter just as you normally would.

Drain the carburetor float bowls by turning off the fuel petcock and running the bike until the engine dies. You can also drain the float bowls by opening their drain screws, which are located at the bottom of each carburetor's float bowl, but be careful not to let gas drip onto hot surfaces. Fill the fuel tank to the very top; this prevents corrosion from forming on the inner surfaces of the gas tank. Finally, add a fuel-stabilizing additive to the tank. Alternatively, you could completely empty the fuel tank and then spray the inside of the fuel tank with a rust inhibitor.

Unscrew the spark plugs and pour in a single tablespoon of clean engine oil. Using either the electric starter or the kick-starter, spin the engine over a few times to spread the oil around. Inflate the tires to their recommended pressures, and, if possible, place the motorcycle on blocks so the tires are off the ground. Finally, remove the battery and store it in a warm place, and your bike is ready for winter.

In the spring, you'll need to replace the battery, refill the float bowls by turning the fuel petcock to the On or Prime position, and again change the oil. If you've done everything right, your bike should start right up.

The Least You Need to Know

- Buy quality tools—it's less expensive in the long run than buying cheap tools.
- Before working on your bike, make certain it's properly supported so that it doesn't fall on you.
- Don't use automotive antifreeze in a motorcycle.
- Overtightening your chain can cause as many problems as not tightening it at all.
- Clean your bike regularly and store it carefully.

Rx: Repair

In This Chapter

- Deciding whether to take your bike in or fix it yourself
- Saving money by removing your own wheels
- Fixing potentially dangerous brake problems
- Replacing your chain and sprockets

In this chapter, I tell you about more in-depth repair procedures than I went over in Chapter 16. I explain how to perform the most common repairs you will encounter, such as changing tires, replacing brake pads, bleeding brake lines, and replacing chains and sprockets. On most bikes, the procedures generally follow those I outline here. There will be minor differences, which is why you'll also need a repair manual. For more specific repairs, you're going to have to rely solely on your repair manual.

If you can master working on your own bike, you will attain new levels of freedom and autonomy. And you'll save a pile of money. But mastering these procedures will take much time and effort on your part. You'll need to invest in the proper tools. You'll need a safe place to work. And you'll need patience.

Take It In or Do It Yourself?

Should you take your bike in to have someone else work on it, or should you do the work yourself?

A lot of that decision depends on whether you can find a shop you trust. (As I mentioned in Chapter 7, you should have done your research on this before you bought your bike.) A good, trustworthy shop will have trained mechanics with the right tools for every situation. But a bad shop can bung up your bike worse than you could yourself—and then charge you a lot of money for it.

MOTORCYCOLOGY

Remember that properly supporting your bike is even more important when performing the repairs in this chapter than it was when performing the maintenance procedures in Chapter 16.

If you learn to do the work yourself, you'll never be at the mercy of some shop's schedule for getting your bike fixed. And you'll develop skills that could prove valuable in an emergency. But you'll also have to buy a lot of expensive equipment.

There are benefits to both methods of repair. Ultimately, you'll be the only person who can decide which method is best for you.

Where the Rubber Meets the Road: Tires

Tires are one of the items you need to inspect each time you ride. Look over your tires each morning, checking for cracks, cuts, irregular swelling, and objects such as shards of glass or nails embedded in the tread. Check tire wear—a tire that looks okay one morning can be noticeably worn the next, especially if you've been riding hard or the air temperature has been high (tires wear faster when the pavement is hot).

Worn tires impair your bike's handling, especially in the rain, and are more likely to suffer catastrophic failure than newer tires. Your tires should have wear bars that appear as the tires age, but chances are, your tires' performance and safety will have begun to deteriorate long before the wear bars appear. Tires wear down the middle first, and as much as many of us love to corner, the reality is that modern roads require us to ride straight, a lot. When they're really worn in the center, they'll start to resist when you try and lean the bike over.

Get in the habit of checking the air pressure in your cold tires before each ride. A sudden loss of air indicates a potentially serious problem. Minor fluctuations in air pressure are normal and are often caused by changes in the air temperature. If your air pressure is a little low, inflate the tire until it reaches the pressure recommended in your owner's manual. If it is drastically low, examine the tread for a hidden nail or some other object that may have punctured the tire.

If a tire is punctured, repair is possible. You can patch a tube or put a plug in a tube-less tire, but I don't recommend either maneuver, except as a way to get your bike to a repair shop. The consequences of a blowout are too great. Replacing a tire or an inner tube is much cheaper than undergoing months of painful physical therapy.

Removing the Rear Wheel

If you need a tire replaced, you should let a repair shop with the proper equipment do the job. That equipment is too specialized and too expensive for most amateur mechanics to have in their own shops, and the consequences of incorrectly mounting a modern tire are too great. But when you need to change a tire, you can save a lot of money by removing the wheels yourself and bringing the wheel assembly into a shop.

MOTORCYCOLOGY

When removing the axle, make certain that you are passing the axle through the swingarm in the correct direction. Many axles have a big end on one side and a securing nut on the other. If the axle won't move in the direction you are tapping, or if it stops moving abruptly, make certain that you're not trying to push it through the swingarm in the wrong direction.

The method for removing motorcycle wheels differs with each bike, depending on the method of securing the axle, the drive system, and the brake system. Some bikes require the disassembly of suspension components or bodywork. The method described here is for a chain-driven motorcycle with disc brakes. Consult your repair manual for specific details.

1. **Remove the axle.** To do this, remove the split pin securing the axle nut in place, and then undo the nut. Some axles may have additional pinch bolts securing them in place that aren't obvious upon first inspection of the assembly. Make certain that you have loosened or removed all bolts holding the axle in place, and gently tap the axle through the swingarm with a soft-face mallet, which helps protect the axle threads from damage.

   Once you have the axle past one side of the swingarm, it should move freely through the wheel. A couple of things may hinder its progress. If the chain is too tight, it may pull the wheel forward, causing the axle to bind. If this is the case, loosen the axle adjustment bolts, being careful to adjust the bolts on both sides an equal amount. If the wheel falls down a bit after you move the axle through one side of the swingarm, it will also cause the axle to bind. You may have to support the wheel with your knee while removing the axle to prevent this.

Some bikes will require you to unhook the rear shocks from the swingarm, allowing it to drop low enough for the axle to clear the exhaust pipes. In extreme cases, you may have to remove the exhaust pipes entirely.

Be gentle when tapping the axle through the swingarm. If it takes more than a light tap, chances are, something has not been properly loosened.

2. **Next, remove the wheel.** Remove the spacers between the wheel and the swingarm, making notes of their location. To help remember their locations for reassembly, I lay them out on a shop towel, along with the axle, in the exact order they go on the bike. Push the wheel forward and unhook the chain when there is enough slack. Move the chain away from the wheel. You may need to remove the chainguard to allow you to move the chain free of the wheel.

You may have to remove some items to get the tire to clear the swingarm.

On shaft-drive bikes, wheel removal is usually easier than on chain-driven bikes. The main difference is that you pull the wheel away from the pinion housing to unhook it from the drive system rather than pushing it forward and removing the chain.

You may have to undo the brake caliper to make room to remove the wheel. If you have to do so, hold the caliper while you remove the wheel, and then make certain that it is securely supported until reassembly. Don't let the caliper hang by its hose.

3. **When you have had the tire changed and the wheel balanced, reassemble by reversing the process.** Don't forget to install a new split pin to lock the axle bolt in place. Make certain that everything is properly assembled before riding, and stop to check all the bolts frequently the first few times you go riding.

 STEER CLEAR

Never ride hard just after you have mounted new tires. New tires are horribly slippery for the first few dozen miles, so ride with extra caution while breaking them in. At first, they may have less traction than the ones you just replaced.

Removing the Front Wheel

Removing the front wheel is similar to removing the rear wheel, except that it's a bit easier because you don't have a drive system to deal with or a swingarm to work around. You may have to remove a speedometer cable, though.

Because you won't have to work around a swingarm or drive system, the front wheel is easier to remove than the rear wheel on most bikes.

To remove the wheel, first unhook the speedometer cable, if necessary. Then remove the axle. On many bikes, the easiest way to do this is to undo the end caps at the bottom of the fork, allowing the axle along with the entire wheel-tire assembly to drop out the bottom. If it works that way, simply roll the tire ahead, remove the axle nut, and pull the axle out. Other bikes require you to remove the axle nut and push the axle through the wheel to remove the assembly, much as I discussed doing with the rear wheel. Either way, note the location of any spacers between the wheel and the fork.

You may have to remove the brake calipers to remove the front wheel. If so, make certain that you don't let them hang by their hoses. While your front wheel is off, don't operate the front brake lever; if you do, the brake pads will close in on each other, making it very hard to fit the brake rotors between the brake pads during reassembly.

To reassemble, just reverse the procedure.

Tires can prove to be major wallet drainers. Motorcycle tires cost much more than their automotive counterparts, approaching $300 apiece for premium sport radials. And they won't last nearly as long as a car tire. A person who logs a lot of miles can easily expect to run through at least one set of tires per year.

A Screeching Halt: Brakes

In all my years of riding, I've seen only two people get killed in motorcycle accidents, both on a racetrack. One of them was killed when his front brake lever came off. This illustrates just how important your brakes are. If even the least complicated part of the system fails, it could cost you your life.

There are two kinds of brakes: *disc brakes* and *drum brakes*. Most modern bikes use disc brakes in front. Many also use disc brakes in back, but some still use drum rear brakes. Disc brakes slow your motorcycle by squeezing pistons inside a caliper, which is attached to your frame or fork and doesn't rotate, against a disc attached to your wheel, slowing both the disc and the wheel it is attached to. Drum brakes work by expanding the brake shoes—stationary, crescent-shaped devices inside your wheel hub—against the inner surface of the hub, which is part of the rotating wheel.

With disc brakes, you will need to periodically change the brake pads, which are metal-backed fiber pads located at the ends of the pistons in the calipers. These pads are the surfaces that actually contact the brake disc, and they wear down over time. With drum brakes, you will need to replace the shoes as they wear down.

CYCLE BABBLE

Many bikes use a combination of **disc brakes** on the front and **drum brakes** on the rear. This combination is especially common on cruisers. Disc brakes use stationary calipers that squeeze pads against discs that rotate with the wheel, while drum brakes use crescent-shaped brake shoes that expand against the inner surface of the wheel hub.

Checking Brake Pads

The procedure for checking pad wear varies according to the design of the caliper. Some allow you to simply look between the caliper and the disc, but many designs have a cover on top of the caliper that can be pried off with a screwdriver. This gives you a clear view of the pads. Some designs require you to remove the caliper entirely to inspect the pads.

If the brake-pad material is wearing thin, it is time to replace the pads. Sometimes the material will change in texture over time, especially if the pads have been subjected to extreme heat or some contaminant. If you notice a decrease in your brakes' performance, you should replace the pads, even if they appear to have enough material on them.

On many calipers, you can visually inspect the pads by popping off a cover on the top of the caliper with a pair of pliers.

Replacing Brake Pads

Again, the procedure for replacing brake pads varies from caliper to caliper, so the instructions presented here are *just a general guide.*

STEER CLEAR

When the caliper is removed from the disc, or when you remove the pads from the caliper, do not squeeze the brake lever. Also be careful not to contaminate the caliper or pads with brake fluid, oil, or dirt because this can cause your brakes to malfunction.

On some designs, the correct procedure doesn't require you to remove the calipers. Others require you to do so. This is usually accomplished by removing the two bolts holding the caliper to its carrier or to a fork leg. However you do it, make sure you keep all the parts scrupulously, surgically clean, including the brake pads themselves, the master cylinder caps, and the caps' rubber diaphragms. Most manufacturers sell their own brand of aerosol cleaners and lubricants, usually including something for cleaning ignition contact points or brake parts. Use it as freely as you would water.

The pads are held in place by pins that pass through the caliper body. The pins are retained by some sort of clip or by a split pin. First remove the clip or pin, being careful not to lose any pieces; they don't come with the new pads. When you are unfamiliar with the procedure, it helps to take notes or digital pictures to remind you of the order in which you removed parts.

Remove the pads with a pair of pliers, and insert the new pads. Because your new pads will be thicker than the old, worn pads, you may have to ease the pistons back into the calipers. This should require little force. If you need to use something to push a piston back in the caliper, use something soft, such as a wooden stick, instead of a metal object, such as a screwdriver, because the metal can damage seals and the surface of the piston.

While the pads are out, visually inspect the pistons' dust seals for any tears.

After you have inserted the pads, simply reverse this procedure, referring to your notes or photos for the correct order of assembly. If your brake uses clips to retain the pad pins, you can reuse those. If you have a split pin retaining the pins, use new split pins instead of reusing the old ones.

Because the old pads were worn, you may have to move the pistons back into the calipers when replacing brake pads.

MOTORCYCOLOGY

A certain amount of grooving in the disc surface is natural, but if it becomes too grooved, braking performance can diminish and pad wear can accelerate. The only repair for a grooved disc on a bike is replacement, an expensive proposition.

When you check your brake pads, you should also check your discs (these are the metal rotors the caliper presses the pads against). If you replace your pads before they become too worn, your discs should last a long time. But if your pads wear down too far, they can damage the discs. You can check your disc by looking at it and feeling its surface for irregularities.

Checking Shoes

The only way to check the brake shoes is to remove the wheel from the bike, which I explained earlier in this chapter. After you remove the wheel, pull the backing plate from the brake drum. This should be so loose that it will fall off on its own if you tip the wheel upside down—but don't do that, because the fall could damage the brakes.

The springs holding the brake shoes in place are strong, so be careful not to pinch your fingers when removing and replacing shoes.

It's difficult to judge the wear of the brake shoes by visual inspection, because you really don't know what they are supposed to look like. Rely on your manual to provide you with information on acceptable shoe-wear limits.

Replacing Shoes

The brake shoes are held in place by strong springs, as well as clips on some designs. Remove the clip, and squeeze the brakes together to release the tension on the springs. Remove the springs and lift the shoes out. Install the new brake shoes by reversing the procedure. Just as with replacing disc-brake pads, keep everything frighteningly clean.

Two strong springs hold the brake shoes in place.

MOTORCYCOLOGY

The distance between the rear wheel and the engine varies slightly as the bike moves up and down on its suspension. The rear-wheel assembly is sprung— that is, it moves with the suspension. This is why you need to leave some free play in components connected to both the rear wheel and the frame or engine, like the rear drum-brake lever and the drive chain.

Adjusting your brake levers can decrease your reaction time in an emergency, saving your life.

Brake-Lever Adjustment

Many bikes come with adjustable brake and clutch levers, items that improve both comfort and safety because they allow you to react more quickly in an emergency. Some handlebar levers adjust by rotating a numbered dial located at the lever pivot.

The pedal angle on your foot brake often is also adjustable, and finding the proper angle can make a huge difference in your reaction time and your riding comfort. On drum rear brakes, the angle is usually adjusted by a movable stop, a bolt located near the rear of the pedal. This bolt usually has a lock nut similar to that used on the rear-axle adjusting bolt. On disc rear brakes, the adjusting bolt will be part of the lever connecting the brake pedal to the master cylinder, and it works in much the same way as a drum-brake lever adjuster.

On drum brakes, you will have an adjustment for free play located on the lever that actuates the brake shoes. You will need to tighten the nut on the end of the connecting rod as the brake shoes wear. Be careful not to overtighten the free play, or suspension motion might accidentally activate the brake. You need to keep enough free play to allow the bike to move up and down on its suspension without activating the brake.

A Bloody Mess: Bleeding the Brake Lines

Disc brakes operate by moving hydraulic fluid from the master cylinder—the reservoir to which the brake lever is connected—to the calipers. The fluid, which comes in several varieties that can't be intermixed (the variety your bike needs is stamped on its master-cylinder reservoir cover), is one of the nastiest substances you will ever encounter. It disintegrates paint and does nasty things to the human body.

It also absorbs water, meaning that if you have a leak in your system, you have to fix it immediately because water makes the fluid mushy and decreases your braking power. Even if you don't have a leak, atmospheric moisture will condense in your brake system over time, so you'll need to replace the fluid every couple of years anyway.

STEER CLEAR

Never use brake fluid from a container that has been opened—it may contain moisture absorbed from the atmosphere. Always use a fresh container. And make certain that you're using the correct type for your brake system. The cover of your master cylinder will be marked DOT 3, DOT 4, DOT 5, or DOT5.1, referring to the type of fluid needed. Use *only* that type of fluid.

After you replace the fluid, you'll need to bleed the air out of the braking system. (Sometimes you'll need to do this even when you don't change the fluid, just to get air out of the system.) This is a messy job that can do damage to both you and your bike, so take your time when performing this procedure. To bleed the brakes, follow these steps:

1. **Remove the reservoir cap at the top of your master cylinder by unscrewing the screws holding it in.** This cap has a rubber diaphragm underneath it. Remove this to expose the fluid. You may want to wrap a cloth around the bottom of the master cylinder to capture leaked fluid before it reaches any painted metal or plastic parts. Keep the reservoir cap and its rubber diaphragm fetishistically clean.

2. **Fill the reservoir with fluid.** Use only fluid from a sealed container (old cans of fluid absorb water from the atmosphere), and use only the fluid your braking system was designed for. Be careful not to spill because the fluid will wreak havoc on the bike's finish. Then replace the diaphragm.

3. **Bleed the brakes.** There will be an odd-looking nipple on your caliper. Put one end of a clear plastic tube over the nipple, and put the other end of the

tube in a jar with some hydraulic fluid inside. Loosen the nipple approximately one turn, and squeeze the brake lever gently, causing fluid to flow through the tube. Tighten the nipple and release the lever. If you see bubbles in the tube, repeat the process until they disappear. Refill the reservoir and refit the rubber diaphragm before squeezing the brake lever. Repeat this procedure for each caliper.

You'll need to have a length of clear plastic tubing on hand to bleed your brakes without making a mess.

Chain and Sprocket Replacement

As mentioned in Chapter 16, modern O-ring chains last much longer than the conventional roller chains used in the past, but they also cost much more to replace. Proper maintenance—keeping the chain clean, well lubricated, and properly adjusted—can significantly increase the life of your chain, but sooner or later, you'll need to replace it. And when you do, you'll often need to replace the sprockets to which the chain is connected.

Chains either have a repair link, also known as a master link or a split link—a link that can be disassembled for chain repair—or else they are of the continuous-loop variety. Replacing a continuous-loop chain requires special tools and is best left to a professional. The following procedure applies to chains with split links.

1. **Clean the chain and sprocket area.** This is the dirtiest, grimiest area on your bike. Cleaning the area will make your job much easier.

2. **Remove anything that blocks access to your sprockets.** You will have to remove the rear wheel and the casing covering the front sprocket. You may also have to remove your chainguard and other items.

3. **Disassemble the chain's repair link.** Using your pliers, squeeze the spring clip off of its pins. Then you can remove the side plate and push the link out the other side. You can now remove the chain.

4. **Remove the sprockets.** The bolts and/or nuts holding the sprockets on will be tight and difficult to remove, and they may also be locked by bendable tabs that require straightening. It might be easier to loosen the bolts on the rear sprocket when the wheel is still mounted on the bike. To do this, have someone apply the rear brake and help stabilize the bike, and break the bolts loose before removing the wheel. Once the bolts and/or nuts holding the sprockets on are removed, you should be able to lift off the sprockets.

The instructions for assembling your chain's split repair link will be provided with the chain.

It might be easier to break loose the bolts on the rear sprocket before removing the rear wheel.

5. **Replace the sprockets and coat the bolt threads with a locking compound, such as Blue Loctite.** Then tighten the bolts to the torque specs in your owner's manual or shop manual. Finally, reinstall the rear wheel assembly.

6. **Put on the new chain.** The new chain will be slightly shorter than the old one (which stretched over time), so you'll need to adjust your rear axle accordingly, remembering to turn the bolts on either side of the wheel evenly to maintain wheel alignment. Place a newspaper under the chain so that it doesn't get dirty if you drop it, and then feed the chain over the rear sprocket, along the top of the swingarm, and then over the front sprocket. This will allow you to connect the chain beneath the swingarm, where you'll have more room to work.

You'll need to loosen the chain adjusters to connect the chain because the new chain will be shorter than the old one. Make certain to move both adjusting bolts the same distance, to retain proper wheel alignment.

7. **Assemble the split/master link with the rubber O-rings.** (The chain's manufacturer will include instructions for doing this with the chain.) Then insert the split link through the two ends of the chain, connecting the chain. Place an O-ring over each exposed pin, put the side plate over the pins, and push the retaining clip over the pins, making certain that the closed end of the clip faces toward the chain's direction of travel. This means that the closed end will be facing the rear sprocket if you're working on the part of the chain that lies under the swingarm.

8. **Adjust the chain to the proper tension,** as described in Chapter 16, and then make certain that all bolts are tight. The chain might require readjusting quite a bit when it is new, so check the tension more often than normal.

> **STEER CLEAR**
>
> Make certain that you replace the split/master link retaining clip's round, closed end facing the direction the chain travels. In that position, the split link retaining clip has its open end facing away from the chain's direction of travel. If the split end is facing the direction in which the chain moves, road debris could wedge between the clip, causing it to come loose and leading to the loss of your chain.

As you perform these procedures, you will get a better idea of your mechanical abilities. You may find that you have a knack for doing your own repair. If so, cautiously branch out, performing more of your own repairs.

Even if you can afford to have someone else do all this work, if you learn to perform your own maintenance and repair, you'll derive more satisfaction from the motorcycle ownership experience.

The Least You Need to Know

- Check your tire pressure before every ride.
- New tires are slippery and need some time to be broken in properly before they provide all their potential traction.
- Always use the brake fluid your brake system was designed to use, and use only brake fluid from a sealed container.
- When replacing the split link in a drive chain, make certain that the round, closed end of the retainer clip points in the direction in which the chain moves.

Customizing and Collecting

In This Chapter

- Why customize your bike?
- Types of custom motorcycles
- Setting goals for customizing your bike
- What to look for when collecting motorcycles

In 1885, Gottlieb Daimler cobbled together the Einspur, the first gasoline-powered, purpose-built motorcycle. The vehicle was just a test bed for his engine, and as soon as he had a motor strong enough to power a four-wheeled vehicle, he abandoned his Einspur. History is a bit unclear about what happened to the vehicle after that. My guess is that it fell into the hands of the first motorcycle enthusiast, who promptly customized the thing.

Motorcyclists have been customizing their machines since the beginning of the sport. Whether we ride a mass-produced Universal Japanese Motorcycle (UJM) or a price-less collectible bike, we can't resist personalizing our machines.

Motorcyclists also like to collect motorcycles. People collect bikes for different reasons. Some collect bikes as investments, although the value of such investments has not been proven. Most of us collect bikes just because we like them. (Motorcycles seem to follow you home sometimes.)

In this chapter, I'm going to help you decide whether you should customize your bike and how to get started. I'm also going to explain the basics of collecting bikes. I'll offer advice on which bikes may be good investments, but mostly I'm going to try to help you find motorcycles that make you happy. Ask any serious collector, and he or she will tell you that's what it's all about.

Why Customize?

Originally, people modified their motorcycles to improve them in some way. In the early years of the sport, for example, many motorcyclists added a windshield, some saddlebags, or perhaps a sidecar to their bikes.

After World War II, customization in the United States focused on improving performance. Young American men and women had been exposed to lightweight, high-performance European motorcycles during the war. When they came home, the old domestic bikes just didn't cut it. Most motorcycle riders had to figure out alternative methods to get higher performance out of their bikes.

How'd they do it? They simply lightened their bikes, removing every nonessential part they could unbolt or cut off with a torch. This became the pattern for customization in this country, and to this day, the *bobbers*, as the original chopped customs were called, set the pattern for American-style custom bikes.

 CYCLE BABBLE

The custom bikes American riders built after World War II were called **bobbers** because owners cut off, or "bobbed," much of the bodywork.

As the performance levels of stock motorcycles climbed, it became less necessary to customize a bike to attain more speed. But people now customize for other reasons, too.

Motorcyclists often customize for style. In the cruiser world, modifications such as lowering a bike's suspension, altering its steering geometry, and adding *ape-hanger* (tall) handlebars, have come to define the terms *custom* or *chopper* for many people. Ironically, most of the common modifications actually detract from a bike's performance, but scores of people do these things to their bikes anyway.

Recently there has been a big growth in the custom scene for sportbikes. The typically younger riders of such bikes have been watching the chopper custom scene and thinking that they can do it just as well. These bikes obviously have a whole new twist on custom style, and can be very innovative. However, they can be just as hard to ride as the customs from the cruiser scene.

But there's an alternate movement in the realm of motorcycle customization. Many people still modify their bikes to increase their usefulness. People add aftermarket suspension components to improve a bike's handling. They mount windshields, more comfortable seats, and hard luggage to make a motorcycle a better long-distance tourer. They add aftermarket air filters and exhaust systems, not only to make their bikes faster, but also to make them more efficient.

CYCLE BABBLE

The term **ape hangers** was coined at the height of the custom-bike movement to describe tall handlebars that forced the rider to reach skyward to grasp the controls, making the rider adopt an apelike posture. Some states have laws limiting the height of these handlebars.

Comparing Customs

Ask a typical American to describe a custom bike, and he or she will most likely describe the radical chopper-type bike. Such bikes account for the largest segment of customization in the United States, but elsewhere in the world, other types of customs have been more prevalent. In the past few years, some of the other styles of customs have been gaining in popularity in the United States, including *streetfighters* (also known as hooligan bikes), which have long been popular in Europe.

CYCLE BABBLE

Streetfighters are usually sportbikes that have had their plastic fairings removed. Originally this was done by owners who had crashed their bikes and stripped off all the broken plastics (it was cheaper than replacing the panels). Now that streetfighters have become cool, people remove perfectly good bodywork to attain the same look. Streetfighters are very popular in Europe, where they originated.

Choppers

Choppers define American motorcycle style. The original bobbers were American hot rods, stripped-down Harleys, and Indians built for speed. As other, faster motorcycles became available, custom Harleys evolved from the bobbers of the 1940s into the choppers of the 1960s. By then, chopper style had become carved in stone: extended forks; high handlebars; a low, fat tire on the back; a tall, skinny tire up front; and a tall backrest or sissybar.

STEER CLEAR

I don't recommend building a chopper-type custom yourself. Such bikes tend to be so foul-handling that they are unsafe. Riding a motorcycle is challenging enough on a bike you can steer. If you want to own such a machine, I recommend buying one from an established customizer who knows what he or she is doing when building the bike.

In the 1970s and 1980s, choppers evolved into low riders, becoming longer and lower. Now low-rider customs are more common than traditional choppers, although the original choppers' style has made a strong comeback in the past few years.

The original bobbers were either Harleys or Indians. When the British began exporting large numbers of bikes to the United States in the 1950s, these, too, became popular bikes to chop. Initially, customizers also chopped Japanese bikes, but by the early 1980s, Harleys once again ruled the custom-bike market in the United States. However, during the early 2000s, a new wave of Japanese V-twin cruisers was also becoming the basis for customs, and now Japanese bikes are undeniably a force of their own in the custom scene. Today you can buy factory-designed aftermarket customizing parts for a variety of both Japanese and American cruisers.

Although typical choppers with extended forks looked pretty groovy, the bikes handled so poorly that they were unsafe to ride.
(Photo © 1998 Darwin Holmstrom)

Harley-Davidsons have long been the motorcycles of choice for customizing projects, but in recent years, Japanese bikes, such as this Honda Shadow, have become more popular among customizers.

(Photo © 1998 Darwin Holmstrom)

Café Racers

While Americans were busy chopping their Harleys, the Europeans took a different approach to customization. For many postwar Europeans, motorcycles were the only form of transportation to which they had access. In Europe, motorcycles were (and still are) used more frequently as practical daily transportation than in the United States.

Thus, customization tended to be more heavily focused on practical improvements. That, combined with the more liberal attitude toward riding fast in many European countries, meant that Europeans were more interested in building faster, better-handling customs than they were in adding higher ape-hanger handlebars and taller sissybars.

In the 1950s and early 1960s, a discernible European style of custom began to emerge. These bikes were inspired by European race bikes. Owners moved their footpegs toward the rear and lowered their handlebars, often using "clip-on" handlebars that bolted directly onto the fork tubes. This placed the rider in a crouched, forward-leaning position. Some owners adapted small fairings to their bikes to mimic the fairings used by racers.

These bikes became known as café racers, supposedly because their owners hung out in cafés and raced each other from café to café. Such bikes have always had a cult following in the United States, a following that continues to grow over time. There are probably more café racers in the United States right now than at any time in history. In some cities, such as Minneapolis and San Francisco, the popularity of café racers rivals that of custom Harleys.

When taken to the extreme, café racers can be as uncomfortable to ride as choppers. But when modified correctly, café racers handle much better than choppers. Another benefit of building a café racer instead of building a chopper is that it's much cheaper. To build a respectable chopper, you'll need to start with either a Harley-Davidson or one of the big Japanese cruisers—an expensive proposition either way.

You can do a very nice café custom job on just about any older Japanese motorcycle—bikes you can pick up for less money than you'd spend on tax and a license for a big new cruiser. Though if you want to build the ultimate café racer, you should go and find a British classic bike to begin with.

Café racers, such as this Rickman-frame Honda 750 from the mid-1970s, have long been popular in Europe and are gaining popularity in the United States as well.

(Photo © 1998 Darwin Holmstrom)

Streetfighters

While Yankees progressed from choppers to low riders, in Europe, café bikes evolved into streetfighters: stripped-down, hopped-up road warriors of the type the original postwar customizers in this country might have devised if they had had access to modern technology.

Streetfighters are all about function, and the first ones had no bodywork, no fancy paint, and no chrome—in fact, sometimes they were purposefully left scruffy.

As sportbikes became increasingly complex, they also became increasingly expensive to buy and more expensive to repair after minor crashes. Insurance companies began writing off perfectly functional sportbikes rather than replacing expensive bodywork.

European motorcyclists started rescuing those damaged bikes, but instead of replacing expensive bodywork, they just trash-canned all the plastic. Like American customizers in the 1940s, they chopped off all the extraneous parts, replacing only what was needed, such as the headlight. In fact, they often bolted on a couple of headlights. When the whole thing was ready, they applied a coat of flat-black paint (to protect the surfaces of the exposed metal, not for any cosmetic reasons) and then went out and rode the wheels off these streetfighters.

These bikes proved to be so popular that the manufacturers got into the act. A variety of companies began marketing sporting bikes without any bodywork, but no one got the streetfighter look down as well as Triumph. The latest Speed Triple embodies the streetfighter look.

Triumph nailed the streetfighter look with its latest Speed Triple.
(Photo courtesy of *Motorcyclist* magazine)

Custom Sportbikes

The biggest growth scene in recent years has been in the world of sportbikes. The scene started with young guys buying Japanese supersport machines, and riding them into the ground, often damaging them while riding wheelies and other stunts.

Ultimately, this was so antisocial that it started to burn itself out, though something positive grew out of the ashes. Young people had finally started getting into motorcycles. Right now the motorcycle world is rejuvenated with young blood, and most of the newer riders don't want to just blend in.

Mixing the fast-and-furious import car scene with all the *Biker Build Off* chopper customs they'd seen on television, they created custom sportbikes. Go to any bike night around the country and you'll see Gixxers (Suzuki GSX-Rs), Busas (Suzuki Hayabusas), and a wide array of other sportbikes, all customized beyond recognition. The most common modifications are lowered suspension and a stretched swingarm, to make the bike look long and low—plus custom paint and massive back wheels and tires. In this scene, the wilder, the better.

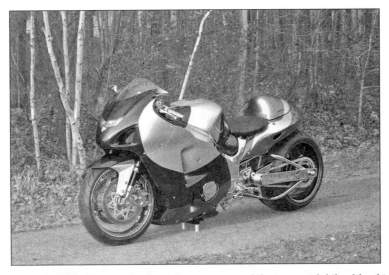

Builders like Ricks Motorcycles shape the custom sportbike scene with bikes like this radical Suzuki Hayabusa.

(Photo courtesy of Simon Green)

So You Want to Customize Your Bike ...

If you are interested in customizing your bike, you need to ask yourself a few questions:

- **What do I want from my bike?** Do I want to improve some functional aspect, such as comfort or handling? Do I want to improve my bike's performance? Do I just want to change my bike's appearance? What you want from your bike will guide you when deciding what changes to make.

- **What compromises am I willing to make to get what I want?** A motorcycle represents a series of compromises made by the designers and engineers who created it. They made those compromises for a reason. Altering one aspect of your bike can cause unintended consequences in some other aspect. Honestly assess what you are willing to sacrifice before making any changes.

- **How much am I willing to spend?** There are many small, inexpensive alterations you can make to your bike that will improve its comfort, handling, appearance, and performance. But making any of the popular major alterations usually costs a lot, and there's no guarantee you'll achieve your desired results. Before embarking on a major modification of your motorcycle, make certain that you know what you want, that your intended modification will achieve that goal, and that the results will be worth what they'll cost you.

Only after you've answered these questions should you make any major modifications to your bike.

STEER CLEAR

Don't make drastic modifications to your bike until you are certain of your goals. Making a radical alteration that turns out to make the bike less appealing can be an expensive misstep.

By nature, customizing is a personal process. Only you know what you want and need from your bike. Part of your task as a new motorcyclist will be to learn as much as possible about your bike. As you become more familiar with your machine, you'll have a better idea of how to modify it to suit you.

I would start out small. Identify an aspect of your bike you'd like to improve, such as style. Perhaps you can add a colored windshield or chrome parts. Make incremental changes when possible. That will help you avoid making serious mistakes that will be difficult (and expensive) to correct.

Discussing various methods for modifying your bike will fill a book in itself. Fortunately, there are many fine books available on the subject. You can order most of these from Whitehorse Press or Motorbooks (see Appendix C).

Classic, Collectible, or Just Old? Collecting Motorcycles

Ride long enough, and you'll notice something about motorcycles: no one can own just one. Becoming a motorcycle collector is an insidious process. It starts when you buy a better bike but can't quite bring yourself to sell your trusty old one. Then you'll decide to explore a different aspect of riding, such as off-road riding or touring, so you'll buy a bike suited for that purpose. But you still won't be able to part with the other two. Then you'll run across a pristine example of a classic bike you've always wanted, and you'll just happen to have enough money to buy it, so ....

STEER CLEAR

Don't collect motorcycles because you think you'll make money. You won't. Even if you pick a winner, you'll be lucky to recoup the money you spend on repairs, upkeep, and maintenance. If you want to get rich, try some other avenue. If you want to collect motorcycles, collect bikes you like.

By this time, you're too far gone to turn back. Like it or not, you're a collector. But it could be worse. Peter Egan, who writes for *Cycle World* magazine, once wrote that everyone needs at least four motorcycles: one for touring, one for sport riding, one for riding off-road, and one classic bike to keep it all in perspective. So go ahead and indulge yourself. Motorcycles have gotten much more expensive in recent years, but they are still cheap compared to cars. And they take up a lot less space.

Collector's Choice

In the late 1980s and early 1990s, some investors decided British motorcycles were going to rapidly appreciate in value, and overnight, the price of Triumphs, Nortons, and BSAs skyrocketed. Many of the people buying these bikes were not motorcyclists: they were investors out to get rich.

Some people did get rich off of the entire debacle, but for the most part, it wasn't the investors—it was the people who sold the motorcycles at inflated prices. The Brit-bike boom lasted a few years, and then prices declined. British bikes still cost more than they used to, even when their prices are adjusted for inflation, but they're back down to somewhat reasonable levels.

The lesson to be learned from all this is that you shouldn't buy a bike solely as a financial investment. It's a risky proposition, at best. Even if you get lucky and buy a bike that does increase in value, it probably won't increase enough to cover the expenses you incur while you own it.

If you're interested in a particular type or brand of bike, you can look for a particular model or year that may someday be worth more than other models or years, but that is a secondary consideration. When deciding what to collect, it's a whole lot more fun to just buy bikes that you really like.

What Do You Like?

Nobody else can tell you this! Before you start collecting bikes, ask yourself what you like. Do you like classic Japanese bikes? Do you like the rugged efficiency of BMWs? How about the fluid style of Italian sportbikes? Or the simple elegance of British bikes? Perhaps you like classic American motorcycles. Whatever your style, your individual preferences are of key importance when you begin collecting bikes.

What's Your Mechanical Skill Level?

How much time and energy are you willing to devote to the upkeep of your bikes? An American or British bike will require a lot more work to keep running than a Japanese bike or a BMW. Italian classics will fall somewhere in between. Know your abilities before you start buying bikes with maintenance requirements that you are unprepared to deal with.

What's Your Budget?

You also need to ask yourself how much you're willing to spend. With the exception of Japanese bikes, any of the motorcycles mentioned in this chapter will take a serious bite out of your bank account. You can still pick up a decent British bike or a BMW for under $5,000, but if your taste runs toward Italian or American bikes, you'd better have considerably more cash available.

You can still find nice, older Japanese bikes for fairly low prices, though. The prices of a few early models, such as Honda's Benly Super Sport 125, have shot through the roof. But you can still pick up a mid-1970s CB750 for around $3,500, and you can find clean examples of other Japanese bikes for less than that. Few of these bikes will ever have any serious investment value, but they're fun to ride and easy to maintain, and they make great projects for café chops.

What Constitutes a Classic?

Classifying a bike as a classic is an almost mystical process. To be a true classic, a bike needs to have just the right combination of rarity, competence, and charisma to tickle collectors right in their reptilian stems.

Some bikes are firmly established as classics. No one questions the status of bikes such as Moto Guzzi's V7 Sport, Ducati's 750 Super Sport or Mike Hailwood Replica, Harley's Knuckleheads and Panheads, Indian's Chiefs and Fours, any Brough or Vincent, BMW's R60s, Ariel's Square Fours, Norton's Commandos, or BSA's Gold Stars. But to get one of these bikes, be prepared to shell out some serious cash. And be prepared to wait, because there are only a handful of some of these bikes on U.S. soil, and most of those are owned by collectors who have little interest in selling them cheap.

If you decide to fork over the big bucks to buy a classic, make certain that you're getting the real thing. For example, earlier Triumph Bonnevilles are much sought after by collectors, while collectors tend to show little interest in the later models with dry-sump oil reservoirs in their frames (rather than in a separate tank). And if you do invest your life savings in a round-case Ducati 750 SS, make certain that you're getting the real thing, because other Ducati models can be converted into convincing SS replicas.

One way to tell a true round-case Ducati 750 SS from a fake is to check the frame. Real production 750 SS models had their frame numbers stamped on the left-rear engine-mount gusset, rather than on the steering head per the 750 GT and 750 Sport, the common donor bikes for SS clones. As well, genuine production 750 Super Sport engines carried serial numbers ending in DM750.1 rather than just DM750 for the GT and Sport. Given that subtleties like these can account for huge differences in value, your best bet is to hire a recognized expert to authenticate such machines.

This service may not come cheap, but if you have enough money to purchase bikes of this sort, you can certainly afford to authenticate your investment.

How else can you tell whether a bike is for real? Read all you can about a particular bike before buying one. If a bike's really a classic, there will be a plethora of books about it. Appendix C lists the names and addresses of a couple of publishers who specialize in motorcycle books. Go online or call and get their catalogs, and you'll find books on virtually every type of classic bike.

 STEER CLEAR

When shopping for a classic bike, make certain you're getting the real thing. Buying a fake can be one of the most expensive mistakes you'll ever make.

If you're interested in collecting classic bikes, get in touch with your local antique motorcycle club. Members of such organizations can provide you with more knowledge about classic motorcycles than any other source. And these people love motorcycles. You'll find no shortage of advice, and you may even be able to find someone who can help you locate the exact bike you're looking for.

Future Classics?

Given the scarcity and cost of true classics, collecting might seem out of most people's reach. And it can be a real gamble. Your odds of losing money are much greater than your odds of making money. That's why I recommend buying only bikes you like and bikes you will use.

That doesn't mean you can't have a lot of fun and possibly even make some money someday. There are useful bikes that qualify as great buys right now that might become classics sometime in the future.

Say, for example, that after you've become a proficient rider, you decide to buy a hardcore sportbike. You can buy any of the Japanese sportbikes.

Or, for about the same price as a modern 600cc Japanese sportbike, you can buy a classic Ducati 900 SS. The 600cc might be a bit faster than the Ducati, but remember the Ducati is already faster than you'll ever be able to ride on public roads. And it's easier to ride fast than most 600cc sportbikes. In other words, it's more sportbike than you'll ever be able to use in the real world. It will require more maintenance, and you'll need to know a mechanic skilled in adjusting its exotic valve gear, but down the road, it may be worth the bother.

Hang on to the Ducati for 10 or 20 years, and then compare its value to the value of a 20-year-old run-of-the-mill Japanese 600. While the 600 will likely be worth far less, the Ducati will probably be worth at least what you paid for it, provided that you've taken good care of it. And if that particular model of Ducati appreciates, as some people speculate it might, you could come out ahead. If you factor in your maintenance costs and inflation, you still may have done better investing in stocks and bonds, but a Ducati is much more fun to ride than a few hundred shares of some tech stock.

By nature of their rarity or oddity, other bikes may someday become collectibles—bikes such as Yamaha's GTS1000, a sport-tourer with an automotive-style front suspension instead of traditional forks, and Honda's audacious six-cylinder CBX. But if you buy one of these, do so because you want the bike. That way, you'll have more fun, and you won't be disappointed if you don't make a fortune.

The Least You Need to Know

- Some modifications can make a motorcycle dangerous to ride.
- Get to know your bike and what you want from it before modifying it.
- If you want to get rich, invest elsewhere, not in classic motorcycles.
- When shopping for a classic, make certain you're getting the real thing.

The Motorcycling Community

So far, I've concentrated on you and your motorcycle. From a safety perspective, that's the most important part of riding, because when you're out on the road, you're all you have to depend on.

But there's much more to motorcycling than just solitary riding. You have now become part of an extended family: the motorcycle community. Probably because of the shared sense of adventure and self-reliance this sport instills, riders of bikes of all stripes—from scooters to tourers and from sportbikes to dirtbikes—share a genuine common denominator: the joy of moving on two wheels.

They congregate to share this passion socially in many ways—at races and in rallies, at charity cruises, and on a Sunday-morning ride. In this part, I'll tell you about different aspects of that community, what it has to offer, and where you can find it.

Join the Club: Motorcycle Clubs

In This Chapter

- What motorcycle clubs can offer you
- The different types of motorcycle clubs
- The importance of the American Motorcyclist Association
- Finding a motorcycle club that's right for you

Motorcycles and motorcycling have fascinated me for as long as I can remember. When I was six years old, I was already figuring out a way to get a motorcycle for myself. Not long after I finally got my first bike, I discovered an aspect of motorcycling I hadn't even considered before: the motorcycling community. I started to hang out with other kids who had motorcycles, and we began riding together.

The main benefit of joining a motorcycle club is camaraderie. Motorcyclists often feel out of place around nonmotorcyclists, like the odd gearhead in the crowd. Motorcycle clubs provide social outlets for motorcyclists, a place we can get together with our own kind and talk about riding and bikes without having to worry about boring each other. A club is a nexus where the motorcycling community comes together.

Whatever your interests, you'll find a motorcycle club with members who share those interests. In this chapter, I discuss different types of clubs and what these organizations have to offer you.

How Motorcycle Clubs Were Born

A lot of the disaffected young people returning to America from World War II—people unable or unwilling to assimilate into mainstream American society—banded together to form the infamous outlaw motorcycle clubs. One such club, the Booze Fighters, became the model for Johnny's Black Rebels Motorcycle Club in the film *The Wild One*. Another of the postwar outlaw motorcycle clubs to gain some notoriety was the Hell's Angels.

The Japanese invasion led to another development in the motorcycle club scene. With all those nice people out riding around on their Hondas, it was only natural that some would form clubs. Which they did, by the thousands. Today you'll find clubs devoted to every make of bike ever built, from Aermacchi to Zundapp, along with hundreds of clubs for specific models.

Today there's a motorcycle club for just about every segment of society. You'll find motorcycle clubs for members of different ethnic groups, motorcycle clubs for computer geeks, motorcycle clubs for trike devotees, and motorcycle clubs for women. Along with the traditional outlaw motorcycle clubs, you'll find law-abiding clubs for police officers and firefighters. There are clubs for recovering alcoholics and clubs for people who like to get falling-down drunk. There are even scooter clubs.

Structured clubs allow motorcyclists to pool resources and achieve things individual bikers could not. In the early years of motorcycling, clubs often centered on competition. Racing clubs were able to maintain racetracks and organize events much more efficiently than individual motorcyclists. That's still the case today, and race-promoting organizations tend to maintain clublike atmospheres.

Types of Clubs

Categorizing clubs is as difficult as categorizing human beings, always a tricky and dangerous endeavor. When you divide people into groups, you end up placing people in the wrong category as often as you place them in the correct category. At best, that's confusing; at worst, it can be hazardous to your health. Placing members of the Bandidos Motorcycle Club in the same category as the Hell's Angels Motorcycle Club might seem logical to an outsider, but certain humorless members of the two groups might not find it amusing. With that in mind, I'll attempt to describe the general categories of motorcycle clubs. (Note that you'll find contact information for many of the clubs mentioned in this chapter in Appendix C.)

Off-Road and Trail-Riding Clubs

A major challenge faced by off-road riders is finding a place to ride. Very little land remains open to trail riders. Off-road and trail-riding clubs often maintain trail systems for members. Even clubs that don't maintain their own trail systems will be able to help you find public or private land where you can ride. Off-road clubs usually conduct organized rides for members and often organize competitive events.

Off-road clubs exist in most areas of the country. For example, the Panhandle Trail Riders Association (PANTRA) maintains a trail network for its members to use in north Idaho and eastern Washington.

Other off-road clubs focus on organizing competitive events. Without clubs such as the Sacramento, California–based Polka Dots Motorcycle Club, for example, which puts on several races and enduros each year, few off-road events would take place.

Off-road clubs may have higher dues than some other types of clubs, but maintaining trails and promoting events is an expensive business. If you like to ride off-road, membership dues in a good club can be the least expensive way to gain access to a good trail system.

Racing and Sportbike Clubs

Sportbike clubs are similar to off-road clubs in function, but tend to be less labor intensive, because sportbike club rides usually take place on public roads, so there are no trails to maintain. Sportbike clubs often organize sport tours for members, and some clubs arrange access to regional racetracks. The only way many riders can afford access to a closed-course racetrack where they can practice high-performance riding is through a club that arranges the rental of track time.

Antique-Motorcycle Clubs

If you appreciate, collect, or restore antique motorcycles, often also referred to as "vintage" or "classic" motorcycles, you'll find membership in one of the many antique-motorcycle clubs around the country essential. When restoring a bike, you can search for years for just the right carburetor you need to get your bike running or for the exact fender or tail lamp for your specific model and year. By using the extensive network of experts found in antique-bike clubs, you can make that process considerably easier. And if you can't locate a part through contacts made in an antique-bike club, club members can probably help you find someone who can make the part for you.

Woody Carson, national director of the Antique Motorcycle Club of America, and his one-of-a-kind 1925 Indian Prince LX2.
(Photo © 1998 Darwin Holmstrom)

Many antique clubs are organized under the umbrella of the Antique Motorcycle Club of America (AMCA), a not-for-profit organization founded in 1954. Worldwide membership in the AMCA is now more than 10,800; many members attend AMCA national meets held around the country each year. The club also publishes its own 88-page magazine, which comes out four times annually.

Make- or Model-Specific Clubs

Many clubs were formed by fans of a particular brand or model of motorcycle. Some of these clubs, such as the BSA Owners Club, were organized around brands or models of motorcycle that are no longer produced and could be classified as antique clubs as easily as make-specific clubs. Other make-specific clubs, such as the Harley Owners Group (HOG), tend to have a heavy ratio of people who own new bikes in their ranks. New bikes need less technical support than older bikes, so clubs such as HOG serve more as social outlets than as practical sources of parts and information.

HOG, a factory-sponsored club with affiliates worldwide and 1 million members, is one of the best-known motorcycle clubs in the world. HOG has helped fuel Harley's spectacular comeback as much as technological improvements to the bikes themselves. HOG helped Harley-Davidson foster a tight-knit community among its customers that, in turn, helped foster customer loyalty that borders on fanaticism.

BMW owners form another tightly knit community of riders. And these folks take their riding seriously. Many Beemer owners put tens of thousands of miles on their bikes every year and often rack up more than 100,000 miles on their machines. Some owners have been known to put 200,000 miles, 300,000 miles, or even more on a single motorcycle. Serious motorcyclists like this deserve a serious club, and the BMW Motorcycle Owners of America (BMW MOA) is indeed a serious organization. It puts on some of the finest rallies in North America and produces a monthly magazine that rivals any motorcycle journal you'll find on the newsstands.

Similarly, the Honda Rider's Club of America (HRCA) is home to an enthusiastic group of—naturally—Honda riders of every stripe. The HRCA also has its own digital magazine, *Red Rider.*

Often clubs devoted to a single popular model will emerge, like the Sandcast Only Owners Club that's devoted to early Honda CB750s with their "sandcast" aluminum engine cases. Sometimes clubs will organize around a particular type of engine used by a company, such as the Airheads Beemer Club (ABC), a club for owners of BMW motorcycles powered by air-cooled boxer motors. This group was organized in response to the increasing complexity and cost that accompanied BMW's recent technological advances.

MOTORCYCOLOGY

Older air-cooled BMW boxer twins are called *Airheads,* while newer air-and-oil-cooled boxer Beemers are called *Oilheads.* There are motorcycle clubs organized by and devoted to the interests of owners of Airheads and Oilheads.

Then there are make-specific clubs that could just as easily be categorized as sport-riding clubs, organizations like the Crazed Ducati Riders of Massachusetts. Some might argue that there is no difference between a Ducati rider and a sport rider. (Some might also argue that Crazed Ducati Riders is redundant, but that's another story.)

The most useful make- or model-specific clubs are clubs devoted to orphan bikes—rare bikes that are no longer in production—such as the Nimbus Club USA celebrating the intriguing Danish machines. Such clubs can be invaluable sources of parts and technical information.

Another group that fits this category is the Turbo Motorcycle International Owners Association (TMIOA). The TMIOA was started in 1987 originally for owners of Honda's CX Turbo motorcycles, but in December 1988, it broadened its focus to include coverage of all the factory turbocharged motorcycles. Turbo sportbikes were built by all the Japanese manufacturers in the early 1980s, but they all suffered from mechanical problems, to some degree, and never became popular. Now these bikes are sought after by collectors, but parts availability is a serious problem, especially given the history of mechanical troubles in such bikes. Clubs devoted to turbo bikes can save a turbo owner a lot of time and money when it comes to keeping his or her bike on the road.

Touring Clubs

Joining a touring club is a great way to get travel tips and advice from motorcyclists who have actually been there (regardless of where "there" is). You'll learn things from members of touring clubs that you won't learn anywhere else, such as where to find good restaurants and hotels, how to find the best roads, the locations of speed traps, and roads to avoid.

Sometimes touring-oriented clubs center on a particular model of touring bike, such as Honda's Gold Wing or Yamaha's Venture. One such group, the Gold Wing Road Riders Association (GWRRA), is the world's largest club devoted to a single motorcycle marque. GWRRA members organize some of the most extravagant club gatherings in the United States.

Locale-Specific Clubs

Often clubs form with no common denominator other than location. Motorcyclists just want to get together with other people from their area who ride, regardless of what they ride or how they ride. Such clubs can provide you with information on riding in an area you won't find anywhere else, an especially valuable service for new riders. The WetLeather motorcycle club of the Pacific Northwest, for example, defines itself as "a food group, with motorcycles."

Female Motorcyclist Clubs

Women have been riding motorcycles as long as men, although never in as great numbers. And women have had their own motorcycle clubs almost as long as men. Organizations such as the Motor Maids, Inc., have long been a part of the motorcycling scene.

But in recent years, the number of women who ride has grown, and now more women ride their own motorcycles than ever before. As more women enter the sport, the number and variety of women's motorcycle clubs has grown.

One of the largest women's groups is Women On Wheels (WOW). When WOW was founded in 1982, women who rode their own bikes were still exceptions, oddities in the motorcycling community. WOW provided an outlet for these women, a place where they could get together with other female riders. Today there are more than 90 WOW chapters all across the United States.

In the past few years, more specialized women's motorcycling clubs have emerged, such as Curve Unit, a club for women sportbike riders.

Age-Specific Clubs

A trend that has gained momentum as the baby boomers age is the rise of age-specific clubs, organizations composed of motorcyclists who have reached a certain age. For example, the Retreads Motorcycle Club International, Inc., consists of riders who are at least 40 years old.

These days there are plenty of riders older than 40—sometimes a lot older. Although the Older Bikers Riding Club (OBRC), which is active in five states, does not stipulate that its members be of a certain age, its motto is telling: "Enjoying the sunset of our lives."

Spiritually Oriented Clubs

In recent years, Christian motorcycling clubs have multiplied prolifically. The Christian Motorcyclists Association (CMA), one of the largest of these organizations, can be found at rallies and events around the United States.

Christian motorcyclist groups do a great deal to promote a positive image of motorcycling to the general public. If you are so inclined, joining such a club would be an ideal way to combine your spirituality and passion for motorcycling.

Christians aren't the only group to combine their spiritual beliefs with motorcycling. There are Taoist and Buddhist motorcycle clubs, and there are pagan motorcycle clubs. There is even one group, the Bavarian Illuminati Motorcycle Club (BIMC), which quotes the Western mystic Aleister Crowley in its club bylaws. The club has very little of what could be called structure, but members do receive a suggested reading list that includes *The Illuminatus! Trilogy*, by Robert Shea and Robert Anton Wilson, and *Programming and Metaprogramming in the Human Biocomputer*, by John Lilly, M.D., as well as an eclectic collection of books on motorcycling and mysticism.

Activity-Oriented Clubs

A variety of clubs combine other interests with motorcycling. Sometimes these clubs combine motorcycle-related interests. If you're interested in motorcycling and camping, for example, you can join the International Brotherhood of Motorcycle Campers (IBMC), a group dedicated to riders who camp out rather than stay in motels when they tour on their motorcycles.

Other clubs combine motorcycling with unrelated interests, such as the Motorcycling Amateur Radio Club (MARC), composed of motorcyclists who are also ham radio operators.

Motorcyclists who have access to a computer can even join virtual motorcycle clubs, organizations such as Cyberspokes.com. These are clubs for people who love to ride but also like to surf the Internet.

Socially Active Clubs

Many motorcycle groups form to support certain causes and hold poker runs and other events to raise funds for charity. One such group, the Honda Rider's Club of America, organizes numerous Ride for Kids events each year to raise money to help children with brain tumors.

Another club that raises a lot of money for a specific charity is the Women's Motorcyclist Foundation Inc. (WMF). In 2004, the WMF partnered with SportBike Track Time in a program called "On Track for a Cure" for breast cancer, with participants raising cancer research money for every mile ride on a track.

Profession-Related Clubs

Often motorcyclists in certain professions form motorcycle clubs with other members of their profession. One of the most famous clubs of this type is the Blue Knights International Law Enforcement Motorcycle Club, a club composed of law-enforcement officials. Formed in 1974, today the Blue Knights Club has over 20,000 members in 635 chapters spread across 29 countries.

Creative Clubs

People are getting more creative when forming motorcycle clubs. Often these are just groups dedicated to having fun, such as the Motorcycle Singles Club, located in

California. As its name suggests, this club encourages single women and men to meet, ride, and share their love of motorcycling.

Other groups solely devoted to having fun have appeared around the country. The Slimey Crud Run (SCR) pays tongue-in-cheek homage to some of the more oily machines of yesteryear—such as Velocette and Indian, along with many others—on which participants make their way twice a year from town to town in southern Wisconsin.

There are clubs for curmudgeon motorcyclists, and there are clubs for vampires who ride, such as three chapters of the Vampires Motorcycle Club. There is even a club for riders who don't like to drink. Alternative MC is an organization dedicated to riding sober—or as succinctly put by the club's motto, "No booze, drugs or attitudes welcome." The club has 22 chapters from Texas to Florida and up to Pennsylvania.

The American Motorcyclist Association

No single group plays a more influential role in motorcycling in the United States than the American Motorcyclist Association (AMA), a 245,000-member organization founded in 1924.

The AMA sold its Pro Racing division in 2008 but remains the world's largest amateur motorsports-sanctioning body. Forty percent of its members are currently or have previously been involved in competition, and the active members participate in some 3,000 events a year across the United States. These events encompass the entire motorcycle-racing spectrum and include events as diverse as amateur motocross, road racing, dirt-track racing, and hill climbing, with competition classes for a wide range of motorcycles, rider skill levels, and often different ages, too—from grade-school kids to senior riders. If there's motorcycle racing taking place in the United States, the AMA is probably involved.

Perhaps even more important than its promotion of racing is the work of the AMA Government Relations Department, which works harder than any single organization to make riders aware of bad laws and anti-motorcycling discrimination at the local, state, federal, and corporate levels. You'd be amazed at some of the anti-motorcycle legislation proposed at all levels of government, as well as the discrimination to be found in the workplace. Fortunately for all of us, during its over 85 years of existence, the AMA has developed successful methods for dealing with discrimination against motorcyclists. Even if you join no other motorcycle organization, I highly recommend joining the AMA.

Finding a Club

One of the best ways to locate a club in your area is to contact the AMA and get a list of AMA-chartered clubs in your area.

If you know of a local place (such as a bar, café, or motorcycle shop) where motorcyclists hang out, you can ask if the folks there know of any local clubs. The Internet is also a terrific resource for finding motorcycle clubs, especially some of the more off-the-wall organizations.

You can also check Appendix C for contact information for some of the national motorcycle groups that may be able to put you in touch with local groups in your area.

After you've found a club, look into it before joining. Attend a couple of meetings and visit with members. Perhaps you might even go for a ride with them. If you enjoy the time you spend with members, chances are you'll enjoy being a member.

Joining a club may not be a necessity for enjoying the sport of motorcycling—motorcycling is, in the end, a solitary activity—but it can greatly enhance the experience. The enthusiasm club members have for riding is infectious and can motivate you to explore new areas of the sport. And if you live in a climate where you can't ride for long periods of time each year, meeting with your motorcycle club can help you make it through the long winter months.

The Least You Need to Know

- Club memberships can be practical as well as fun.
- Clubs can be great sources of hard-to-locate parts and information.
- Many clubs do a great deal of work supporting causes other than motorcycling, such as breast cancer research.
- Joining the AMA is the best way you can ensure the future of motorcycling.

The Open Road: Touring and Rallies

In This Chapter

- Preparing your bike for a trip
- Planning your trip
- Packing gear on your bike safely
- Learning about motorcycle rallies around the country

I enjoy all aspects of riding, from commuting to work to trail riding, but I enjoy touring on a bike most of all. I find nothing more thrilling than cresting a hill and seeing a new expanse of world open up before me. Whether I'm exploring the Sand Hill region of Nebraska, the High Desert in Southern California, the lush Ozark Mountains of Arkansas, or the wheat fields of Minnesota, I never get bored when I'm traveling on a bike.

In this chapter, I share with you some of the tips I've learned over the course of my trips.

I also talk a bit about where to go on your motorcycle (as well as where not to go). And I discuss different motorcycle-related events, such as rallies, you can attend.

Any Bike Is a Touring Bike

If you have a dependable motorcycle, you can travel on it. Ed Otto, a competitive long-distance rider, rode 11,000 miles on a Honda Helix *scooter* during the 1995 *Iron Butt Rally*, one of the most grueling long-distance motorcycle rallies in the world.

CYCLE BABBLE

The **Iron Butt Rally** is arguably the most grueling long-distance motorcycle road rally in the world. Participants ride around the perimeter of the United States, often including side trips that take them hundreds or even thousands of miles out of their way. Finishing the rally requires that you ride at least 11,000 miles in 11 days. Top-10 finishers often ride 12,000 to 13,000 miles in that time.

Of course, some motorcycles make better tourers than others. Selecting a bike to tour on is an individual choice. It doesn't matter how well a motorcycle works for other riders—what matters is how well it works for *you*. How well does your motorcycle fit you physically? Is it comfortable on daylong rides? How well do its power-delivery characteristics suit your riding style?

You also need to feel comfortable with the reliability of your bike. You don't want to get stranded in the middle of some unfamiliar urban area or isolated mountain road on a bike. Before you decide to take a bike on an extended trip, you should know its mechanical condition. If you do travel on a bike that has a tendency to break down, you should be familiar enough with the bike's mechanics to perform some basic repair work on the side of the road.

Piaggio's BV Tourer 500 scooter might not be the ideal mount for 1,000-mile-a-day rides, but at a more relaxed pace, it can make a fine traveling companion.
(Photo courtesy of Piaggio Group USA)

Planning a Trip

I have a tendency to overplan trips, marking out each gas stop on my map, along with my estimated time of arrival. But some of my best motorcycle tours have been the least planned. I once went on a meandering two-week trip through Wyoming and Colorado with a friend who is perhaps the least organized human being I've ever met.

Once I let go and gave control to a higher power (in this case, my buddy's disorganized ways), I had the most relaxing trip of my life. And I saw more of the country I rode through than I ever had before. I discovered that the most entertaining road is the road to nowhere.

Touring Range and Fuel Stops

But even on the road to nowhere, you have to prepare at least a minimal amount. Most motorcycles have small gas tanks and can travel only a short distance between fuel stops, at least when compared to cars. You need to plan your trip so that you know you'll be able to find fuel when you need it.

MOTORCYCOLOGY

Learn to predict whether a town will have an open gas station by checking its population. State road maps always list the names of all the towns in the state, along with their populations. A town with a population of 500 or more should have a gas station, but the station may be closed in the evenings and on Sunday. To find an open gas station after hours or on a Sunday, you'll need to find a town with a population of 1,000 or higher. Make sure you plan your course accordingly.

Some bikes have more touring range than others, depending on the size of their fuel tanks and what kind of gas mileage they get. For example, a bike with a 4.7-gallon tank that gets 36 miles per gallon on average can travel 169.2 miles before you have to start walking, while a bike with a 3.7-gallon tank that gets 54 miles per gallon on average can go almost 200 miles before refueling.

Touring and sport-touring motorcycles generally have big fuel tanks, but sometimes they burn so much gas that you really don't have that great a range. Cruisers tend to have smaller tanks, but some cruisers, especially the V-twins, use less fuel, so they can travel nearly as far. Some bikes with exceptionally small tanks, such as older

Harley-Davidson Sportsters, can barely travel 100 miles before they start sucking air out of their tanks.

Not only is having to constantly refuel your bike time consuming and annoying, it can also be dangerous. In many areas in the United States, especially in the West and Southwest, you can easily ride 150 miles between gas stations. These are isolated areas, and if you were to run out of fuel in such a place, you would probably be eaten by buzzards before someone found you.

STEER CLEAR

When traveling through isolated areas such as the American West, it's better to err on the side of caution when planning your fuel stops. It's better to refuel too often than to not refuel often enough.

Even if you aren't going any place in particular, keep your bike's range in mind when deciding which roads to take. Don't push your luck when it comes to refueling. If you are getting low on fuel and pass a gas station, refill your tank. If you decide to wait until the next town, you could find that the town has no gas station.

Keep in mind that your fuel mileage can vary, depending on conditions. If you are riding fast, into a headwind, or have a heavy load, you can count on running out of fuel sooner than if you are traveling more slowly or carrying a lighter load.

Preparing Your Bike

Throughout this book, I've tried to stress the importance of properly maintaining your motorcycle. When traveling long distances on a bike, this is especially important. If your bike were to break down in an isolated mountain pass, you could freeze to death before someone found you. Making certain your bike is in good shape before you take a trip serves an economic purpose as well. Having a breakdown far from home can be much more expensive than having your bike fall apart while commuting to work. When you break down in an isolated area, you don't have the luxury of shopping around for the best prices. You may get stuck paying a high motel rate just to have a roof over your head while you're waiting for repairs. And you also don't have the luxury of finding a mechanic you trust.

Your best bet is to get your bike in as good shape as possible before taking a trip. Study the procedures in Chapters 16 and 17. Make certain that you perform all routine maintenance. Here's a list of procedures you should always perform before an extended trip:

- Change the oil.

- Have your battery load-tested.

- Check your coolant and chain tension.

- Tighten every nut and bolt on your bike.

- Replace leaky fork seals, as well as worn bearings and bushings in the frame.

- Replace worn shocks and sacked-out fork springs.

- Pay close attention to your tires. If there is the slightest possibility that your tires will wear out on your trip, replace them before you go.

What to Bring?

No matter what I tell you, you will probably overestimate the amount of clothing and gear you'll need when you take your first motorcycle trip. But here are my suggestions for all you need for a safe, comfortable ride.

The Clothes Make the Motorcyclist

On my first extended trip, which I took many years ago, I brought a couple of different jackets (for riding in a variety of weather conditions), along with five or six complete changes of clothing, including some dressy clothes in case I wanted to go out to eat or on a date.

Now I bring a couple of pairs of jeans, a couple of turtlenecks, a couple of sweatshirts, and a couple of T-shirts. I may bring three T-shirts if the weather is hot or if I plan to be gone a week or more. And I bring pretty much every pair of underwear and socks I own. If I go out for a nice dinner, I wear my cleanest pair of jeans and the turtleneck with the fewest holes in it.

Your best bet is to travel light on a bike. Bring only clothing you'll wear. And you'll always seem to wear less than you bring. As you become a more experienced motorcycle traveler, you'll find that you bring less clothing on each successive trip.

Tools You'll Use

Although I pack fewer clothes for each trip, I find that my list of must-bring gear grows each year. Every time I've needed an item I didn't have, I've included that item on following trips.

I always bring a small selection of extra tools, even when I'm on a new bike. The toolkits that come with most bikes will do in a pinch, but I always like to have an extra set of combination spanner wrenches, a couple of pliers (needle-nose pliers and Channellock pliers), a ratchet, and a small selection of sockets. I also include a cigarette lighter, a small selection of nuts and bolts (including some for connecting my battery cables to my battery), some electrical connectors, a roll of wire, zip ties, and a couple of rolls of tape (friction and duct tape).

Safety First: First Aid

I also carry a first-aid kit with me. I make certain that the kit includes the following items:

- A selection of bandages, including gauze bandages
- Adhesive tape
- An antibiotic of some sort
- Something for bee stings

This is a list of the absolute minimum amount of items a first-aid kit should include. If you can pack a more complete kit, you should do so, even if you need to leave something else behind to make room for it.

For the Scenic Routes: Photographic Equipment

I'm a photographer and always bring my camera equipment when I travel, which presents some challenges on a bike. The greatest of these challenges is weather protection. If you have watertight hard luggage, this is not as much of an issue, but riders with soft luggage will have to come up with a way to keep the rain off their camera equipment. Before a trip on which I'll be using soft luggage, I buy a box of the most durable garbage bags I can get (the kind for bagging leaves seems to be the toughest) and then double-wrap my cameras in these bags. Gallon-size zipper-lock food bags are also good.

MOTORCYCOLOGY

Always buy a large box of heavy-duty garbage bags before going on a motorcycle trip. You'll be amazed at the uses you'll find for them. I place my clothes in them and then put the garbage bag in my saddlebags. Not only does this protect my clothes from getting wet, but it also makes it easier to pack and unpack my saddlebags. I also wrap my sleeping bag in garbage bags. If you've ever had to spend a night in a wet sleeping bag, you'll see the value of this practice.

Another option is to use small point-and-shoot cameras when you travel. You can keep these in your vest pockets or fairing pockets, where they'll stay dry and be ready when you need them.

If you pack your camera in your luggage, whether you have soft or hard luggage, be careful not to place it in a location where it will bounce around. Just the vibration from your bike can pound expensive cameras to pieces; if they bounce around in your trunk or against your shock absorbers while in your saddlebags, you could end up with very expensive paperweights instead of cameras. To protect your equipment, pack soft items, such as towels, clothing, or pillows, around it to absorb shocks and vibrations. A pair of thick socks makes a decent shock-absorbing slip cover for your camera in a pinch—as long as the socks aren't full of sand from your trip to Sleeping Bear Dunes.

STEER CLEAR

Make certain that your load is secure when packing a bike for a trip. If something falls off, it could get caught in your wheel or chain, causing you to lose traction and crash.

Carrying your camera in a fanny pack or carrying a point-and-shoot camera in your vest pocket can eliminate much of this problem, though be aware—anything you carry that's directly attached to your body can amplify your injuries if you come off. Personally, I don't carry anything like house keys (that could pierce me) in my pockets while I'm riding.

Protective Gear

I always wear a full-face helmet with a visor when traveling. Not only does a full-face helmet provide superior protection in an accident, but it also provides superior protection from the elements and superior comfort.

The most versatile piece of protective gear you can own is a waterproof riding suit like Aerostich's Darien jacket and pants (mentioned in Chapter 9). These suits eliminate the need for rain gear, freeing up a lot of luggage space, and they provide unmatched versatility. With all liners in place, such suits provide excellent cold-weather protection; yet with the liners removed and all vents opened, they are the best hot-weather gear you can buy. This is especially important when traveling in high mountains, where temperatures can vary by 50 or 60 degrees in just a few miles.

You Can Take It with You: Packing Your Bike

Once you've decided what to bring, you'll need to figure out how to bring it with you. Packing techniques are more important than you might think. If your gear falls off your bike, the best you can hope for is that you'll just lose a few items. A more likely outcome is that your gear will get caught in your wheels or chain, causing you to crash.

Luggage

To provide enough carrying capacity for touring, you'll need to have some sort of luggage. Most bikes will accept soft saddlebags and a tankbag; these items are the easiest and most economical way to provide extra carrying capacity on your bike.

STEER CLEAR

When mounting soft luggage on your motorcycle, make certain that your luggage doesn't come into contact with your exhaust pipes, or you could lose your belongings in a fire.

Some bikes won't accept soft luggage because of the shape of their tailpieces or because their exhaust pipes ride too high. This is especially problematic on sport-bikes. Some bikes won't accept tankbags, either, because of the shape of their gas tanks. If this is a problem on your bike, you can buy tailpacks that strap onto the passenger's portion of your seat. If you can't mount soft luggage and you don't have a passenger seat on your bike, you'll need to carry all your belongings in a backpack or choose a different bike for traveling.

A few companies, such as Givi, make hard luggage for many motorcycles. This luggage is expensive, and mounting it can prove quite a challenge, but the convenience of hard luggage makes it a worthwhile investment.

*Soft luggage, such as this tankbag, tailpack, and saddlebags, all from Chase Harper,
can convert just about any motorcycle into a tourer.*

(Photo © 1998 Darwin Holmstrom)

*If soft luggage won't fit on your motorcycle, you can carry your gear in a tailpack,
such as this Supersport Tail Trunk from Chase Harper.*

(Photo courtesy of Chase Harper)

This Givi mounting system with hard luggage can make a motorcycle significantly more useful.
(Photo courtesy of Givi USA, Inc.)

In addition to soft luggage and a tankbag, I strap a duffel bag to the passenger seat of my bike. This provides all the carrying capacity I've ever needed.

Camping

If you choose to camp rather than stay in motels when you travel, you can save a lot of money, but you also need to bring a lot of extra gear. The bulkiest items you'll need to pack are your tent and sleeping bag. But if you use your head when packing, you can use these items to help make your load more secure. I tell you how to pack your camping gear in the next section.

Loading Up

Before attempting to pack your bike, go to your nearest bike shop and buy at least four bungee nets. Bungee nets are stretchy webs made of nylon ropes with metal hooks that attach to your bike. They are the most wonderful devices ever invented for motorcycle touring, especially if you camp out.

Use a pyramid design when packing a load on a bike—put the widest, stiffest pieces on the bottom, and put the narrower, spongier items toward the top. My own method is to lay my duffel bag crosswise on the passenger seat, so that the ends of the bag are resting on my saddlebags. Behind that, I lay my tent, also crosswise. I then place a bungee net over the two items, tightly securing it in the front and in the rear.

STEER CLEAR

Check your loads, including your soft luggage, frequently when traveling on a bike. The vibration from your bike can loosen hooks and straps. If you find a strap or a bungee hook that has worked its way loose, take the time to adjust it. The consequences of luggage flying loose can be deadly.

Then I lay my sleeping bag in the nook created between the tent and the duffel bag. Often a single bungee net won't go all the way around my sleeping bag and still solidly attach to the bike, so I'll secure the bungee net in the front of the load and stretch it as far over the sleeping bag as it will go. Then I'll hook the rear of the bungee net to the hooks of the bungee net holding the tent and duffel bag in place. If the top net won't reach the hooks of the bottom net, I'll hook it to a place on the bottom net where the nylon cord is doubled up. Next, I firmly attach another bungee net to a secure point behind the load and hook it to the front of the bungee net covering the sleeping bag, again trying to attach it to the hooks on the other net. The fourth bungee net is a spare, since they sometimes stretch or break.

Unless your luggage is waterproof, packed clothes are likely to get soaked if you ride in the rain for long. It's a mediocre solution at best to sleeve your luggage in plastic trash bags (tempting as this seems), because the wind at highway speeds can rip them open. A better bet is to pack your clothes in the bags, and then store these inside your luggage.

Different size loads require variations on this theme. If you're traveling two-up, you'll need more carrying capacity. Unless you are riding an ultimate-behemoth touring bike or you're pulling a trailer (neither of which I recommend until you're an experienced rider), you should probably consider not camping when traveling two-up.

Using a luggage rack also requires you to alter your methods of packing. A luggage rack can increase your carrying capacity and provide you with more secure points to attach bungee nets, but make certain that the rack is mounted securely, and don't overload the rack.

First, attach the widest and stiffest items at the base of your load. Next, attach
narrower, softer items.
(Photos © 1998 Darwin Holmstrom)

You may have to make adjustments to the method described here, but if you structure
the load so that it is solid and securely attached to the bike, using a pyramid method
to keep your center of gravity as low as possible, you should be fine. Check your load
frequently (including the straps attaching your soft luggage to your bike); if anything
starts to loosen, take the time to adjust and tighten it.

Pacing Yourself

Traveling on a motorcycle drains you physically much more than traveling in a car.
It's important that you receive proper nutrition and rest when riding.

Unfortunately, fine dining isn't easy on the road. Road food is notoriously unhealthy
and doesn't provide the kind of energy you need for touring. Try to eat as many
carbohydrates as you can. Have pancakes instead of an omelet for breakfast. (And eat
all your toast.) Have salads for dinner instead of steaks.

Most important, make certain that you drink enough water. If you drink just soda or
coffee, the caffeine in those drinks actually depletes your body's supply of water. Get
in the habit of buying a bottle of water each time you stop for gas instead of buying

a can of soda. Onboard water systems are increasing in popularity. Aerostich Darien jackets even have a pocket sized to hold a hydration system.

When riding long distances, exhaustion can creep up on you, diminishing your riding skills. You may not even be aware it is happening. This is especially problematic on hot days and can cause otherwise safe riders to make mistakes. As I've said repeatedly, you can't afford to make mistakes on a bike.

You need to be aware of your mental and physical condition. When you feel yourself getting tired, stop. Find a rest area and stretch your legs. Pull into a convenience store or gas station, buy some juice and a bag of peanuts, find a shady spot in the parking lot, and sit down for a bit. If you are out in the middle of nowhere, find a crossing or turnout where you can park your bike, and then find a shady spot to lean against a tree, or lie down in the grass and watch some clouds go by. Take a nap, if you feel like it. It may slow down your schedule, but if you continue riding when you're exhausted, you might never get where you're going.

Motorcycle Madness: Rallies

So now that your bike's all dressed up, you probably want someplace to go. Just about any place makes a good destination for a motorcycle tour—a visit to friends, to relatives, or just to nowhere in particular. If you have no particular destination in mind, you might want to attend a motorcycle rally. Rallies make a logical destination for a bike trip. While the trip is its own reward on a bike tour, rallies are hard to beat, as far as destinations go.

There are rallies for cruiser fans, rallies for tourers, rallies for sportbike riders, and rallies for antique bikes. There are Norton rallies, Moto Guzzi rallies, Ducati rallies, and BMW rallies. Whatever your interests are, you can find a rally where you'll meet hundreds, or even thousands (in some cases, hundreds of thousands) of like-minded riders. Rallies are places where you can go and revel in all aspects of motorcycle culture.

Major Rallies

Motorcycle rallies have distinct personalities. Some are mild mannered and relaxed, while others are obnoxious and just plain rude. Most fall somewhere in between. The biggest, loudest, rudest rally of all is Bike Week at Daytona.

Daytona Bike Week

Held during the first week of March each year in Daytona Beach, Florida, Daytona Bike Week is the wildest party in the United States.

Daytona began as a racing-oriented event, and racing still plays an important role in the week. The Daytona 200 is the main draw, but you also can catch Supercross racing, flat-track racing, and off-road competition in an event called the Alligator Enduro. As well, the American Historic Racing Motorcycle Association (AHRMA) organizes some of the best historic racing in the country at Daytona.

But it's the variety of other activities that gives Daytona its unique character. All kinds of motorcycle-related events take place during Bike Week, like the WyoTech Annual Brute Horsepower Shootout dyno contest (where one modified Suzuki Hayabusa cranked out an amazing 569 horsepower), the Alligator Mystery Tour, the Adrenaline Crew Stunt Show, flea markets, swap meets, burnout and loud-pipe contests, and nearly countless bike shows, including the Rat's Hole Custom Bike Show.

The nonmotorcycling activities are what really make Daytona infamous, including many that are not exactly family oriented. In addition to the ever-present live bands, freely flowing beer, and wet T-shirt contests, you'll be able to take in the American Arm Wrestling Competition, the World Famous Ratmate Contest, Coleslaw Wrestling, his and hers tattoo contests, and naturally, the Bikini Bombshell Contest.

Daytona is not a destination for the easily offended, nor is it a place for anyone with a low tolerance for loud Harley-Davidsons or the anti-everything-but-Harley attitude of some Harley owners. But if you're looking for the ultimate all-in-one motorcycle event, you have to check out Daytona Bike Week at least once.

Black Hills Motorcycle Rally

The annual Black Hills Motorcycle Rally is held in Sturgis, South Dakota, and so over the years this major weeklong event has simply become known as Sturgis. It is somewhat tamer than the Daytona Bike Week, generally attracting an older crowd, but calling it a family event is still a bit of a stretch. Let's just call it a Midwestern version of Daytona.

As in Daytona, racing was the original purpose for the gathering at Sturgis, but over the years, the spectacle of the rally began to eclipse the racing. Competition now includes drag races, a Harley XR1200 racing experience, and the creative Buffalo Chip Mud Races.

But also like Daytona, it's all the other events taking place that give Sturgis its character. Main Street during the rally becomes a sea of black leather and denim, swirling around the vendor booths lining the sidewalk.

One of the best things about the rally at Sturgis is riding in the Black Hills of South Dakota. The roads in the Black Hills offer terrific riding any time of the year, but during Bike Week, you'll be sharing those roads almost exclusively with other motorcyclists.

Sturgis gained a reputation in the 1970s as a wild party spot for outlaw bikers, but the wild days are history. Like the motorcycling public in general, Sturgis is becoming more mature.

Laconia Motorcycle Week

Laconia, New Hampshire, hosts the last of the three top American bike weeks. Like both Daytona and Sturgis, there are several different race events to enjoy: you can catch a hill climb, some flat tracking, Supercross, and vintage racing at New Hampshire International Speedway.

Also just like the others, you'll find a big downtown gathering of motorcycle people getting crazy. Laconia really does have the most incredible surroundings, though. In almost every direction, there are twisty mountain roads, and every time you pull in for gas or some food, you'll find how great the locals are. If you've got a sportbike and like riding the curves, this is a can't-miss summer destination.

Other Rallies

As motorcycles become more popular, appealing to more diverse and ever larger numbers of riders, motorcycle rallies multiply and become more diverse. There are rallies scheduled at certain times of the year, such as Biketoberfest. There are rallies devoted to all brands, such as the Mother Road Rally on historic Route 66. There are even cultural motorcycle rallies like the Roundup, which began as a rally for African American riders but now encompasses any rider who just wants to have a good time.

Most motorcycle clubs (like those mentioned in Chapter 19) hold national rallies. Women On Wheels holds its International Ride-In each summer at various locations around the country. The Christian Motorcyclists Association holds several rallies each year. The Retreads Motorcycle Club, International, Inc., has a big get-together each summer, as do the Harley Owners Group, the BMW Motorcycle Owners of

America, the Moto Guzzi National Owners Club, and just about every other group you can imagine.

The American Motorcyclist Association holds its Vintage Motorcycle Days (VMD) at the Mid-Ohio Sports Car Course in Lexington, Ohio, each July, and this event provides some of the most spectacular vintage racing in the country.

One of the more entertaining events held each year is the Davis Motorcycle Rally, held in New Hampton, Iowa, every September. This family oriented rally offers much the same experience as other touring-bike orientated rallies like Americade, but with a bit more elbow room: only about 4,000 motorcyclists attend Davis each year, rather than the 50,000 at Americade. Another small rally that provides big entertainment is the Sportbike Rally in Parry Sound, Ontario. This is a great place for Yanks to go and see Canadians take on the sport.

One of the great things about all rallies is that you get to meet interesting people, many of whom you encounter again and again over the years. While the motorcycle community is growing, it's still a relatively small group, and sooner or later, you'll meet just about everybody, from Willie G. Davidson to celebrities to a couple from your own hometown.

The Least You Need to Know

- Any dependable bike that you are comfortable riding can be a touring bike.
- While it's fun to be spontaneous when traveling on a bike, you should at least plan where you'll make your next fuel stop.
- Make certain that your bike is in top running condition before you take a trip, and don't take off on questionable tires.
- Sloppy packing on a motorcycle can lead to your gear falling off and getting caught in your wheels, causing you to crash.
- Attending rallies is a great way to meet other members of the motorcycling community.

Trikes and Electrics

In This Chapter

- What three-wheeled motorcycles are all about
- How trikes differ from normal motorcycles
- The difference between trikes, reverse trikes, and sidecars
- How electric motorcycles work
- Capabilities of electric bikes
- How to tell if an electric bike is right for you

Maybe you're a different breed of cat, or dog, or humanoid. We already know that's true because you're reading this book on motorcycles, and furthermore, you're now dabbling at least one toe into a chapter on three-wheeled and electric motorcycles. How feng shui is that!

In America, motorcycling is all about following your own path. Unlike in some other countries, where small motorcycles and scooters represent some folks' best opportunity for motorized transportation, in the United States cars are, face it, the *de facto* method of getting around. (That is, unless you live in a city with good mass transit or which is bicycle-friendly.) Because cities, schools, and businesses are already set up to handle large volumes of cars, riding a motorcycle really becomes an optional pursuit. And since you're obviously just the type to take a risk and explore this wonderful sport, you might also be the type to explore it on three wheels, or with a nearly silent, smooth, and "carbon-free" electric motor providing the grunt.

Read on for the inside skinny on three-wheeled motorcycles of every stripe, followed by the essential story on electric bikes.

When Three Wheels Are Just Right

As Snowball the pig said in George Orwell's *Animal Farm*, "Four legs good, two legs bad." He was, of course, talking about animal-kind versus mankind. But now that the subject has come up, where do the three-legged (or actually three-wheeled) animals among us, namely *trikes*, stand? After all, they exist smack between motorcycles and cars, and as a result take some thinking, some adapting, and some openness to accept and adopt. But after reading this section, you may be inclined to go try one, and maybe even buy one. When that happens, you'll be among a select breed of riders.

CYCLE BABBLE

A **trike** can take three different forms: two wheels in front and one back; two wheels in back and one in front; or two wheels in line, like a regular motorcycle, with the third wheel located on the right side.

What all of this psychobabble means is quite simply that, like Goldilocks' middle bowl of porridge, the new crop of three-wheel scooters and motorcycles—often simply called trikes—are just right for some people. Offering the wind-in-your-face excitement of a motorcycle with the improved stability of a multiwheeler, the growing number of three-legged machines is finding homes in America's garages. From a small 244cc Piaggio MP3 three-wheeled scooter to a giant 1.7-liter Harley-Davidson Tri-Glide touring machine, and from a racy Can-Am Spyder to a big custom Chevy V8-powered chopper, the range of available three-wheeled machinery is as wide as the Kansas prairie.

So how do you know if a three-wheeled motorcycle is even right for you? Reading this section is a good way to find out. But in brief: if balancing a motorcycle is a daunting proposition to you, a three-wheeler might be a good place to start. However, there are only a few that combine light weight and a low price, one example of which is the Piaggio MP3. Occupying the middle ground in both size and cost are three-wheeled sidecar rigs from the Indian company Royal Enfield and the Russian company Ural. Can-Am and Harley-Davidson produce larger and more expensive three-wheelers.

Trikes Through the Ages

Why do three-wheelers even exist, anyway? The answer goes back almost a century in the United Kingdom and Europe, where petrol and cars were expensive, and the roads were narrow. Here, riding motorcycles for everyday transportation made good sense because they were small and maneuverable, affordable, used very little fuel, and were taxed at a lower rate than automobiles.

Can-Am's swoopy Spyder is the modern interpretation of a nearly century-old two-wheels-in-front trike format, popularized by Morgan in the early 1900s. These days this format is called a "reverse trike."
(Photo courtesy of *Motorcyclist* magazine)

To expand their utility, around a century ago motorcycles sprouted a third wheel and a sidecar (later with a protective top and windshield for rainy days) that enabled them to transport an entire family, or groceries and supplies, all on the cheap. Another approach was the Morgan trike of the early 1900s, which featured a two-seat cockpit, a steering wheel, a front-mounted engine, two steerable front wheels and a single rear wheel. It was half car, half motorcycle—and just right for inexpensive, versatile transportation.

While America never needed nor adopted such devices, as the decades passed and technology evolved, a naturally evolving market finally made room for trikes here in the United States, and today there are several intriguing styles available.

Three-Wheeled Combinations

Amazingly, a greater variety of trike designs are available than any other form of street-legal vehicles:

- Traditional trikes use repurposed motorcycle architecture that places a motorcycle-style wheel and fork in front and a pair of drive wheels in back.

- Another approach features two wheels in front and one wheel in back. This is often referred to as a "reverse trike." Some experts regard this as the best platform because it can corner left or right equally well (unlike a motorcycle with an attached sidecar), and because it has two wheels that steer and carries most of its weight on those wheels.

- The third design attaches a sidecar to the right side of an existing motorcycle.

I offer more details on all three of these designs in the following sections.

As a group, trike owners seem to enjoy getting out on the open road and going places. Accordingly, these adventurous souls often fit their machines with a travel trunk and even tow a trailer so they can bring along camping and cooking equipment, cold-weather riding gear, or clothes and supplies for an extended trip. The thrill is in being out in the elements touring the countryside, while also having all necessary comfort items close at hand.

Trikes: One Wheel in Front

Essentially an Electra Glide touring motorcycle with dual rear wheels, the Harley-Davidson Tri Glide design recalls the early days of Harley's *meter maid* police three-wheelers. The lavish modern Tri Glide Ultra Classic, and its more modest relative the Street Glide, features a single steerable front wheel with handlebar and foot controls like a motorcycle's, and the company's V-twin engine powering dual rear wheels.

 CYCLE BABBLE

The term **meter maid** recalls an era when female police officers rode motorized trikes and gave out a loving bumper crop of parking tickets.

This type of trike offers three-wheel stability and eliminates the need to balance a bike that could topple over without the rider's strength and finesse to hold it up. Naturally, no sidestand or centerstand is required, and the Tri Glide, priced at about $30,000, also features a reverse gear. That's a good thing, because at 1,174 pounds, you wouldn't want to push the Tri Glide backwards into a parking space.

Numerous aftermarket companies offer their own unique-construction trikes as well as conversions for other motorcycles, including the Honda Gold Wing, a large and luxurious six-cylinder touring motorcycle. Regardless of the brand, though, three-wheelers are nearly always larger, heavier, more complex, and more expensive than their two-wheel counterparts.

Harley-Davidson is the leading original equipment manufacturer (OEM) to adapt motorcycle-style architecture to three wheels. The result is the Tri Glide Ultra Classic, a big V-twin powered tourer built for long and memorable days on the road. (Photo courtesy of Harley-Davidson Motor Co.)

Reverse Trikes: Two Wheels in Front

With motorcycle-style seating, two steerable wheels in front, and a single drive wheel in back, the Can-Am Spyder series grants a wind-in-your-face motorcycle ride experience with no need to learn the tricky balancing act a two-wheeled bike requires, and no need to master using a sidestand or centerstand.

In case you wondered, the Can-Am Spyder RS and RT take their design inspiration from an unlikely source—snowmobiles! But when you think about it, the parallels are right there: a snowmobile has two skis for steering in front, a handlebar for turning, and a single drive track in back. Capable of commuting to work, taking a Sunday morning ride, or traveling cross country, the 929-pound Spyder also occupies the far end of the motorcycle spectrum in terms of size and cost, around $20,000.

On the more affordable side lives the Piaggio MP3 250, 400, and 500 model range. Weighing as little as 450 pounds with a starting price of around $7,000, the MP3 popularized three-wheel scooter travel when it debuted in 2006. While the MP3 does share its two-wheels-in-front design with the Can-Am Spyder, even a casual glance at the two machines reveals an important difference: the Can-Am's front wheels are positioned far apart, and the Piaggio's are positioned close together. This means that the Can-Am essentially steers like a car; the vehicle remains fairly "flat" in corners and does not lean inward like a motorcycle. On the other hand, because the MP3's front wheels are set close together the vehicle steers just like a motorcycle, with the rider leaning into the corners. They are two very different cups of Darjeeling, but the MP3 is one that a lot of riders apparently enjoy—the company says the model range accounts for 30 percent of the Piaggio division's annual scooter sales.

One of the more novel inventions of the last decade is Piaggio's MP3, which features two wheels in front, one in back, and still leans like a motorcycle. The twin front wheels can be locked in the upright position for stability when parked.
(Photo courtesy of Piaggio Group Americas, Inc.)

The difference between the Can-Am Spyder and Piaggio MP3's "two-wheels-in-front" design and the Harley Tri Glide "one-wheel-in-front" style is mostly handling. While the physics are complex, the bottom line is that the Can-Am and Piaggio "reverse trike" designs offer sporty performance up to and including some spirited cornering, and traditional trikes like the Harley are more for straight-line cruising and touring.

Sidecars: Motorcycle + Sidecar

The last form of three-wheelers is the traditional motorcycle with a sidecar bolted on via a series of steel connecting arms. Precious few motorcycle manufacturers offer a sidecar as standard equipment, with the Russian company Ural being an exception. India's Royal Enfield also offers a sidecar as a factory option.

Royal Enfield, an old British motorcycle nameplate, is now manufactured in India. You can use the single-cylinder Bullet with a bolt-on $3,000 Cozy sidecar to expand your passenger-carrying capacity or to eliminate the need to balance in the traditional motorcycle sense.
(Photo courtesy of Classic Motorworks Ltd.)

There are a number of advantages to riding a motorcycle with a sidecar. One is that you don't have to balance like on a two-wheeler (although motorcycles with sidecars do require finesse to ride, including the creative use of *body English*). It also won't tip over when you stop, and you'll never need to struggle to hold it upright at a traffic light—even if your legs are on the shorter rather than longer side, or if you're disabled. If you like to travel with passengers, then you can put one in the sidecar, and maybe another one behind you on the seat if you like. Sidecars likewise offer a great place to store cargo, such as if you want to run to the nursery on a Saturday morning to get a few flats of geraniums. And finally, you can always detach the sidecar and enjoy using a standard motorcycle anytime you like (though you have to be qualified with tools, or else use a qualified mechanic, to do so).

CYCLE BABBLE

Body English describes how a person uses particular body motions to accentuate or improve the outcome of a certain physical maneuver. You might use body English to direct a bowling ball down the lane, to help spin your partner on the dance floor … and to turn a sidecar.

Three of the more prominent makers of three-wheelers include Can-Am, Harley-Davidson, and Piaggio. You can find out more about their offerings, along with those of other companies, at the following websites:

Trikes	www.harley-davidson.com/en_US/Motorcycles/ tri-glide-ultra-classic.html
Reverse trikes	http://spyder.brp.com/en-US
	www.piaggiousa.com/scooters.php
Sidecars	www.enfieldmotorcycles.com
	www.imz-ural.com

In addition, there are numerous area and regional clubs for three-wheel devotees. But a good national club to try is Trike Riders International, which is devoted to activities and fellowship for trike riders of all stripes. Find them at www.trikes.org.

MOTORCYCOLOGY

In North America at least, sidecars are mounted on the right side of the motorcycle so that the rider (or operator if you prefer) of the motorcycle occupies the left side of the vehicle, nearest to opposing traffic. Can you imagine what would happen if sidecars were mounted on the left side? You might take Aunt Edna for a ride, and then forget for a moment your bike was connected to a sidecar at all, nearly running her smack into the grille of an oncoming taco wagon. You don't want to go there, because you'd probably kiss that $5 bill in your annual birthday card goodbye.

Safety Is Still a Priority

While three-wheelers may appear easier and safer to operate than a standard motor-cycle, like motorcycles they still require training, practice, and skill—and can equally subject you to injury if you make a mistake. So whether you're considering three wheels or two, take a Motorcycle Safety Foundation course before you set foot (or tire, actually) on public roads on any type of motorcycle. You certainly will be glad you did. (See Chapter 10 for information on motorcycle safety courses.)

STEER CLEAR

Three-wheelers are significantly larger and heavier than their two-wheeled motorcycle cousins. If you have no riding experience at all, steer clear of buying the biggest and most luxurious three-wheeler you can find as your first motor-cycle. It's better to take a Motorcycle Safety Foundation course (see Chapter 10), gain adequate riding experience on a smaller three-wheeler like the Piaggio MP3 range, and then move up to Big Momma when you're really ready.

Rise of the Electric Voodoo Machines

Long ago and far away in youth's 'hood, there was a kid who had ingeniously built an electric motorcycle. It was a hybrid, actually, a minibike frame with an old washing-machine electric motor mounted where the old putt-putt mower engine originally lived. It worked great, too. He could go round and round on the driveway just as far as dad's orange hedge-trimmer extension cord would let him reach.

Fast-forward maybe four decades, and we have the new kids on the block creating computer-designed and -operated electric superbikes capable of sizzling acceleration, triple-digit top speeds, a range of up to 100 miles between charges, and a carbon footprint of precisely zero (although this is somewhat paradoxical, because there's carbon in the batteries, carbon in the steel, and so on). In fact, Zero is the name of one of the pioneers of electric bikes. This company, together with others called Brammo, KTM, Mission One, and Roehr, are pushing a bow wave of excitement for electric bikes, and they're quickly touching all the bases, from superbikes to off-road playbikes to everyday commuter bikes. With prices ranging from below $10,000 for a Brammo or Zero commuter bike, to nearly $35,000 for the Roehr eSuperBike RR with twin motors, 96 horsepower, and premium European chassis components, there is already something for literally everybody.

Understand Your Motivation

But back to the term "zero carbon footprint" for a few moments. If your motivation in buying an electric motorcycle—or any electric vehicle, for that matter—is the notion of making zero impact, you should probably expand your world view a bit. While admittedly a solar-powered electric motorcycle, which charges its batteries directly from the sun (or perhaps wind or renewable biofuel), is technically possible, that's not how things work in the real world, at least currently. Modern photovoltaic panels of the type you could affix to your vehicle are not currently powerful enough to charge it outright. You still need high-voltage household current, or else current from a charging station, to do that. So while the machine in question may be able to whisk down the road with zero internal-combustion emissions, the electricity to power it still most likely came from a fossil-fueled or nuclear-powered plant.

That said, many believe that electric vehicles are our future, and if you squire around town on a new electric motorcycle, you can definitely take pride in being the first of a new breed of tech-savvy buyers.

It Takes Energy to Move

If you want to get all simple about it, the whole point of having an engine in a motorcycle is to do the work that your legs would otherwise do, for example, on a bicycle. In other words, to turn the back wheel. Whether your goal is to go to the corner store for some Twinkies or else to rocket around the Daytona speedway in a professional race, at the end of the day you need power to turn the back wheel for you. You already read about how normal motorcycle engines provide this in Chapters 5 and 6.

Unless you were drawing pictures of motorcycles instead of listening to your teacher in Physics 101, you might remember the law of conservation of energy, which says that energy cannot be created or destroyed, but it can change forms. Thus, the traditional internal-combustion engine turns the potential energy contained in gasoline into thermal energy (those neat little explosions inside the cylinders), accompanied by a large change in volume (a chemical change), and finally into kinetic energy (the rotation of the crankshaft and driveline) to turn the back wheel. Naturally, this is what sends you whistling down the road.

Amazingly, the same thing goes for an electric motorcycle, only instead of residing in the fuel tank in the form of gasoline, the potential energy is stored in the battery pack as chemical energy. When you turn the throttle, this chemical energy is turned into electricity, and then into kinetic energy as the motor turns, driving through a simplified transmission to turn, *voilà*, the back wheel.

No Such Thing as a Free Ride (Yet)

Here's an example of the shell game that can be played with the whole "green revolution" argument in transportation. It's entirely possible to charge up a seemingly clean electric motorcycle (or car) using a dirty, filthy gasoline-powered generator that has no catalytic converter or other emissions equipment, and which runs on oil bought from some foreign nation or dug out of a sensitive seabed off our own shores. So while the end result is a vehicle zipping down the road with no tailpipe emissions, emissions aplenty were created while the "green" motorcycle's battery was charging. Not everything is as it appears.

Bottom line: before you sign the papers to adopt the notion that electric vehicles are totally emissions free, you might want to consider where the energy comes from to charge them up. And for that matter, where all the silicon, steel, aluminum, carbon, lithium, plastic, rubber, petrochemicals, and other materials come from to design, build, and bring them to you.

MOTORCYCOLOGY

Both gasoline engines and electric motors need energy to run. The traditional gasoline engine uses the potential energy stored in gasoline, where the electric motorcycle uses the potential energy stored in batteries. The end result is the same: both types of powerplants turn the rear wheel to move you forward.

Electric-Bike Technology

They may look all modernistic and techie with their sculpted body panels, but underneath, electric motorcycles actually share quite a lot with traditional motorcycles. They still have a chassis (usually steel or aluminum) like a regular bike, suspension systems consisting of a front fork and rear swingarm, hydraulic disc brakes, lights and a horn, handlebars, seating, fenders, and hand and foot controls. And once underway, they are every bit as much a "motor cycle" as, well, a real motorcycle.

For some people, the hardware lurking beneath those body panels may be a bit mysterious. Fear not though, because electric motorcycles are, in principal at least, simpler than gasoline-powered bikes. They have way fewer mechanical components and, with the exception of the inner workings of their various electronic boxes (which we won't go into here), are quite easy to get your head around. So here goes.

Batteries

The go-to battery for heavy lifting that we all grew up with is the lead-acid battery. This is the same type that starts your car and powers the lights and TV in your RV. Motorcycles use them, too, for starting the engine and operating the lights and accessories.

But these old faithful batteries don't have the high energy-to-weight ratio that's desirable for powering a vehicle swiftly and for long distances. The old lead-acid batteries can provide plenty of power, but such an electric motorcycle would be way too big and heavy to be practical.

That's why a newer form of electric battery technology has been adopted for the crop of electric motorcycles now emerging. They use *lithium-ion batteries* of the type that power your cell phone, laptop computer, and digital camera, only much larger, of course. Producing about 3.6 volts per cell compared to the 2.1 volts from a lead-acid battery and 1.5 volts for a common alkaline flashlight battery, the primary advantage of lithium-ions is their high energy density, light weight, quick recharge time, and long life. Although expensive, these traits make them ideal to power electric motorcycles.

CYCLE BABBLE

Lithium-ion batteries produce electricity by the reaction between a carbon anode (positive terminal), a metal oxide cathode (negative terminal), and a lithium salt electrolyte (conductor).

The "energy density" (the ability to store energy) of lithium ion far surpasses traditional lead-acid car-type batteries, or even nickel-metal hydride batteries. This is a crucial deal for electric bikes because, unlike a car, there isn't a huge amount of space available to store large batteries. So having an efficient, small, lightweight one is better. As of this writing, the latest electric motorcycles can go about one hour or 100 miles on a single charge. Maximizing operating range and having the ability to provide quick, convenient recharges may make or break the widespread adoption of electric vehicles.

The term "recharge time" refers to how long it takes to recharge a depleted battery pack. Depending on the size of battery pack and the type of current available (120 volts or 240 volts), recharging can take anywhere from 90 minutes to 6 hours or more.

MOTORCYCOLOGY

Wired in series, the lithium-ion battery packs in the emerging cadre of electric motorcycles produces from less than 100 volts up to 300 volts. The battery pack normally is service free for the life of the batteries, which can range from 500 recharges up to 2,000 recharges. At this point the battery pack needs replacement.

Electric Motor

The motors in the new electric motorcycles are specifically built for the job. Using up to 96 volts (higher voltage makes short work of hard jobs), they rotate from 0 to 6,000 rpm or more and, unlike gasoline engines, typically produce their maximum torque at very low rpms (theoretically 0 rpm). This means they can accelerate really quickly from a standstill or from low speeds, such as is required around town. Most electric motorcycles use one electric motor, but some, such as the Roehr eSuperBike, use two. Electric motors are not yet as powerful as a topflight superbike engine, but the highest-output ones can still spur a motorcycle well above 100 mph. Normally it is maintenance free—or nearly so.

The Roehr eSuperBike has not one but two electric motors, with a claimed output of 96 horsepower—nearly as much as a modern four-cylinder 600cc sportbike.
(Photo courtesy of Roehr Motorcycles)

Controller

The electric controller is akin to the throttle on a normal motorcycle; it determines how much current is fed to the electric motor. The twist grip connects to a potentiometer, a device that interprets the throttle position selected by the rider, and turns it into an electrical signal. Electric controllers contain circuitry that gets hot, and some require cooling fans and/or air ducts to draft the heat away from them (along with the battery pack and electric motor itself). The controller is mounted out of sight, beneath the bodywork of the motorcycle. Normally the controller is also normally maintenance free.

Transmission

Unlike a normal gasoline-powered motorcycle, an electric motorcycle has no need for a clutch or a traditional gearbox. That's because the electric motor does not need to idle like a gasoline engine to be ready to ride. It can simply be stopped while awaiting the rider's decision to turn the throttle and go. Also unlike gasoline engines, electric motors theoretically have an almost totally flat power curve, and they also produce power from 0 rpm on up to their maximum rotational speed. That means that multiple gearbox ratios are not required to achieve a fully functional machine.

The electric motor may drive the rear wheel through a belt or chain. But on the horizon are electric motors built right into wheel hubs that may further reduce weight and improve efficiency.

Zero Motorcycles started with an off-road playbike, then expanded to an assortment of models including the street-legal Zero S and this dual-sport Zero DS.
(Photo courtesy of Zero Motorcycles)

Regenerative Braking

An electric motor spins when you hook it up to a battery. But did you know that same electric motor will also *produce* electricity if you spin its armature with a power drill or even your fingertips? The same electromagnetic induction that powers the motor also can produce power! That's the principle behind regenerative braking. When you're sailing down the road and close the throttle, the more sophisticated electric vehicle controllers can turn the still-spinning motor into a generator, sending current back into the battery pack and increasing your travel range.

MOTORCYCOLOGY

Five current brands of electric motorcycles include Brammo, KTM, Mission Motors, Roehr, and Zero. As this book went to press, none of the major motorcycle makers had followed suit, but it's probably only a matter of time before they do. You can find out more about the currently available offerings at the following websites.

- www.brammo.com
- www.ktm.com
- www.ridemission.com
- www.roehrmotorcycles.com
- www.zeromotorcycles.com

A great source for up-to-the-minute news and information about electric motorcycles is a website called PlugBike.com.

Should I Ride Electric?

The new and growing field of electric motorcycles is very exciting. Their performance and operating range are growing quickly, up to the point where some of them are looking like pretty good alternatives to regular gasoline motorcycles. Here is a handy list to use to determine if one is right for you:

- **Affordability.** New technology always costs more, so can you reasonably afford it? The purchase price is typically higher than comparable used or new gasoline bikes. You'll probably also want to verify whether you can get collision and comprehensive insurance for it, on top of the compulsory liability insurance your state no doubt requires. But on the flip side, electric motorcycles may be eligible for attractive tax credits. Check with a qualified tax accountant in your state to find out.

- **Travel Requirements.** At least in our current highway system, there are precious few charging stations available for electric vehicles. If you plan to travel more than half the distance of an electric motorcycle's estimated travel range, you'd better figure out how you're going to charge up the battery midtrip so you can get home again.

- **Service.** If you buy an electric vehicle and it has a service need (either under warranty or after the warranty expires), how is that going to get handled and who is going to pay for it? You don't want to be stuck in Syracuse with an electric bike that can only be repaired in Reno.

- **Climate.** Batteries get as sleepy as a garter snake in cold weather, and so living in a temperate climate makes good sense if you plan to use the vehicle year-round. But then again, you wouldn't be riding any type of motorcycle in Fargo in December, now would you?

 STEER CLEAR

Unless your daily mileage requirements are within the range of the battery pack on an electric motorcycle, don't count on it as your primary transportation. Otherwise you might run out of juice before you can get home, stranding you or delaying your trip while you find a place to recharge.

The Least You Need to Know

- Three-wheelers come in three different configurations: trikes, reverse trikes, and sidecars.
- Trikes do not handle like a car or a motorcycle; they have their own peculiar style.
- Trikes typically cost more than their two-wheel scooter and motorcycle cousins.
- Electric motorcycle technology is evolving at a rapid pace.
- Battery range remains one of the primary concerns of electric-bike practicality.
- Electric motorcycles still use energy—it's just electrical energy rather than energy from gasoline.

Biker's Buying Guide to New Bikes

The editors of *Motorcyclist, Motorcycle Cruiser, Sport Rider,* and *Super Streetbike* magazines produce an annual buyer's issue that lists all street-legal motorcycles for sale for the current year, along with technical specifications, prices, and editors' comments. This guide is more than worth the few dollars it costs on the newsstand. But the equation gets even better in *The Complete Idiot's Guide to Motorcycles,* because we've included the core elements of this buyers' guide here as well.

The recommendations that follow may vary from those of the magazine staff because this book is judging the bikes using different criteria. The magazine publishes its guide for experienced motorcyclists; in contrast, by and large the following recommendations are geared toward helping new riders. Bikes are evaluated using the following criteria:

- **Ease of use.** Learning to ride is difficult enough without choosing a difficult motorcycle to learn on. In evaluating the bikes in this guide, a premium has been placed on power characteristics (because you will find smooth throttle control to be easier on bikes with a broad, smooth powerband) and on ease of handling.

  Note that ease of handling is not the same as outright handling prowess. When I discuss ease of handling, I'm talking about how maneuverable a bike is in the kind of situations in which you will ride. A bike might be the best-handling machine on the racetrack but be a real handful when you practice braking and swerving in a parking lot. Bikes that combine smooth power and easy handling earned a "Recommended—Beginner" rating.

- **Versatility.** You probably aren't going to go out and buy several bikes right off the bat, so your first motorcycle should be capable of serving you in a variety of situations. It should also be a bike you can grow with, rather than a machine you'll want to ditch midway through your first season of riding.

- **Ease of maintenance.** Few people have an unlimited expense account to maintain a fleet of bikes, so ease of maintenance has been taken into account in these bike recommendations.

- **Fun.** Because motorcycling should be fun, selecting a bike based solely on its practicality would be foolish. Incidentally, style is also included under the category of fun. That's because style is strongly a matter of opinion, and this book's opinion of what looks stylish may vary from yours. If you like the way a bike looks, don't worry about what anyone else thinks about it.

The descriptions of the many motorcycles within this buying guide are all self-explanatory, but you'll also notice that some bikes are marked as "recommended." To make this book useful beyond the learning stage of your motorcycle ownership experience, the recommendations are broken down into three categories:

- **Recommended—Beginner.** These are bikes that should be both safe and unintimidating to you once you've completed your initial motorcycle training.

- **Recommended—Intermediate.** Motorcycles in this category will be more challenging to ride than the beginner group, but will be great bikes to move up to once you've clocked up some miles on two wheels.

- **Recommended—Experienced.** Finally, these are the machines that really need some skill to ride safely, but are among the best of the best at what they do. They're the bikes we aspire to.

All of these recommended bikes are featured in the color section, too, so you can take a closer look at them. By the way, it's much easier to clean drool off the shiny colored paper, so don't hold back.

This appendix lists virtually all readily available street-legal motorcycles for sale in the United States, including dual-sport bikes that are at home on the dirt or the street. Excluded are competition bikes such as motocross and trials motorcycles, because such focused machines aren't relevant to most people. This appendix is divided into two sections: Cruisers and Tourers; and Sportbikes, Sport-Tourers, and Standards. Each section leads off with a general description of the types of motorcycles contained therein. And finally, within each category, motorcycles are organized alphabetically by manufacturer. Happy reading—and riding!

Cruisers and Tourers

Since the advent of the touring cruiser, the line between touring bike and cruiser has blurred. With a couple of exceptions, most touring cruisers and touring bikes are too heavy and cumbersome for a novice rider, but the cruiser category provides ample examples of terrific first motorcycles. Most cruisers are on the heavy end of the motorcycle spectrum, but their low seat height and low center of gravity (especially the V-twin-powered machines) can mask that weight, making them feel much lighter when they're moving. Also, the relaxed power output of most V-twin engines is ideal for newer riders trying to learn smooth throttle control. Generally, most motorcycles of 1000cc or more are going to be too big, too heavy, and too powerful for novice riders. There are, of course, exceptions, and I've noted them.

Aprilia Cruisers and Tourers

Aprilia MANA 850/GT ABS

The MANA 850 is designed as "a bike for all seasons" that puts "safety, versatility and easy riding first." The key is a seven-speed transmission that can be operated manually, or function automatically in three different modes. The MANA GT ABS adds an anti-lock braking system (ABS) and a half fairing with adjustable windshield. A generous top box is also available.

BMW Cruisers and Tourers

BMW K1200 LT

If your idea of fun is touring the country on a two-wheeled luxury liner, take a long, hard look at BMW's K1200 LT. A higher-output, liquid-cooled inline-four makes 116 horsepower and 86 pound-feet of torque, while a trick, electrohydraulic centerstand helps with parking. Just a few of the niceties you'll enjoy while earning your Iron Butt certificates.

BMW K1300 GT

BMW's K-series inline-four motorcycles received additional displacement; a wider, stronger torque curve; and more peak horsepower last year. Built for high-speed sport touring, the K1300 GT also features ABS as standard equipment, and options include a xenon headlight, the latest ESA II electronically adjustable suspension, and traction control.

BMW R1200 RT

One of our all-time favorite sport-tourers is BMW's R1200 RT. The RT offers standard saddlebags (optional top box), ABS, superb wind and weather protection, and plenty of power with its 1170cc air-cooled boxer engine, which makes 110 horsepower. With the RT's low center of gravity, handling and maneuverability are also exceptional.

Can-Am Cruisers and Tourers

Can-Am Spyder RT/RT Audio/RT-S

Can-Am's innovative Spyder trike touring lineup starts with the base RT model. The midlevel RT Audio and Convenience model adds AM/FM audio with iPod integration, fingertip shifting, heated passenger grips, and secondary gauges. The RT-S boasts upgraded trim, adjustable rear suspension, and LED and fog lights.

Ducati Cruisers and Tourers

Ducati SportClassic GT 1000 Touring

Ducati's SportClassic range of bikes features the Italian company's proven air-cooled two-valve 90-degree V-twin for simplicity and light weight. As such, even when equipped with its standard windshield and chromed luggage rack, the versatile GT 1000 Touring weighs only 407 pounds dry, giving it a definite handling advantage.

Harley-Davidson Cruisers and Tourers

Harley-Davidson CVO Ultra Classic Electra Glide

The full-dress Electra Glide is the only bike that matters for many tourers, and now here comes the rich Ultra Classic Electra Glide from H-D's prestigious Custom Vehicle Operations. Priced just slightly below the value of Fort Knox, the CVO Electra Glide features a standard GPS unit, a heated leather seat and handgrips, a choice of custom paint jobs, and a powerful 110-cubic-inch Screamin' Eagle mill.

Harley-Davidson CVO Street Glide

Rumble into any town between San Diego and Sturgis, and you'll get instant respect aboard Harley's *ne plus ultra* Street Glide. Newly developed by The Motor Company's inventive Custom Vehicle Operations, the CVO Street Glide packs a Twin Cam Screamin' Eagle, slammed front fender, custom paintwork and seating, LED lighting, oversize saddlebags, and special Agitator wheels.

Harley-Davidson Tri Glide Ultra Classic

With a special three-wheel frame and power from a 103-cubic-inch air-cooled Twin Cam V-twin engine, the Tri Glide Ultra Classic is an entirely different way to tour. Boasting comfortable two-passenger seating, generous storage capacity from a top box and rear-opening trunk, and an optional $1,195 electric reverse gear, it's ready to chase the horizon.

Harley-Davidson CVO Softail Convertible

With its Screamin' Eagle 110 CI V-twin engine, custom seat and paintwork, and Stinger chromed 18-inch wheels, the 2010 CVO Softail Convertible from the H-D Custom Vehicle Operations matches the best work of custom shops at a fraction of the price. Innovations include a detachable compact fairing, passenger seat, and saddlebags, so you can dress it up or go light and lean.

Harley-Davidson Street Glide Trike

The new Street Glide Trike is designed for touring luxury with the low-slung cool of a Harley Street Glide cruiser. Motivated by a 103-cubic-inch Twin Cam V-twin driving through a versatile six-speed gearbox (with an optional electric reverse gear), the Street Glide Trike also features a large fairing for wind protection, a rear-opening trunk offering 4.3 cubic feet of storage, and reduced steering effort.

Harley-Davidson CVO Fat Bob

New in 2010 from Harley's Custom Vehicle Operations, the CVO Fat Bob is nothing less than a customized Dyna Fat Bob on mechanical steroids. It features a 110-cubic-inch Twin Cam Screamin' Eagle engine pumping out a claimed 113 pound-feet of torque, a high-flow air filter, diamond-cut aluminum controls, leather seats, a denim-colored frame, and an attention-getting choice of paint jobs.

Harley-Davidson Electra Glide Ultra Limited

Consummate luxury meets the open road with Harley-Davidson's prestigious Electra Glide Ultra Limited. Its rubber-isolated 103-cubic-inch fuel-injected V-twin engine simply makes the miles melt away, and so do the comfortable front and rear touring seats, heated handgrips, floorboards, and full-coverage touring fairing and lowers. Command central features complete instrumentation and switchgear.

Harley-Davidson Ultra Classic Electra Glide

If you're looking for a premium Milwaukee tourer, here it is. A large fairing with Lexan air deflectors and vented lowers, a Harman/Kardon audio system, and plush seats create a cocoon of comfort for rider and passenger alike. Expansive luggage capacity and a 6-gallon fuel tank put the entire continent within reach, while four-piston brakes, optional ABS, and security system boost confidence.

Harley-Davidson Softail Rocker C

With ultraclean lines, plenty of chrome, and a flame paint job, the Softail Rocker C is unlike anything else that's rolled off Harley's assembly line. The Rocker C is powered by The Motor Company's counterbalanced Twin Cam 96B pushrod V-twin and features a trick two-into-one seat that provides a custom solo-seat look with the versatility of adding a passenger when you so choose.

Harley-Davidson Electra Glide Classic

The Electra Glide Classic captures a classic '60s touring look with fully modern features, including Harley's rubber-mounted Twin Cam 96-cubic-inch pushrod V-twin engine with fuel injection, a six-speed transmission, cast-aluminum wheels, plush suspension, and triple disc brakes with optional ABS. Like most Harleys, the Electra Glide Classic is available in a host of color combinations.

Harley-Davidson Street Glide

The Street Glide is all about a clean, uncluttered look—and plenty of custom-cool touring chops. It features a bat-wing fairing with solo headlight; a short, smoked windscreen; and integrated mirrors. Four-piston brake calipers also come standard, while ABS is optional. The 2010 version included a new 18-inch front wheel, a revised fifth gear, and a redesigned rear fender.

Harley-Davidson Road Glide Custom

The Road Glide Custom is all about making a statement—and a big one. From its audacious shark-style fairing to color-matched saddlebags, this Glide commands you to look at what it's got goin' on. For 2010 the Road Glide added minor upgrades, including a new custom-style taillight and a quieter helical-cut fifth gear. Cruise control, ABS, and a security system are optional.

Harley-Davidson V-Rod Muscle

The V-Rod Muscle is the flagship of the Harley's VRSC lineup. Its high-tech 1250cc DOHC, sequential-port fuel injection, liquid-cooled V-twin engine sends a claimed 86 pound-feet of torque through a five-speed gearbox and belt drive. The V-Rod Muscle stands alone with unique satin chrome straight-shot dual side exhausts and a choice of black or solid-color paint options.

Harley-Davidson Road King/Classic

Think of the Road King as the minimalist's full-dress tourer. Favoring a fork-mounted windshield over a full fairing, and minus the passenger back-rest and top trunk, the Road King strips interstate travel down to the bare essentials—while retaining the performance of H-D's rubber-mounted Twin Cam 96-cubic-inch V-twin. The Road King Classic adds spoke wheels, leather saddlebags, and more paint choices.

Harley-Davidson Heritage Softail Classic

The Heritage Softail blends retro aesthetics with a load of touring features, including touring-style fenders, a detachable Lexan windscreen, comfortable passenger seat with padded backrest, and studded leather saddlebags. It's all powered by H-D's potent Twin Cam, fuel-injected 96-cubic-inch V-twin with a six-speed transmission. Special wheels and solid, two-tone and custom paint jobs are optional.

Harley-Davidson Softail Custom

If you like the classic, chromed, laid-back chopperesque look, the Softail Custom may be a good choice. With an ape-hanger handlebar, a 21-inch chrome-spoked front wheel, a king-and-queen saddle with integrated backrest, and a Fat Bob fuel tank, the Softail Custom is classic Harley-Davidson. Take your choice of six paint combinations, including thee different two-tones.

Harley-Davidson Softail Cross Bones

Designed to combine the soul of postwar bobbers with contemporary 2010 engineering, the Softail Cross Bones features a black ape-hanger handlebar, springer front suspension, a sprung solo seat, and generous floorboards. All of this style rides on top of Harley's proven 96-cubic-inch air-cooled Twin Cam 96B counterbalanced engine for a uniquely powerful ride.

Harley-Davidson Softail Deluxe

The Softail Deluxe is one nostalgic Hog, receiving numerous upgrades a few years back and returned in 2010 with H-D's potent Twin Cam 96B fuel-injected engine. Whitewalls front and back turn on chrome-spoked wheels, while a low seat height of just 25.9 inches makes this one of Milwaukee's lowest Big Twins. Options include chromed aluminum wheels and your choice of solid colors or two-tone paint.

Harley-Davidson Night Rod Special

The Night Rod Special is H-D's sportiest V-Rod, with an upgraded, black-on-black, 1250cc, 60-degree V-twin and brushed, straight-shot exhaust with black caps and black shields. The Night Rod Special also comes with a slipper clutch, four-piston brakes (with optional ABS), a 5-gallon fuel tank, and red-striped rims. A choice of three different two-tone paint jobs is standard.

Harley-Davidson Softail Fat Boy/Lo

Thoroughly revised three years ago, the Fat Boy returned in 2010 with Harley's 96 CI fuel-injected engine powering through a six-speed transmission and bullet-hole 17-inch disc wheels, the rear of which is ringed by a burly 200mm-wide tire. Choose the Fat Boy Lo for sinister black-finished fork covers, tank, fenders, wheels, headlight, oil tank, and exhausts—and a superlow seat height.

Harley-Davidson V-Rod

The V-Rod is Milwaukee's high-tech power cruiser, and features an exotic 1250cc DOHC, liquid-cooled, eight-valve, Revolution V-twin that pumps out a claimed 84 pound-feet of torque. It also offers a slipper clutch, spoked front and semi-disc rear wheels, and options including ABS and a security system. Black paint is standard, but extra-cost colors, including two-tone, are also available.

Harley-Davidson Dyna Fat Bob

With its long tail section, the Dyna Fat Bob is a bit reminiscent of Harley's iconic Super Glide of the early '70s. But the Fat Bob goes much further with twin headlights, double-barrel Tommy-gun exhausts, machined and slotted disc wheels, and stainless steel drag handlebars. Power is from a fuel-injected Twin Cam 96 V-twin feeding through a six-speed transmission and durable belt drive.

Harley-Davidson Dyna Wide Glide

Long and low, with a kicked-out chromed fork, a 21-inch front wheel, and black rims, the Dyna Wide Glide looks better than ever. The Wide Glide retains its trademark wide front fork, drag-style handlebar, shortened front fender, and Tommy-gun paired exhaust setup. A fat 180mm rear tire, side-mounted license plate, and spectacular optional flame paint job also help set it apart.

Harley-Davidson Dyna Super Glide Custom

Begin with a basic Dyna Super Glide, apply massive amounts of chrome, and you have the Dyna Super Glide Custom. Powered by a Twin Cam 96 pushrod V-twin and detailed with chrome accents and beautiful chrome spoke wheels, the Super Glide Custom is available in six colors, including a trio of two-tone combos. Improvements for 2010 included a revised fifth gear and new Michelin tires.

Harley-Davidson Dyna Street Bob

Harley-Davidson's Street Bob epitomizes the old-school bobber look with a tall ape-hanger handlebar, black bodywork and rims, and brightly chromed wheel spokes. The Street Bob puts power to the ground through a six-speed transmission and features a generous 4.7-gallon fuel tank and low-down solo saddle. Vivid Black is standard, and color paint is available for an extra $375.

Harley-Davidson Dyna Super Glide

The Super Glide is Harley's basic big twin, with a silver Twin Cam 96 1584cc V-twin featuring sequential fuel injection and a conventional fork topped by a bullet headlight. The Dyna frame surrounds that engine with rubber mounts and midmount foot controls for comfy ergos. For 2010 the Glide got a new helical-cut fifth gear and new Michelin Scorcher tires.

Harley-Davidson Sportster Forty-Eight

With its all-black chassis, black-finished engine cases, low suspension, and compact 16-inch black wheels, the new Forty-Eight has a slammed-down look that's part drag-racer and part custom-shop special. Power comes from Harley's fuel-injected 1203cc Evolution engine driving through a five-speed gearbox and belt final drive. Two color paint jobs and a security system are the only options.

Harley-Davidson Sportster Nightster

Harley's Sportster Nightster provides an in-your-face style straight out of the '60s. It features old-school fork gators, a chopped rear fender, side-mounted license plate, and lowered suspension for an essential look all its own. The Nightster is powered by a rubber-mounted 1203cc V-twin and is available in four colors, including a pair of two-tone paint jobs, and includes sultry black wheels.

Harley-Davidson Sportster 1200 Low/Custom

The Sportster 1200 Low is a close-to-the-tarmac 1203cc Sporty with a seat height of just 28 inches, midmounted footpegs, and a wide handlebar that's pulled back toward the rider for comfort. This direct '57 Sportster descendant is available with standard cast-aluminum or optional spoke wheels. The Sportster 1200 Custom boasts a classic 21-inch front wheel for a more raked-out look.

Harley-Davidson Sportster Iron 883

Looking like it just came out of a rat-rodder's garage, the Iron 883 features more blacked-out parts than any other bike in the Harley lineup. Based on the venerable 883 Sportster, the Iron 883 provides the essential Milwaukee V-twin experience, with no frills attached. It's also priced attractively, with a $305 security system as the only option. Estimated fuel economy ranges from 45 to 60 mpg.

Harley-Davidson Sportster 883 Low (Recommended—Intermediate)

Milwaukee's base-model Sportster 883 Low is the least expensive way into the Harley-Davidson club. The 883 Low features a rubber-mounted, air-cooled, 883cc V-twin engine; low-rise handlebars; and solo saddle. Iconic Sportster features include staggered shorty exhausts, a peanut fuel tank, and a low single saddle. After 53 years of production, the Sportster remains an American classic.

Honda Cruisers and Tourers

Honda Gold Wing (Recommended—Experienced)

Quite possibly the most competent, capable touring motorcycle in the world, Honda's venerable GL1800 Gold Wing comes in several trim levels: Audio Comfort, Audio Comfort Navi XM, Audio Comfort Navi XM ABS, and Airbag. All are powered by Honda's smooth and powerful 12-valve, 1832cc opposed-six with low maintenance shaft final drive.

Honda DN-01

Borrowing design cues from sportbikes, sport-tourers, and cruisers, Honda's outrageous DN-01 blurs the boundaries between established motorcycle genres. It features an efficient 680cc V-twin engine coupled to an ingenious transmission that can be used in automatic or five-speed manual mode. A long wheelbase and low seat height provide an ultralow look.

Honda VTX1800T/N/F

Honda's VTX1800 comes in several flavors. The classic VTX1800N has valanced fenders, a teardrop tank and headlight, and staggered dual mufflers, while the touring VTX1800T adds a windscreen, passenger backrest, and large saddlebags. The sportier VTX1800F has stripped-down styling, a bobbed front fender, and unique 18-inch wheels and tires.

Honda Fury/ABS

In 2009 Big Red unleashed one of the most audacious factory choppers yet. In addition to offering an exceptionally clean overall design, the Fury boasts a kicked-out front end and a wheelbase of nearly 6 feet, a hidden single shock rear suspension that provides an authentic hard-tail look, a big 200/50-18 rear tire, optional ABS, and typical Honda attention to detail.

Honda 1300 Custom Interstate

A stylish cruiser designed for long-distance riding, the new Interstate differentiates itself from its Sabre and Stateline brethren with a standard touring windscreen, full-size floorboards, heel-toe shifter, leather-covered hard bags, and chrome fork covers for good measure. Pearl Blue paint is unique to the Interstate, but no ABS is currently offered.

Honda 1300 Custom Sabre/ABS

Replacing the VTX1300C from 2009, Honda's 2010 Sabre is a more polished, contemporary-looking middleweight cruiser. Its 1312cc V-twin engine is derived from the Honda Fury chopper and features "Pro Street" dragster-inspired styling, fuel injection, and maintenance-free shaft drive for ease of ownership. ABS is optional.

Honda 1300 Custom Stateline/ABS

The 2010 Stateline is part two of Honda's new 1300 Custom lineup. It replaces the Sabre's clean chopper-style 21-inch front wheel with a beefier traditional 17-incher, along with fully valanced fenders, for a more classic look. Like the other 1300 Customs, the Stateline's 52-degree liquid-cooled V-twin engine has fuel injection and three valves per cylinder. ABS is optional.

Honda Shadow Phantom (Recommended—Beginner)

You'd be hard pressed to find a more custom-looking lightweight cruiser than Honda's 2010 Shadow Phantom. Balancing its sinister black finish and retro-style touches are a civilized new fuel-injected engine that offers strong performance as well as supreme user friendliness. The 745cc liquid-cooled V-twin engine powers through a five-speed gearbox and shaft drive.

Honda Shadow RS

New in 2010, the Shadow RS combines the prowess of a back-roads naked bike with the looks and street credibility of a cruiser. Fuel injected like the Shadow Phantom, the RS offers abundant V-twin torque and a nice exhaust note through its chrome-plated staggered exhausts, but distinguishes itself with chain final drive for a more sport-bike-type riding experience.

Honda Shadow Aero

Full-size aesthetics and middleweight performance make the Shadow Aero an attractive option for budget-minded folk. The Aero is powered by a 745cc, six-valve V-twin breathing through dual exhausts. With a 25.9-inch seat height and lower dry weight, the Shadow Aero is a good choice for cruising newcomers or smaller riders.

Honda Shadow Spirit 750

The chopper-styled Spirit 750 is powered by a liquid-cooled, 52-degree, 745cc V-twin and, like its Shadow Aero cousin, uses low-maintenance shaft drive to transfer power rearward. However, the Spirit features old-school spoke wheels instead of the Aero's cast-aluminum rims. It's available in four colors, including a pair of cool flame variations.

Honda Rebel (Recommended—Beginner)

The 2008 Honda Rebel returns virtually unchanged and remains a staple at rider-training facilities throughout the country. The 234cc, air-cooled parallel-twin provides reliable power, while five speeds and chain final drive put power to the ground. A reasonable price and superlow 315-pound dry weight make the Rebel an excellent choice for beginners.

Hyosung Cruisers and Tourers

Hyosung GV650/SE

The GV650 cruiser is the middleweight cruiser cousin of Hyosung's GT sportbike series. Featuring an inverted fork, digital speedometer, and LED taillights, the GV650 is powered by the same fuel-injected, liquid-cooled, 647cc V-twin as the GT lineup, and offers a five-speed transmission and belt drive as well. Two-tone paint and even a Special Limited Edition are also available.

Hyosung GV250

As the kid brother of the GV650 cruiser, the diminutive GV250 features an eight-valve, 249cc V-twin engine that's fuel injected for 2010, with improved intake and exhaust efficiency. The GV250 still features valanced fenders, a low seat height, and a 3.7-gallon fuel tank for extended range, but Hyosung claims the riding position is improved thanks to a longer fork and lower bars.

Kawasaki Cruisers and Tourers

Kawasaki Vulcan 1700 Voyager/ABS

The Vulcan 1700 Voyager takes up where the Vulcan 1700 Nomad leaves off to provide the consummate full-dress touring mount. Along with its potent 1700cc fuel-injected and liquid-cooled V-twin, it offers a full touring fairing and lowers, and a trunk with integrated passenger backrest. Niceties include plenty of chrome plating, a choice of paint colors, and optional ABS.

Kawasaki Vulcan 1700 Nomad

Introduced last year, the Vulcan 1700 Nomad slots into the Kawasaki lineup just below the Vulcan 2000 Classic LT to provide a thoroughly competent touring rig at an affordable price. Standard features include a 103.7-cubic-inch liquid-cooled V-twin engine, a touring windshield, roomy hard saddlebags, a comfortable dual saddle, front and rear floorboards, and a passenger backrest.

Kawasaki Vulcan 2000

With its four integrated projector-type headlights inside a stylish chrome shell, the Vulcan 2000 is a distinctive power cruiser boasting a 2053cc, liquid-cooled, fuel-injected pushrod V-twin. Kawasaki's biggest V-twin is built for all-day riding comfort, thanks to roomy ergonomics and a bucket-style seat. The single-shock rear suspension is likewise adjustable for enhanced ride quality.

Kawasaki Vulcan 2000 Classic/LT

In traditional fashion, the Vulcan 2000 Classic's cylinders feature a matte-black finish and polished fins. A traditional headlight, buckhorn bar, and plush passenger seat make for a comfortable two-up cruising platform while the stupendous torque powers you down the road. The Classic LT light tourer adds studded seats, leather saddlebags and backrest, passenger floorboards, and a windscreen.

Kawasaki Vulcan 1700 Classic/LT

The Vulcan 1700 Classic joins graceful styling with modern digital fuel injection, a six-speed overdrive transmission, and dual-piston brake calipers for a full quotient of looks and performance. The Classic LT model adds a protective windshield, studded leather seat, passenger backrest, and newly upgraded saddlebags. Both models have improved heat management and paint options for the 2010 model.

Kawasaki Vulcan 900 Classic LT

Take the basic Vulcan 900 Classic and add touring features such as studded leather saddlebags, custom studded seats, a comfortable passenger backrest, and an adjustable windscreen, and you have Kawasaki's 900 Classic LT. The Classic LT model not only soaks up long-distance mileage, it provides a big-bike look and feel at a true bargain price.

Kawasaki Vulcan 900 Custom

Introduced in 2007, the fuel-injected 900 Custom is Kawasaki's midsize cruiser. The chrome-laden dragster look-a-like is complimented by a wide, 180mm, 15-inch rear tire and narrow 21-inch cast wheel up front to successfully blend the versatility of a midsize cruiser with plenty of bad-boy drag style. A Special Edition with black-out components and color-coordinated wheels is $300 more.

Kawasaki Vulcan 900 Classic (Recommended—Intermediate)

The Vulcan 900 Classic was introduced in 2006 and features the long and low styling of the larger Vulcan 2000 Classic. Curved engine fins add style to the 903cc, eight-valve V-twin. Veterans and entry-level riders alike will find the agile 900 friendly and fun, while those on a budget will appreciate its affordable price and premium features such as electronic fuel injection.

Kawasaki Vulcan 500 LTD

The Vulcan 500 LTD is the only parallel twin in Kawasaki's cruiser lineup. Lighter and less expensive than its V-twin brothers, the LTD makes an excellent ride for beginners looking for an entry-level cruiser. The rev-happy engine, coupled with the bike's compact size and affordable price, make it a fun little scoot that returns an estimated 50 mpg.

Kawasaki Eliminator 125

As the smallest cruiser in the Kawasaki lineup, the Eliminator 125 is ready to return a claimed 95 mpg with its thrifty 124cc, air-cooled, single-cylinder engine. Handling is likewise easy, thanks to a feathery wet weight of only 320 pounds—less than half that of many cruisers. Neat styling, electric starting, and easy-on-the-wallet pricing add to the appeal.

Moto Guzzi Cruisers and Tourers

Moto Guzzi Norge 1200 GT

With its curvaceous bodywork, protective fairing, integrated hard saddlebags, and standard ABS, the Moto Guzzi Norge 1200 GT is serious about its role as a Gran Turisimo machine. An upgraded version of Guzzi's perennial 90-degree pushrod V-twin architecture, the 1151cc powerplant is both fuel injected and air cooled, and powers through a six-speed gearbox and shaft final drive.

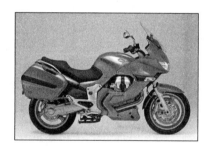

Moto Guzzi California Vintage

Moto Guzzi's California Vintage has been popular for years, and even the LAPD used them at one point. This classic-looking tourer features Guzzi's legendary 1064cc V-twin with low-maintenance shaft drive and a five-speed transmission, while also featuring a large windshield, supplemental fog lights, Brembo brakes, a stylish two-tone dual saddle, and plenty of chrome.

Royal Enfield Cruisers and Tourers

Royal Enfield Bullet G5 Military

If you're into stealth touring, or perhaps on a quest to find D. B. Cooper, the Bullet 500 Military from Royal Enfield may be just what you need. In homage to its World War II military heritage, it's finished in olive drab and comes equipped with durable panniers. Fuel economy is estimated at 85 mpg, thanks in part to modern fuel injection.

Suzuki Cruisers and Tourers

Suzuki Boulevard C109R/RT

The Boulevard C109R and C109RT have a unique style all their own. Powered by a fuel-injected, liquid-cooled, eight-valve 1783cc V-twin tuned for ultralow rpm torque and with low-maintenance shaft drive, the C109RT model features a standard windscreen, leather saddlebags, and a backrest for an additional $1,200. Both models feature Suzuki's combined front/rear braking system.

Suzuki Boulevard M109R/R2/Limited Edition

Suzuki's M109R power cruiser features a 1783cc, liquid-cooled, eight-valve V-twin. There's also a single-shock rear suspension, cast wheels, an inverted fork, and sportbikelike radial-mounted brake calipers. The M109R2 features a distinctive headlight, while the Limited Edition adds unique graphics and polished components for an extra $300.

Suzuki Boulevard C90/T

The Boulevard C90 is based on Suzuki's old Intruder 1500 LC, but upgrades that platform with a GSX-R type electronic fuel-injection system. The C90 also features shaft final drive and a five-speed transmission. For weekend travelers, the C90T model features a windscreen, saddlebags, and backrest for an extra $1,000.

Suzuki Boulevard M90

Dramatically styled and motivated by a lusty 1462cc, liquid-cooled V-twin engine, the Boulevard M90 not only has a street-savvy appearance and performance, but the technology to back it up. Its inverted fork and link-type rear suspension were inspired by the company's GSX-R sportbikes, while its fuel injection ensures crisp operation in all weather conditions.

Suzuki Boulevard S83

Suzuki's Boulevard S83 is based on the old-style Intruder 1400 and features an air-/oil-cooled, six-valve, 1360cc V-twin with twin 36mm Mikuni carburetors that really crank out the torque. The S83 has shaft final drive and weighs just 535 pounds, which makes it exceptionally agile and lots of fun.

Suzuki Boulevard C50/Special Edition/T

Suzuki's middleweight cruiser boasts an 805cc V-twin and classic valanced fenders, dual saddles, and a crisp LED taillight. The C50 Special Edition adds stylish cast wheels for $200 extra, while the touring-oriented C50T gets a standard windscreen, saddlebags, and a passenger backrest for an additional $1,300. The C50 Special Edition and C50T also offer two-tone paint schemes.

Suzuki Boulevard S50/M50/Special Edition

The chopperlike Boulevard S50 has a liquid-cooled, twin-carbureted, 805cc V-twin that delivers plenty of power through a low-maintenance shaft drive. At just 478 pounds and with a seat height under 28 inches, the S50 is user-friendly and maneuverable. The more performance-oriented Boulevard M50 and M50 Special Edition have fuel injection, an inverted fork, and cast wheels.

Suzuki Boulevard S40

Based on the tried-and-true Savage 650 from years past, Suzuki's affordable S40 provides an exceptional level of comfort, affordability, and reliability. It's powered by a four-valve, 652cc single and is the only cruiser in Suzuki's broad line to use belt-drive as opposed to shaft-drive systems. A low dry weight of 381 pounds promotes easy handling.

Triumph Cruisers and Tourers

Triumph Rocket III Touring

Revised in 2009, Triumph's powerful Rocket III Touring bike continued in 2010 with an audacious 2.3-liter triple engine and an interstates-for-breakfast appetite for travel. Dedicated touring features include a big detachable windshield, luxuriously padded seats, front and rear floorboards, and hard bags. Optional ABS, and a choice of colors and accessories, adds to the appeal.

Triumph Rocket III Roadster (Recommended—Experienced)

Now with a claimed 163 pound-feet of torque—which Triumph says surpasses any other motorcycle on the market—the redesigned 2010 Rocket III Roadster adds a healthy dose of streetfighter to its original cruiser DNA. Besides its revised 12-valve, 2294cc triple engine, this new Roadster boasts more comfy ergonomics and rear suspension, standard ABS, and plenty of sinister black paint.

Triumph America/Speedmaster

A shrouded front fork gives the America a radical chopper look, while its traditional-looking, 865cc, air-cooled, V-twin engine provides a distinctly different sound than typical V-twin cruisers. Forward-mounted footpegs and controls ensure a relaxed riding position. The Speedmaster features unique cast-aluminum wheels, a contoured solo seat, flat handlebar, and shorty exhausts.

Triumph Tiger/ABS/SE

All new back in 2007, the Tiger shares the powerful and smooth 1050cc inline-triple with Triumph's Sprint ST, tuned here for low and midrange power. The Tiger wears 17-inch wheels front and back, and is exceptionally comfortable, with a wide and accommodating seat for two-up excursions. ABS is available, or you can choose the SE with standard ABS. All 2010 Tiger models come with locking hard bags.

Ural Cruisers and Tourers

Ural Gear-Up

Recalling its military upbringing, Ural's Gear-Up is as content on a hunting or fishing trip as it is cruising back roads. With available forest or desert camo paint schemes and an engageable sidecar drive, the Gear-Up is a unique sidecar package capable of going nearly anywhere. Other Ural sidecar models include the Tourist, Retro, Patrol, and Red October Limited Edition.

Victory Cruisers and Tourers

Victory Vision Arlen Ness

Bike builder Arlen Ness created his own limited-edition Victory Vision with diamond-cut cylinder heads, a hand-stitched leather seat, custom paintwork, and Ness Signature chrome. But underneath the dazzling finishes, the Arlen Ness model is pure Victory Vision—contemporary engineering wrapped in memorably unique bodywork that's designed for both show and go.

Victory Cory Ness Jackpot

Bike builder Cory Ness was commissioned by
Victory to style this limited-edition Jackpot.
The tricked-out Jackpot features custom Fireball
Red paint, "Evil 7" billet wheels, a hand-stitched
leather seat, an individually numbered build plate,
and plenty more. Power comes from Victory's
106-cubic-inch, fuel-injected V-twin with special
diamond-cut cylinders and heads.

Victory Vision Tour/ABS

With a huge 29 gallons of luggage capacity and
powered by a 106 CI fuel-injected motor driving
through a versatile six-speed transmission, the
Vision Tour is one serious hauler. Its long list of
standard touring features includes a full-coverage
fairing, a power windshield, and multifunction
instrumentation. Options include ABS and a choice
of solid, pearl, or two-tone paint jobs.

Victory Jackpot

The Jackpot is the custom version of the Vegas
and uses Victory's torquey 106-cubic-inch air-/
oil-cooled, fuel-injected Freedom V-twin. It features
a superwide 18×8.5-inch rear wheel and 250mm
tire, unique five-spoke wheels, and distinctive
graphics. The Jackpot also sits exceptionally low to
the ground with a seat height of just 25.7 inches.

Victory Hammer/Hammer S

Victory's Hammer S appeals to riders looking to
flex their biceps with a clean, powerful muscle
cruiser. An inverted fork, dual front disc brakes,
semi-upswept dual exhausts, meaty 250mm-wide
rear tire, and standard tachometer all serve notice
that the Hammer S means business. The Hammer
offers more eye candy in the form of additional
bright-work and dramatic Blue Ice paint.

Victory Vision Cross Country

Victory's new Cross Country is designed to cruise or tour. This stylish bagger defines itself with a powerful 106-cubic-inch fuel-injected Freedom V-twin engine, a six-speed gearbox, a touring fairing, and 21 gallons of storage capacity. Creature comforts include front and rear floorboards, electronic cruise control, and even an MP3-compatible sound system. Three paint schemes are available.

Victory Vision 8 Ball

With a futuristic look, the new 2010 Vision is Victory's latest entry into the luxury cruising/ touring market. It features a fuel-injected 106-cubic-inch Freedom V-twin mated to a six-speed overdrive transmission and smooth-running belt drive. Unique features include highly stylized fairing (with a low "bagger-style" windscreen) and bodywork, extra-long exhausts, and an ultralow seat height.

Victory Hammer 8 Ball

Victory calls the new 2010 Hammer 8-Ball "Raw American Muscle" for good reason. It's powered by Victory's 100-cubic-inch Freedom V-twin engine, detailed with a black-out handlebar and wheels, and pushed down the highway by a six-speed overdrive transmission, durable belt drive, and a massive 250mm-wide rear tire. An inverted front fork and four-piston brake caliper add real performance credibility.

Victory Vision Cross Roads

Debuting in 2010 was the Vision Cross Roads, a stylish light tourer with heavyweight credentials, starting with a big 106-cubic-inch fuel-injected V-twin engine rated at 92 horsepower and a heavy-duty 106 pound-feet of torque. As its name implies, the Cross Roads is built to travel with a generously large windscreen, a useful 21 gallons of weather-proof storage capacity, and an air-adjustable rear shock spring.

Victory Kingpin

Starting with the Vegas, Victory designers added dramatic bodywork that looks like it was sculpted by the wind. Power comes from a 1634cc, air-/oil-cooled V-twin engine, while highly stylized wheels, staggered chrome exhausts, and brightly polished engine fins add plenty of curb appeal. The Kingpin is available in a choice of solid or two-tone colors.

Victory Vegas

The low-slung Vegas is powered by Victory's trademark 100-cubic-inch Freedom V-twin with a six-speed transmission and belt drive. It features a 21-inch front wheel and 18-inch rear wheel, and sports a removable passenger seat and multi-LED taillight. For 2010 the Vegas has a 1.3-inch lower seat, more rear-set foot controls, and a more pulled-back handlebar for improved ergonomics.

Victory Kingpin 8-Ball

The Kingpin 8-Ball has a bad-boy look all its own, thanks to a blacked-out Freedom 100-cubic-inch fuel-injected V-twin engine, aluminum wheels, fork, handlebar, tank, and fenders. The engine powers through a five-speed overdrive transmission. Other features include Victory's dramatic Stingray wheels, a bright LED taillight, and a new seat that puts you 1.3 inches lower to the ground.

Victory Vegas 8-Ball

The Vegas 8-Ball is the least expensive cruiser in the Victory lineup and hosts an array of attractive features, such as the 100-cubic-inch Freedom V-twin engine with five-speed transmission. Blacked-out bodywork, fork sliders, triple clamps, handlebars, and wheels give the Vegas 8-Ball plenty of attitude, while a new 1.4-inch lower seat and more rearward control placement make it easier to handle.

Yamaha Cruisers and Tourers

Yamaha Royal Star Venture S

The Royal Star Venture S is Yamaha's big touring rig. Powered by a torquey, smooth 1294cc V-4 with low-maintenance shaft drive, it provides real comfort and reliability, and is fully prepped for long hauling with a four-speaker sound system with CB radio/intercom/CD player. Both the front fork and link-type rear suspension are air adjustable for different load conditions.

Yamaha Star VMAX

Successor to the fast and furious original 1985 V-Max, the 2009 VMAX boasts a humungous 1679cc, fuel-injected V-4 engine. It also adopts Yamaha sportbike technology, including Yamaha Chip Controlled Throttle and Yamaha Chip Controlled Intake to smooth power delivery and improve torque spread. The audacious power-cruiser styling is unmistakable.

Yamaha Star Stratoliner S/Deluxe

The Star Stratoliner S uses the Roadliner's powerful and refined air-cooled, 1854cc, fuel-injected V-twin for its sleek design, strong performance, and durability. Featuring hard bags, a backrest, and a large windscreen, it's ready to travel in style. New in 2010, the Stratoliner Deluxe added a sleek bagger-style fairing with integrated audio system and color-matched hard bags—and tons of authority.

Yamaha Star Roadliner S

The popular Roadliner S features loads of polished chrome, including (but definitely not limited to) engine covers, fork, and fork covers, plus polished aluminum wheels. It is also powered by the same smooth, torquey, fuel-injected, 1854cc V-twin as the Stratoliner and features a quiet and reliable belt drive. "Neo-streamline" design gives the Roadliner S a distinctive look.

Yamaha Road Star Silverado/S

The Road Star Silverado cruiser is retro-styled, with fat 16-inch diameter wheels and tires, valanced fenders, and roomy leather-covered saddlebags. Power is provided by a torquey, air-/oil-cooled, 1670cc V-twin featuring electronic fuel injection. The premium Road Star Silverado S features plenty of chrome accents, passing lamps, and locking hard saddlebags for an additional $600.

Yamaha Star Raider/S

Yamaha's Star brand set out to create a chopper with improved functionality and reliability. Both Raider models feature an air-/oil-cooled, 1854cc V-twin with plated cylinders and forged pistons, along with an aluminum chassis tuned for agile handling. The Raider S adds polished chrome to its triple clamps, fork sliders, air-box cover, engine covers, headlight housing, and handlebar risers.

Yamaha Road Star S

The Road Star S is Yamaha's mainstay cruiser, built around a robust and reliable 1670cc, eight-valve, pushrod air-cooled V-twin. It boasts twin discs up front, low-maintenance belt drive, and a bright LED taillight for visibility. Numerous chrome accents include front fork and brake master cylinder, switchgear, and levers. Floating floorboards add to comfort on long trips.

Yamaha V Star 1300 Tourer

The heart and soul of Yamaha's V Star 1300 Tourer is a throaty-sounding, liquid-cooled, 1304cc V-twin. Like other Star motorcycles, it merges authentic cruiser styling and modern engineering to create a highly useful light-duty touring rig, complete with leather-wrapped saddlebags, windshield, and passenger backrest. Upgrades for 2010 included a new handlebar and seat and more chrome.

Yamaha V Star 950 Tourer

The V Star 950 Tourer begins with the V Star 950's 942cc, air-cooled, overhead-camshaft V-twin engine and single-shock steel chassis, and then adds a windshield, leather-wrapped hard saddlebags, and a passenger backrest for comfort. The result is a very competent and affordable tourer that works as well as it looks. Throw in $200 more for shimmering Seashell paint.

Yamaha V Star 950 (Recommended—Intermediate)

Introduced in 2009, the V Star 950 features the larger Roadliner's "neo-streamline" styling on a smaller, easier-handling and more affordable platform. Motivation comes from a fuel-injected V-twin powering through a five-speed gearbox and belt final drive. The V Star 950's standard color is Candy Red, but $200 extra buys your choice of Raven or Pearl White paint.

Yamaha V Star Custom

The V Star Custom is long, low, and chopperesque—and the lightest of the Star middleweights at 513 pounds wet. It's essentially a stripped-down V Star Classic with a narrower and larger-diameter front wheel, smaller fenders, and lower seat. The compliant suspension and pullback handlebar make a comfortable and affordable cruiser, while a generous 4.2-gallon fuel tank extends your range.

Yamaha V Star Classic/Silverado

The V Star Classic offers a lot of value for the dollar, with a torquey and efficient 649cc, four-valve V-twin, roomy seating, elegant full steel fenders, wide wire-spoke wheels, a chromed fork, classic retro styling, and less weight to manage compared to larger cruisers. The Silverado adds a touring windshield and studded seats, saddlebags, and passenger backrest.

Yamaha V Star 250 (Recommended—Beginner)

The smallest of Yamaha's V-twins, the V Star 250 (formerly the Virago) is powered by a 249cc, air-cooled V-twin. It features plenty of chrome, a five-speed transmission, and chain final drive. Weighing just 324 pounds, and with an MSRP under $4,000, the V Star 250 is an attractive and affordable entry into cruiser motorcycles.

Sportbikes, Sport-Tourers, and Standards

Most sportbikes make poor first bikes because they tend to be hard edged and single-mindedly focused on riding fast. But many of you reading this book will eventually end up on sportbikes, and there is some logic in learning to ride on the type of bike you intend to ride later. Fortunately, there are some very good sportbikes that also make good tools for perfecting your riding skills. Foremost among these bikes is Suzuki's pair of SV650s: the naked SV650 and the more sporting SV650SF, which features a more racy riding position and a small fairing. One thing to keep in mind when considering a sportbike, however, is that most of these bikes have at least some plastic bodywork, and some bikes have extensive bodywork. That bodywork could be very expensive to replace if you have even the slightest tip-over … and you'll probably have at least one slight tip-over while learning to ride. Some insurers also charge more to cover sportbikes because of the replacement cost of the plastic panels.

The sport-tourer category is something like the potpourri category on the game show *Jeopardy:* it contains everything from gigantic touring bikes such as Honda's ST1300 to lighter-weight, sportier machines like their Interceptor. Most of these bikes are too bulky for a beginner, although some, such as BMW's F800ST, are reasonably slender and lightweight. Others make flat-out terrific first bikes.

The standard category is even more of a mixed bag, but it provides the most versatile bikes for a beginner. Generally, these bikes are naked (without bodywork), although more manufacturers are now including a small fairing. Also, some naked bikes, such as Ducati's Monster 696 and the previously mentioned Suzuki SV650, make terrific sportbikes. So don't get hung up on labels. Forget what other people think. Decide what type of bike most appeals to you, and go for it.

Aprilia Sportbikes, Sport-Tourers, and Standards

Aprilia RSV4 R/Factory (Recommended—Experienced)

The RSV4 is Aprilia's ultimate sportbike, powered by a new 65-degree V-4 with 177 horsepower at the crank. Upgrade to the 182.5-horsepower Factory, and you get Ohlins suspension, carbon-fiber bodywork, forged wheels, adjustable frame geometry, and more.

Aprilia RSV 1000 R/Factory

Powered by Aprilia's 60-degree, fuel-injected V-twin, the RSV 1000 R delivers 143 horsepower and sports a fully adjustable Ohlins fork and Sachs rear damper. The Factory is exceptionally well equipped with fully adjustable front and rear Ohlins suspension and an Ohlins steering damper.

Aprilia Tuono 1000 R/Factory

"The World's Best Wheelie Machine" is back again with the new-generation V60 fuel-injected V-twin fed by ram air and producing a claimed 139 horsepower. The Factory adds fully adjustable Ohlins suspension, forged wheels, and Brembo Gold radial-mounted brakes.

Aprilia Dorsoduro 750

Developed in cooperation with Aprilia Racing, the Dorsoduro is Aprilia's first 750cc supermotard. It's powered by a 92-horsepower, 90-degree V-twin, with a torque peak of over 60 pound-feet at an accessible 4,500 rpm. An alloy and steel trellis frame ties it all together.

Aprilia Shiver 750

The Shiver is the naked variant of the supermoto-themed Dorsoduro. With its alloy-and-steel-trellis combination frame, the Shiver has a distinctive look. With 95 ride-by-wire horsepower on tap, the Shiver offers three different selectable throttle response modes.

Aprilia SXV 4.5–5.5

Aprilia slugs it out in the street and supermoto market with V-twin power in the form of the SXV 4.5 and 5.5. Both feature an innovative 77-degree V-twin with programmable fuel injection. The chassis is a rigid tubular steel structure aimed at exceptional responsiveness. The 5.5 features a larger and more powerful 549cc engine.

Benelli Sportbikes, Sport-Tourers, and Standards

Benelli Tornado 1130

Benelli's line-topping Tornado 1130 blends supersport styling in with the company's unique three-cylinder powerplant. With a claimed 160.9 horsepower, the Tornado has considerable poke. Chassis bits are well spec'd too, with a Marzocchi fork, Extreme Technology rear shock, and Brembo brakes.

Benelli TNT Sport/EVO

The TNT Sport and Sport EVO are Benelli's premiere streetfighters. Power comes from the familiar 1130cc triple, in this instance tuned for a claimed 127.4 horsepower at a low and accessible 9,250 rpm. Like the Tornado supersport, the TNT Sport/Evo have a Marzocchi fork, Extreme Technology rear shock, and Brembo brakes.

Benelli Café Racer

When you just gotta have something unique, Benelli offers the Café Racer. If its gold-and-maroon paint scheme doesn't get your attention, its wild styling and snaky tubular frame and swingarm surely will. A 135-horespower version of the familiar Benelli triple provides the motive force.

Benelli TRE K/TRE K Amazonas

With it partial fairing, the TRE K is designed to offer greater comfort in the long haul. Like the Benelli naked bikes, it retains the same comfortable upright riding position. For all-surface fun, the TRE K Amazonas has spoked wheels along with unique bodywork.

Benelli TNT

Benelli's most affordable model is the edgy TNT. Power comes from a 135-horsepower version of the same 1130cc engine that drives all Benelli models. It's also got a Marzocchi fork and an Extreme Technology rear damper with adjustable rebound damping.

Bimota Sportbikes, Sport-Tourers, and Standards

Bimota DB7

The Bimota DB7 takes full advantage of Ducati's powerful 1098 Testastretta Evoluzione engine through an innovative chassis design. It features a hybrid oval tubular trellis frame, a swingarm linked directly to the engine for rigidity and handling predictability, a carbon fairing, and forged wheels.

Bimota Tesi 3D

First introduced in 2006, the Tesi 3D was developed by Bimota in Rimini, Italy, and is available in limited quantities in the United States. Featuring a swingarm-type front suspension, the Tesi 3D has a trellis-type frame and suspension arms. Typical of Bimota, the Tesi has mouthwatering details everywhere you look. Power is supplied by a torquey, air-cooled Ducati V-twin.

Bimota DB5R

The most focused machine in the DB5 series is the striking "R" model. Powered by the Ducati 1100DS air-cooled twin, the DB5R has a tubular steel and alloy frame that helps keep the dry weight down to a feathery 375 pounds. Premium Ohlins suspension and Brembo brakes (twin radial calipers up front) complete the package.

Bimota DB6R

If the terms "sexy," "exotic," "Italian," and "naked" are meaningful to your next motorcycle purchase, look no further than Bimota's DB6R. It's powered by Ducati's air-cooled Desmo 1100 engine and features a dry slipper clutch, a host of carbon-fiber goodies, and specially developed forged alloy wheels.

Bimota DB5S

Powered by the Ducati 1100DS air-cooled twin, the Bimota DB5S biposto (two-seater) is designed to offer serious sporting performance coupled with room for two. Derived from the DB5 Mille, the DB5S has a tubular steel and alloy frame, along with the premium components you'd expect from Bimota.

Bimota DB6 Delirio

Feel like getting naked? The DB6 Delirio is the *au naturel* version of the Supersport DB5S. That means Ducati 1100DS air-cooled twin power, and an intricate tubular steel and alloy chassis and swingarm. A 50mm Marzocchi fork is up front, with a fully adjustable Extreme Tech Mono Shock in back.

BMW Sportbikes, Sport-Tourers, and Standards

BMW R 1200 HP2 Sport

The BMW R 1200 HP2 Sport features the most powerful production boxer motor ever designed, with double-overhead camshafts helping to produce an impressive 133 horsepower. Front and rear suspension is fully adjustable Ohlins, and braking is handled by radial-mounted Brembo calipers.

BMW HP2 Megamoto

The HP2 Megamoto is based on the HP2, but with a supermoto spin. The Megamoto offers a 113-horsepower version of the air-cooled, 1170cc boxer engine (with standard Akrapovic exhaust!) and features 17-inch wheels front and back with a fully adjustable Ohlins shock and a Marzocchi front fork.

BMW K 1300 S

The performance king of the BMW K line is the K 1300 S. With 175 horsepower hitting at just 9,250 rpm, the S is brimming with accessible power, and lots of it. Narrower and more aerodynamic, the new S rolls on a fat 190mm-wide rear tire. Clutch-free shifting, electronically adjustable suspension, and stability control are optional.

BMW R1200 GS/Adventure (Recommended— Experienced)

With 105 horsepower, mucho packing capacity (with BMW's well-designed luggage), long-travel suspension, and true long-haul comfort, the R1200 GS—and taller, even more adventurous Adventure—continue to advance the adventure-touring concept BMW pioneered long ago. Around the world or around the block, these two do it all.

BMW S 1000 RR (Recommended—Experienced)

BMW enters the serious superbike fray for the first time with the S 1000 RR. Though conventional in concept, its execution is jaw dropping, with a claimed 193 horsepower, four riding modes, and available race ABS and dynamic traction control, including a unique lean angle sensor. This 403-pound missile is the real deal.

BMW R1200 R

The do-everything R1200 R is powered by a 109-horsepower boxer twin that offers plenty of easily accessible power. For more forgiving handling, it's equipped with BMW's integral ABS and ASC (automatic stability control). The R1200 R is packed with features such as optional heated grips and on-the-fly electronically adjustable suspension.

BMW F 800 GS (Recommended—Intermediate)

The BMW GS family features a middleweight in the lineup with the F 800 GS. With its 798cc parallel-twin with 85 horsepower, six-speed transmission with chain final drive, and switchable ABS, the F 800 GS is the most off-road-oriented GS to date. Wide pegs and a low center of gravity make the GS very maneuverable.

BMW F 800 ST

The F 800 ST is BMW's middleweight sport-tourer, featuring an 85-horse, liquid-cooled, 798cc parallel-twin and a full fairing with a high windshield and touring-oriented ergonomics. Twin Brembo disc brakes with optional ABS ensure plenty of stopping power, while optional touring cases and heated grips provide plenty of storage and comfort.

BMW F 650 GS

Despite the 650 in the name, the street-oriented F 650 GS is powered by the same basic 798cc parallel-twin you'll find in other 800 models. Go figure. Here, it makes 71 horsepower, and is paired with six-speed transmission, chain final drive, and optional switchable ABS.

BMW G 450 X

BMW's serious dual-sport missile is the G 450 X. Full of exotic engineering, the X has a stainless steel frame, concentric swingarm pivot and countershaft sprocket, and a laid-down single liquid-cooled cylinder. With a foot of suspension travel at each end and a feathery 245-pound dry weight, the X is ready for the rough stuff.

BMW G 650 GS

Decked out in traditional GS go-anywhere kit, the G 650 GS provides a lighter-weight, lower-cost passport to adventure. Powered by a 53-horsepower liquid-cooled single working through a five-speed transmission, the GS is stopped by standard ABS. Heated handgrips are also standard.

BMW G 650 Xcountry

The superversatile G 650 Xcountry features BMW's 53-horsepower single mated to a five-speed transmission, chain final drive, and a Marzocchi telescopic fork. With a round headlamp, round side panels, and anodized black wheels, the Xcountry is cutting-edge cool. And at just 326 pounds (dry), the Xcountry is also highly maneuverable.

Can-Am Sportbikes, Sport-Tourers, and Standards

Can-Am Spyder RS/RS-S

In 2007 Can-Am stirred up the sportbike establishment with its dramatic three-wheeled Spyder. Powered by a fuel-injected, 998cc V-twin, the RS model has traction and stability control, ABS, and a reverse gear. The RS-S model adds fingertip shifting, plus special wheels, seats, and Pearl White paint.

Ducati Sportbikes, Sport-Tourers, and Standards

Ducati 1098R Bayliss LE

In celebration of Troy Bayliss's 2008 World Superbike Championship, Ducati is offering just 500 copies of the 1098R Bayliss LE. A true racebike with lights, it features Ducati's 1198cc Testastretta Evoluzione L-twin, producing a claimed 180 horsepower and weighing just 364 pounds. A full-race Termignoni exhaust is included.

Ducati Multistrada 1200/ABS/s Sport/s Touring

Powered by 1198 Testastretta engine that pumps out a claimed 150 horsepower, the completely new Multistrada 1200 is Ducati's ultimate do-it-all machine. Push-button control of engine mapping and traction control boosts versatility. Move up to the Sport, and you get electronically adjustable ABS and suspension settings. The Touring version adds saddlebags.

Ducati 1198/S (Recommended—Experienced)

With a Testastretta Evoluzione engine producing a claimed 170 horsepower and nearly 100 pound-feet of torque, and packing a dry weight of just 377 pounds, the 1198 offers true hyperbike performance. Fully adjustable Showa suspension is standard, while the 373-pound S model gets upgraded Ohlins suspension front and rear and traction control.

Ducati Streetfighter/S

Ducati is taking it to the streets with the new Streetfighter. Its Testastretta Evoluzione engine produces a claimed 155 horsepower and 85 pound-feet of torque. With a dry weight of just 373 pounds, the Streetfighter promises heaps of naked fun. Showa suspension is standard, while the 368-pound S model gets upgraded Ohlins suspension and selectable traction control.

Ducati 848/Nicky Hayden Edition

Want a piece of Ducati Superbike magic for a bit less coin? The 848 may look a lot like an 1198, but beneath the skin this is a truly unique middleweight. Weighing just 370 pounds, the 134-horsepower, liquid-cooled 848 blends track-day reflexes with good streetability. The Nicky Hayden Edition comes with a flashy commemorative paint job.

Ducati SportClassic Sport 1000 S/biposto

Patterned after Ducati's '70s-era café racers, the Sport 1000 S features a fully adjustable Marzocchi inverted fork, and twin, fully adjustable Sachs rear shocks. Power comes via Ducati's Desmodromic four-valve twin producing over 90 horsepower and nearly 70 pound-feet of torque. It's also available in biposto (two-seat) configuration.

Ducati Hypermotard 1100/S

Ducati's Hypermotard arrived in '07 to rave reviews. The wide bar allows big-time flickability, while the long seat allows easy fore/aft movement for maximum control. Suspension duties on the extratrick S-version are handled by a 50mm titanium nitride-coated fork and an Ohlins shock. These cool twins crank out a solid 90 horsepower.

Ducati Monster 1100/S

Powered by a 1078cc, air-cooled twin with 95
horsepower and a robust 75.9 pound-feet of torque,
the Monster 1100 is a regular riot. Brembo brakes
front and rear handle stopping duty, while a fully
adjustable Showa fork and Sachs shock keep the
chassis stable at speed. Choose the S to upgrade to
Ohlins suspension.

Ducati SportClassic GT 1000

Ducati's SportClassic range of bikes features retro
styling and the Italian company's proven air-
cooled, two-valve, 90-degree V-twin for simplicity
and light weight. At only 407 pounds dry, the GT
1000 makes the most of the claimed 92 horsepower.
An upright riding position makes the GT comfortable and versatile.

Ducati Hypermotard 796

Ducati's littlest (and most affordable) Hypermotard
is the brand new 796. Powered by a new 796cc
engine that spins out 81 horsepower and 55.7
pound-feet of torque, the 368-pound Ducati promises a good time on just about any kind of road. An
APTC "wet" clutch has a slipper-type action for
drama-free downshifts and a light lever action.

Ducati Monster 696 (Recommended—Beginner)

Ducati's affordable base Monster is the 696. With
fresh style and a high-mounted pipe, it looks the
part of the urban hooligan. Nearly 80 air-cooled
horsepower pushing just 355 pounds means
mayhem is sure to ensue. A host of accessories are
available through Ducati dealers to let you build
the perfect beast … er, Monster.

Fischer Sportbikes, Sport-Tourers, and Standards

Fischer MRX

With exotic styling and an American-made alloy frame and swingarm, Fischer's MRX is a unique middleweight sportbike. It's powered by a liquid-cooled, 647cc, 90-degree V-twin that produces a claimed 77 rear-wheel horsepower and 52 pound-feet of torque. Suspension includes a 43mm inverted fork and Ohlins rear shock.

Harley-Davidson Sportbikes, Sport-Tourers, and Standards

Harley-Davidson Sportster XR1200 (Recommended—Intermediate)

The XR1200 brings Harley-Davidson's legendary dirt track heritage to life, and puts it in your driveway. The 1203cc, air-cooled Evolution engine thumps out 73.9 pound-feet of torque at 4,000 rpm. Pushing 562 pounds, acceleration is solid if not dazzling. An upside-down fork and triple discs complete the package.

Honda Sportbikes, Sport-Tourers, and Standards

Honda ST1300/ABS

Blending sport and touring attributes, Honda's ST1300 is hugely capable and features a velvety-smooth, longitudinally arrayed V-4 and a high level of comfort, in addition to a motorized adjustable windscreen, removable hard bags, and comfy seat. The ABS version costs $1,200 more.

Honda VFR1200F (Recommended—Experienced)

Honda's latest tour de force is the all-new VFR1200F. Powered by a 76-degree V-4 that borrows from MotoGP technology, the ultimate VFR has torque-compensating shaft final drive and all-day comfort. A conventional six-speed transmission is standard, with a multimode Dual Clutch Automatic Transmission version offered as an upgrade.

Honda CBR1000RR/ABS

Honda completely revamped its flagship literbike back in '08. With more power, dual-stage fuel injection, a revamped bodywork package surrounding an all-new twin-spar aluminum frame and MotoGP-style exhaust, Honda clearly took dead aim at ruling the superbike class. Combined ABS is once again available in the 2010 model.

Honda Interceptor/ABS

Redesigned several years ago and tweaked every year since, the Interceptor remains one of the most competent all-around sportbikes on the market. Comfy ergonomics, a smooth and capable 16-valve V-4, and proven reliability make it an ideal choice for sport-touring enthusiasts. It's available in black only; ABS is available for an extra $1,000.

Honda CBR600RR/ABS

Completely overhauled in '07, Honda's CBR600RR leapt to the top of the middleweight class with a more powerful engine with dual-stage fuel injection, a lighter frame, and an electronic steering damper. At just 410 pounds brimming with gas, the 600RR is a formidable package. It's available in two color schemes, with ABS as a $1,000 upgrade.

Honda XR650L (Recommended—Beginner)

Honda's long-running XR650L might be more than a decade old, but it shouldn't be discounted as a nonperformer. On the contrary, it's a fantastic motorcycle, especially in the dirt, where its XR600 heritage comes to the fore. It's tall (seat height is 37 inches), but it'll go just about anywhere you point it.

Honda CRF230L/M

The CRF230L is a good choice for riders who need multisurface versatility. The rugged air-cooled engine starts with the push of a button, and light weight and a low seat height make this an excellent beginner's bike. The supermoto-themed CRF230M is targeted at the commuter crowd.

Hyosung Sportbikes, Sport-Tourers, and Standards

Hyosung GT650R

Think of Hyosung's GT650R as China's answer to Suzuki's popular and functionally excellent SV650SF twin. A liquid-cooled, four-valve, 647cc V-twin forms the core of the GT650R, while the trick-bits list includes adjustable rear-mounted footrests and a digital speedometer. Four color combinations are available.

Hyosung GT650/S

The GT650 features a liquid-cooled, eight-valve, 647cc V-twin with a claimed 79 horsepower and six-speed transmission. It offers an upright and roomy riding position, single-shock rear suspension, and inverted fork. The S model adds a half fairing for greater wind protection.

Hyosung GT650

The GT650 is the naked version of the half-faired GT650S with an upright and roomy riding position. A single-shock rear suspension and inverted fork keep this one smooth and stable, while dual discs help slow everything down. It's available with a black frame and black or blue paint.

Hyosung GT250R

The GT250R joined South Korea's Hyosung line in 2007 and returns again as an entry-level sportbike. It includes a 249cc, 27-horsepower, air-cooled V-twin engine with a five-speed transmission. You'll also find trick componentry like an inverted fork for a price well under $4,000. It's available in four color schemes (two are two-tone).

Hyosung GT250

Hyosung's GT250 naked bike is reasonably well equipped considering its modest price. You get a 249cc V-twin, a five-speed transmission, inverted fork, disc brakes front and rear, and a large halogen headlight to bore holes into the night. A low seat height makes it a viable option for beginners.

Kawasaki Sportbikes, Sport-Tourers, and Standards

Kawasaki Concours 14/ABS

The Concours 14 combines the fire-breathing, 1352cc inline-four of the ZX-14 with impeccable handling and comfort. The result is a world-class sport-tourer. An aluminum chassis, radial brakes, inverted fork and ram-air induction are built into a sport-touring package that loves to rack up miles. An ABS version is available.

Kawasaki ZX-14

Returning in 2010 was Kawasaki's exceptionally fast and smooth ZX-14, which vies for Ultimate Sportbike honors. It's powered by one of the most potent engines ever slipped into a sportbike chassis—a liquid-cooled, 1352cc, 16-valve inline-four producing 160-plus rear-wheel horsepower. It's offered in red, or in two-tone titanium/black.

Kawasaki ZX-10R

All new in 2008, Kawasaki's flagship superbike, the ZX-10R returned with a 16-valve, fuel-injected, 998cc inline-four tuned for spectacular high-rpm performance. Developed with help from Japanese superbike racer Akira Yanagawa, the ZX-10R chassis provides a level of handling equal to that of a racer.

Kawasaki Z1000

Reincarnated for 2010, the Z1000 returned with fresh and aggressive style and a host of feature advances. Its inline-four is tuned for massive midrange, and bolts into a stiffer alloy chassis. The inverted front fork is fully adjustable, and the rear suspension offers preload and rebound adjustability. Available in black or white, the Z1000 has standard digital instrumentation.

Kawasaki ZX-6R

Reworked, revamped, and revitalized back in 2009, Kawasaki's ZX-6R gained midrange power and shed an impressive 22 pounds. A Showa "big piston" fork works with a mass-centralized chassis and repositioned engine to speed reflexes while boosting rider confidence. Choose from black, red, or two-tone green/black.

Kawasaki Versys (Recommended—Intermediate)

The Versys, based on Kawasaki's successful Ninja 650R, uses a liquid-cooled, eight-valve, 649cc parallel-twin mated to a six-speed transmission. Semi-long-travel suspension features a 41mm fork and a gull-wing-style swingarm help make the Versys a competent all-arounder. For the 2010 model, there's new styling, rubber engine mounts, and an adjustable windscreen.

Kawasaki Ninja 650R

Introduced in 2006, the exceptionally user-friendly Ninja 650R returned in 2009 with over 40 updates and refinements, including improved suspension and new styling. The liquid-cooled, 649cc parallel-twin delivers plenty of rip in a compact package, and handling is stellar—great for beginners and a seriously fun motorcycle for everyone else.

Kawasaki ER-6n

In yet another remix of Ninja 650R DNA, the ER-6n packs familiar virtues into a rowdy naked package. Power comes from a liquid-cooled, eight-valve, 649cc parallel-twin mated to a six-speed transmission. Muscular bodywork includes a unique instrument cluster with a multifunction LCD screen.

Kawasaki KLR650

For over 20 years, the big KLR has been the choice of dual-sport riders seeking reliable and fun on- and off-road performance. In 2008 a new and improved KLR arrived, with a 41mm fork and redesigned UNI-TRAK rear suspension. For the 2010 model, the KLR carries over with the same rugged versatility that's made it legendary.

Kawasaki KLX250SF

Want an affordable 250 with a supermoto spin? The new KLX250SF builds on the foundation of its dual-sport counterpart S model. Radial sportbike tires on 17-inch wheels improve pavement grip, while a big 300mm front disc slows it down. Lowered suspension is specially tuned for the street.

Kawasaki Ninja 500R

Despite being around since 1987 (as the EX500), Kawasaki's Ninja 500R returns largely unchanged. But why mess with success? From roadracing to sport-touring to commuting, the Ninja 500R is up to the task. The liquid-cooled parallel-twin is bulletproof, and at $5,499, the 500R is an excellent value.

Kawasaki KLX250S

Updated in 2009, the KLX250S featured new wheels, brakes, and suspension. Power comes from a fuel-efficient liquid-cooled single that starts with the push of a button. It's paired with a six-speed gearbox. An engine-driven balancer helps smooth vibes on the highway. Take your pick of black or green.

Kawasaki Super Sherpa

Interested in doing a little bit of everything? The Super Sherpa is designed to handle a wide variety of terrain and be a good fit for all kinds of riders. The air-cooled single is docile and durable and sips gas to the tune of 63 mpg. It's relatively light weight and low seat height make the Super Sherpa easy to manage.

Kawasaki Ninja 250R

After the arrival of an all-new Ninja 250R in 2008, the 2010 model returned with the same great attributes. The high-revving, liquid-cooled, eight-valve powerplant is tuned for smooth power delivery and features a two-into-one exhaust. Fuel economy is spectacular, and so is bodywork that echoes the look of bigger Ninja models.

KTM Sportbikes, Sport-Tourers, and Standards

KTM 1190 RC8 R/R Akrapovic/R Red Bull

If the garden-variety RC8 leaves you yawning, consider the RC8 R. A bump in displacement and other tweaks wake up the motor to a claimed 170 horsepower. Race-sec WP suspension, superlight Marchesini forged wheels, and carbon bits sweeten the deal. Choose the Akrapovic or Red Bull version and you also get unique graphics and a racing kit.

KTM 1190 RC8

With 152 V-twin horsepower squeezed into a compact, 406-pound package, the RC8 is sure to drain your adrenal glands. The steel trellis frame carries WP suspension at both ends, and braking is by Brembo. For the 2010 model, shifting and fork calibration has been improved.

KTM 990 Supermoto R/T

For rabid mountain swervery and general street riding, KTM offers the 990 Supermoto R. With a claimed 115 horsepower pushing 417 pounds, the Supermoto promises lively acceleration. Want more road-going comfort and utility? The T version comes with soft luggage, larger fuel tank, and a roomier dual saddle.

KTM 990 Super Duke

With a claimed 118 horsepower crammed into a compact, lightweight package, KTM's 990 Super Duke is naked aggression on wheels. WP suspension front and rear keeps the Super Duke tracking true, and Brembo radial calipers slow it down. Take your pick of black or KTM orange.

KTM 990 Adventure/R

KTM's restyled 990 Adventure is the epitome of the hard-core open-class dual-sport. Long-travel suspension and a more powerful 999cc, fuel-injected V-twin mean you have virtually no limits to your route or destination. The R-model features different graphics and an even more aggressive chassis.

KTM 950 Super Enduro R

If you want to do it all … and do it big, the KTM 950 Super Enduro R may be just the ticket. With the relentless power of a liquid-cooled, 942cc V-twin, this beast is built for the wide-open spaces. Brembo brakes and WP suspension with 10 inches of travel ensure this KTM is up to the worst you can throw at it.

KTM 690 Duke

The KTM 690 Duke started the trend toward production supermotards. The 2010 model is driven by a powerful liquid-cooled, 654cc single producing a claimed 65 horsepower. Other trick bits include a 48mm inverted fork, radially mounted Brembo calipers, and cast 17-inch wheels.

KTM 690 Enduro R

Serious off-road capability is the mission of the 690 Enduro R. Think of it as a roadable dirtbike. Powered by a 654cc, liquid-cooled single with a six-speed gearbox, the Enduro R offers broad-band power. WP suspension front and rear with nearly 11 inches of wheel travel helps soak up the rough stuff.

KTM 690 SMC

The Supermotard 690 SMC is powered by a 654cc, four-valve single and wears street-oriented 17-inch spoked wheels. New patented technology allows tubeless tire to be fitted. WP suspension is standard front and back: a 48mm inverted fork and an adjustable monoshock. Weighing just 305 pounds (dry), the SMC is sure to be a blast on tight roads.

KTM 530 EXC/Champion's Edition

KTM's competition enduro powerhouse is the 530 EXC. Like its 450 sibling, it also happens to be street legal. With a torquey and rev-happy 510cc single mated to a dirt-serious chassis, the big EXC is highly competitive. For the 2010 model, it has a new frame, along with gearbox, suspension, and brake upgrades. The Champion's Edition has unique graphics, plus other features.

KTM 450 EXC/Champion's Edition (Recommended—Intermediate)

Here's a serious competition enduro that also happens to be street legal. Powered by a liquid-cooled, 449cc single and weighing just 251 pounds, the 450 EXC is all about off-road performance. For the 2010 model, it has a new frame, along with gearbox, suspension, and brake upgrades. The Champion's Edition has unique graphics, plus other features.

Kymco Sportbikes, Sport-Tourers, and Standards

Kymco Quannon 150

Taiwan's Kymco features a wide range of scooters, but they also offer this pretty slick-looking light-weight sportbike. Powered by a 149cc SOHC single with forced-air cooling, the Quannon 150 sips fuel, squeezing 70 miles out of every gallon. It's just $2,999, yet you still get an aluminum perimeter frame, front and rear disc brakes, and a full fairing.

Moto Guzzi Sportbikes, Sport-Tourers, and Standards

Moto Guzzi Griso 8V

Moto Guzzi's most advanced model is the Griso 8V. With its new SOHC V-twin with four valves in each cylinder, it develops a claimed 110 horsepower at only 7,500 rpm. The rest of the Griso is modern, too, with fully adjustable suspension front and rear, radial brake calipers, and a torque-compensating shaft drive system.

Moto Guzzi V7 Café Classic

Climb aboard the "Way Back Machine" for a trip to 1967. The V7 Café Classic has style and proportion of the original V7, recast with more modern technology. The 744cc, air-cooled V-twin has the traditional Moto Guzzi look coupled with trouble-free EFI.

Moto Guzzi Stelvio 1200 ABS

For those seeking adventure, both on the road and off, Moto Guzzi offers the Stelvio 1200 4V. Powered by a classic Moto Guzzi V-twin that develops 103 horsepower at a relaxed 7,250 rpm, the Stelvio is a great travel companion. Shaft drive reduces maintenance, while a standard windscreen improves comfort.

MV Agusta Sportbikes, Sport-Tourers, and Standards

MV Agusta F4CC

Want the maximum possible MV magic? Simply sign up for the "Special Production" F4CC. The "CC" stands for famed designer Claudio Castiglioni. Over 90 percent of the components are "tailor made," including items like a one-off mechanical slipper clutch and a titanium exhaust system. Bring lots of money!

MV Agusta F4 RR 312 1078

MV Agusta's flagship superbike was new and improved in 2009, with a larger engine that kicks out 190 horsepower and pushes the sleek beauty to a claimed 193.88 mph. Chassis capability comes via Marzocchi's inverted 50mm R.A.C. (Road Advanced Component) fork and Brembo forged aluminum wheels, with Y spokes.

MV Agusta Brutale 1078 RR

Back in 2009, MV put additional brutality into the company's top street fighter. The Brutale 1078 RR has a 1078cc engine than slugs out 154 horsepower (up 20 over the previous model). Featuring a Marzocchi inverted fork and the fine details that have made MV legendary, the Brutale 1078 RR is pure Italian beauty.

Royal Enfield Sportbikes, Sport-Tourers, and Standards

Royal Enfield Bullet 500 Classic G5/Deluxe G5/Classic C5

Royal Enfield's new fuel injected, unit-construction engine churns out a claimed 27.2 horsepower and pushes top speed to 82 mph. A single front disc and rear drum brake slow it down. Choose the retro look of the Classic G5, Deluxe G5, or truly vintage Classic C5.

Royal Enfield Bullet 500 Classic/Deluxe/Electra X

The Bullet 500 is a classic Brit bike by way of India. Its 23-horsepower, 499cc, air-cooled engine has a Mikuni CV carburetor and starts with a robust kick. You'll top out at a claimed 75 mph. You also get a five-speed transmission and a double-leading shoe front drum brake. The Bullet Deluxe adds chrome; the Electra X has '70s style and a front disc brake.

Suzuki Sportbikes, Sport-Tourers, and Standards

Suzuki Hayabusa

All new in 2008, Suzuki pulled out all the stops with its hyperspeed Hayabusa flagship. A heavily revised engine with displacement bumped to 1340cc, all-new aerodynamic bodywork, a redesigned chassis, suspension, and radial-mount brakes make the 'Busa the fastest possible route to a speeding ticket. Available in white, black, or silver.

Suzuki B-King/ABS

The B-King was an all-new motorcycle for 2008, and a close cousin to Suzuki's Hayabusa flagship. Powered by the same 1340cc fuel-injected inline-four as the Hayabusa, the B-King leaves little to the imagination with an intimidating appearance that includes twin underseat exhaust pipes. ABS is an extra $600.

Suzuki GSX-R1000

Redesigned back in 2009, the GSX-R1000 got a clean-sheet engine design with more torque and horsepower across the rev range, plus it allows a shorter wheelbase. The twin-spar chassis was new, too, and is paired with a meaty Showa "big piston" fork and fully adjustable Showa rear shock. Mouthwatering!

Suzuki GSX-R750

Arguably one of the world's best track bikes for the masses, the GSX-R750 has heaps of go-fast features like fully adjustable suspension, a back-torque limiting clutch, and an electronic steering damper. The engine management system allows the rider to choose from three settings to match the conditions.

Suzuki GSX-R600

Suzuki's formidable middleweight sportbike features a free-revving inline-four with a three-mode selectable engine management system and a servo-controlled exhaust system. A back-torque limiting clutch smoothes deceleration, and the GSX-R rides on fully adjustable suspension.

Suzuki V-Strom 1000

For adventure-touring types who spend a lot of time on the tarmac, but who occasionally hit the odd fire road, the V-Strom is the ideal machine. Its eight-valve, 996cc V-twin provides abundant midrange torque, and it's all-day comfy. Many accessories are available, including hard luggage and top case.

Suzuki Bandit 1250S/ABS

Suzuki's Bandito Grande has been a favorite for years. All new in 2007, the Big Bandit featured a torquey and smooth liquid-cooled, fuel-injected, 1255cc 16-valve inline-four that's never at a loss for asphalt-spitting power. A six-speed transmission with ideal highway gearing is standard, while ABS adds $500.

Suzuki GSX650F

If you love GSX-R styling but can't stomach the steep insurance or contortionist riding position, Suzuki's GSX650F might be the ticket. Power is via a fuel-injected, liquid-cooled, 16-valve 656cc inline-four mated to a six-speed transmission. A comfortable seat and upright riding position ensure all-day comfort.

Suzuki SV650SF/ABS

The SV650SF has a full fairing and is powered by Suzuki's popular, smooth, and torquey 645cc V-twin. At just 438 pounds full of gas, the SF is lightweight and agile, and features a much more aggressive riding position than its naked brother—it's almost GSX-R-like. ABS is available for an additional $500.

Suzuki V-Strom 650/ABS

The V-Strom 650 is the little brother of Suzuki's liter-class adventure tourer, and every bit as capable. It's actually more capable off-road, and quite possibly more fun to ride due to its lighter weight and confidence-inspiring nature. The V-Strom 650 uses the SV's grin-producing and flexible V-twin. ABS is an extra $500.

Suzuki Gladius (Recommended—Intermediate)

Here's a fresh branch on the SV family tree: the Gladius. Power comes from the much-beloved 645cc V-twin, paired with a six-speed cog-box. A steel-tube trellis frame ties together basic preload-adjustable front and rear suspension. With a sensible control layout and an accommodating seat, the Gladius offers livable comfort.

Suzuki DR-Z400SM

With the versatility and performance of its dual-sport brother (the DR-Z400S), the DR-Z400SM adds 17-inch spoked wheels and aggressive supermoto styling. The result is a supernimble, lightweight machine that's a blast on any type of tight, twisty tarmac. It's available in black or white.

Suzuki DR-Z400S

The DR-Z400S forms the basis for Suzuki's Supermoto machine, and for good reason. The dirt-focused DR-Z400S successfully combines light weight with good agility and handling. It's an ideal choice for riders looking for a dirt-worthy dual-sport. It's not for the short of inseam, however, with a seat height of 36.8 inches.

Suzuki SV650/ABS

The SV650 reminds us all just how fun and affordable street riding can be. Powered by a torquey and smooth 645cc, eight-valve V-twin, it's got useable power galore. The upright riding position makes it comfy for all-day riding, and at a buck less than $6,000, it offers great value. ABS is available for an extra $600.

Suzuki GS500F

If you like the GSX-R look but are new to the sportbike market—or you're still developing your skills—take a look at Suzuki's GS500F. For under $6,000 you get decent engine and chassis performance with time-proven reliability—all in a tastefully styled package that looks for all the world to be a GSX-R.

Suzuki DR650SE

The DR650SE is a remarkably versatile motorcycle, powered by a smooth and durable air-cooled single with the magic button—electric starting! With substantial ground clearance and compliant suspension, the DR is as comfortable on rocky two-track trails as it is commuting to work or school. Fuel economy is great, too.

Suzuki DR200SE

If you're looking for an unintimidating entry into motorcycling that is equally comfortable on the street as on trails, the DR200SE is an excellent choice. Powered by a reliable, air-cooled 199cc single, the SE has reasonable power and plenty of suspension travel to go along with its relatively low seat height.

Suzuki TU250

Basic, easy to ride, and oh so fuel efficient, the new TU250 has classic standard style. An ideal beginner bike, the TU is light, low, and easy to manage. Power comes from a low-maintenance, 249cc, air-cooled single that starts with a touch of a button. Fuel injection makes for easy starting and precise throttle response.

Triumph Sportbikes, Sport-Tourers, and Standards

Triumph Sprint ST/ABS (Recommended—Experienced)

Triumph's powerful sport-touring Sprint ST received a host of upgrades in 2007 that included raised bars, a higher windscreen, and improved heat control. The Sprint ST is powered by Triumph's potent 1050cc inline-triple and definitely leans more toward sport than touring. ABS is available.

Triumph Tiger/ABS/SE

All new back in 2007, the Triumph Tiger shares
the powerful and smooth 1050cc inline-triple with
the Sprint ST, tuned here for low and midrange
torque. The Tiger is shod with 17-inch wheels
front and back, and is exceptionally comfortable,
with a wide and accommodating seat for two-up
excursions. ABS is available, or you can choose the
SE, with standard ABS and luggage.

Triumph Speed Triple

A perennial favorite of ours, the hooligan Speed
Triple has a 1050cc, 12-valve triple featuring liquid
cooling, while radial-mount two-piston front brake
calipers provide fierce stopping power. With 131
claimed horsepower at 9,250 rpm, the hardest part
of riding the Speed Triple is keeping the front tire
grounded.

Triumph Daytona 675

The Daytona 675 got significant changes back in
2009, starting with three more horsepower—up
to a claimed 126 horsepower peak output from
its 675cc, fuel-injected triple. It also got a revised
engine control unit that plugs into an accessory
quick-shift kit, fully adjustable suspension, radial-
mount monoblock front brake calipers, and 7
pounds less weight.

Triumph Bonneville T100 (Recommended—Beginner)

Featuring electronic fuel injection, the T100 is
the premium version of the Bonneville roadster,
with hand-painted coach lines and chrome engine
covers. Other neat features include a tachometer
and peashooter-style dual exhaust pipes. The T100
also gets a two-tone paint scheme to maintain that
old-school legendary Brit-bike look.

Triumph Street Triple/R

Blend the prowess of the Daytona 675 and the attitude of the Speed Triple and you have the Street Triple 675. Powered by a 675cc, 12-valve inline-triple, it offers an upright riding position with street-fighter looks. The Street Triple R features fully adjustable suspension, four-piston front brake calipers, an upside-down fork, and special paint and graphics.

Triumph Thruxton

Triumph's Thruxton is a tribute to the home-built café racers of the '60s, with adjustable front and rear suspension, aluminum rims, and a floating front disc brake. The 865cc, eight-valve V-twin features hot cams and free-flowing upswept exhaust, while race-inspired clip-on handlebars, rear-set footpegs, and firmer suspension tuning add to the appeal.

Triumph Scrambler

Straight out of the '60s à la Steve McQueen is Triumph's ultraretro Scrambler. It shares the same 865cc, eight-valve V-twin with the Bonneville and sports upswept dual exhaust canisters complete with protective heat shielding. Also boasting modern electronic fuel injection, the 2010 model is available in a pair of retro two-tone color combinations.

Triumph Bonneville/SE

Triumph's fuel-injected 865cc Bonneville is a retro-roadster styled after the famous Bonnies of the '60s. In 2009, it got even more period looking with 17-inch aluminum wheels, shorter fenders, a lower and narrower seat, and unique silencers. The Bonneville SE adds a matching speedo and tach, polished engine covers, and a chromed tank badge.

Yamaha Sportbikes, Sport-Tourers, and Standards

Yamaha FJR1300A/AE

Yamaha's FJR1300A and FJR1300AE sport-tourers offer an exhilarating riding experience with over 140 horsepower on tap. The big FJR features a push-button adjustable windscreen with an anti-scratch coating. Both models come standard with ABS, while the AE version features electronically controlled clutchless shifting.

Yamaha YZF-R1/LE

Yamaha's flagship sportbike borrows tons of technology from the company's YZR-M1 MotoGP racer. A cross plane crankshaft optimizes power delivery while producing a unique sound. Fly-by-wire throttle control has rider-programmable mapping, while plenty of titanium and magnesium components help reduce weight. The new LE has Fiat Yamaha team graphics.

Yamaha YZF-R6 (Recommended—Experienced)

The YZF-R6 features an aluminum frame and swingarm, Yamaha Chip Controlled Throttle (YCC-T), Yamaha Chip Controlled Intake (YCC-I), a magnesium subframe for improved mass centralization, and even a built-in lap timer. For the 2010 model, the high-revving, 599cc, DOHC inline-four engine gets a remapped engine control unit and a longer, quieter muffler.

Yamaha FZ1

Want massive superbike power together with a more comfortable riding position and lower insurance rates? Meet the FZ1. Radically styled, this naked bike sports numerous performance goodies such as a 20-valve motor, inverted forks, and a single-shock rear suspension. Its upright riding position, dual saddle, and cockpit fairing provide all-day comfort.

Yamaha YZF-R6S

The YZF-R6S is a competent and versatile sportbike with less extreme ergonomics than Yamaha's ultrahigh-performance YZF-R6. Based on a previous-generation R6—likewise with AMA Supersport championship-winning credentials—the R6S offers an affordable and more comfortable alternative to today's narrowly focused race-bike replica 600s.

Yamaha FZ6 (Recommended—Intermediate)

Updated in 2007, the FZ6 carries on with two enticing color options, Deep Blue and Raven (black). It's still powered by an R6 motor tuned for enhanced midrange punch, and features a trick under-seat exhaust. The cockpit fairing offers riders a decent amount of wind protection, and the upright riding position is comfortable for all types of riding.

Yamaha WR250X

All-new back in '08, Yamaha's supermoto-inspired minithumper features technology from Yamaha's off-road and sportbike gene pool. Built for the street-oriented hooligan, the WR250X is powered by a fuel-injected 250cc single with titanium valves, and sports 17-inch spoke wheels, fat grippy rubber, and a wet weight of 300 pounds.

Yamaha WR250R (Recommended—Beginner)

Closely related to the WR250X supermoto bike, the dual-sport WR250R brings more off-road capability. Good power (for a 250) and a six-speed transmission helps out off-road, and when cruising up to the speed limit (and beyond) on the highway. And it starts with the push of a button. Long-travel, fully adjustable suspension front and rear make it highly competent.

Yamaha XT250

All new back in '08, the XT250 dual-sport machine offers contemporary styling, an efficient air-cooled motor, and a refined chassis with decent suspension travel (while retaining a reasonable seat height), all at an attractive price. Plenty viable for both street and off-road duty, the XT250 also features electric starting, two-up seating, and 2.6 gallons of fuel capacity.

Yamaha TW200

Although not the toughest-looking dual-sport on the market, the TW200 makes up for it by creating its own kind of silly fun, with those big tires bouncing over the sand dunes and trails like whirling basketballs. Superdurable and nearly bulletproof, the TW will provide years of fun for riders of all skill levels. It also returns an estimated 78 mpg!

Zero Sportbikes, Sport-Tourers, and Standards

Zero S/DS (Recommended—Beginner)

And now for something completely different. Zero Motorcycles offers two street-legal machines, the supermoto-themed S and the dual-sport DS. Both are powered by a lithium-ion battery array and an electric motor. With a claimed 4-hour recharge time and 50-mile range, both Zeros can hit 67 mph.

Biker's Buying Guide to Used Bikes

Appendix A listed just about every new streetbike sold in the United States, some of which can honestly be called bargains. But as you may have noted, even the so-called bargains will require you to lay out some serious cash before you can park one in your garage.

If the price of a new bike is beyond your means, you needn't worry much; the used-bike market can help get you on two wheels.

While some motorcyclists trash their machines, most keep them in fairly good condition. Many of the used bikes you'll find will be in nearly the same shape as a new bike.

Chapter 7 showed you how to make certain a used bike is in sound mechanical shape. Now this appendix lists some used bikes that will make exceptional first motorcycles.

Because used-bike prices vary according to a variety of factors, from the condition of the bike to locale, value estimates are not included in this guide. But generally, you can count on the notion that bikes costing more new also tend to cost more used. Just as a new MV Agusta costs more than a new Kawasaki, a used MV Agusta costs more than a used Kawasaki.

As with the "Biker's Buying Guide to New Bikes" in Appendix A, used bikes are listed alphabetically, by make. Only bikes manufactured since 1982 are included. However, some good, dependable motorcycles were manufactured before that time, and if you find one that runs well and is in good shape, you shouldn't pass it up just because it's older. But be aware that you will have more mechanical trouble with older bikes than with newer bikes. In addition, technological advances from the early 1980s to the present make motorcycles manufactured since then safer and more practical.

For more information, the *Black Book Motorcycle Value Guide* is one of the best sources we've found for accurate used-bike prices. Published monthly, the guide goes for $88 for a year's subscription, and individual copies can be purchased for $24 by calling Black Book National Auto Research at 1-800-554-1026, or visiting www.blackbookusa.com on the web. The services of *Kelley Blue Book* can also be a big help, because you can determine a used bike's current trade-in and retail values on the web. Go to www.kbb.com/motorcycle.

Aprilia

Aprilia has been selling motorcycles in the United States for over a decade now. Although there aren't a ton of used Aprilias on the market, there are a few. More recent models are better.

Pegaso

Aprilia's Pegaso makes a terrific first bike, if you can find one. While it presents itself as some sort of dual-sport, this one works best on the street. Although a few injected versions were imported into the United States, the simpler carbureted version is a much smoother and easier ride.

BMW

Like new BMWs, used Beemers tend to cost more than most other bikes, but they are well worth the extra money. The care with which these bikes are built means they tend to last longer than most other motorcycles.

R850R/R1100R/R1150R/R1200R

BMW's least expensive Oilhead bike, the R model (available in 850cc, 1100cc, 1150cc, and 1200cc versions), makes a terrific first bike, the kind we like to recommend. That is because it is a competent machine that will serve riders well long after they graduate from being novices to experienced riders.

R80GS/R100GS/R1200GS

These big Beemer dual-sports, the original leviathans of the trailbike world, might be a bit of a handful for a new rider, but their torquey, tractable engines and overall balance make them much easier to ride than other bikes of similar engine displacement. These are expensive motorcycles, but they tend to last a long time.

R80/R80ST

This is a street-only version of the original R80GS dual-sport. The R80s are even easier for an inexperienced rider to learn on than the GS series because they have lower seats—a factor that seems to make new riders feel more secure. The R80s are relative bargains, too.

K75/K75S/K75C

These bikes use three-cylinder versions of BMW's unique flat, four-cylinder engine. They are rather large bikes for a beginner, but as with the R80 and R100 boxer twins, their power-delivery characteristics make them easy to ride. Also like the Boxers, they tend to cost more than most other used bikes.

F650

We heartily recommend the original carbureted version of BMW's F650 as a first bike. In fact, we recommend it as a second, third, or forty-fifth bike because it is that good. Built on the same assembly line as Aprilia's Pegaso, this bike differs from the Aprilia in having a four-valve head rather than Aprilia's five-valve head, but BMW's version puts out even more power than the Aprilia, so apparently it gets on just fine without that extra valve.

Buell

Former road racer Erik Buell did what many dream about and few achieve—he started his own motorcycle company. Eventually acquired by Harley-Davidson, only to be shut down during the economic downturn of the late 2000s, Buell nonetheless made an imprint that will long be remembered.

Blast

Specifically designed as a newcomer's bike, the Blast has everything necessary to attract a whole new segment of motorcyclists to the Harley fold. Built for a decade, the 492cc single-cylinder streetbike represents an excellent value today—not to mention potential as a future collectible.

Ducati

Ducati builds pure-blooded sportbikes, and this single-minded passion has helped the company develop an image and following that's much larger than the relatively small volume of bikes the company produces.

Monster 696/800/900

The long-running Monster lineup represents an excellent value for Ducatis. Light, low, and uniquely styled, the Monsters are easy-to-ride bikes that are suitable for beginning riders but will also reward experts with their performance. Later models are fuel injected.

Honda

Honda is another manufacturer that makes motorcycles of exceptional quality. You'll find a lot of nice used Hondas out there—no surprise since the company is a household name.

CB750 Nighthawk

This slightly newer Nighthawk model is a fantastic all-around motorcycle, and a clean used example represents an excellent value.

CB650SC/CB700SC Nighthawks

If you're looking for a good, inexpensive inline four-cylinder Japanese motorcycle, have a look at Honda's original Nighthawk series. Many motorcyclists prefer them to the newer 750 Nighthawks simply because they have shaft drives, while the newer Nighthawks have chains. Even with shaft drives, they are some of the best-handling motorcycles of their day. Some riders take issue with their 16-inch front wheels, which make these bikes seem a bit twitchy in some circumstances, although many novices prefer the maneuverability those same wheels provide.

NT650 Hawk GT

These little V-twin sportbikes have become more popular since Honda stopped importing them to the United States. They are more fun on a twisty road than just about anything. The only drawback is that they're a bit cramped for riders over 6 feet tall.

NX650

Back in the late 1980s, Honda decided to produce a dual-sport that didn't look like one—or like anything else the motorcycling world had seen before. The result was the unique NX650, a streetbike based on Honda's XL600R dual-sport. Honda created a rather interesting and useful street thumper, one that will cost you a fraction of the price of the cheapest new 650 single.

XL350R/XL500R/XL600R/XR650L

In their day, these simple bikes were among the nicest trailbikes around. Today their traditional air-cooled engineering has been surpassed by a new generation of liquid-cooled dual-sport bikes, but considering that used XLs are highly affordable, you can probably learn to live with it.

XL600V Transalp

This V-twin dual-sport, which was imported into the United States only in 1989 and 1990, is one of the best all-around motorcycles produced those years and is easy for a beginning rider to master.

FT500/VT500 Ascots

These are two different bikes. The FT uses an air-cooled, single-cylinder engine derived from the XL500 dual-sport, while the VT uses a liquid-cooled V-twin lifted from the 500 Shadow. Both make excellent first bikes.

VF500C V30 Magna/VF500F Interceptor

Both these bikes use different versions of the same engine. The Magna surrounds the engine with one of history's most elegant little cruisers, while the Interceptor is among the finest-handling motorcycles built in the mid-1980s.

VT500/VT600/VT700/VT750/VT800/VT1100 Shadows

The Shadow cruiser line contains some of the most reliable motorcycles manufactured in the past couple of decades. VT700 Shadow models combine striking looks and genuine comfort with the low maintenance of a shaft drive and hydraulically adjusted valves. They actually rival many of the new midsize cruisers as all-around motorcycles.

Kawasaki

Because Kawasaki has a reputation as a high-performance company, many Kawasaki motorcycles will have seen hard use. But they are rugged bikes that can withstand a lot of abuse.

Vulcan 800/Vulcan 800 Classic/Vulcan 800 Drifter

Kawasaki's 800cc Vulcans make great first bikes. Their hardtail-look rear ends, created by hiding the shocks, give them a low center of gravity that allows for easy handling at parking-lot speeds. The Vulcan 800 looks like a 1970s-era chopper, the Vulcan 800 Classic recreates the look of a 1950s-era touring bike, and the Vulcan 800 Drifter recalls the classic streamlined Indians of the 1940s. All were discontinued in favor of the current Vulcan 900 series, but this now makes them an even better bargain on the used market.

Vulcan 750

If you can get past the styling of this one, you'll find a great motorcycle underneath. Kawasaki produced this high-tech, liquid-cooled lightweight cruiser for many years, only recently discontinuing it as the market evolved.

KLR600/KLR650

Kawasaki's perennial KLR liquid-cooled dual-sport bike got a major redo for 2008, but any of the models dating back to the mid-1980s are good basic motorcycles. Adept on city streets, freeways, or not-too-difficult trails, these single-cylinder bikes appeal to beginners and experts alike.

Ninja 600R/Ninja ZX-6R

Debuting in the mid-1980s, the Ninja 600 established the pattern for modern 600 sportbikes, with a liquid-cooled inline four-cylinder engine, perimeter frame, and sexy roadrace-style bodywork. Kawasaki has been building the Ninja 600 for over a quarter century now, with many improvements along the way. But make no mistake: all of them are serious sporting motorcycles.

KZ550/KZ550 LTD/KZ550 GPz/KZ550 Spectre

Kawasaki's air-cooled 550 four-cylinder bike was impressive when it first appeared, and it's still a useful machine. Reliable as a claw hammer, the 550 still has enough power to get you into serious trouble with legal authorities. The best of the bunch is the GPz, which predated the current 600cc sportbike class.

Ninja 500

Kawasaki has made incremental improvements to its 500 Ninja over its long production run, but the original is still a good bike. A 10- or even 20-year-old model will cost far less than what you'll pay for a brand-new one.

454 LTD/Vulcan 500

These ancestors to the Vulcan 500 LTD are fast little cruisers, but many people question their styling. If you don't mind the way they look, they are useful bikes.

Eliminator 250

If you can find one, this nifty little twin-cylinder cruiser shares its engine with the EX250 Ninja, meaning that it is a snappy bike. These motorcycles are easy to ride, plenty fast, and, with their small bikini fairings, just about the cutest bikes ever made.

Ninja 250

Kawasaki sold the same basic Ninja 250 for years, which means that an older one is just as good as a newer one if it's been cared for. And since motorcycle values tend to drop off as the years go by, an older 250 Ninja in excellent condition can be an incredible deal.

Eliminator 125/Eliminator 250

For fun, easy-to-ride cruising, you'd be hard pressed to find a better value than Kawasaki's venerable Eliminator 250 and Eliminator 125. Low-slung, lightweight (the current Eliminator 125 weighs only 320 pounds), and inexpensive on the used market, they're a great gateway to casual motorcycling. Kawasaki discontinued the Eliminator 250, but the Eliminator 125 carries on.

Suzuki

Suzuki has built some unique, often highly functional motorcycles, but earlier in the company's history designers occasionally created bikes that the buying public has not warmed up to. One famous example was the rotary-engine RE5 of the 1970s. On the other hand, the company's recent record of racing championship leaves no doubt about their capabilities.

VX800, Intruder, VZ800 Marauder

These capable motorcycles might be a bit much for most new riders, but those who feel comfortable with bikes of this size will also find them best buys.

GS550E/ES/L/M/GS650G/GL/GS650M Katana

Any of Suzuki's air-cooled four-cylinder 550s and 650s of decades past make excellent, dependable bikes as long as they've been well kept and, hopefully, parked in a garage. But as these models are admittedly now older, expect them to need small repairs more frequently than newer motorcycles.

SV650/SF

At only 370 pounds, this fun-to-ride V-twin sportbike is easy to handle for beginners and exciting enough for experts. It's also been around for a few years, so there should be an ample supply of used ones available. This one is definitely a best buy if you can find the right bike.

GS500E/F

Everything stated about these bikes in Appendix A goes for the used versions, except the price. These bikes have been popular with commuters, tourers, and even roadracers, so if you buy a used GS500E or GS500F, make certain that it hasn't been raced.

GSF400 Bandit

Some people consider the smallest Bandit, built between 1991 and 1993, one of the best-handling motorcycles ever made. You have to rev the snot out of its little four-cylinder engine, but when you do, it goes like the wind.

DR-Z400S/SM

Suzuki was the first of the major motorcycle companies to introduce a modern liquid-cooled dual-sport bike. Sharing engineering with the dirt-only DR-Z400E, the S model was fully street legal and freeway capable, while still being good off-road. The DR-Z400SM model was introduced later and featured grippy supermotard street tires, a larger front brake, and other performance tweaks. Suzuki still builds and sells all three models, and used ones can be bargains.

DR200SE/DR350S/SE/DR650S/SE

Like Honda did with its XR/XL lineup, Suzuki stuck with air-cooling for its single-cylinder line of DR dual-sport bikes. The result is a simple and trouble-free machine that can go just about anywhere. Because the engineering has not advanced that far since the bikes were launched years ago, a used version in good shape is just about as good as a brand-new one.

Boulevard GZ250/S40

The single-cylinder GZ250 and S40 serve as the entry points for Suzuki's line of Boulevard V-twin cruisers. Displacing 652cc and 249cc respectively, they represent a viable option for riders wanting to start cruising.

Yamaha

Yamahas are rugged, well-constructed bikes, and they all carry a little DNA from Yamaha's extraordinary racing heritage. While bikes like the monstrous VMAX and R1 superbike generate a lot of the press for Yamaha, a host of smaller bikes quietly provide excellent usability and value.

FJ600

Although it was considered a sportbike in its day, the FJ seems like a standard now. With its frame-mounted half-fairing and sporty riding position, this bike is still striking. If you can find a clean example, buy it. The FJ600 predates Yamaha's current YZF-R6, which is a very serious sportbike.

XJ550 Seca/Maxim/XJ650 Seca/Maxim/XJ700 Maxim

Yamaha's first four-cylinder midsize engine series, which powers all these bikes, set new standards for performance when introduced in the early 1980s and has proven rugged and dependable over the years. Though older now, these models should be quite inexpensive, and if in good condition they'll provide good performance and service.

Yamaha V Star 250

Although it's the smallest bike in Yamaha's Star cruiser lineup, the V Star 250 represents an excellent value in a used bike. That's because it's utterly unique with its 250cc V-twin engine—a tiny replica of the big-bruiser V-twins that sometimes surpass 2 liters. Take that, big dogs!

XT200/XT225/XT250/XT350/XT550/XT600

These bikes trace their roots all the way back to the original big Japanese thumper, the XT500 of the 1970s. Air-cooled, reliable, and easy to maintain, the XT series is also fun to ride and a willing companion for all sorts of travel adventures. Pick the engine size based on what you want to do with the bike, choosing a smaller displacement for around-town riding and a larger displacement for freeways and touring.

Throughout this book, I've discussed what a wonderful community of people you will meet when you become a motorcyclist. This appendix tells you how to get in touch with that community. I list the addresses of some major clubs and organizations, and I also tell you where you can find all the books, videos, accessories, and other paraphernalia you'll want and need.

Motorcycle Safety Foundation (MSF)

The Motorcycle Safety Foundation is a national nonprofit organization sponsored by the U.S. distributors of BMW, Ducati, Harley-Davidson, Honda, Kawasaki, KTM, Piaggio/ Vespa, Suzuki, Triumph, Victory, and Yamaha motorcycles. I've tried to stress the value of taking a Motorcycle Safety Foundation RiderCourse, but in case I haven't made myself perfectly clear, taking such a course can save your life. No other action you can take will help you have a safer motorcycling career. To find a RiderCourse near you, contact:

Motorcycle Safety Foundation
2 Jenner Street, Suite 150
Irvine, CA 92618
1-800-446-9227
www.msf-usa.org

American Motorcyclist Association (AMA)

If taking an MSF RiderCourse is the most important thing you can do to help make you a safer rider, joining the AMA is the most important thing you can do to safeguard your rights as a motorcyclist. Contact the AMA at:

American Motorcyclist Association
13515 Yarmouth Drive
Pickerington, OH 43147
1-800-AMA-JOIN
www.ama-cycle.org

Clubs and Organizations

As I said in Chapter 19, joining a club can be your best way to get in touch with your local motorcycling community. The following list gives you the names and addresses of just a few of the thousands of clubs available.

Blue Knights International

As its name implies, the Blue Knights International Law Enforcement Motorcycle Club, Inc., is a club specifically for law enforcement officials. There are currently 635 chapters and over 20,000 members in 29 states. To find the chapter nearest you, contact:

Blue Knights International
38 Alden Street
Bangor, ME 04401
207-947-4600

BMW Motorcycle Owners of America (BMW MOA)

BMW MOA has chapters across the country, in addition to Canada, Europe, South America, and in the Armed Forces worldwide. The club puts on some of the best rallies you'll find anywhere. It also publishes the *BMW MOA Anonymous* book, which lists members willing to help other members on their travels, plus an excellent monthly magazine. You can contact its national headquarters at:

BMW Motorcycle Owners of America
PO Box 3982
Ballwin, MO 63022
636-394-7277
www.bmwmoa.org

Christian Motorcyclists Association (CMA)

As I said in Chapter 1, motorcycling is a spiritual activity—so much so that some people like to formally combine it with their religion. If you would like to do the same, a great way to do so is by joining the CMA. These folks put on some terrific events and have chapters all across the country. Contact them at:

Christian Motorcyclists Association
PO Box 9
Highway 71 South
Hatfield, AR 71945
870-389-6196
www.cmausa.org

Gold Wing Road Riders Association (GWRRA)

GWRRA is the largest club in the world devoted to a single motorcycle: the Honda Gold Wing. Membership is open to owners of the ultimate touring behemoth, as well as Honda Valkyries. You can contact GWRRA at:

Gold Wing Road Riders Association
21423 North 11th Avenue
Phoenix, AZ 85027
www.gwrra.org

Motor Maids, Inc.

Motor Maids is not only one of the oldest clubs for female motorcyclists; founded in 1940, it's one of the oldest motorcycle clubs, period. Today there are some 1,200 Motor Maids members, many of who attend the club's annual convention. Contact them at:

Motor Maids, Inc.
PO Box 1654
Toccoa, GA 30577
www.motormaids.org

Retreads Motorcycle Club International, Inc.

Retreads Motorcycle Club International boasts a membership of 5,000 motorcyclists, and all of them have at least two things in common: they have reached the age of 40, and they love to ride motorcycles. If you are interested in locating a club near you, just go to the club's home page:

Retreads Motorcycle Club International, Inc.
528 North Main Street
Albany, IN 47320
http://retreads.org

Ronnie Cramer's Motorcycle Web Index

This site has a wonderful listing of motorcycle clubs and organizations. If there is a club—or even a type of club—you're looking for, you should be able to find it here. The site also includes useful links for motorcycle insurance, art, clothing, films, and other subjects. Check it out at:

www.sepnet.com/cycle

Turbo Motorcycle International Owners Association (TMIOA)

The TMIOA is a club for owners of the exciting but short-lived factory turbocharged motorcycles from Honda, Kawasaki, Suzuki, and Yamaha. You can contact them at:

Turbo Motorcycle International Owners Association
http://turbomotorcycles.org

Women On Wheels (WOW)

This motorcycle club for women includes some of the most enjoyable motorcyclists imaginable. If you are a female motorcyclist, you would be well served by joining your local chapter of WOW. To find your nearest chapter, contact Women On Wheels at:

Women On Wheels
PO Box 83076
Lincoln, NE 68501
1-800-322-1969
www.womenonwheels.org

Books

You can learn anything you've ever wanted to know about motorcycles and motorcycling by reading one of the tens of thousands of books available on the subject.

Motorbooks

Motorbooks publishes and distributes books on all aspects of vehicular culture, from antique tractors to airplanes. It also produces and distributes an incredibly diverse collection of motorcycle books. You can order books or a catalog at:

Motorbooks
Quayside Publishing Group
400 First Avenue North, Suite 300
Minneapolis, MN 55401
1-800-826-6600
www.motorbooks.com

Whitehorse Press

A division of equipment supplier Whitehorse Gear, Whitehorse Press publishes and distributes books on motorcycles and motorcycle travel, and its catalog contains one of the most complete selections of motorcycle-related books and products you'll find anywhere. To obtain the latest Whitehorse Gear catalog, contact them at:

Whitehorse Gear
107 East Conway Road
Center Conway, NH 03813-4012
1-800-531-1133
www.whitehorsepress.com/books

Suggested Reading

The following list includes some of the most important books you can read when starting out as a motorcyclist.

Against the Wind—A Rider's Account of the Incredible Iron Butt Rally
Ron Ayres
Whitehorse Press, softbound, 1997, 240 pages
This book gives you an inside look at what it is like to compete in one of the most demanding motorcycle endurance events in the world. Ayres's storytelling skills make what is already a fascinating story even more fun to read.

Bodies in Motion: Evolution and Experience in Motorcycling
Steven L. Thompson
Aerostich, 2008, 400 pages
If you've ever wondered why riding a motorcycle feels good, there is an explanation deeper than "because it just does." Author Steven L. Thompson took years researching the topic on a scientific level, concluding that, genetically, "sensation seekers" thrive on the same types of stimulus that helped our evolutionary ancestors survive. The book also includes a precedent-setting vibration study of nine iconic motorcycles.

A Century of Indian
Ed Youngblood
MBI Publishing Company, hardbound, 2001, 156 pages
This beautifully photographed book tells the story of Indian motorcycles through the "Century of Indian" exhibit at the Motorcycle Hall of Fame Museum. Youngblood developed the book in conjunction with his work developing the exhibit and penned the informative yet entertaining text that accompanies the photography.

Ducati Story: Racing and Production Models 1945 to the Present Day
Ian Falloon
Haynes Publishing, hardbound, 2006, 224 pages
During the past two decades, many books have been written about Ducati. This is one of the best of those books. *Ducati Story* is a case study in how to build the finest high-performance motorcycles in the world and how *not* to conduct a business. Motorcyclists and business types alike should find this a fascinating book.

Harley-Davidson Evolution Motorcycles
Greg Field
MBI Publishing Company, hardbound, 2001, 192 pages
This book covers Harley history from The Motor Company's precipitous decline and near bankruptcy in the late 1970s and first half of the 1980s to its resurrection and eventual return to the number one position in the American market. Author Greg Field has done a fantastic job researching company history and the history of the Evolution engine family, the series of engines that powered Harley's remarkable comeback.

Harley-Davidson in the 1960s
Allan Girdler and Jeff Hackett
MBI Publishing Company, softbound, 2001, 96 pages
Author Allan Girdler and photographer Jeff Hackett document the history of the most important American motorcycle company of all time during the tumultuous 1960s.

Hell's Angels: A Strange and Terrible Saga
Dr. Hunter S. Thompson
Random House, Inc., softbound, 1999, 276 pages
Hunter S. Thompson may be more famous for his excessive lifestyle than for his writing, but long after everyone has forgotten about his excesses, his writing will live on. His command of the English language rivals that of any author, living or dead, and when he chooses to write about motorcycles, so much the better.

Honda Gold Wing
Darwin Holmstrom
Whitehorse Press, softbound, 2001, 96 pages
The story of the Gold Wing is, in many ways, the story of American motorcycling, making this a worthy read for anyone interested in the sport.

How to Set Up Your Motorcycle Workshop: Designing, Tooling, and Stocking
Charles G. Masi
Whitehorse Press, softbound, 1996, 160 pages
This book can save you a lot of headaches (as well as a lot of aches in other places) when doing your own motorcycle maintenance. Masi even manages to make the subject entertaining, with his offbeat sense of humor.

Jupiter's Travels
Ted Simon
Jupitalia Productions, softbound, 1996, 450 pages
What were you doing from 1973 to 1976? Author Ted Simon was riding around the world alone on a Triumph Tiger. Now in at least its umpteenth printing, *Jupiter's Travels* is an intelligent and thoughtful look at the soul of the world through a motorcyclist. Incredibly, Simon did the trip again in 2001 at 70 years of age, and followed up his original book with *Dreaming of Jupiter.*

Motorcycle Owner's Manual: A Practical Guide to Keeping Your Motorcycle in Top Condition
Hugo Wilson
DK Publishing, softbound, 1997, 112 pages
This book won't replace a good repair manual specifically for your bike, as the author himself admits, but it serves as an excellent additional source of information. General procedures are explained much more clearly than in most manuals, and the photos are easier to follow.

The Motorcycle Safety Foundation's Guide to Motorcycling Excellence: Skills, Knowledge, and Strategies for Riding Right
Motorcycle Safety Foundation
Whitehorse Press, softbound, 1995, 176 pages
If you can't take a RiderCourse, at least buy the Motorcycle Safety Foundation's book, which is a collection of its instructional material. These folks know what they're doing, and they know how to save lives.

One Man Caravan
Robert Edison Fulton Jr.
Whitehorse Press, softbound, 1996, 288 pages
In this book, Fulton chronicles his 17-month around-the-world motorcycle trip, which he began in 1932. In this fascinating story, Fulton gives the reader an idea of what it was like to tour on a motorcycle in the days before electric starters and gas stations on every corner.

World Superbikes: The First 20 Years
Julian Ryder, photographs by Kel Edge
Haynes Publishing, hardbound, 2008, 224 pages
When World Superbike racing first began in 1988, journalist Julian Ryder left the Grand Prix circuit to cover the new series. He's been doing so ever since, and now he's written a book chronicling the first two decades of the immensely popular series. His in-depth knowledge of the racers and the sport in general make this a gripping book, and Edge's photography is superb.

Zen and the Art of Motorcycle Maintenance: An Inquiry into Values
Robert M. Pirsig
Bantam Books, softbound, 1974, 380 pages
(distributed by Whitehorse Press)
I try to reread Pirsig's motorcycle classic at least once a year, and each time, it is like reading a different book. It may prove a tough read for those without a philosophical bent, but it is worth the effort.

Web Pages

You can find literally hundreds of motorcycle-related web pages on the Internet, including ones that update their content on a daily basis. The great thing about these webzines is that they have absolutely up-to-the-minute news. When a company releases a new model of motorcycle, you don't have to wait months to see it on the cover of a magazine because it is instantaneously broadcast over the Internet. Within minutes of the finish of a national or international race, you can log on to one of the racing-oriented sites such as www.speedtv.com or www.superbikeplanet.com and get the standings. And don't forget Twitter—you might be surprised what comes up when you type in the name of your favorite bike.

While there are a nearly infinite number of motorcycle-related web pages on the Internet, here is a list of a few favorites, along with their web addresses. This is a subjective listing, so do your own research because you may find magazines that you like far better than the ones listed here.

- American Motorcycle: www.americanmotorcycle.com

- Dirt Rider: www.dirtrider.com

- Hot Bike: www.hotbikeweb.com

- MotoGP: www.motogp.com

- Motor Cycle News: www.motorcyclenews.com

- Motorcycle Cruiser: www.motorcyclecruiser.com

- Motorcycle Daily: www.motorcycledaily.com

- Motorcycle Online: www.motorcycle.com

- Motorcyclist: www.motorcyclistonline.com

- Motoworld.com: www.motoworld.com

- PowerSports Network: www.powersportsnetwork.com

- Roadracing World: www.roadracingworld.com

- SPEED: www.speedtv.com

- Sport Rider: www.sportrider.com

- Superbike: www.superbikeplanet.com

Recommended Viewing

From chopper culture to racing to travelogues, there's no shortage of motorcycle entertainment available on DVD these days. But programs having to do with rider safety should be at the top of every motorcyclist's must-watch list. This program, in particular, is highly recommended:

Street Smarts: The Advanced Course in Urban Survival
Produced by Paul Winters and David West
Nothing compares to taking an MSF RiderCourse, but if you choose not to do so, at least buy these three videos—they may save your life. Much of the material presented in the videos is covered in a RiderCourse, and while you won't benefit from individual instruction and instructor feedback, you'll at least be able to see how it's done. Ideally, you should take a RiderCourse *and* buy these videos. Considering what's at stake, the relatively low cost of these videos represents one of the best investments you can make.

Parts and Accessories

In the long run, you're better off buying as many motorcycle supplies as you can from your local dealers, but often you won't be able to find what you want locally, and you'll have to look elsewhere. The following list provides you with names, addresses, and phone numbers where you can find just about anything you need.

Aerostich

To get one of Aerostich's fantastic riding suits, you're going to have to go directly to the source and give owner Andy Goldfine a call. Even if you're not in the market for a riding suit, you should contact him and get a copy of the Aerostich catalog, which contains the most useful collection of quality riding accessories you'll find anywhere. It is also the most entertaining catalog you'll ever read.

Aerostich/RiderWearhouse
8 South 18th Avenue West
Duluth, MN 55806
1-800-222-1994
www.aerostich.com

Bike Bandit.com

Bike Bandit is an Internet seller of OEM (original equipment manufacturer) parts for most major motorcycle brands, as well as aftermarket products, apparel, tires, manuals, and tools. Contact them at:

Bike Bandit.com
1-888-339-3888
www.bikebandit.com

Chaparral Motorsports

Chaparral has one of the widest selections of gear and accessories for both on- and off-road riding you'll find anywhere. Contact them at:

Chaparral Motorsports
555 South H Street
San Bernardino, CA 92410
1-800-841-2960
www.chaparral-racing.com

Dennis Kirk, Inc.

Dennis Kirk has been around for 40 years now, and advertises an amazing 150,000 items in stock for off-road, Harley-Davidson and metric bikes. Plus, they get your stuff to you fast, with free shipping on some orders. Contact them at:

Dennis Kirk, Inc.
955 South Field Avenue
Rush City, MN 55069
1-800-969-7501
www.denniskirk.com

J&P Cycles

If you have a Harley-Davidson and want to chop it, if you have a basket-case Harley chopper and want to refurbish it, if you want to spiff up your Harley, or if you just want to build a complete motorcycle from parts, you'll find everything you need to do so in the J&P Cycles catalog. It has parts for Honda Gold Wings and metric bikes, too. Contact them at:

J&P Cycles
13225 Circle Drive
Anamosa, IA 52205
1-800-397-4844
www.jpcycles.com

JC Whitney

If you're a careful shopper, you can get some killer buys on motorcycle accessories from JC Whitney. Although inexpensive, some of the items JC Whitney carries are of surprisingly high quality. You can contact them at:

JC Whitney
1-866-529-5530
www.jcwhitney.com

National Cycle, Inc.

National Cycle builds some of the finest aftermarket windshields and fairings you can buy. You can purchase products from any shop or catalog, but if you call the folks at National Cycle and order direct, they can help you select the windshield or other accessories such as exhausts, saddlebags, and luggage that best fulfill your needs. Contact National Cycle at:

National Cycle, Inc.
2200 South Maywood Drive
PO Box 158
Maywood, IL 60153-0158
1-877-972-7336
www.nationalcycle.com

Sport Wheels

Billed as the country's largest motorcycle liquidation center, Sport Wheels features an enormous inventory of used parts in rural Jordan, Minnesota. If you ever need something—whether it is a part or a complete motorcycle—and can't find it, give them a call. You can contact Sport Wheels at:

Sport Wheels, Inc.
3301 166th Street West
Jordan, MN 55352
1-800-821-5975
www.sportwheel.com

Tuners and Builders

As a new rider, you really don't need to make your motorcycle any faster than it is; most of today's bikes offer plenty of performance right out of the crate. But if you do want more power, the following people can help you out.

Graves Motorsports, Inc.

Chuck Graves knows a thing or two about building fast bikes. Working closely with Yamaha, Graves-tuned bikes have won multiple championships, and the organization has funneled much of what they learned into parts you can buy today. Contact him at:

Graves Motorsports, Inc.
7629 Densmore Avenue
Van Nuys, CA 91406
818-902-1942
www.gravesport.com

Hahn RaceCraft, Inc.

Bill Hahn's claim to fame is building motorcycles for drag racing. For a price, he'll help you build what will without a doubt be the quickest motorcycle in town. Contact him at:

Hahn RaceCraft, Inc.
205 Beaver Street
Yorkville, IL 60560
630-553-6830
www.hahnracecraft.com

HyperCycle

If you want to legally ride your sportbike at the limit, HyperCycle can slot you into a track day at four different Southern California circuits. A three-group format allows riders to circulate with others of comparable skill, and one-on-one instruction is provided. The company can also modify your bike for even better track performance. Contact them at:

HyperCycle
818-988-8860
www.hypercycle.com

Mr. Turbo

Mr. Turbo builds horsepower-boosting turbo kits for big Kawasaki and Suzuki road burners, as well as a universal turbo kit that can work on a wider variety of engines. Contact them at:

Mr. Turbo
4014 Hopper Road
Houston, TX 77093
281-442-7113
www.mrturbo.com

Racing Clubs

The following is a list of clubs that can help you get started in motorcycle road racing. But even if you don't want to arc around corners with your knee skimming the ground, attending the races they organize can still be a blast.

American Federation of Motorcyclists, Inc.
6167 Jarvis Avenue, #333
Newark, CA 94560
510-796-7005
www.afmracing.org

American Historic Racing Motorcycle Association
2375 Midway Road SE
Bolivia, NC 28422
910-253-9738
www.ahrma.org

Central Motorcycle Roadracing Association
PO Box 101177
Fort Worth, TX 76185-1177
817-570-9779
www.cmraracing.com

Central Roadracing Association
2845 Harriet Street, #203
Minneapolis, MN 55408
612-332-4070

Mid-Atlantic Road Racing Club
14408 Chantilly Crossing Lane, #675
Chantilly, VA 20151
703-786-2987
http://marrc.nova.org

Motorcycle Roadracing Association, Inc.
PO Box 40187
Denver, CO 80204
303-530-5678
www.mra-racing.org

Northeast Sportbike Association (NESBA)
PO Box 70
Mohnton, PA 19540
610-750-6909

Oregon Motorcycle Road Racing Association
503-221-1487
www.omrra.com

Utah Sport Bike Association
PO Box 26791
Salt Lake City, UT 84126
www.utahsba.com

Washington Motorcycle Road Racing Association
PO Box 94323
Seattle, WA 98124
www.wmrra.com

WERA Motorcycle Roadracing, Inc.
2555 Marietta Highway, #104
Canton, GA 30114
770-720-5010
www.wera.com

Willow Springs Motorcycle Club
PO Box 911
Rosamond, CA 93560-0911
661-256-1234
www.wsmcracing.com

High-Performance Riding Schools

Besides taking the Experienced RiderCourse from the Motorcycle Safety Foundation, the best way to improve your riding skills (and your chances of having an injury-free riding career) is to take a course in high-performance riding. Whether you are going racing or you just want to hone your street-riding skills, taking a quality high-performance riding course can teach you things that can save your life. Usually these schools are expensive, but if they can make you a better (and safer) rider, they are worth the money.

Although most of these schools have their headquarters in the American Southwest, many conduct classes at different racetracks around the country, making it easier for riders to attend. Call or write for a schedule of class dates and locations.

BMW Performance Center Motorcycle Training
300 Chestnut Ridge Road
Woodcliff Lake, NJ 07677-7731
1-888-345-4269

California Superbike School
940 San Fernando Road
Los Angeles, CA 90065
323-224-2734
www.superbikeschool.com

CLASS Motorcycle Schools
320 East Santa Maria Street, Suite M
Santa Paula, CA 93060
805-933-9936
www.classrides.com

Hallett Advanced Rider Training
PO Box 69
Hallett, OK 74034
918-356-4814
www.hallettracing.net

Moto Ventures
951-767-0991
www.motoventures.com

Schwantz Motorcycle Riding School
6075 Barber Motorsports Parkway, Suite A
Birmingham, AL 35094
1-866-223-5649
www.schwantzschool.com

Skip Barber Superbike School
PO Box 1629
Lakeville, CT 06039
860-435-1300
www.skipbarber.com/superbike_school

STAR Motorcycle School
562-802-7061
www.starmotorcycle.com

Cycle Babble Glossary

ABS (Anti-Lock Brake System)   A system that detects when a wheel is not turning and releases pressure to the brake on that wheel, preventing a skid.

aftermarket   The sector of the market that sells parts and accessories other than original equipment manufacturers (OEMs).

Airheads   A term for older, air-cooled BMW boxer twins.

ape hangers   A term describing tall handlebars that force the rider to reach skyward to grasp the controls, making the rider adopt an apelike posture.

backrest   A cushioned pad that adds comfort and security for the passenger.

bagger   A cruiser-style motorcycle equipped with saddlebags and an abbreviated fairing.

belt-drive system   A final-drive system that transmits power to the rear wheel via a toothed rubber belt.

Big Twins   The engines in larger Harley-Davidson bikes.

blind spot   The area not shown in a rearview mirror.

bobbers   The custom bikes American riders built after World War II. The owners cut off, or bobbed, much of the bodywork.

body armor   The protective padding in motorcycle clothing.

bottom end   The bottom part of the engine, where the crankshaft and (usually) the transmission reside.

boxer   A two-cylinder engine with the pistons opposing each other, resembling fists flying away from each other.

brakes (disc and drum)   Disc brakes use stationary calipers that squeeze pads against the discs that rotate with the wheel. Drum brakes use horseshoe-shape brake shoes that expand against the inner surface of the wheel hub.

café racer Motorcycles modified to resemble racing motorcycles from the 1950s, '60s, and '70s. They are called café racers because their owners supposedly raced from café to café in London, where the bikes first appeared in the 1960s.

cam A shaft with eccentric lobes on it that opens the valves. More formally known as a camshaft.

carbon fiber A high-tech material favored in many motorcycle applications because it is extremely strong and light.

carburetor A device that mixes fuel with air to create the charge burned in the combustion chamber.

cases The two clamshell-like metal halves containing the bottom end of the engine.

CE approval A European standard of certification for motorcycle clothing.

centerstand A stand that supports the motorcycle in an upright position.

centerstand tang A small lever attached to the centerstand.

chain-drive system A final-drive system that transmits power to the rear wheel via a roller chain.

chassis The combined frame and suspension on a motorcycle.

chopper Once used to describe a custom motorcycle that had all superfluous parts chopped off in order to make the bike faster, a chopper today is a type of custom bike that usually has an extended fork, rigid or hidden rear suspension, and high handlebars.

clip-ons Handlebars that attach directly to the fork tubes, rather than to the top yoke.

clutch A device that disengages the engine from the transmission, allowing a rider to feed in power gradually and change gears smoothly.

combustion chamber The area at the top of the cylinder where the fuel charge burns and pushes the pistons down.

coming on the cam The term used when a four-stroke reaches its powerband.

coming on the pipe The term used when a two-stroke reaches its powerband.

connecting rods Rods that attach the pistons to the crankshaft's offset journals. The pistons' up-and-down movement is converted into rotation movement through the swinging motion of the journals.

constant-radius turn A turn with a steady, constant arc. In a decreasing-radius curve, the arc gets sharper as you progress through the curve, while in an increasing-radius curve, the arc opens up.

contact patch The area of your tire that actually contacts the road while you ride.

cordura   A synthetic outer material used to make motorcycle clothing.

counterbalancer   A rotating eccentric weight inside an engine that cancels some of the engine's vibration.

countersteering   The way you use the handlebars to lean the bike into a turn. If you want to turn right, you push the handlebars to the left, and vice versa.

cowling   A piece of bodywork that covers the engine area.

crotch rocket   A term some people use to refer to sportbikes.

crowns   The tops of the pistons.

cycle   The up-and-down motion of the piston. The terms *cycle* and *stroke* are used interchangeably when referring to engine types.

cylinder block   A hollow aluminum casting containing one or more hollow cylindrical sleeves.

cylinders   The hollow cylindrical sleeves in the top end of an engine inside of which internal combustion occurs.

decreasing-radius curve   A turn in which the arc gets sharper as you progress through the curve.

direct injection   A fuel-injection system that pumps fuel directly into the combustion chambers, rather than the intake ports.

dirtbike   Bikes intended for off-road use that aren't legal to ride on public roads. Sometimes the term *motocross* or *enduro* is used to distinguish pure dirtbikes from dual-sport motorcycles that are also street legal.

discs   The metal rotors that brake calipers press their pads against to create braking force.

double-cradle frame   A bike frame with two steel tubes cradling the engine from below.

dresser   A motorcycle set up for long-distance touring.

dual-sport   Street-legal motorcycles with varying degrees of off-road capabilities. Also called dual-purpose motorcycles.

eccentric journals   Used to attach the connecting rods to the crankshaft.

ergonomics   The science used to design devices, systems, and physical conditions that conform to the human body. This is a prime consideration when designing a motorcycle.

Evolution (Evo)   Harley-Davidson engine with aluminum cylinder and head castings, introduced in 1984.

fairings   The devices mounted at the front of a motorcycle to protect the rider from the elements. These range from simple, Plexiglas windshields to more complex and encompassing body panels.

false neutral   When you fail to engage gears and the transmission behaves as though it is in neutral, even though it isn't.

flat cylinders   Cylinders arranged in a flat, opposing configuration, such as those found in the flat-four- and flat-six-cylinder engines used in Honda's Gold Wings.

foot paddling   The way an unskilled rider walks his or her motorcycle around at low speeds.

forks   The metal suspension assembly that connects the front wheel to the rest of the motorcycle.

four-cylinder bike   A motorcycle with four cylinders.

fuel-injection system   A system that forcibly injects fuel into the cylinder head's intake ports. Differs from carburetors, which rely on the vacuum created by the pistons to draw the charge into the intake ports.

gearhead   A person with a strong interest in all things mechanical; a motorcyclist.

gearset   A set of gears, usually paired on two different shafts, within a bike's transmission.

grab rail   The rear-mounted handles that a passenger holds on a motorcycle.

high-siding   The outward flinging motion that occurs when a motorcycle loses traction, and then suddenly regains it, during a turn. This is the most dangerous kind of crash.

horsepower   The scientific measure of an engine's ability to perform work. Also referred to simply as power.

hydroplane   When tires start to float on top of water, causing them to lose contact with the road's surface.

increasing-radius curve   A turn whose arc opens up as the curve progresses.

inline-four   An engine with four cylinders in a row.

inline-triple   An engine with three cylinders in a row.

Iron Butt Rally   The most grueling long-distance motorcycle rally in the world. The rally challenges riders to travel at least 11,000 miles in 11 days.

kick-start   The method of starting a motorcycle without an electric starting system.

knucklehead   A term for Harley-Davidson's first overhead-valve twin, introduced in 1936.

L-twin engine   A V-twin engine with its cylinders splayed apart at a 90-degree angle, which creates a smoother-running engine.

lane splitting   Riding between lanes of traffic on a freeway or other road.

laying the bike down   A crash in which you and the bike slide to the ground together.

lugging the engine   Letting the rpm fall below the engine's powerband.

manual transmission   A device consisting of a set of gears (the gearset) that alter the final-drive ratio of a vehicle to enable an operator to get up to speed.

naked bikes   Bikes without any type of fairing.

oil line   The spilled trail of oil in the center of a busy road.

Oilheads   Newer, air-and-oil-cooled BMW Boxer engines.

open-class   When referring to street-legal sportbikes, open-class designates motorcycles with engines that displace more than 800 cubic centimeters of volume.

original equipment manufacturers (OEM)   The companies that build the bikes.

orphan bikes   Bikes built by companies that are no longer in business.

overbore   When you overbore your engine, you machine out the cylinder sleeves and install oversize pistons, effectively increasing your engine capacity.

overhead-cam system   A system wherein the camshaft is located in or above the cylinder head. There are single-overhead-cam (SOHC) and double-overhead-cam (DOHC) designs.

panhead   A term for Harley-Davidson's aluminum-head V-twin engine with hydraulic lifters, introduced in 1948.

parallel-twin engine   A two-cylinder engine with its cylinders placed side by side in an upright position.

pillion   The passenger seat of a motorcycle, or the actual passenger who sits behind the rider.

pistons   The slugs moving up and down within the cylinders.

ports   The passageways inside the cylinder head through which air and fuel enter the combustion chamber and exhaust gases exit.

powerband   A certain rpm (revolutions per minute—how many times per minute an engine's crankshaft spins around) range in which an engine makes most of its power.

primary drive   A drive system—via gears, chain, or belt—connecting the engine's crankshaft to its clutch, and from there to its transmission.

pushrod system   System in which the cams are generally located in the bottom end and activate the valves through long rods, called pushrods, and rocker arms.

radial   When used to describe a tire, refers to the way the cords of a tire are constructed.

rain grooves   Channels cut into a road's surface to help water run off the road during a rainstorm.

regenerative braking   Converts braking energy into electricity to recharge batteries on an electric bike.

repair link   A link in some motorcycle chains that can be disassembled for chain repair.

repli-racers   Hard-edged sportbikes. These motorcycles are characterized by riding positions that tuck the rider into an extreme crouch, forcing him or her to crouch over the fuel tank.

revolutions per minute (rpm)   The number of times the crankshaft spins around each minute. Often the term *revs* is used, especially in conversation.

riding two-up   Carrying a passenger on your bike.

rocker arms   Devices that work like upside-down teeter-totters and push the valves open.

rubber-mounted   Engines that use a system of rubber cushions and/or jointed engine mounts to isolate engine vibration from the rider.

saddlebags   Soft or hard storage bags that affix to the sides of the motorcycle near the rear wheel. Construction ranges from pliable leather or synthetic materials to rigid plastic or aluminum.

shaft-drive system   A final-drive system that transmits the power to the rear wheel via a drive shaft.

shovelhead   A term for Harley's third-generation overhead-valve V-twin engine, introduced in 1966.

sidecars   Small carriages attached to the side of a motorcycle to provide extra carrying capacity.

single   A motorcycle engine with one cylinder.

sissybar   A tall decorative vertical structure located behind the passenger's portion of the saddle. May double as a backrest, or as a place to affix luggage.

slipping the clutch   The term used to describe only partial engine drive propelling a motorcycle.

snicking The act of shifting a well-functioning transmission. A transmission that doesn't snick into gear is described as sloppy-shifting.

solid-mounted Engine that is bolted directly to the frame tubes.

splitting the cases Taking apart the cases to repair the motor. *See also* bottom end.

sport-tourer A motorcycle that combines the comfort and carrying capacity of a touring bike with the handling and power of a sportbike, with a larger fairing and hard, lockable luggage.

sportbike A motorcycle designed for optimal speed and handling characteristics, often with extensive bodywork.

springer fork Forks with large, exposed springs to dampen the impact of road irregularities.

squid Someone who rides a sportbike on the street as if he or she were on a racetrack.

steering geometry The geometrical relationship between the steering axis and the front axle.

sticky A term used to describe tires with very good grip.

stoppie Using the front brake to lift the rear wheel of a motorcycle off the ground while stopping.

streetfighter A bare-bones sportbike, stripped of all extraneous body work (also called a hooligan or naked bike).

stroke The up-and-down motion of the piston.

stunt riding Riding wheelies and similar maneuvers on motorcycle.

supermoto A type of dirtbike or dual-sport bike with wheels and tires from a roadbike.

suspension The forks and shocks (and technically tires) of a motorcycle. The suspension springs, together with the tires' sidewalls and air pressure, all support the motorcycle.

tappets Small metal lifters located between the cams and the pushrods or valve stems.

telelever system The most successful alternate front suspension, made by BMW, which transfers the shock-absorption function of a hydraulic fork to a shock absorber located behind the steering head.

thumper Bikes with large-displacement, single-cylinder, four-stroke engines.

top end The upper part of the engine, which contains the pistons, cylinders, and valve gear. Also contains the induction system, which mixes an air-and-fuel charge for the combustion chamber.

torque   A twisting force and, in a motorcycle, a measure of the leverage the engine exerts on the rear wheel.

touring bike   A larger motorcycle equipped for longer rides with a fairing, saddlebags, and a trunk or rack.

track days   Organized group riding at a race track.

traction   A tire's ability to grip the road.

travel   The distance that suspension components—the forks and shocks—move when the bike rides over bumps.

trike   A three-wheeled motorcycle. Trikes may have one wheel in front and two in the rear, or two wheels in front and one in the rear.

twin-spar frame   A bike frame with two steel or aluminum spars (flat beams) that pass around or over the engine.

two-stroke engine   An engine whose power cycle consists of just two movements, or strokes: the piston moves down, drawing in the fuel-air charge, and then up, squeezing the charge for combustion.

two-up   A term for carrying a passenger on your motorcycle.

unitized transmission   A transmission (often referred to as a unit transmission) that is an integral part of the engine's bottom end.

Universal Japanese Motorcycle (UJM)   During the 1970s, the Japanese became so identified with the four-cylinder, standard-style motorcycle that this term was coined to describe them.

V-4   An engine of four cylinders, arranged in a V-shape configuration, with two cylinders on each side of the V.

V-twin   A two-cylinder engine with its cylinders placed in a V shape. These engines can be placed either transversely (crosswise) or longitudinally (lengthwise) in the motorcycle frame.

valve guides   Metal tubes that position the intake and exhaust valves.

valve train   The system of valves that lets the air/fuel charge in and the exhaust gases out.

valves   Tulip-shaped valve train components with a round metal stem and a broad, tapered head. Cams open and close the valves to let fuel charge in and exhaust gases out.

vanishing point   The furthest visible point in the road.

wheelie   Using engine power to lift the front wheel of a motorcycle off the ground while accelerating.

Index